THE TRAILSIDE KILLER'S
TRAIL OF TERROR

San Francisco and northern California lay under a thickening fog of fear. Beginning in 1979, a series of savage rape-murders of young women in the Golden Gate area signalled the presence of a monstrous serial killer. Yet one of the most massive manhunts in U.S. history found only fresh victims.

At last the law closed in on David Carpenter, whose thick glasses and shy stammer concealed an insatiable sexual appetite and a murderous anger. This is the detailed story of the hideous crimes, the gripping manhunt, the sensational series of trails, and, above all, the secret self of the killer who *almost* got away with murder . . . again and again. . . .

"A thorough and engrossing account of a violent sociopath."

—*Publishers Weekly*

MURDEROUS MINDS

☐ **THE SLEEPING LADY:** *The Trailside Murders Above the Golden Gate* **by Robert Graysmith.** The law finally caught David Carpenter, whose thick glasses and shy stammer concealed an insatiable sexual appetite and a murderous anger. This is the detailed story of the hideous crimes, the gripping manhunt, the sensational series of trials, and the secret self of the killer who *almost* got away with it. (402553—$5.99)

☐ **DEATH SENTENCE:** *The Murderous Odyssey of John List* **by Joe Sharkey.** The riveting story of mass-murderer John List, who savagely killed his mother, his wife and three children—then "got away with it" for eighteen years! One of the most chilling true crimes of the century. (169476—$4.95)

☐ **THE SEARCH FOR THE GREEN RIVER KILLER by Carlton Smith and Tomas Guillen.** In this book you will meet the young women who died hideously. You will meet the men hunting for their killer. But there is one person you will not meet. The Green River Killer himself. Like London's Jack the Ripper, this one is an unsolved serial murder case. (402391—$4.99)

☐ **FATAL VISION by Joe McGinniss.** The nationwide bestseller that tells the electrifying story of Dr. Jeffrey McDonald, the Princeton-educated Green Beret convicted of slaying his wife and children "A haunting story told in compelling detail."—*Newsweek* (165667—$5.95)

THE
SLEEPING
LADY

The Trailside Murders Above the Golden Gate

Robert Graysmith

Illustrated by the Author

AN ONYX BOOK

ONYX
Published by the Penguin Group
Penguin Books USA Inc., 375 Hudson Street,
New York, New York 10014, U.S.A.
Penguin Books Ltd, 27 Wrights Lane,
London W8 5TZ, England
Penguin Books Australia Ltd, Ringwood,
Victoria, Australia
Penguin Books Canada Ltd, 2801 John Street,
Markham, Ontario, Canada L3R 1B4
Penguin Books (N.Z.) Ltd, 182-190 Wairau Road,
Auckland 10, New Zealand

Penguin Books Ltd, Registered Offices:
Harmondsworth, Middlesex, England

Published by Onyx, an imprint of New American Library, a division of
Penguin Books USA Inc. Previously published in a Dutton edition.

First Onyx Printing, April, 1991
10 9 8 7 6 5 4 3 2 1

 REGISTERED TRADEMARK—MARCA REGISTRADA

PRINTED IN THE UNITED STATES OF AMERICA

Dedication

This book is dedicated to the memory of Elizabeth "Ellie" Wigner (1957–1988), who came from the peaks of Switzerland, spoke five languages, and was the kindest and most beautiful of women.

Contents

viii   CONTENTS

Foreword

The Sleeping Lady, Mount Tamalpais, towers—steadfast and dispassionate—above the Golden Gate, an implacable sentry between San Francisco Bay and the open Pacific. The Sleeping Lady stretches eastward, clashing against the grain of the surrounding ridges and lower coastal peaks that run northwest to southeast.

According to Harold Gilliam, environmental writer, "Nowhere else on Earth could there be a more dramatic juxtaposition of a metropolis and a mountain. I have always suspected that this mountain has entered deeply into the collective experience of the people of San Francisco and probably helped shape the character of the city itself." Only half a mile high, the mountain appears so lofty because it has no foothills. "Take away Tamalpais," it is said, "and what is left of Marin County would hardly fill a wheelbarrow."

For roughly five thousand years there had not been a murder on Mount Tamalpais. During the first four thousand years or so the peaceful Tamal Indians, the area's sole inhabitants, clustered their reed houses only as far as the base of the blue peak. They were in terror of the upper mountain and never ventured there. Evening would find these hunters and gatherers basking in the sweat-house or toiling in front of smoking fires, grinding plump black acorns to fine meal. But at nightfall their collective gaze would rise toward the summit, where they feared powerful and deadly spirits walked the trails.

After the rush for gold people kept from the top until 1897, when the mountain was finally tamed and exotic mansions such as Coffin House and Owl's Nest were sunk into the green rock and a curvilinear mountain railway climbed to an inn at the summit. Mark Twain, Jack London, and Robert Louis Stevenson were known to have strolled through Tamalpais's silent ribbons of mist. The trees of the Sleeping Lady had been toppled in 1849 and the flash fires of 1906, 1913, 1922, and 1945 had almost deforested the triple peaks. However, these calamities were inconsiderable compared to the human tragedy to come.

In the summer of 1979 the tranquility of the mountain's green and blue slopes was shattered when the first re-corded homicide on Mount Tamalpais occurred. Soon af-terward serial killings and rapes on the parkland trails began. A handsome, dark-haired man with a hawklike profile was glimpsed stabbing a woman hiker to death. This young man, later dubbed the Trailside Killer, van-ished as completely as if he had never been, while at the same time a troubled, stuttering man, an ex-convict, walked the trails with a confidence that eluded him in daily life. Oddest of all, the stammering man was listed on the state computers as still being in federal prison.

As the search for this unknown man continued, the residents of the idyllic communities that ringed the mountain and the sprawling nine counties, ninety cities and towns of the Bay Area, became fearful. The killer's unpredictable crimes swept the hikers from the winding trails and isolated canyons of Mount Tamalpais. "The area is so beautiful," one nature lover cried in anguish, "and now it has fallen under the rule of a madman."

The Trailside case became one of the great manhunts of the twentieth century and eventually involved the FBI, and the law enforcement agencies of Marin County, San Francisco, Santa Cruz, San Jose, and Daly City. Slowly the killer moved over the wooded paths of the Golden

Gate National Park Reserve, eventually migrating south to Santa Cruz and intruding on some of the most dazzling areas on earth—a haunting mountain, a floating island, and a dark forest of the oldest living things. The massive investigation made and smashed careers as lawmen fought the killer and one another in their long, frustrating search for justice.

Missing young women, a coven of avenging witches, a pair of bloodstained glasses, an elusive .38-caliber revolver, a "mystery" .44-caliber gun, a discarded knife, and a gold-yellow jacket as tantalizing to the police as the Golden Fleece—all became pieces in the intricate puzzle.

For twenty-six years a determined woman sought to convince authorities that her intuition about a man from her past was correct, that he was a killer.

"There were more victims than just the people who were shot," Santa Cruz police inspector Stoney Brook told me. "There were the people who lived who were hurt beyond repair. This investigation took a toll on all involved like I've never seen before. Whatever it was that I had going for me all those years, this one just had me whipped."

There would be two of the most unusual and costly trials in U.S. history. From the beginning of the crimes the records in the Trailside case were sealed from both public and press by court order, and it is finally with this book that the full story can be told. After four years of writing, researching, illustrating, and interviewing, I have completed a journey that brought me in contact with dedicated detectives and lawyers, courageous survivors, and the darkest side of the human soul.

With the last page of *The Sleeping Lady* written I took a hike with a friend, leaving from Fairfax where a vegetarian rock-and-roll club called the Sleeping Lady once stood. He took me to the back side of the mountain in late afternoon—the extreme western watershed area, past the Bolinas-Fairfax Road, which was the part of the mountain that had remained untouched by the Trailside Killer. "It's a lonely environment," said my friend, "more shadows than the rest of Tamalpais and dense, dark woods and darker ravines, tall redwoods and open magic meadows." As we walked he told me the legend of the Sleeping Lady. "It concerns both abduction and death. It seems that shortly after the creation of the world a golden sun god fell in love with an Indian maiden. As he swept her up in his arms to carry her off to his home in the sky, he stumbled over Mount Diablo, the woman slipped from his grasp, and both plunged to earth—she to her death.

"The indentation created by the fallen god became a valley that filled with ocean waters, San Francisco Bay, and the spot where the maiden touched ground assumed her profile in the shape of a mountain. The place where she lay, forever reposed in the sleep of death, became ghostly Tamalpais, her face and her reclining form clearly visible in the long mountain ridge beside the water. The low drifting summer fog that moves in from the Pacific and around the mountain is said to be a gentle blanket with which the sun god is cloaking his lost love."

Every book has its own color—the story of the Trailside case carried with it an undeniable hue of gold, from the gold jacket the killer wore to the golden bridge that carried him into the parklands. Finally my friend and I came to a large canyon where a spectacular triple waterfall spilled into three separate pools in the granite rock. "You should see it with the sunset shining through it," he said, taking a deep breath, "like a cascade of gold!"

—ROBERT GRAYSMITH
San Francisco, September 1989

Acknowledgments

With heartfelt thanks for loyal support, both inspirational and emotional, to the following—Pamela Kibrick, Margot Alexandra, David Martin, Aaron Vincent, and especially Peggy Smith for being so patient. Without Inspector Stoney Brook this book would not have been possible. Thanks to Marion Irving, Richard Wood, Sergeant Rich Keaton, John Posey, Ann Harrington, Lieutenant Don Besse, Kathy Derby, Sergeant Walt Robinson, Sheriff Charles Prandi, Supervisor Gary Giacomini, Margie Goodman, Shelby Lynne and Doug Smith, Mike Waller, Don Rose, Sergeant Ken Womack, Marilyn Hansen, Joyce and Jerry Stowers, Martha and Marsha Gaddini, Reno Taini, Leroy Looper and Kathy Sofos, Shane Williams, Dave Toschi, Dr. Edward Shev, Inspector Margaret Hartman, Lulu of the Lloyds, Joe Henard, Jim Toland and Laura Baty Toland, Joey and John R.E. Toland, Teresa Allen, Gerry Lee Bell, Susan Bergman, Carolyn Parker, Richard Millman, Lisa Blakely, Bob, Peggy, Ben, and Nicholas Cooper, Mel Torme, a true crime buff, Lee Pullins, Emily, Jason, Brisy, Stephanie Hendricks, Linda Zimmerman, Penny Wallace, Esther Scott, Sheila Kelly, Sharon Fox, Tannith Lee, Betsy Lombard, Ann Carter, Kandi Leonard, Ruth McLay, Elizabeth McBryde, Nikki Bengal, the gang behind the counter at the Owl and the Monkey, Gene, Kathleen and Somerset, Shayne, Diana, Britta Engel, John Sennet and Jordan, Ele Lozares, Julie, Fred, Luba and Leah Reeves, Lee Rodgers, Dave McElhatton, Robert McCormick, Alex Bennett and Christy Frazier, Herb Caen, Dave Mitchell, Dr. R. William Mathis, Bob MacKenzie of KTVU-TV, Bruce A. Thabit, Mike Kilpatrick, Lee Gertler, Chris Dittmar, Gladys Wenzel,

Roger Ruben and Joe Moreland, Chip Proser, Sam and Patricia Hookano, Susan Johnson, Bill and Lance, Bruce Bellingham, Del, Dr. Roy Minstzer, "Nuge," Robert Verhaeg, Bill Thomson, Barb Hauser, Kit Artig, Millicent Chase-Lalanne, Mike Stoye, Steve Sharpe, Joseph Mario Balbi, Paul Vietzke, Lawrence Cain, Linda M., Agnes Lourdes Livingston, Pete DeMarco, Deborah Barr, Dan Strone, my agent, Amy Mintzer, and, of course, Dick Marek, my editor, whose unfailing insight and direction cleared the tangled trail to the top of the Sleeping Lady.

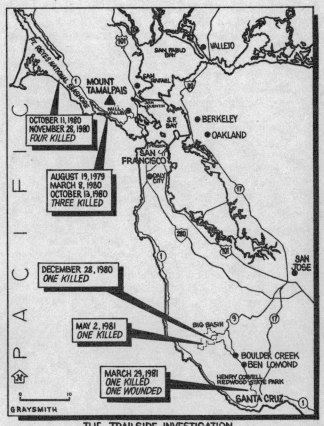

PT. REYES NATIONAL SEASHORE

VALLEJO

SAN PABLO BAY

SAN RAFAEL

MOUNT TAMALPAIS

MILL VALLEY

SAN QUENTIN

S.F. BAY

BERKELEY

OAKLAND

SAN FRANCISCO

DALY CITY

SAN JOSE

BIG BASIN

BOULDER CREEK
BEN LOMOND

HENRY COWELL
REDWOOD STATE PARK

SANTA CRUZ

OCTOBER 11, 1980
NOVEMBER 28, 1980
FOUR KILLED

AUGUST 19, 1979
MARCH 8, 1980
OCTOBER 13, 1980
THREE KILLED

DECEMBER 28, 1980
ONE KILLED

MAY 2, 1981
ONE KILLED

MARCH 29, 1981
ONE KILLED
ONE WOUNDED

PACIFIC

N

0   10

GRAYSMITH

THE TRAILSIDE INVESTIGATION

PART ONE

THE
MOUNTAIN

A spot of cloudy gold lit first upon the head of Tamalpais, and then widened downward on its shapely shoulder; the air seemed to awaken, and began to sparkle; and suddenly "The tall hills Titan discovered," and the city of San Francisco, and the bay of gold and corn, were lit from end to end with summer daylight.

> —Robert Louis Stevenson,
> from the deck of the Oakland Ferry
> on San Francisco Bay

All around beneath me was spread for a hundred miles on every side, as far as the eye could reach, an undulating country of clouds. . . . It was such a country as we might see in dreams, with all the delights of paradise. There were immense snowy pastures, apparently smooth-shaven and firm. . . . The earth beneath had become such a flitting thing of lights and shadows as the clouds had been before.

> —Thoreau, 1844

GRAYSMITH 1981

GOLDEN GATE BRIDGE FACING NORTH INTO MARIN COUNTY

1

Roberta:
1955

Even the ice plant introduced by the Golden Gate Park Rangers was hard-pressed to tack down the drifting sand dunes of mile-long Baker's Beach, a secluded place with a background of pines and cypress near San Francisco's Presidio.

Darting seagulls, fish-diving cormorants, swifts, and tattlers soared over the treacherous surf, spray exploded against the jutting rocks while just offshore was a larger black rock, Helmet Rock, and beyond that, to the north, Marin County.

During the summer evenings, after the occasional bonfires on the beach have died, a concentrated form of glittering, luminous protozoa, "light of the night," turns the evening tide a glowing pink, and any tired bather who chances to wade through this radiant surf and then crosses the sand leaves behind, if only for a fleeting moment, a series of ghostly, phosphorescent, and tantalizingly insubstantial footprints.

On a blustery, mid-February morning, the dark puffs of fleeing clouds hung to the north above the red clay Marin Headlands. Over the years the wind had blasted mountains already riddled with World War II storage tunnels and gun placements and worn them green at the water's edge, while the more distant peaks of the mountain were bluer and several shades lighter than the closer ridges. Forbidding weather had chased the multicolored sailboats and skiffs from the bay, and olive-drab waves whipped to a froth along the beach. A long freighter, the *Fleetwood*, was headed seaward.

In the freighter's rigging there was a soft, almost imperceptible whisper, and Roberta could feel beneath her feet the throb of screws turned by two fuel oil-driven, DR-geared steam turbines. As she glanced over her shoulder the chilly wind caught her short hair and whipped one dark lock into her eyes. She brushed it away.

She gazed toward the green waves lathering the nearby rocky shore in the gray, imperfect light and then down at the choppy, nearly black waves alongside the ship. Balanced against the winds that lashed the deck of the bleak freighter, she clung to the railing at the stern, victim of both an oily seasickness and an anger that had overtaken her almost from the instant the crew had cast off from the pier.

Roberta could feel the strength of the fearsome six-knot current as the ship was swept under the Golden Gate Bridge toward Japan. Two hundred and twenty feet above, a fog horn boomed out. Beneath the span, to the south, the San Francisco side, a graceful steel arch most were not aware of, a hidden bridge, pitted by the corrosive salt spray, curved over old Fort Point where there was a second set of pylons, anchors for the slender cables of the bridge.

In the water farther out from the hidden bridge stood the South Tower, seventy-five stories high and a twin to a tower over four thousand feet away on the Marin side, marking the boundary between counties. It is, however, an imperfect twinship. While the North Tower, which oversees the abandoned light station at Lime Point, was constructed on solid ground, the South Tower was built over a thousand feet from the shore in water sixty-five feet deep and locked in a concrete-poured bedrock one hundred feet below the surface.

As the freighter cleared the underside of the bridge Roberta could see the rounded peaks of Marin's Mount

Tamalpais,* known as the Sleeping Maiden or Sleeping Lady. The alignment of the peaks produces an awe-inspiring sight when seen from the proper angle, most particularly from San Anselmo to the north and especially on the evenings when the fog comes billowing in through the Golden Gate. Then Tamalpais takes on the amazingly lifelike appearance of the full-length figure of a woman, reclining at a forty-five-degree angle, which fills the whole of the western horizon. With her toes arching toward the town of Corte Madera, she seems to be resting on a gray bed.

Roberta turned from the triple-peaked mountain and carefully studied the freighter—its weathered wood, its three decks, its radar, its two masts and bulky, welded iron framework of faded red and bitter green standing out against the spray. The *Fleetwood* was a heavily refitted refrigerated cargo ship, a reefer, and its most distinctive features were the two large mast houses, three-quarters aft and amidships. These contained the indispensable refrigerating machinery that chilled the cargo—fruit was being carried out this time. The long, slender vessel had a high freeboard, a long superstructure, and precise longitudinal framing at both its bottom and its decks.

As the ship lifted and lowered in the waters the sting and salt of the spray served only to fan Roberta's anger, an anger that had been growing ever since she and her two children had boarded shortly before. It was unlike her to take an immediate dislike to anyone, certainly a dislike that seemed to be as irrational as the distaste she felt toward the stuttering young purser. But he would not leave her fourteen-year-old daughter, Shelby Lynne, alone. Years later she would still recall the intensity of her feelings.

As in a dream, the freighter moved heavily past angular hills in the direction of the Point Bonita Coast Guard Lighthouse. To her right Roberta could see Baker's Beach

*Tamal (land near the bay) and pais (mountain). Before 1850 it was called Table Mountain, Mount Palermo, Tannel Bume, Bay Mountain, and Tamales Mountain, but after that time known as Mount Tamalpais. Its name may have derived from the Spanish *mal-pais* (badlands) or might signify the land of the Tamals, a Lacatuit tribe who held the peaks in great reverence.

and the San Francisco Military Presidio. Two hundred years earlier this whole area around San Francisco had been a combination of vast meadowlands, gigantic salt-water and freshwater marshes, swamps, and great oak-bay forests all crosscut and intertwined by rushing channels. In those days the water table lapped so close to the surface, only a foot or two away, that the land was wet and spongy with sweeping stands of unconquered bunchgrass that could swallow a man. A wildlife habitat having no equal once thrived in these rich lands: an array of dark sea lions and white pelicans, cormorants, gulls, geese, and black-ringed ducks. Even whales were washed ashore, and then both Indians and grizzlies alike would feast.

To the Indian inhabitants the world was a profusion of magical objects—streams, trails, rocks, waterfalls—all alive with will and individual personality, sharing a kinetic kinship with the environment. Each object in this ancient universe was embodied with a life force, dreams were as genuine as waking life, and the gods resolutely stood only a whisper away on the other side of consciousness.

Tamalpais itself essentially was a place of awe and veneration to the tribe who lived at its base, the Tamals. They believed violent spirits inhabited the peaks of the mountain and reverently built their earthquake-resistant, flexible thatched huts no closer than the foot of it. Perhaps The People, as they called themselves, were right not to climb Tamalpais. When settlers came and moved up the side of the Sleeping Lady their world would change dramatically forever.

Soon the elk were gone, along with the bald eagles, antelope, wolves, condors, grizzlies, and even, with the draining of the ponds and marshes, the geese, ducks, steelhead, and salmon. Eventually The People were obliterated as well, left to wither away in the missions of the last century. Virtually slaves, after 1880 there were only fifty left, one of the oldest, an unknown Ohlone Indian at Mission Dolores, crying out, "I am all that is left of my people. I am all alone . . . my people were once around me like the sands of the shore—many, many."

As the freighter moved beyond the lighthouse Roberta watched the blue and green mountain. Beneath it, to the north, was Stinson Beach, where Roberta's family had a summer home. Roberta herself was a fifth-generation San Franciscan, and the family was once in the social register. Her great-grandfather had owned the original Gray Line bus company and, once, all of Tanforan. She watched Tamalpais until she could no longer see it as a separate shape; it had blended into the surrounding landscape. Perched on the horizon like a cutout, the ship seemed to hang for half an hour on the edge and then disappeared into the bad weather ahead.

Roberta's husband, John, a merchant seaman, had worked on the *Fleetwood* as chief engineer sailing with Pacific Far East Lines. Bringing with her two of their children, Shelby Lynne and Robert Dwayne, who was nicknamed Rocky, she was on her way to join him in Japan, where he was working. A third son, towering, crewcut John Jr., was in college and couldn't make the trip.

"I wasn't in the same room with my mother," Roberta's daughter recalled over thirty years later. "I had a stateroom all to myself with two or three bunks, one after another. There was a bathroom, and I remember that because it was the only time I've ever been seasick in my entire life. There was just this endless bumping up and down. My mother's cabin was across the companionway, and then there was a stairway between her room and mine. She and Rocky slept on bunks alongside each other at one end. There must have been a toilet and shower in their room because there was in mine."

The trip should have been a pleasant vacation, but by the second day out Roberta had become exasperated, concerned, and irritated enough over the twenty-five-year-old purser's interest in her daughter to learn his name, David J. Carpenter.

Clutching the railing she made her way across the slippery deck, through a dark passageway, up a brief flight of stairs, and down into an abbreviated corridor that led to the captain's cabin. The door was open.

The captain's suite was divided into three parts, each segment twice the size of the preceding one. The parts consisted of a small, untidy bathroom, a Spartan bedroom equipped only with a bunk and two chests, and the captain's dayroom, the largest space of all.

The dayroom was furnished with a tan leather chair, an

overstuffed sofa flanked by flowered upholstered chairs,
and a teakwood tea table. Above the paneled desk hung
polished nautical instruments Roberta did not recognize.

Spotlighted by a tall chrome floor lamp, the spacious
cabin's sole illumination, was a uniformed man, bent over
his work at the desk. In the heat of the room his forehead
glistened. Roberta was certain this man, caught in a circle of light like some circus performer, was the captain.
At this moment he was performing a balancing act with
a small bowl of tea, which he drank periodically and with
obvious pleasure, the steam curling up and around his
lips. Oblivious to her, he continued, between sips, to
methodically work on the papers before him. In the darkness outside the circle of light the shortwave crackled.

With her ring finger Roberta tapped firmly on the extreme edge of the tan metal door, received no response,
and then rapped with greater force. The black-haired,
older officer at last acknowledged her.

She had intended to start quietly, reasonably, but all
her irritation rushed out in a torrent—"I want you to
keep your purser away from my daughter!" The captain's
shoulders tensed. The older man's sea-toughened face
lifted and gazed in her direction.

"Your purser," she continued, "has taken an un-
wholesome interest in my little girl and I've come here
to ask you to say something to him about it. I want you
to tell him to keep his hands to himself."

Serenely the senior officer explained to her that the
purser's job was to entertain the passengers. Carefully he
told Roberta that Carpenter meant well.

"Surely, you don't pay him to put his hands all over
the passengers? He's continually putting his arms around
my girl." The thought of the purser's hands made her
shiver. To her they seemed extraordinarily large. "The
company has an obligation to the adult passengers, especially the parents. He's always giving her candy and
patting her. I want him ordered away from her."

During her plea the captain's head had bobbed up and
down in silent agreement, but now with a barely noticeable shrug he bent over once more, his attention seized
by an array of worksheets. Dismissed and unsatisfied Ro-

berta went topside again. He thinks, she said to herself, that it's my imagination.

She looked upward, smelling the salt in the spray spun off the ocean. The shoreless sky, which that morning had begun as pale yellow, had transformed itself into gentle pink by noon. Even the air, to Roberta, seemed warmer than usual. She felt an electricity in the air and on her skin. To the east, banks of vertical rain clouds, lined up like soldiers in rows seventy miles long and ten miles wide, were joined only by lines of slashing rain. By late afternoon winds churned up the sea and, amid rain and blinding spray, began to make a howling noise. Set out in bold contrast to the heaving black waters, irregular silver flakes of foam flew about in all directions and showered down like a hundred thousand white flowers over the ship.

In the *Fleetwood*'s wireroom the flat, horizontal beam of the ship's rotating antenna had mapped out a typhoon on the cathode-ray tube of its storm detector unit and punched out a thin, yellow paper tape to show its shape.

"The storm," Shelby Lynne, Roberta's daughter, recalled years later, "continued from the time we left the Golden Gate Bridge and followed us all the way across the Pacific and never ceased until we were two days out of Japan. At one point during the storm something amazingly big hit us—we went up, up and back and forth, and then sideways and down. We never did learn what it was, waves crossing or something. There was just this hollow roar as the sea leaped and the ship dived."

For days the weather was so rough and the waves so sharp and high that all twelve of the passengers were compelled to huddle together, feeling damp and claustrophobic, just below the *Fleetwood*'s bridge, playing hearts and Scrabble at the gaming tables. To Roberta this was the most difficult past of the voyage—being in proximity to the troubling young purser, David Carpenter.

On the tenth night in the lounge Roberta had put down her magazine and walked to the window. As she stood watching the slanted rain beating against the glass, and feeling each forward roll of the *Fleetwood*, Carpenter entered. He was framed perfectly in the circular glass. The purser was five foot, ten inches tall and Roberta guessed he weighed in the neighborhood of 160 pounds.

Granted Carpenter was immaculate in his tan ship's uniform. She watched this night as he touched each of his fingers together and contemplated them, something she had seen him do often. Until this moment it had been Roberta's theory that the purser's hands appeared so abnormally large to her because of their extraordinary whiteness. However, as she studied them closely, the answer came to her. His hands appeared so white, and in their whiteness so enormous, because there was not a solitary hair upon them. She could not discern even a tracery of fine hair about the knuckles.

Carpenter rose from his chair, talked to Roberta's daughter again, and then, with a wave of his hand, left the dining room. The close and constant contact with him and the storm were slowly wearing Roberta down.

When on the following day Carpenter was back with her daughter, she sought out the captain again. Nothing had changed. He was still at work when she told him how uneasy the stammering young purser still made her feel.

"Precisely what does he do?" asked the captain, putting both elbows on the teak desktop.

"He's friendly only to my daughter, Shelby Lynne, pays no attention to my son Rocky at all. It's not something I can readily describe to you. It's just something about him, nothing overt. He's just constantly putting his arms around her shoulders, rubbing her neck, touching, giving her things—just overly interested in her."

There was silence. Roberta could hear the loud tick of the clock, the roar of the ocean outside. Suddenly she was aware the captain had gone back to his mountain of forms, tilting his head from side to side as if to view his work from exactly the right angle.

"He's simply *too*—friendly."

Again no reaction.

Roberta left, once more unsatisfied. Over the next few days, in the confines of the small lounge, she learned her opinion of Carpenter was strongly divergent from that of the other passengers. They not only liked him but all seemed to feel sorry for him.

It might have been because the man suffered from both poor eyesight and a crippling stutter. The crew had long been in the habit of finishing his sentences for him. Midway in the voyage the passengers had taken to doing the same. Roberta thought Carpenter was liked because he had an ability to gain sympathy and had a talent for manipulating people.

Strange and abrupt, a light sometimes would flash from the purser's eyes, changing the reposing hazel color to hard gray—an alteration of personality as profound to Roberta as a shadow cast over the face of the moon.

As they entered an area of first spotty and then dense fog on the night of their seventeenth day at sea, Roberta realized they were near Japan. She went on deck to catch a glimpse of land lights but could see nothing but grayness floating just above the water. The prow of the ship cut through the shrouds of fog and parted the thin mist to the east. For a while Roberta walked the deck, and then she went to bed.

The next day was the final day of the voyage, and Roberta went to the bow of the ship to bask in her first taste of sun in quite a while. Ahead she could see gulls, land, a sort of rocky presence, where the four mountainous islands of Kyushu, Shikoku, Hokkaido, and Honshu, the Japanese archipelago, loomed. Within hours, drawn irresistibly into port by the Kuroshio current, they would be docking in Yokohama and the trip would be over, which would mean a welcome departure from the purser.

A wind from the east caressed her face, and in the white light she wondered what it was that made her both fear and detest the friendly young man. In all it was a combination of a mother's protectiveness, woman's intuition, and some indefinable feeling. Between Roberta and the purser there existed a relationship in which nothing happened, a battle in which no blows were struck and where one of the combatants was unaware of the struggle.

At one point during the voyage Roberta had caught Carpenter writing a phrase in her daughter's memory album and had made a mental note to see what it said, but had been sidetracked. It would be five years before she would have occasion to read what the purser had written, but in all that time Roberta never forgot the stuttering man. Their brief meeting was one that would obsess and trouble her for over a quarter of a century.

2

The Purser:
1960

On one of the brightest, sunniest mornings of the summer, Tuesday, July 12, 1960, at 8:30 A.M., David Carpenter drove up San Francisco's Green Street in his 1953 Oldsmobile. In the sunlight the *Isla de los Alcatraces*, Isle of the Pelicans, floated in the bay to the north—Alcatraz, the crumbling federal prison, entering its last days. Farther north was Angel Island with its deer and light station.

Even though he had only turned thirty in May, Carpenter could see in the mirror that his hair was thinning. Above his full lips, flaring nostrils, pug nose, and luminous hazel eyes, his forehead had grown high. He ran his hand through the fine brown hair feeling the flattened angle at the back of his skull. His teeth were crooked, front to back, and cut at various angles.

Carpenter had passed the intersection of Octavia and Green near Allyne Park for the third time when he saw, as he had expected, an acquaintance, Lois DeAndrade, strolling from the Green Street apartment she shared with three other women. She was on her way to the bus stop across the street. Lois was employed as a secretary for

Foote, Cone and Belding, an advertising company that had done business with Pacific Far East Lines, where the purser worked.

Silvia Ortman, one of the company's clerks, knew them both. "He'd come off the ships and come into the office. He'd sit there and yak with all the girls," she said, "He really acted like a nice guy. He was funny. We were all clerks and he was a purser on one of the ships.

"Hopeless," she recalled. "He really stuttered a lot. I think that was from his father beating him practically to death. You see, I knew Elwood, his father, because he was our mail guy in the office for years. He was a little old man. He seemed really nice, but you never know what goes on in the heart. David's childhood was pretty painful.

"Since we knew his dad real well, when David wasn't out to sea they'd let him come in and work in the mail room with some of the kids. At that time Lois worked in the office of Hawaiian Textron down from where I worked. She was a darling girl."

Carpenter had started with the lines on the first of March in 1952, had been in the U.S. Coast Guard,* and during a period of diligent enterprise had climbed from purser-trainee and clerk on both passenger ships and freighters to become a clerk in charge of military shipments and assistant to the vice-president of the main office.

Lois, who had lived in San Francisco for a dozen years, initially had met David Carpenter through a mutual friend in July of 1958 and become friendly enough with him to have coffee with him on four or five occasions. Consequently she was not surprised when, on June 7, 1959, her thirty-first birthday, he invited her to his Westlake home for dinner. Carpenter's wife, Ellen, made Lois a sumptuous meal and even baked a birthday cake. And several months later, when the purser learned Ellen was pregnant with their third child, he phoned Lois at her Green Street apartment to tell her the good news.

The brakes on Carpenter's car squealed as he pulled

---

*Merchant Marine #2-1017-574, Travel Book #BK-58179.

up alongside the attractive secretary. His face brightened as he called out to her.

"Why don't I give you a lift to work?" Carpenter said as he opened the passenger door for her.

Lois smiled. "No, but thanks." Though Lois had not seen Carpenter for almost nine months, the purser periodically called her. "He used to ring me up every couple of months or so," she said later, "to see how I was doing and catch up on current boyfriends and just to chat. Normally I would go to the bus stop with my roommates, but my roommates were late that morning, so I went to the bus stop by myself. I didn't recognize the car or the person at first, and when David called to me I turned around. I was surprised to see him in the area and I said, 'What are you doing here?' And he said he was driving around and around the block. He wasn't sure where I lived, but he was hoping he would see me, and that his wife had a new baby and he wanted me to come and see the infant."

The purser continued to insist. Circe Anne had been born a little under a month earlier and Carpenter explained that since Ellen and the infant were at the Presidio visiting an old army friend, a captain, this would be a good opportunity for Lois to see the new child.

"Thanks, but I have to work," she explained.

"Look, it'll only take a few minutes. I'll be glad to drive you downtown right after the visit."

Lois looked at her watch and reluctantly agreed. "He was so crestfallen," she remembered, "and I felt sorry for him, and I didn't want to refuse. And he said his wife would be so disappointed. It would only take five minutes he promised and then he would drive me straight to work."

Those who knew the purser during this period portrayed him as being bright, with a pleasant personality and great sense of humor. But also he had a reputation for being sexually aggressive in his relations with women. On numerous occasions, various women were placed in the position of having to fight off his advances.

Carpenter had married five years earlier, on November 5, 1955, and lived with his wife and three children in Pacifica. However, he was plagued with sudden terrifying rages, and these were fueled by an unquenchable sexual drive, money worries, and inability to communicate because of his severe speech impediment.

Anxiety and tension escalated when he anticipated trouble, was embarrassed by being forced to converse with people in authority, or was frustrated. Attempting to deny the stammering, to suppress it, enslaved and haunted the young man.* However, when Carpenter was alone, talking to himself, speaking with children, singing, shouting, whispering, reading aloud, or speaking in unison with others he had no difficulty with his speech. In any totally spontaneous situation he was fluent. He had his good days and bad days.

His problems were not lost on his superiors at the shipping lines. An efficiency report stated: "He had no difficulty getting along with other people other than his terrific temper due to his speech difficulty whenever he had to handle public relations at the company."

As Lois and Carpenter drove slowly westward along the remaining blocks to the Presidio the man talked glowingly of his wife and their courtship days.

"You two will have time for a chat," he said, taking his eyes from the road. The worn tires hummed in the yellow light.

The reality was that the purser was miserable in his marriage. He said later, "My wife was not interested in anything but local neighborhood gossip. I got very bored with her and only stayed around because we had three children."

In the early fifties Carpenter had gotten to know two Daly City sisters, Wilhemina and Ellen May Heatlie, and he began to make romantic overtures toward Wilhemina. The relationship ended when he was rebuffed.

The jilted man first badmouthed Wilhemina among their mutual friends and then turned his attentions to Ellen. Carpenter began to show up at the Irvington Street address to take the younger sister out, and in 1955 the nineteen-year-old girl and the twenty-five-year-old purser

---

*Five times as many boys as girls stutter, the same ratio as dyslexia. Marilyn Monroe, Fred Astaire, Thomas Jefferson, Winston Churchill, Moses, and Aristotle all stuttered.

were married by Judge Horn in San Francisco with their
friend William Burge acting as witness.

With each child, Ellen and David Carpenter moved to
a larger place. When the first, Michael David, was born
at St. Joseph's in September of 1956 they moved to
Apartment 15, 90 Forest Grove, in Westlake. A second
child, Gabrielle Louise, was born on July 3, 1958, after
Carpenter had become a shipping lines clerk and ceased
his wandering at sea, which had bothered Ellen, and the
family moved to Apartment 23, 60 Lynnewood Drive.
Ellen was a model of the fifties wife—she stayed home,
she didn't drive, and Carpenter picked out their house
for her. As plans for a third child were made he signed
a deed of trust for Robert and Lillian Clancey's Pacifica
property in September of 1959 in the amount of
$4,705.37. Circe Anne was born June 17, 1960, after the
family had moved to 380 Mina Lane.

Only one thing suppressed his rage, held the worst
elements of his personality back, and released the tension and frustration—intercourse three times a night.
Then, when this did not hold him in check, there were
incidents of violent outbursts which, afterward, Carpenter would claim not to have been aware had happened.

"We drove down Lombard toward the Presidio," recalled Lois, "and he started driving up one street and
down another street and he couldn't seem to remember
where he had left his wife and new baby. And I thought
that was kind of funny. And I said, 'I've just really got
to get to work,' and he said, 'No. Wait a minute. I think
I remember where it is,' and we kept driving around."

Lois realized there was something unusual about the
purser today. "His speech was very clear. He did not
stammer at all. David had a really bad stammer. And
from the time he picked me up, the whole while, he did
not stammer."

The purser followed Lombard right onto the heavily
wooded base; the Presidio with its smorgasbord of military functions was the oldest active military installation
in the United States.

Carpenter pulled slowly by Letterman Hospital. Ahead
and far to the stuttering man's left, hidden by trees, was

the Officers' Club, the oldest adobe building in San Francisco.

Carpenter continued to speak in a slow and deliberate manner as the road merged into Lincoln Boulevard. Northwest, then west, then southwest the meandering road twisted. Past the military cemetery sped the little car swinging west under the Highway 101 overpass. Lois now had no idea where they were headed. The trees grew heavier, darker.

Carpenter continued to drive aimlessly. At about half-past nine Jewell Wayne Hicks, a military policeman on duty, noticed a 1953 Oldsmobile circling about the army installation. He decided to check on it, thinking the driver was lost, but by the time he reached the curve in the road he had lost the auto.

Lois and Carpenter were now near Crissy Field, where the fireworks celebration was held each Fourth of July, and headed into a secluded warehouse area. The purser turned onto an isolated street that led to a battery site to the west of Crissy, adjacent to a lonely beach.

"Oh, man, I think I'm really in trouble," said Carpenter as he eased the Olds to a stop in front of a white bunker-type building.

In the distance Lois saw the Golden Gate Bridge, looking impressive but almost unreal in the sunlight. Framed behind it was the peak of Mount Tamalpais, the bay beneath alive with colored sails. When Lois turned to look at Carpenter she was aware of an odd look in his eyes. He had grown silent and said nothing when Lois complained she had to get to work.

"By then," Lois recollected, "I was really nervous, so I started to get out of the right-hand side of the car and started to run. And he said, 'What's the matter? Where are you going?' and he got out of his side, and he grabbed me and put me back in the car.

"He straddled my body, a knee on either side, and reached into the glove compartment and pulled out a knife and a rope. He told me to be quiet and if I was quiet he wouldn't kill me, but if I made any noise he would."

Reaching over Lois he opened the glove compartment where he had a package of clothesline. Tearing off the wrapping with his teeth he unraveled the nylon line and began to bind the struggling woman. Lois fought back until Carpenter took out a knife and put it to her throat saying, "If you make any more noise or continue to struggle, I'll kill you." As he repeated this his voice grew husky and his phrasing became more meticulous. After a pause he said seriously, "I don't want to hurt you, Lois, but I'll kill you if you're not quiet."

Bewildered, Lois looked up into his eyes. "David, what's the matter with you? You're my friend." She pleaded to know what was happening, and finally Carpenter cried out, "I have this funny quirk that's got to be satisfied." Lois was to say later, "Perhaps David went crazy. I was so terrified I don't think I moved after that."

Partially tied, pinned to the seat by Carpenter's knees, Lois saw him reach under the seat and pull out a hammer. She was in despair until she happened to look up. "I saw there was a road up above. And I saw a vehicle go by, and instinctively I guess I went for the horn. And the knife was there. And I lunged like this and I guess I honked the horn. I screamed."

Carpenter struck out at her with his knife. Lois was able to deflect it with her right hand, but the blade lacerated the tendons of her fourth and fifth fingers. With her left hand, Lois succeeded in getting the door open and tumbled out, her purse spilling out lipsticks and coins as she followed close behind it. However, she fell in a crouch, and as her heels gained solid ground, she began running.

Carpenter, armed with the claw hammer, bounded after her, catching up within a few steps. He raised the hammer over his head and, in a powerful arc aimed at Lois's head, swung. A second time Lois deflected his blow. She heard the sound of her watch crystal smashing.

The next time Carpenter hit her. Later Lois would not recall actually being hit by the hammer but would remember the number of blows. Barely conscious, she called out for help, and in the distance Jewell Wayne Hicks heard her.

When the military policeman heard Lois's screams he was driving up the narrow green road. He slammed on his brakes and slid sideways in the grass, leaving skid marks in the dark turf. Hicks saw the Oldsmobile parked under a tree down an incline in the underbrush, but because he was approaching from the driver's side of the vehicle the struggling couple on the opposite side were out of his line of vision. From the sounds below, Hick's assumed a rape was being committed, so he came out of his jeep with his riot baton in one hand and the other hand on his holstered, blue-steel .45–military automatic.

As Hicks ran he could see the other side of the auto. A man was on top of a woman, holding her down with his knees, and striking her with a hammer. Even as Hicks charged him he continued hitting. The MP shouted for the young man to stop and back away. There was still no reaction from Carpenter. Later, Hicks said, "Even when he saw me coming down the hill, he kept hitting her." All Lois knew was someone else was there and Carpenter had ceased his battering. She had been hit at least six times.

Hicks was right on the purser now and the man ran to the back of the Olds, dodging and swinging at the MP, hitting him with a numbing blow on the left forearm. The policeman leveled his gun at Carpenter, ordering him to drop the hammer.

"I recall being down on the ground," said Lois, "and being hit on the head. It was all so fast. And I remember I heard a sound or was aware of something else or someone else being there and then he stopped hitting me. And then I thought I saw two people. My vision was blurred. I just knew that someone was there."

At Hicks's second command of "Back away! Drop your weapon!" Carpenter complied, and the hammer fell into the short grass. The military policeman could see Lois was breathing, but with a rasping noise, and he was certain she had sustained a fracture. The skull was obviously broken in two places.

In a flurry of action Hicks marched Carpenter to his car, leaned into the vehicle to radio for help, and communicated their location and the need for immediate medical aid. As the MP was speaking, the purser withdrew a fountain pen–type gas gun that fires a .38-caliber shell and discharged it at the officer. All Jewel Wayne Hicks could see was a puff of white smoke, a flash; all Jewell Wayne Hicks could hear was the sound of a shot being fired point blank at him. The slug missed. Hick's cheek was burned by gas.

The MP, eyes smarting, fired through the billowing cloud of gas in the general direction of David Carpenter. The first shot missed, but as the purser turned to run, Hicks fired two more shots. These connected, striking Carpenter in his abdomen and in his leg. The man was knocked off his feet and into the thick underbrush. He clutched his side in agony. The MP heard the purser's voice call out in a stammer, "Don't shoot: You've hit me."

"I heard a gunshot," said Lois in retrospect, "and I tried to get up on the side of the car. I got in the car, locked the doors, and the windows were down. I got behind the wheel of Carpenter's car and tried to start it, but my fingers were hanging. I couldn't turn the key. The next thing I knew there was an MP there who was picking me up in his arms, and it was just all so confusing."

A second patrol car arrived and two MP's leaped out. "They tried to put me in the back of the patrol car," said Lois, "and David was in the back of the car, and I wouldn't get in the car. And they kept saying, 'It's OK, it's OK.' And Carpenter said to me, 'It's OK. I won't hurt you anymore. I won't hurt you now—I can't hurt you.' "

As the patrol car raced over the tree-lined streets Lois was given some aid for her head injuries and Carpenter for his bullet wounds. The purser, dazed and distracted, eyes blinking dully, had a look reminiscent of someone in a dream.

Lois was hurt seriously. She was found to have a fractured skull that was depressed bilaterally on either side. There were three lacerations on each side caused by the six blows Carpenter had struck. Visually the surgeons could see her skull was broken in two places.

Lois's injuries were so extensive that she had to undergo immediate brain surgery. During the operation surgeons were concerned about brain damage but were unable to gauge the extent of the wounds at that time. Small tantalum plates were fashioned for both sides of her head, and portions of the skull were removed to repair the damage done. Tendon grafts were done on her fingers, but these would prove ultimately unsuccessful. Carpenter, under the custody of a U.S. marshal, was also hospitalized and moved from Letterman Hospital, on the Presidio, across the Golden Gate Bridge into Marin County to the more secure San Quentin prison hospital.

Roberta was now living in Ben Lomond to the south of San Francisco where she boarded horses for the local children. Roberta, who didn't ride, had taken over the stable mainly to please her youngest daughter, who loved horses. She had remodeled an old house and enclosed the front porch to form a dining room, which overlooked the black-cottonwood-flanked San Lorenzo River and where she sat this gloom-ridden, rain-wrapped July morning two days after the Presidio attack. Roberta folded open the morning paper to see the face of the purser staring back at her.

At least it appeared to be him; the age was right. It seemed the man had been involved in a violent crime in the thick, secluded woods of San Francisco's military Presidio. Roberta pushed her half-eaten breakfast aside, poured a second cup of coffee, which she ignored, and leaned forward to study the picture of the arrested man. He seemed very much like the ship's purser she remembered from her trip to Japan, right down to the thick glasses and precise military brush, short haircut. His head was tilted into the shadow of his hand, his wedding ring catching the bright gleam of the exploding flashbulb that had illuminated the hospital picture. The purser was in a wheelchair, wearing an ill-fitting dark robe and light gray pajamas, his long feet stretched out in the white hospital slippers.

The man slumped in the wheelchair seemed collapsed in remorse, and his hands covered his eyes as if to blot out everyone else. In his lap lay an earlier edition of a newspaper with a story about the attack partially visible. However, Roberta was a perceptive woman, and she leaned closer to the photograph to look at the expression on the face under the hand. Then she sensed his thoughts were of himself only, his anguish from his wound, his pain from being caught—pale-white lips were clinched in a smile while in the background reporters stood in a semi-circle, pencils and pens poised over notebooks.

Roberta turned her attention from the picture to the small story that accompanied it. It was headlined:

HIGH BAIL FOR HAMMER ATTACKER

Bail of $25,000 was set for David Joseph Carpenter, a shipping lines clerk accused of a hammer attack on a pretty secretary.

FBI Agent Frank E. Denholm appeared before U.S. Commissioner Joseph Karesh to file a complaint charging assault with attempt to commit murder and to request the high bail.

The clerk and his victim, Lois DeAndrade, 32, of 1832 Green Street, were both reported in "satisfactory" condition yesterday by their physicians.

Miss DeAndrade, who suffered a fractured skull in the hammer beating Tuesday at the Presidio, is a patient at Franklin Hospital.

The thirty-year-old clerk, of 380 Mina Lane, Pacifica, was shot two times by a military policeman who was attracted by Miss DeAndrade's screams.

Miss DeAndrade told authorities that the suspect had offered her a ride to work then drove to a secluded area of the Presidio and attacked her with a knife and a hammer.

Roberta realized she had been correct in her initial assessment: there was no doubt that the hammer attacker and the purser from her Japanese vacation were the same man. An urgency now seized her, and in the drab morning she hunted down her daughter's vacation diary. With thick fingers she anxiously thumbed to the entry from the *Fleetwood*'s purser to her child, Shelby Lynne. "To you from me, David Carpenter on the USS *Fleetwood.*"

For a while Roberta sat with the scrapbook in her lap, watching the rain collect on the painted trim outside the kitchen window and dripping off drop by drop.

On August 3, 1960, Carpenter was sufficiently recovered from his bullet wounds to be booked into the San Fran-

cisco City Prison by the United States Marshal's Office
and charged with assault with the intent to commit murder. During the time of his hospitalization he claimed
not to remember the attack on Lois. A report on the
purser's mental and physical condition was made before
U.S. Commissioner Karesh. Because the court-ordered
psychiatric examination of the defendant had not been
completed, a further hearing was set for August 25.

At the new hearing Carpenter's attorney, Franklyn
Brann, argued that the psychiatric study was superficial
and a second study was ordered by the judge. By October
8 Brann had decided how to try the case. He explained
to Judge Oliver J. Carter that insanity would be raised as
a defense.

On October 26 the purser was indicted by the federal
grand jury on four counts. The first was assault with intent to commit murder on the person of Lois DeAndrade,
the second charge was assault with a deadly weapon; the
claw hammer was specifically mentioned in the indictment. The third and fourth counts were assault with a
deadly weapon upon the person of Jewell Wayne Hicks.*
Along with the claw hammer, the gas gun, which contained a .38-caliber live round of ammunition, was being
considered a deadly weapon.

On October 31 Carpenter appeared in U.S. District
Court and pleaded Guilty only to the second count, assault with a deadly weapon on Lois. To the remaining
charges he pleaded Not Guilty. Brann attempted to have
counts one, three, and four of the indictment dismissed,
but all without success.

By Wednesday, December 7, 1960, a jury was paneled. The purser was tried on counts one, three, and four.
The two charges of assault with a deadly weapon carried
a five-year maximum penalty each and the assault with
intent to commit murder carried a twenty-year maximum.

The two court-appointed psychiatrists had testified that
Carpenter was mentally competent to stand trial on the
pending charges. This pretty much defused Brann's strat-

*All counts were a violation of Title 18, U.S. Code, Section 113 (a)
and 113 (b).

egy, and he and his client had an earnest discussion at the beginning of the trial. During the deliberations Brann and Assistant U.S. Attorney William P. Clancy, Jr., had a conference and requested to see Judge Louis E. Goodman in his chambers.

Cloistered from the jury, Brann plea bargained, explaining his client was willing to change his pleas on counts three and four to Guilty if count one of the indictment was dismissed. Goodman agreed to drop the assault with intent to murder charge and entertained the two guilty pleas. When the judge returned to the court he dismissed the jury.

Goodman's first move was to order the purser to the federal medical facility at Lompoc for a ninety-day psychiatric study. Since Carpenter continued to say he was suffering from amnesia, no one, from the superficial examination done so far concerning his mental health, had the slightest idea why the purser had done what he did.

However, the next time he appeared before Goodman, on March 9, 1961, for the sentencing, Carpenter's memory of the violent hammer and knife attack had at last returned. During a showing of Hitchock's movie *Psycho*, he explained to Goodman, it had all come back to him. The judge bent his head and continued reading through the psychiatric report on the defendant. He came to a portion that stated the defendant suffered from a "sociopathic personality disturbance."

As Goodman commented on the "brutality of the defendant and the past record of his sexual aggression" his eyes strayed across the courtroom, where the purser's twenty-four-year-old wife solemnly held their infant child. Grimly he sentenced the purser to five years on count two, five years on count three, and four years on count four, to run consecutively for a total term of imprisonment of fourteen years. Since the attack had been on federal property the purser was committed to the U.S. Penitentiary at McNeil Island, Washington.

Ellen filed a divorce complaint against her husband in the county clerk's office for San Mateo County in Redwood City, giving the date of separation as July 12, 1960, the day of the attack. As community property she listed the 1953 Oldsmobile used in the attack, household furniture and furnishings, and charged the purser with extreme cruelty and "wrongfully inflicting upon her grievous mental suffering." Since Ellen had no money for a lawyer she was granted counsel to handle the divorce. Additionally she requested reasonable child support and alimony and custody of the three children.

On August 27, 1962, a final judgment of divorce was entered on the grounds of extreme cruelty, and Carpenter was ordered to pay Ellen one dollar per month for child support and an equal amount for her maintenance. She also received all listed community property, and a restraining order was placed in force against the prisoner to prevent him from annoying or molesting the children or Ellen.

Carpenter, now prisoner number A 28796-M, had been received into federal custody at McNeil Island on April 12, 1961, where the final judgment of divorce reached him August 27, 1962.

Carpenter's future behavior was foreshadowed in his pattern of exchanging, depending upon the situation, one reality for another. First he had told Dr. Rappaport that he had amnesia. With his next psychiatrist, Dr. Diamond, he presented what he considered a more plausible explanation of the Presidio stabbing and clubbing. He told Diamond he was having an affair with Lois and the entire incident was a lover's quarrel. In 1964, just before his first parole hearing, he gave a new version of the attack—"I just snapped . . ." As always, Carpenter, with his uncanny ability to read people and manipulate the system, chose the story most amenable to the questioner. He returned in 1966 to the affair version and then finally, in his last interview on the Presidio assault, placed the full blame on Lois, claiming that *she* had stabbed him first. In addition, it was the MP, Hicks, who had panicked.

When the papers reported Carpenter had been given a sentence of fourteen years, Roberta, in Ben Lomond, must have breathed a sigh of relief. Her brush with the purser, however brief, however minor, had left her shaken and obsessed. Roberta began to see his face behind every unsolved crime in the news and continued to report her suspicions to incredulous police over the years.

3

The Purser: 1969–1970

On the surface, prison seemed to have had little effect on the purser. Though he was refused parole at his first hearing in 1964, the authorities were forced to release him when his mandatory parole date was reached on April 7, 1969, and, after serving nine years, the minimum sentence, Carpenter found himself leaving McNeil Island.

From April 29 on, records of the federal probation office in San Francisco show faithful and obedient compliance on the part of the purser. For a while he resided with his stepbrother, William, on Las Palmos Drive and began studying welding at the John O'Connell Vocational School. A month later he reported he had moved to Langton Street and had starting receiving grants from the Manpower Development and Training Act.

Carpenter began attending a group therapy class, and his probation officer saw this as a valiant attempt on the ex-con's part to get to the bottom of his troubling emotional problems. At these classes he met Helen, who was five years younger than himself and a clerk typist at a college. She had been divorced in 1964, and the pair began to date.

On August 8 they were married, with Carpenter's stepbrother in attendance. The purser moved in with Helen at Apartment 304, 1140 Sutter Street and in October notified his parole officer of the change of address and his new phone number. Uncharacteristically, in December, he broke off communications with the parole board even though his probation was not set to expire until January of 1974.

Helen, a naturally high-strung woman driven to the edge of a nervous breakdown, had gone to Hawaii at the beginning of January in 1970 to relax, leaving her husband behind to spend his spare time driving aimlessly through the south bay.

The pressure within him began to reach insurmountable proportions since the safety valve of sex within marriage was not there during his wife's absence. Though Carpenter hid it well, his self-control had eroded to a dangerous degree. Some sort of crisis was building within him, and he began to make plans.

The troubled purser plunged southward down the scenic highway toward Santa Cruz, an uncontrollable urge driving him on a route that would encompass Boulder Creek, Oakdale, and eventually the Mother Lode. As the traveler fled on this January 27 from the pressure, from crimes not yet committed, he rolled his windows down, feeling the cool wind in has face under the bright skies.

He stopped along the way, splashed water in his face, and cooled the back of his neck, and then, on Highway 280, his attention was caught by an attractive young woman as she drove past. He followed irresistibly and forced her car off the road. After one quick look at his eyes, she charged into the undergrowth to hide. The purser called out to her in a clear, angry, and unstuttering voice to come back, but was answered only with silence. He waited, listening, hearing only the sound of wind rustling the dry needles in the nearby pines as night came on.

Finally, Carpenter drove on southward. He skirted the edges of small sleepy towns in his 1965 Volkswagen, spinning along Highway 9, toward Boulder Creek. At

10:15 P.M., just ten miles from the town, Carpenter's headlights picked up a lone auto moving sluggishly along the road ahead of him.

By now desperate, he pressed down on the accelerator until the two-door sedan was bearing down on the slower-moving car. The driver of the other car, nineteen-year-old Cheryl Lynn Smith, was just returning from her parents' house to her home in Boulder Creek. She looked up in time to see the onrushing vehicle in her rearview mirror but not in time to avoid being hit.

Unshaken by the collision, Carpenter looked down on the seat next to him where he had thrown a knife he used to cut salami, and his pale hand closed around the handle. When he got out of his car the wheels of the woman's car were spinning in the dirt along the road's edge and a dense cloud of dust had formed. For an instant Carpenter was only an indistinct shadow moving through the cloud. When Cheryl Lynn could see him clearly she lashed out, "Why did you crash into me? Are you drunk or something?"

Carpenter would later claim that the auto accident precipitated the violent string of events that followed, that he was depressed over an unhappy love affair he was having with a San Francisco State student and Cheryl Lynn had suggested he go back. "This set me off," he said afterward.

Carpenter did not respond at first but proceeded to estimate the damage to both vehicles, moving behind her as he spoke, registering his regret for the accident, the knife under his coat. As Cheryl Lynn was examining her own car, her back to him, the purser suddenly reached for her neck.

"I want to rape you—I'll have to kill you if you don't come with me," he whispered.

She felt fingers digging into her forearms, dragging her up the sharp incline of the hillside. Brambles, thistles, and thorns tore at her clothing and nylons and both of her shoes were lost on the hill's steep slope. One shoe went tumbling to the road below and landed next to her car.

Carpenter grabbed at her clothes, forcing her to undress. He had now taken out the knife and, grasping her lowered dress in one large fist, proceeded to pull her the rest of the way up the hill, where he ripped off her remaining garments.

In an effort to escape from him Cheryl Lynn found herself sliding and slipping down the embankment. The purser lunged at her with the blade, striking at her arms and legs. When she saw her blood dripping into the dust she dropped into a crouching position. Abruptly the purser became motionless. The muscles in the girl's right arm had been partially severed, and she could feel other wounds in her left hand as she wriggled away and started hobbling down the incline. Effortlessly, the man caught up with her and grasped Cheryl's bleeding forearms, letting his fingers slip to her wrists.

She finally found the courage to look up at her attacker's face again and was stunned to see how altered it was from when he had first come upon her. His features and his manner had softened, and he became both gentle and solicitous toward her as he wrapped her in his coat and let her walk back to where the cars were. Most of her clothing was left behind on the hillcrest.

"Look," he stammered, "you're hurt and b-b-b-bleeding. Let me follow you home and I'll bandage you up if you make me a promise not to call the police."

She refused and made it back to her car under her own power, got it started, and drove off. She was aware of the beating of her own heart, her own breathing, the stickiness of the car's steering wheel. When she looked in the rearview mirror she froze. The stranger was as good as his word. He was following at a distance.

Just ahead were the welcoming lights of a small Boulder Creek hotel, and she raced toward it. Her attacker kept pace. She had no idea if he was following to see if she was going to be all right or if he was going to repeat the assault. When she reached the lights of the hotel the purser panicked and sped away into the night.

But not before she jotted down YIY 104—his license-plate number.

A doctor was called, and Cheryl was found to have a deep wound of about three inches long in her right tricep and a seriously deep cut on her left palm. A cast was put on her arm, and she began the first of five days of hospitalization.

Carpenter returned to his Sutter Street apartment, carefully changed out of his blood-spattered clothes, left them in a heap on the floor, and packed a bag with new clothes, a hunting knife, flashlight, and electrical cord. He was aware that it would be only a short while before his car was traced because it was registered in his wife's name, and he wasn't surprised when he soon heard banging at the front door—the San Francisco police. Carpenter raced out the rear door of the apartment with his bag, abandoning his wife's car, and walked the entire way to Daly City, where he slept in a deserted house. Unshaven, unwashed, unrepentant, he woke in the Wednesday morning light.

He hitchhiked to Santa Cruz where he was let out near the woods. He passed an abandoned car, mired in the soft iron-colored mud, worked his way down the hillside into a rocky gully and then up a small hillock.

As he walked under the shadows of pines he could see in the distance a thin white trail of smoke from a chimney. He was near Empire Grade Road, and soon he came to another house. He was dazed. He had picked up a chill, and when he got to the house the lifeless air that clung like a shroud to each still leaf in the clearing failed to warm him.

It was 2:30 P.M. when the owner of the house, Mrs. Wilma Joyce McDonald,* a schoolteacher, returned home with her two sons, aged seven and three. She was surprised to see her husband sitting in an easy chair in their front room wearing his robe and holding a 16-gauge shotgun. But the shadowy figure in the chair *wasn't* her husband. It was a stranger wearing his clothes.

The silhouetted man spoke in a clear voice and explained he was wearing the robe because "That bitch last night got excited and there was b-b-blood all over the place."

Carpenter made the mother and the boys lie facedown on the kitchen floor. Eventually he sent the boys to their bedroom and forced the schoolteacher to accompany him.

*The last name of this person has been changed.

They took her car and drove to an empty cabin once owned by his parents from 1934 until 1949 in the Santa Cruz area, near Henry Cowell Redwood State Park, where the purser had stored some of his things. But before he drove the woman back to her children he raped her.

"He told me to put my hands behind my back," she said later, "and, if I would do that he wouldn't hurt me . . ." Afterward his mood had changed. He had carefully wiped the caked mud from his shoe and knees and apologized while he drove her back to her home. He took her husband's hat and a jacket. Stealing the teacher's Mercedes-Benz Carpenter cried out, "I'm sick. I need help. I'm lonely," and he drove off, heading back toward Daly City. At 8:05 the next morning, January 29, Sharon O'Donnell, twenty-five, was accosted by Carpenter in her apartment house parking garage at 355 Park Plaza in Daly City. Holding a rifle on her, Carpenter forced the woman into the Mercedes and tied her hands. While he was switching plates from O'Donnell's VW to the teacher's car O'Donnell was able to get free and run from the garage. Carpenter then stole *her* car and fled. A bloody flashlight, a hunting knife, and a brown electrical cord with one end tied in a slip knot were found in the abandoned Mercedes.

For days the purser hid out in the woods. He had lost his nerve after the failed kidnapping and abandoned O'Donnell's car in Calaveras County. At 11:05 A.M., February 3, Tuesday, Lucille Davis, a cleaning woman, responded to a knock at the back of her employer's residence. Davis opened the door to see Carpenter brandishing a long-barreled pistol at her. He tied her to a bed, robbed her of three dollars, and stole her automobile. Police later theorized that the purser had stolen the gun in Amador City.

Forty-five minutes later Barbara Robb,* a twenty-five-year-old housewife, opened her back door, thinking the man outside was her husband. Pointing the pistol at her, Carpenter pushed his way into her Angel's Camp home and demanded her keys and any money she might have.

*The last name of this person has been changed.

"I have killed before," he said, "and I'll do it again if you don't come with me."

Taking her infant son with them she was forced at gunpoint to drive the purser to an area known as the Sheep Ranch on Avery Road. He took Barbara and her child to a campsite he had hidden in the woods. She was compelled to remove all of her clothing and to submit to an act of sexual intercourse. Afterward Carpenter re-dressed in a different set of clothes, which he had kept at the campsite, and ordered Barbara to drive him to the outskirts of Oakdale. Carpenter was enthralled with the sixteen-month-old child and bounced him on his knee as the mother drove. Barbara could not take her eyes off the blue-steel gun, which lay on the seat between them. Catching her eye, the man smiled. "It's been a long time since I held a baby this small."

Close to Oakdale he had the mother leave him alongside the road. She watched as he walked away and said later, "I remember him as quite kind. He was especially gentle with my baby."

Though Carpenter seemingly acted in a panic, his actions were calculated. "Carpenter's got a bag of tricks with him," recalled one detective years later. "He's got a briefcase or an AWOL bag and he's got in there handcuffs, garrotes, changes of clothing. When he would take these women off he would take them to a spot where he had already designated he was gonna be. When he's through with his crime, it's like Superman going to the phone booth—he changes his clothes, his identity, and he walks right out of the area.

"He was meticulous in how he had these attacks planned. He would be in a jogging suit, take off a victim, rape her in front of her child or whatever, and then when he got through and had her all tied up he'd go into his little bag, open it up, take off the jogging suit and put on a sweater and a pair of shorts and walk out of the park. He was trying to run, but he didn't know where to run to so he'd always go to the woods. Isn't that odd."

Carpenter hitchhiked to Modesto and made directly for the Greyhound bus depot there. At 8:30 P.M. Stanislaus County deputies from the sheriff's office spotted him and he was placed under arrest. He was advised of his rights but declined to make any comment regarding the battery of charges being leveled at him. He was placed in the Calaveras County Jail to await trial.

The purser looked around the small jail. Though he was being held on rape charges, rape was one of his greatest fears.

"Such county jails have tanks that can hold as many as thirty men," he said, "with very limited supervision. Homosexual rape is only one part of what goes on there. The strong take anything and everything, whether it be food off a person's tray, his clothes, his shoes, his money, his canteen, his sex . . . you name it. And you can't say anything because if you do, you are branded a snitch—you could get killed."

Events were not over yet. On Monday, April 27, 1970, Carpenter led an escape of himself and four other inmates. They cut through their cell bars and got out through a skylight. Easily, they all vaulted a fence and loped into the woods. After the break the prisoners huddled together in a wheat field.

At this point Carpenter told the other men some astonishing information. "I am," he proudly stated, "the Zodiac Killer." The other escapees looked from one to the other. They knew the Zodiac was a serial killer whom the police had been searching for since 1966. Zodiac's specialty was taunting the police before and after each murder with a series of macabre letters and cryptographs. The convicts did not believe the purser.

In only a short time bloodhounds sniffed out the fugitives and deputies crunched their way through the dry straw of the field to recapture them. Like the yellow wheat in the deserted field, the accusations against the purser grew inch by inch until the stuttering man seemed about to be swallowed up in his own file.

On May 1, the complicated charges were broken up into two groups—the first, two counts of armed robbery and one count of kidnapping; the second, one count of auto theft and prison escape. For the first group Carpenter was sentenced to five years to life on two counts and one year to twenty-five years to run consecutively. In the second group there were two counts of from six months to five years.

Judge Joseph Huberty said of Carpenter, "I believe that this man is extremely dangerous and that he should be incarcerated for a substantial period of time." Three days later the purser was in prison at Vacaville.

In July the Santa Cruz grand jury returned a five-count indictment against Carpenter, charging him with assault with intent to commit rape on Cheryl Lynn Smith and rape, robbery, and car theft by force and fear against Wilma Joyce McDonald and her kidnapping. The purser pleaded Not Guilty to all counts, and the case was bound over for jury trial. Appearing before the jury at Santa Cruz on October 5, Carpenter withdrew his earlier plea and pleaded Guilty to rape and burglary, by stipulation fixed as first-degree burglary, and, upon motion of the DA, three counts of the indictment were dismissed. As Carpenter stood listening to the questioning, he became breathless, and the long-familiar feelings of humiliation and anxiety grew within him.

"When Carpenter went to the joint," one policeman recalled, "he went for nonsexual offenses. Now that is very important to him. Robbery, kidnapping, crimes of violence—that's what he went in for. He didn't want to go to the joint and have a tail on him when he came out as being a sex offender. Besides in the joint sex offenders are often treated differently."

On October 29, 1970, just before being sentenced on rape and robbery counts, Carpenter told Santa Cruz Superior Judge Charles S. Franich about his severe stammering problem. "I wish you well, sir," Franich replied, "but something has to be done about your overpowering desire for sex."

Carpenter was defended by a Santa Cruz attorney, Jim Jackson, who was aware that the man had once told his parole officer that "During periods of extreme stress my sexual urge rises to such a point that it becomes an overwhelming impulse." Jackson wrote to his client while he was in jail and told his associates that he thought the man was a "sensitive person. I never knew why he did what he did when I represented him. Some people are wicked and heartless. But he was never that way to me. He was easy to get along with and intelligent.''

Judge Franich wrote to the prison authorities to recommend that the purser be given some sort of speech therapy to cure his stuttering. Was there a connection between his stuttering and his murderous attacks? he wondered.

Back in May, when he had first been processed into Vacaville at the Northern Reception Guidance Center and assigned prisoner number B 27305, Carpenter was tested and determined to have an IQ of 125, which placed him in the upper percentile. He also was assessed as having a personality disorder which manifested itself by hostility toward women.

Dr. Ralph Allison, a psychiatrist, examined the forty-year-old Carpenter for a probation report in 1970 and painstakingly constructed a picture of the man from his childhood on. Apparently David Carpenter was the child of strict, demanding parents who seemingly preferred his older brother and younger sister to him. Carpenter's Santa Cruz probation officer, James Solomon, noted in a psychiatric file the prisoner's pathological history dating back to age seven, when he first started stammering: "His parents and siblings were not fond of him at all, being somewhat ashamed of his speech impediment."

Carpenter was naturally left handed but was forced first by his mother and then by a succession of teachers to use his right hand. Fighting against this, the child became openly rebellious. Added to this was the fact that he had suffered from remarkably poor vision since the time he had begun stammering.

David Carpenter's parents, Frances Elizabeth (née Hart) and Elwood Ashley Carpenter, had married in San Francisco on August 6, 1929, when David's father was twenty-nine and his mother twenty-two. Elwood was at the time recovering from the failure of a previous marriage, which had produced a son, William Elwood, who was being raised by his mother in Idaho.

David Joseph Carpenter was born May 6, 1930, at Stanford Hospital in San Francisco while his father was working as a postal delivery driver and the family was living at 1680 Alabama Street. His birth was filed as Registry Number 2793, Certificate Number 8-5147.

Four years later the purser's sister, Anne, was born and the family moved to 152 Sussex Street. Carpenter's childhood, which he described as hellish, was unhappy primarily because of his mother's unloving, inflexible, and exceedingly domineering stance within the family group. It reached such a point that Elwood, Carpenter's father, left home for over a year when David was fourteen. Many of the arguments were over Carpenter's speech impediment, but mystifyingly his mother did not want him to seek treatment for it. Because of this affliction he had few friends during his formative years and was a chronic bed wetter into his early teens.

David's mother made attempts to treat his stammer, but these were tentative at best. Frances Carpenter would go as far as making arrangements at the U.C. Medical Center, but would take him to the door of the clinic, stand for a moment, and then inexplicably take the child back home again. Other times she would arrive too late for the appointment. "He would dwaddle and dwaddle," she would say.

At Glen Park Elementary School Carpenter's life was no better. "I tried," said one teacher. "I tried and tried and I just couldn't get through to him." The physical abuse and emotional neglect during David's developmental years had scarred him, limiting his interaction with others. David would do cruel things like pulling the wings off a fly to shock the other kids. "At school," wrote Dr. Allison, "he was always made fun of . . . because of the stammer and inability to get out answers, even though he was brighter than most children in the school."

Carpenter was so regularly roughed up by his classmates after school, children who resented his role as both teacher's pet and sometimes class snitch, that Frances forbade him to play with other kids after class, and on the rare occasions she allowed children over to the Carpenter home on narrow, twisting Sussex Street, she set arbitrary, often unrealistic, time limits. When these limits were reached the visitor would abruptly be ordered to leave.

Usually the lonely child's afternoons were filled with

a succession of ballet lessons and violin classes. The perhaps excessively well-groomed David could be seen trudging to class, his violin under his arm, dressed in what was called at the time a Little Lord Fauntleroy suit, his precious brown locks lovingly and neatly trimmed by Frances.

Evonne Cary, one of the children on Sussex Street, felt sorry for David, and it was common knowledge among his classmates that the stuttering child's mother beat him. There would be gaps of two to three days when David would be absent from Glen Park Elementary. "Then," recalled Evonne, "when he would come back, he would be covered with bruises from head to toe. He wore short pants, so you could see the black and blue marks on his legs as well as painful welts on his arms and his face. Short pants weren't acceptable then, but his mother made him wear them." Evonne could recall opening her fourth grade yearbook to see the group graduation class photo, and as she peered closely she could see that even on the special day when the class portrait was taken, David distinctly had a black eye.

One summer, Evonne's family camped in Redwood Valley and found themselves situated near the Carpenter family. At breakfast the second day she saw David stumble and break a milk bottle. Frances Carpenter reached for her husband's belt and beat David with the buckle end so brutally that she left welts. To Evonne it seemed that no matter what the stammering child did it wasn't good enough for his mother. As far as Evonne could tell, Elwood Carpenter acted in much the same manner toward his son, but his abuse was mostly verbal. However, around him David would toe the line like a soldier.

It was no wonder, with the combination of physical and verbal abuse, that all of David's attempts to fit in with his peers met with failure. During games he was cast as the villain, though the other children were aware of his rough life. "There was just something about him," said one, "that made him aggravating to be around." Attacked by the larger boys, stammering, weak-sighted, David would retaliate by trying to choke them or, in response to the rejection and pain he felt, would secretly take out his aggressions on small animals. Instead of playing sports he would play chess with the grown-ups, and every adult on Sussex Street knew "that kid is book smart, not street smart."

David's best friend, Robert Gorrebeeck, lived two houses away with his brother, Ray, and could recall that visiting the Carpenter home was tantamount to walking on eggs. "Frances and Elwood had lain down specific rules. It was like you had to make an appointment before you could go over and see him." The strict parents, as far as Robert was concerned, were part of David's problem, but he could name two other reasons the child was so universally disliked. "Partly it was his clothes. They always dressed him up like some fancy pants, and the kids on the block were always pounding the hell out of him. He always looked like he was going to private school. Partly it was because he got such good grades, because he was smart as a whip.

"But after the neighbor kids would get through punching him—he couldn't fight back—his parents would take over. Can you imagine gettin' a beating because you went camping and came home with dirt on your pants? Practically his only friends were the neighborhood girls. He usually had my sympathy, but then he'd do something cruel like twisting the head off some girl's doll. He'd get that stupid smile on his face like it was a prank."

A neighbor child, Paul Anderson, had never seen any of David's beatings but recalled one evening, on an errand for his mother, that he had passed the Carpenter home and heard David screaming. Next day at Glen Park school he saw pink, raised marks on David's face. Paul knew that David was scared of his mother and would become anxious when the special time he had to be home approached. "I'll g-g-get hit," he would cry racing over the curved street toward his home, which was framed by dark green trees on the hillside above.

Carpenter's life continued in much the same manner until in the tenth grade at Balboa High he ran away from home and school and hid in the Santa Cruz mountains in the family cabin at Redwood Grove, the same cabin Carpenter would, as an adult, force the schoolteacher to drive him to in 1970. After his truancy he was expelled from school.

Dr. Allison could trace the young man's difficulties with the law to the age of twelve. At fourteen Carpenter was actually committed to Napa State Hospital for sex offenses. Detectives spoke years later of his many escapes from institutions and how he was drawn to the wilderness of Santa Cruz, where he was suspected of committing burglaries, so many that the neighbors in the Boulder Creek area near Santa Cruz requested they be notified the next time Carpenter left Napa. At the age of seventeen David was sentenced to the California Youth Authority facility at Preston, California, charged with molesting two cousins, an eight-year-old boy and a three-year-old girl, whom he had encountered in a Diamond Heights park and taken to a school bathroom. He allegedly threatened them with a knife and told them, "My dog will bite you if you don't do what I say." Carpenter later denied that he had engaged in oral copulation with the girl but was kept at the facility until he was eighteen and paroled in December of 1948 after being committed to Napa State Hospital for ninety days of study.

His juvenile records show an embittered, incorrigible teenager with five arrests on sex charges, a history of one escape from Juvenile Hall, and an additional two walkaways from the same facility. Carpenter often bragged to the other inmates that he had spent his teen years getting into trouble raping girls. "By the time I was eighteen I had had intercourse fifty times, sometimes with consent, but most often by force," he said.

Dr. Allison asked Carpenter point blank, "When did all of this start?" Carpenter looked across the office desk and said, "I pulled down a little girl's pants for the first time when I was eight years old." Allison looked down in his journal and wrote carefully, "David Carpenter had learned to take out his anger sexually."

As a youth he had been employed driving a truck and doing messenger service around the piers and docks of San Francisco for his father's shipping express business. In the summer of 1950 he was employed as an office boy and messenger for the H.B. Thomas Company on Battery Street.

On August 5, 1950, Carpenter's parents were away from the Sussex Street home, and Carpenter was driving

a seventeen-year-old girl he knew to her girlfriend's house
when he asked her if they could stop by the family residence so she could help him straighten up the living room
before his parents got back. Once inside Carpenter made
sexual overtures toward the girl, but she managed to escape him by locking herself in the bathroom and crawling
out the window.

He was bound over on the charge he had "willfully
and feloniously made an assault upon . . . a female under
the age of eighteen, with the intent to have and accom-
plish the act of sexual intercourse upon said female."
Carpenter pled Not Guilty to the charge. A jury trial was
held on October 10, and he was found Not Guilty.

Allison noted that though the purser had dropped out
of Balboa High in the tenth grade he had completed his
education while serving time at McNeil Island. Santa
Cruz probation officer Solomon told Dr. Allison that the
captured purser at the time "made no attempt to deny
the allegations against him, had been quite cooperative,
and asked only that he be placed in a facility where he
could receive help."

In his report Allison wrote, "During moments of extreme stress, sexual urges often reach such a point they
become an overwhelming impulse." He described the
prisoner as "enterprising, capable, energetic, versatile,
exacting, individualistic, verbally facile, persuasive, and
sentimental. . . . He certainly has poor impulse control."

Dr. Allison did not note Carpenter's most acute attrib-
ute, his genius at reading people, seeing out their most
vulnerable area and then manipulating them.

Allison believed that Carpenter was acting out the ego
of his mother. His mother hated women, hated her own
aunt, Carpenter told Allison, therefore so did Carpenter.
The purser without fail portrayed himself as the victim
of a woman, of women in general. All of his actions
stemmed from this belief. If blame were placed it should
fall upon the woman, the catalyst for his rage.

Allison labeled Carpenter a "mentally disordered sex
offender" and began looking for the "treatable cause"
rather than the symptoms. Could it be Carpenter's stammer? Allison wrote, "If he could get proper therapy for

his stammering we might be able to prevent further catastrophes of this sort.'' Later Allison said that ''we don't have any clear information on why people stutter. Sometimes with a different method of expression, like singing, the stutter disappears.''

Why did Carpenter's stutter disappear prior to and during his sexual attacks? Was there some connection between the stutter and the violence? Most authorities on stuttering say no. A serious stutterer does not tend to be any more aggressive than the average person. Under high emotion, stuttering often disappears. It is believed that in the case of some stutterers their ''nervous systems react to stress by increasing tension in the muscles controlling the larynx.''

Dr. Martin Schwartz of New York University writes, ''There are three major target areas of stress-induced muscle tension. The shoulder muscles, abdominal wall muscles and facial muscles. But about 3 percent of the world's people have a primary target area of tension in the larynx. . . . the result is a spasm in the muscles of the larynx controlling the vocal cords. . . . children develop a stutter as a result of a struggle pattern of trying to force out words through the constricted muscles.''

The fear of stuttering and the fear of certain words can trigger a spasm. Dr. Schwartz had a theory on why some individuals would stop stuttering before and during an angry outburst. Some stutterers don't stutter when distracted by the subject of their anger. Extreme tension would affect every muscle in the body and ''that little signal from the larynx would be overpowered by tension from elsewhere . . . physiological masking.''

At the time of Carpenter's arrest it was also known that there was sometimes a link between brain tumors and murderous attacks. Allison knew of Charles Whitman's ''sudden impulsive outbursts'' prior to his murdering, from an Austin, Texas, water tower, seventeen people in 1960. More recently angel dust, PCP, has been blamed for some homicides.

Allison concluded, ''Whenever Carpenter feels hemmed-in his sexual urge climbs, and the only way he can think straight, to make plans and act on them, is to rape the nearest female.

"He is a very bright man who has many capabilities, and he is not a professional criminal. It would seem worth the state's time and money to try an effective rehabilitation approach for him, for a change."

Carpenter was sent to Folsom Prison on June 17, 1970, and then to San Quentin in a temporary medical transfer from August 2, 1972, until October 18, 1972. He was returned to Folsom, and then on December 4, 1972, transferred to the California Medical Facility at Vacaville until February 28, 1977.

During his time at Vacaville he conformed to all prison regulations, cheerfully performed his assigned work, and did not present any disciplinary problems. Because of this he was kept in medium custody.

"When I was at Folsom and Vacaville," he said later, "I worked a lot of key inmate positions in the 1970s where I was around staff most of the time and a lot of the higher echelon of the prison—lieutenants, captains, and associate wardens. It got to where they treated me like a piece of furniture and talked freely in front of me, which allowed me to learn a lot about the California Department of Corrections.

"At that time, CDC was trying to really build an empire and was frustrated at not being able to expand the way they wanted. I remember back then that things were very mellow—even with the overcrowding and having two men in a cell at a time.

"Everybody had a job, and at that time, virtually all of the work inside of the prison and outside of the prison was done by prisoners; the cost for operating and maintaining the prisons was cheap because of this use of the prisoners.

"But the hardest part of being in prison has to be concern for one's physical safety," Carpenter wrote afterward. "The only out-of-cell activity nowadays for most of the men in the California prison system—other than visits and taking a shower—is to go out to the yard. And it's the yard where most of the trouble, the fighting, stabbings, and killing, takes place.

"More and more, men are being put in a position of having to join some kind of gang simply for survival. But one you join such a group, you have to go along with whatever the group decides to do or your life is now in jeopardy from the group.'' Carpenter generally avoided drugs, drink, and inflammatory racial situations and limited his betting to sporting events while in prison. The system of sentencing had just changed, replaced by indeterminate sentencing. Many of the prisoners were bored and that, said Carpenter, "invariably leads to trouble. Violence becomes a relief from boredom." Carpenter was suffering from emotional problems and was awarded a disability claim by Social Security of $246.30 per month, which was made payable to his mother.

Carpenter pondered what kind of men the system released upon society. "But what happens when prisoners are released who have lived in an atmosphere of violence for years and years? These men are going to come out with no rehabilitation, no skills, and no good feelings for their fellow men. It makes no sense to keep someone locked down the entire time he is in prison and then on the day his term is over release him to society from a locked-down situation."

Carpenter took numerous outside college courses in finance, mathematics, accounting, and philosophy and received top grades. Enrolled in vocational welding and sheet-metal courses he did less well but was constantly improving.

Employed in a clerical capacity within the institution, he did above-average work. At Vacaville he became involved in group therapy and was diagnosed as a bright man who had many capabilities, was not a professional criminal but had a sexual deviation, "sadism (rape) with a passive/aggressive personality."

As his years in prison passed, the purser increased his group therapy activity within the group session to the point where a female co-therapist was utilized to teach him how to cope with his deep-seated hostilities, which in the past he had directed toward women and which were a result of the many problems he had had in his early life with a rejecting mother. His 1973 probation report read: "He was so often beaten as a child that he developed a crippling stutter."

In 1973, Carpenter's seventeen-year-old son, Michael,

stayed at the Carpenter home with the purser's parents and was struck by the fact that there were no pictures of his father there. He was never mentioned and was considered nonexistent. "We didn't have any contact with his side of the family," said Michael, "because of an agreement between him and Mom that he wasn't to contact us while we were growing up." In 1974, Michael, curious went to Vacaville to meet his father for the first time since Carpenter's divorce. After their meeting the purser began writing his son once a week, usually regarding business or finances, and helping him financially structure his life.

At Vacaville in 1975 Carpenter submitted a letter to the psychotherapy group in which he stated that as a result of extensive treatment in the therapy session, especially since utilizing the assistance of a woman cotherapist, "I was able to get down to gut level dealing with my sexual hang-ups and learned how to deal with women on the same level as everyone else. I do not have any hostilities toward women any more nor will I ever have to rape another woman, or use force against them because I feel adequate now and do not suffer from the stresses and strains that I have for these past many years. I am presently working on my speech problems and I feel more confident in myself than at any point in my life."

"Carpenter was the kind of guy," recalled one prison guard, "who could be standing in a rain storm and lie about the weather . . . he could also get people to do things for him under the guise of innocent assignments. He had the habit of creating a colorful or dramatic cover story to hide his dealings, no matter how innocent, with these people."

After his parole from Vacaville in 1977, the purser was released to the federal authorities to serve some two and one half more years for violating the terms of his 1960 assault conviction. Taken by a U.S. marshal he was housed in the Sacramento County Jail and then McNeil Island.

On May 9, 1978, Carpenter was sent from McNeil Island to Lompoc Federal Penitentiary, where he developed a tight circle of four friends—his best friend, a man known by the nickname The Greek, Jeff, Nation, and a bright, likeable, music-obsessed young man who was serving a six-year sentence for bank robbery and considered Carpenter a mentor, Shane Williams. Shane and Carpenter met during the recreation period.

During the time he was at Lompoc a Santa Rosa woman, Mollie Jo Purnell, became Carpenter's pen pal. "I first c-c-c-came in contact with her," he recalled, "when she headed the Amanda Blair Friendship Club. She established a friendship club between men and women to make herself a few dollars . . . and eventually opened it up to prisoners." Mollie also published a pen pal newspaper.

"Mollie," an official said later, "is the type of individual who's going to be a pushover for anything and everything. She was married to a former convict, and I assume she met him in the same way she met Carpenter, through the mail. Her husband, Raymond, committed suicide in August 1978; he shot himself in the bathroom. Mollie was at her most vulnerable when she met Carpenter. Her father had died in March 1978 as well. She had once been a rape victim [December 1978] and was very surprised that Carpenter was not at all sympathetic about her assault. But, like I said, he always picks the right people to do what he wants, just that incredible ability of his to find the right person."

Mollie had several contacts with Shane Williams, beginning in February of 1979. "Shane," Carpenter claimed later, "asked me to have Mollie accept s-s-s-some funds he was going to have sent so they could get some marijuana from this guy in prison who was supplying it. . . . I used to call her two or three times a week from a little room they have at Lompoc. 'I'll let you talk to Shane,' I told her. Shane asked her if she'd please accept some money orders and then send the money to the family of the prisoner who was selling the pot." Shane gave Mollie the cash under the pretext of buying a guitar. A third party was to purchase drugs with the money. "M-M-M-Mollie," said Carpenter, "knew nothing about the nature of the purchase. I just told her I'd like her to do a favor. Shane may have told her the purpose, but it's been so long ago I don't remember."

Because phone records existed, records that would af-

terward be used to develop a case against Carpenter, he
would later claim these (and future conversations and
meetings) concerned marijuana deals. Ultimately the authorities would prove that these calls actually had nothing
to do with the sale or purchase of marijuana. At no time
was Mollie Purnell involved in the traffic of drugs.

"Shortly before I left prison, I think it was in April, I
made another arrangement that Mollie receive funds and
s-s-s-send the funds on. I know the first transaction definitely went through, but I don't know about the s-s-
second."

Using money earned by selling stocks out of his cell
through his mother and sister, Carpenter, as he neared
the end of his sentence, made arrangements to have certain packages mailed to himself in care of Mollie. Sometime between May and the end of July she received a
parcel with no return address, but with a New York post-
mark. It was securely taped and she stored it away in her
closet with the others. However, her curiosity was
aroused, especially after Carpenter warned her against
opening this particular package.

Over a period of days the matronly and much-put-upon
widow studied the parcel from the East Coast. Finally
one day she was driven to open it, carefully peeling back
the tape so that the purser would not know it had been
opened. Mollie saw it was full of wadded newspapers.
As she pushed these aside she saw what she would later
describe as "a large revolver . . . bluish-black."

Quickly Mollie retaped the package as neatly as she
could and replaced it in the closet vowing never to tell
Carpenter what she had seen.

On May 21, 1979, David Joseph Carpenter, under parole
conditions until October 28, 1982, was released to Reality House West at 380 Eddy Street in San Francisco, a
halfway house for federal prisoners. The building had
been the Cadillac Hotel, an elite, Victorian hotel, and
was bought by Kathy Sofos and Leroy Looper on a "no-
money-down basis" in 1969. They had transformed it
into a halfway house. "We worked very hard," remembered Kathy. "We painted everything in sight, we carpeted all the hallways, flushed all those plugged-up

toilets." Kathy scoured and scrubbed, polished and painted, fumigated and decorated the old 159-room building till it stood out among the rundown and boarded-up Tenderloin buildings, a safe harbor in a turbulent sea.

Reality House West sits downtown in the heart of the toughest part of San Francisco. It provides temporary housing for ambulatory mental patients, some eighty senior citizens, detoxifying alcoholics, and approximately forty-five "nonrisk" ex-convicts, who use the house for sixty to ninety days as a "reentry base." There was some worry about putting convicts and seniors together, but the Loopers' contract with the Bureau of Prisons called for nonviolent people in need of a transitional phase, although Kathy thought the bureau sometimes misrepresented some prisoners. Leroy, a linebacker-size New Yorker, knew all the tricks of the cons and the junkies, since he had been both as well as an abused child.

Carpenter was under certain restrictions at the halfway house, he recalled. "You had to check in by 11:00 P.M. if I'm not mistaken. Had to be in until 6:00 A.M., unless you had a job where you had to leave earlier. You could get a weekend pass if you had a place to go."

Carpenter lived in a single, second-floor room that the Bureau of Prisons was paying $17 a day for while he searched for a job and went about getting his life back together with the help of a counselor. The compact room had steam heat, new carpeting, draperies comprised of lace curtains and shades, an old walnut dresser circa 1900, bed, headboard, chair, and walls painted the same color as the building's beige exterior.

Just as maids did their daily room cleaning, Kathy did drug and contraband searches. If she found anything, an IDC (incident) report would be filed. "It depended," she said, "on what we found. If I found a marijuana seed I would probably put the person on restriction, but if I found drugs I would send them back to prison."

On his second day at the halfway house Carpenter called Mollie Purnell specifically to discuss picking up his packages and again throughout the week on May 25, 26, and 27.

Carpenter's twenty-year-old daughter, Gabrielle, had grown up not being allowed to talk about her father. She was working at a car dealership near Reality House and on May 27 Carpenter walked over to see her. "The first time I met him," she later said, "He just walked into the office and asked for me and said, 'Hi, I'm your dad,' and gave me a box of candy." She found in him a nature "that is warm and sensitive toward the needs of other people."

On Wednesday, May 23, 1979, two days after his release from Lompoc, David Carpenter made initial contact with the Department of Vocational Rehabilitation in Oakland, referred to this agency by his new parole officer, Richard Wood. There he was given a physical and psychiatric examination and sent to a speech therapist, D. Wayne Smith, for four hours per week.

At Lompoc Dr. Matheson's records of Carpenter's speech therapy presented a different picture than he had presented to Wood—they showed a steady and successful progression of speaking without impairment. "Improved," it read. "Carpenter speaking with moderate to severe stutter," and the final record entry of March 1979 said, "Carpenter speaking without speech impediment." Why then was the purser still stuttering?

Smith, the therapist, believed Carpenter had never had any real therapy for his speech defect and explained to him that he shouldn't try and hide his stuttering. "First of all, it's impossible to do. I want you to take your time speaking, pause often." He then asked Carpenter what his main speech problems were. "There are three," the balding man replied. "One is talking on the phone, second is talking in front of large groups, and the third is meeting s-s-s-strangers for the first time. I have partial problems with the letter *m*, as in *mother* and *money*." These were two subjects that obsessed Carpenter. "I have particular trouble with *s*. I don't ever remember *not* s-s-s-stuttering."

Smith suggested that Carpenter advertise the fact he stuttered. "Let everyone know. Ask yourself when you're in a situation if your self-image is a positive or a negative one. How do you perceive the person you are talking to? Is your own body energy at low ebb? Learn to accept the worst before it happens and you will lose much of your fear. Be kinder to yourself."

Carpenter had read about using a metronome, and he began experimenting. He learned that when he spoke in a singsong manner he didn't stutter, but it all came apart when he was in a pressure situation.

In an attempt to help his stuttering after his release from Folsom the purser began smoking marijuana. "I did experiment with it when I got out of prison in 1979," he admitted later. "Alas, it really didn't do anything for me speechwise. My stuttering s-s-stayed the same, but my attitude toward my stuttering changed. The more I smoked, the less I cared or let it bother me."

On June 5, two weeks after the purser had come to stay at Reality House West, he joined the Sierra Club and began to hike in groups of fourteen to twenty people on the Sleeping Lady, Mount Tamalpais, on the weekends. Altogether he later claimed to have hiked on Tamalpais twenty-five times, six to twelve of those alone or with his dog, Herman.

Once Carpenter was at Reality House West, his parole officer, Richard Wood, began to work up a release plan: 'Where he's gonna live, work, go to school." Wood called Neil Nevesny in Oakland, who was with the Department of Vocational Rehabilitation. Wood and Nevesny were friends and had done a lot of business together. Nevesny interviewed the purser and found him eligible for their services. Carpenter would attend a common treatment center in Oakland, a facility owned and operated by the Bureau of Prisons. Reality House West, also under contract with the Bureau of Prisons, differed in that it was a private organ and was paid a daily fee for each client.

Nevesny placed Carpenter with a computer printer training school in Hayward. "This guy shouldn't be working around women," Wood warned him.

"Hey, no," said Nevesny. "This is an electric typesetting school, so if he gets a job he's going to be sitting in a room by himself with a typesetter."

"Sounds good to me," said Wood.

By letter, Wood advised the vocational center through Nevesny on June 14, 1979, that because of Carpenter's history of violence he "should not be permitted to maintain a job which provides an opportunity or temptation to injure someone.'' The concerned federal probation officer went on to suggest, ''In the event this man is employed in a position around women and that a woman in that employment was subsequently raped by him without anyone advising the employer of his prior record for rape then there will be grave consequences.'' Such a ''duty to warn'' letter was standard policy, and Wood had written many. Wood felt, ''Even if Nevesny warned them and they still went ahead and said, 'Look we'll place him next to women,' then it's, 'I warned them and that's all I can do.' Basically, you've got to cover your ass.''

On July 23, 1979, Carpenter began the computer printing course at the California Trade School at 25100 Mission Boulevard in Hayward. The course ran for six months at a cost to the state of $2,400. The school was owned and operated by Joseph Elia and Lane Thomsen, and they sometimes hired promising students to teach or work in the school's retail outlet, Econo Quick Print.* Carpenter immediately hit it off so well with the two businessmen that he set his eye on one of these jobs. On July 23 he made a trip to Santa Rosa to see his eldest daughter.

During his first week at the printing school the purser became involved with another student, Nancy Morrison,** who was on federal parole for a narcotics conviction. A relationship developed between the two; since they lived in the same section of San Francisco, the purser drove her back and forth to the school. At the end of July they were going out socially and an odd sexual relationship had developed. Carpenter agreed to pay Nancy a weekly allowance in return for sexual favors. At first he visited her twice a week, but then started to show up more frequently. His attentions were not kinky, but they grew steadily more rough and aggressive. Nancy thought at one point that he was going to crush her during sex. She described him to her friends as ''a horny old man who was turned on by young women.''

Carpenter was undergoing transitional shock at this point. He was used to someone telling him when to get

---

*Located at 25673 Nickle Place, Hayward.
**This name has been altered.

up, when to eat. Like many parolees he had trouble meeting time limits and getting acclimated to the community. On July 30 he told Joe and Lane he had trouble with his eye and was out for the day. "I came back on July 31," he recalled, "but c-c-couldn't work. I had an eyepatch on when I came back to work on August 1, and I could work a full, typical day at the school by August 2. I was there a full six hours. School is 9:00 A.M. through noon, half-hour for lunch, then work until 3:30. If I didn't put the full time in, it could be made up at a later date."

The eye injury provided an excuse for Carpenter to get away to visit Mollie Purnell, his former prison pen pal. Although the purser and Mollie had discussed marriage, the first time they actually met face-to-face was on August 2 when Mollie saw him at the Distribution Center on Pine Street in San Francisco.

She commented on his eyepatch; Carpenter mentioned the packages that had been mailed in care of Mollie. He insisted on coming with her on her route and crowded into her small Honda auto. Mollie completed her rounds for California Couriers by 1:00 P.M. and they headed for Santa Rosa.

Since they had planned to have dinner together they stopped on the way at Speers Market in Forestville. Mollie let Carpenter choose the vegetable. He chose peas with cream sauce, which she hated. She paid for the groceries with a check and they drove to her house. She had the purser wait in her car while she went inside and phoned California Couriers. Returning, Mollie told him she had to go on a special run. "I didn't want to have dinner with him," she said later, "so I told him I wouldn't be available."

Though Carpenter had hinted frequently throughout their trip that he was anxious to pick up his parcels he chose only the one from New York that Mollie secretly knew contained a gun. Carpenter said he would like to go to Marin City, but she took him just to the vicinity of the depot in Santa Rosa.

Monday, August 6, 1979, was a special day. Carpenter was granted a one-day live-out status from the halfway house to attend his parent's fiftieth wedding anniversary celebration, and he played hookey from his trade school classes. ''They were remarried at St. John's Catholic church. Because it was my parents' anniversary a picture was taken there of my three children, M-M-M-Michael, Gabrielle, and Circe, and m-m-myself.'' Tuesday evening he was back at Reality House West.

Mollie wrote him a series of checks dated August 10, 15, and 17 for services in her flea-market sales, and with these, on Friday, August 17, Carpenter opened a savings account at the Continental Savings and Loan* in the Glen Park district where his parents lived.

Carpenter's friendship with his bosses, Joe and Lane, deepened. Eventually he loaned them $2,000 cash for use in their company, Moon Tide, to manufacture drinking mugs. They began to take him in their trailer to Joe Elia's ranch in Mendocino for target practice with their .38-caliber handgun. In the summer of 1979 they left early Friday and stayed at the ranch until late Sunday. At this time a photo of Carpenter wearing a dark windbreaker with a hood was taken by them in front of their trailer. He continued hiking on Mount Tamalpais.

*2855 Diamond Avenue, savings account #2000142.

4

Mill Valley:
Edda, 1979

Lying less than two miles directly beneath Mount Tamalpais, the south Marin County town of Mill Valley is built around an ancient railroad depot from which all its streets radiate. Back in 1896 there were eight miles of track laid in solid rock right up the side of the mountain. A thousand people an hour would take the ferries from San Francisco to Sausalito, link up with the 1.8-mile narrow-gauge electric spur railway, the Tamalpais and Bolinas Line with its bell cast from silver dollars, and crowd the Eastland station to ride Sidney Cushing's deep maroon, gold leaf-trimmed steam train on its zigzag path around 283 curves and over 22 trestles. It was known as "The Crookedest Railway in the World."

At Mesa Junction, halfway up the mountain, the track compressed itself into the shape of a double bowknot in order for the graceful 74,000-pound Shay engine with its six red, open-canopied observation cars and green cable-car caboose to rise one hundred feet in the space of a thousand feet, paralleling itself five times, the track describing forty-two complete circles.

There were moonlit "gravity cars" crowded with top-hatted and bonnetted passengers that would drift silently into the deep redwood canyons of Muir Woods. People drank and danced in those days at The Tavern, just below the East Peak with its fearsome nighttime gales and glorious vista of bay and ocean. They drank on the way up on the train and drank on the way down, their bottles crashing on the green rocks below.

The town is nestled between two creeks. Old Mill Creek is to the south where John Thomas Reed, fresh from Dublin and the first Anglo-Saxon to settle in Marin County, built the peninsula's first sawmill and gristmill in 1836 in Cascade Canyon. The city took its name from the little sawmill of which only nine timbers remain. The tiny creek to the north with the long name is Arroyo Conte Madera del Presidio.

In 1890 the Tamalpais Land and Water Company began to auction off parcels of Mill Valley, then called Eastland after the developer. The population remained small until the great earthquake of 1906, when an influx of San Franciscans doubled it. Even then the number remained under four thousand until after World War II, when summer cabins and tract homes began to climb up the south slope of the mountain. John and Edda Kane lived in one of these homes ten miles north of San Francisco.

Propped in front of the television set, a can of beer in his right hand, John Kane tilted his head to look out onto Miller Avenue. A bright green Sunday morning, August 19, 1979, tempted even him to get out of his chair. But on that day John's arthritis was active again: both knees throbbed and added to the nagging guilt he felt because he was both emotionally and physically disinclined to accompany Edda on her planned four-hour hike of the mountain.

In the late sixties John and Edda had made the move from North Hollywood to Marin County, the fifth richest county in California. Almost immediately Edda had gotten a lucrative job as a Bank of America executive while John began selling sporting goods for a manufacturing firm.

For over five years Edda, forty-four, had belonged to

a hiking group composed mainly of European immi-
grants, the Nature Friends Tourist Club, which owned a
bright Swiss chalet overlooking Muir Woods.

Now it occurred to Edda that one of her friends, Jeanne
Glaser, a club member, might like to go along this Sunday morning, so Edda dialed her. The phone at Jeanne's
rang until Edda guessed that her friend was still at church,
so she decided to go alone.

Edda sprinkled on her footpowder and put on two pairs
of socks. The inner pair was polypropylene; the outer
pair was made of wool. She got her Italian-made Easy
Hikers, new four-pound-plus boots, from the hallway and
began stringing the laces through the D-rings and hooks.
The boots had come from her husband's company. Each
ankle was foam-padded, the shoe portion glove-leather
lined, and the contoured, curve-beveled insoles were also
foam-lined. A sturdy nylon shank ran the length of the
boot to reinforce it. Like most hikers Edda filled a water
bottle and put it in her red day pack.

Across the room John had watched his wife as she
gracefully and efficiently laced up her boots. Edda got
out her walking stick and leaned it against the redwood
door. She used it more for a sense of Zen balance than
anything else. Her short, dark cropped hair shone and
swayed as she bent forward. Her luminously intense dark
eyes looked up at her husband.

Where Edda seemed quick, John, in his early sixties,
seemed slow, where she was sharp and darting, he burned
with a steady flame. She was an exceedingly fast walker
and as a rule chatted energetically as she took her sturdy
rhythmical steps up the mountain of soft stone.

In the summer the trails facing north were best, allowing the hiker to avoid the dust of the dry roads. Though
East Peak and Bolinas Ridge in the summer usually are
kissed by cooled air off the ocean, on that day a warm
wind of twenty-five miles per hour rushed over the park.

John cautioned Edda to be careful and to be home before dark. Edda waved good-bye, started up their VW
Rabbit as her husband waved good-bye in return, and
pulled out into the street. She drove to the parking lot
just below the Mountain Home Inn at the base of Mount
Tamalpais.

Edda reached the East Peak, the highest, and found
the winter winds had thinned the serpentine soil. Far below she could see five, half-full reservoirs* reflecting
back the slate blue of the sky and the eleven cities** that
ringed the mountain. To the North, where the long Bolinas Ridge unfolds, she knew Mount St. Helena and
Mount Shasta lay. East of the wooded valley of Lagunitas
Creek, across San Francisco Bay, stands Mount Diablo.
Unseen, far beyond, is the Sierra Nevada. To the south
were Mount Hamilton and Loma Prieta. Edda looked
westward where the mountain became grassy lowland.
The west slope continues tumbling and rolling right to
Stinson Beach and into the Pacific.

At dusk John went to the window and looked out. Edda
had still not returned. Alarmed he went to the phone,
dialed the county sheriff's office, and reported his wife
missing. The department's veteran detective was dispatched to help in a search for Edda Kane.

"Edda Kane," recalled Detective Sergeant Rich Keaton with the Marin County sheriff's department. "Ah!
That was strange. To be one of the first on the scene.
They had dogs working that night. When we got there it
was pitch black. By the time we got in there and started
to get to our work the area had been dark for some time
and we had to work by flashlight for the most part."

It was dawn when the park rangers phoned John and informed him Edda's car was still in the lot at Mountain
Home Inn. John was stunned. He drove to the parking
lot and with aching legs set out to retrace every step of
the trail to the mountain's summit. As he pushed up the
trail his eyes blurred, his lungs burned, and his arthritic

*The watershed lakes of Kent, Bon Tempe, Phoenix, Lagunitas (the
smallest), and Alpine (the largest), which can hold up to three billion
gallons of water behind dams on the northern slope of the Sleeping
Lady. The 18,000-acre lake country is a different world; the 2,500
acres of the Marin Water District are patrolled by four rangers.
**Encircling the mountain are the cities of Marin—San Anselmo,
Fairfax, Ross, San Rafael to the northeast, Kentfield at the mountain's
eastern foot, Sausalito, Belvedere, and Tiburon at the shoreland, and
clinging to the base of Tamalpais are Greenbrae, Corte Madera, and
Mill Valley.

knees twisted from side to side. Silently he saw eerie illusions cast by the oblique morning light, recalling how many other life forms teemed on the mountain. It was still so early that a red bat with low, white-tipped ears darted briskly in front of him for several yards down the trail. Still the man plodded on, stiff-legged now, his knees locked against the pain.

In the back of his mind must have been the thought that he was not alone on the mountain, there might be someone else on the trail. John would stop, bend his aching knees, and strain his eyes in the dimness, trying to see into each clump of thick shrubbery under the gray oaks. His eyes moved from side to side, scanning the shrubs for any secret they might hold.

As he reached the summit a hollow whisper moaned through the stunted trees and clouds momentarily came between him and the rising sun. Chilled by the cold wind at the peak, he was lost in mist. When it finally cleared he could see the entire bay spread beneath him—an immense silent landscape. Turning, he hobbled down the trails one last time.

Suddenly there was a noise in the brush. John stepped quickly back. Something, some animal, appeared in the path ahead of him. The only impression the distraught man had was one of fierceness—man and unknown beast observing each other. Whatever animal it was plunged into the thicket and was gone. John returned to where the VW sat alone under the gloomy pines and then went home to wait.

As the sun rose, the search began. Dogs and men fanned out, methodically checking each major trail and minor path. A searcher treading behind a black police dog finally reached an area of heavy growth one mile east of Mountain Theatre at 1:30 P.M. Sixty feet uphill from heavily traveled Rock Springs Trail the dog began to sniff the undergrowth of Sargent cypress, manzanita, and oak. The searcher rushed through the plateau areas where the oaks and bays gathered and dipped into the dense underbrush. The dog had found the missing woman. She was in a kneeling position, facedown, as if she had been made to plead for her life before a bullet from a large-bored and powerful weapon had been discharged into the center of the back of her head.

"When we finally came across Mrs. Kane's body all items of a personal nature of hers had been removed with the exception of one sock," recalled Sergeant Keaton. "There she was, in a canopied area, facedown with a bullet wound in the back of her head and void of anything else of her personal belongings, even her glasses. She couldn't see anything without them. Here you are in the sanctity of the mountains and here is this terrible violation. There was no evidence of sexual assault, although oral sex could have taken place.

"We had had other cases where people had been murdered elsewhere and their bodies dumped on Mount Tamalpais, but Edda Kane was actually the very first person killed on Tamalpais." Sergeant Keaton suspected that the killer of Edda Kane had carefully chosen the umbrellalike effect of the trees so he couldn't be seen from above.

It was determined that the high-caliber gun that had killed Edda was a .44, a Bulldog. "The area," said Sergeant Keaton, "where Edda Kane was killed was not immediately roped off, but was later on. We had to bring all of our equipment in by foot."

Since this was the first known killing on the Sleeping Lady, the press descended on Edda's husband. The distraught man sat in his darkened living room on Miller Avenue lashing out his answers, holding his knees in pain, and rocking back and forth. From time to time his eyes would stray to the cartoons on the television across the room. Both the end of John's nose and his smallish eyes behind the dark-rimmed glasses were tinged with red from crying.

"If it hadn't been for my damn knees I would have been with her," he said slapping his legs. "Now I wish to hell I'd done it anyway. I told her I couldn't go on a long hike because of the arthritis. I don't hike much.

"Edda knew every trail on that mountain, loved it, and she wasn't afraid of anybody, anything—in fact, if anything she was almost too innocent. If somebody stopped her on the trail and asked for directions she wouldn't hesitate to help. She was that way.

"It's so senseless," he said, his anger growing.

"That's what makes it so upsetting. The guy took three credit cards and ten dollars. He didn't take her wedding ring. He didn't take her jewelry. He didn't rape her. What the hell did the son of a bitch want?

"The only thing I can figure is that she was at the wrong place at the right time. She was the first murder they have had on that mountain. It was a one-in-a-billion chance!" John could no longer go on speaking, and the press left.

The rangers were equally outraged and puzzled. They were used to simple cases of car break-ins in the lots at the base of Mount Tamalpais, but a murder on the face of the mountain was something else.

"To me it's sad," said thirty-four-year-old park ranger Bob Walker. "It's sad that people can't go hiking and enjoy themselves without worrying about this sort of thing. Maybe you expect these things in the city. But up here you're supposed to be able to get away and enjoy yourself. And be safe.

"Normally the people who go into the back country aren't up to types of things like this killing. Those are done by different people, people who like to stay close to their cars."

The distraught friend of Edda's, Jeanne Glaser, said, "She loved the physical aspect of hiking as well as the quiet and peacefulness. Edda was a very fast walker, but we always talked a lot. It was our one time to talk about any subject; usually we had a running conversation . . . I was at church. I would have gone if I had known she wanted to go." Jeanne felt it was conceivable her presence might have prevented the attack. "But on the other hand, I may have been hurt, too. Whoever did it had a gun, right?"

After Marin County's sheriff's deputies had searched the mountainside thoroughly, they released two composite drawings of a couple of men who had seemed to be acting strangely on the mountain the day Edda was killed. Police were forced to track down and talk to over five hundred hikers to come up with an artist's rough sketches of a hooded man and a blond young man. The hooded man had been seen by a German plastic surgeon who, through his knowledge of the human face, provided an excellent description.

Reporters were put off. The sheriff's office was being more than guarded with information. They would tell the press that they would do lab tests to see if the victim had been sexually molested. Over and over the reporters were told that these tests were still in progress. The sheriff did tell the media that some of Edda's clothing had been taken by the killer. "What clothing?" the sheriff was asked. "*Some* clothing," is all he would say. All the reporters knew was that someone on the mountain had been shot in the head. All reports were ordered sealed by Sheriff G. Albert Howenstein, Jr., who was charged with being the head law enforcement officer of Marin County.

On the same winding street where David Carpenter lived with his elderly father and legally blind mother, a neighbor reported a .44-caliber pistol missing from his closet shelf.

5

Mill Valley: September 1979

As political cartoonist for the largest paper in Northern California, the *San Francisco Chronicle,* I had become acquainted with many policemen and become close friends with a few of the detectives involved in the Zodiac case, an unsuccessful, eleven-year-long search for a serial killer which I wrote a book about in 1986, but which I started to investigate in 1975. Now came an attack on a blameless woman on an umblemished mountain where there had been no previous instance of violence.

I was intrigued with accounts of the tragedy. The crime on the Sleeping Lady had the potential of being a deeply moving story, and as a visual person I was seized by the powerful pictoral metaphor of the gigantic stone form of a woman reposed in death overlooking one of the great cities of the world. And how, I wondered, had it affected the residents of the tiny, idylic communities clustered at the mountain's base? After all, many of these individuals had deserted the urban scene precisely to escape such commonplace violence. Now they discovered the serpent had come to Eden. Practically without being aware of it I had carefully clipped out the two composite suspect sketches, filed them, and made plans to re-create the ill-fated woman's last walk, along whatever trail it might lead me.

It was a beautiful day when I drove across the Golden Gate Bridge to nearby Marin County. Before going up the mountain I walked around tranquil Mill Valley and realized that the mountain must be a constant reminder to the people of the town, insistently forcing the issue of Edda's death back into their minds. As I sat in the bright park by the old Northwestern Pacific Railroad Depot, watching mothers and their babies, I could hear that Edda was the major topic of conversation. I looked up—the haunting face of the maiden in the mountain held its eternal profile. My eyes moved to the thrust of her chest and then followed the long sweep of her body to the peaks of her toes.

Previously, people in Mill Valley had kept their doors unlocked and the police had never dealt with big-scale crime. But now there was a sense of caution among the people, and the town buzzed and crackled with fear from one end to the other—at the bookstores, The Depot, and the Upstart Crow, at the Blithedale Plaza Shopping Center, Old Brown's Store, curvy Throckmorton Avenue, where people gathered at the Carmel Coffee Company, on Corte Madera Avenue, and at Living Food, Inc., on steep, heavily wooded Blithedale Avenue with its white, Victorian houses, and to the north end of Cascade Drive where a thirty-foot waterfall plummets into a redwood canyon and flows back to the old sawmill. Mill Valley offers society, solitude, and wild surroundings. In addition to the shadows cast by the redwoods and bay laurels lining the streets the peak literally casts a shadow over the entire city and at the same time protects the town from ocean gusts, keeping the temperature comfortably between forty-three degrees and seventy-five degrees year-round.

The people of Mill Valley are an assortment of successful business people, farmers, computer whizzes, Hollywood actors and directors, rock stars such as Sly Stone, and singers such as Mimi Fariña and Country Joe McDonald. Edda Kane's death disturbed them all.

Just as Edda had on that sunny Sunday, I drove to Mountain Home Inn where I parked in the twenty-eight-car-capacity public lot at Panoramic Highway across from the Inn.

I started where Edda began the first leg of her climb. The trails that crisscrossed the mountain were the same ones that had been blazed by the settlers and Indians long ago. As I walked the trail I could smell the pines and laurel. The several species of oak, along with the California bay or laurel, buckeye, and big leaf maple, are thickly grouped at the middle of the mountain. But where I was and at the summit they are farther apart and fairly sparse. Although fog sometimes clings to the lower elevations the peak is usually exposed to bright sunlight at 1,500 feet. I passed through the same scrub Edda had walked through. Red-tailed hawks soared through the sky, and I was aware of an abundance of snipes and bluebirds. The wildflowers were not so plentiful. The rhododendrons had virtually disappeared, and the chaparral was decreasing in size on the lower elevations.

The police did not really know which way Edda had taken, so I played it by ear, following each path and trail to the East Peak. About a hundred feet from Mountain Home Inn I came to a fire station and walked onto the fire road for about twenty minutes. It became progressively steeper and rockier as I approached the Old Railroad Grade, which was more level. To my left was a rusting water tank.

Witnesses had seen Edda turn upward on Throckmorton Trail, which climbed directly to the East Peak, and I had gone this way too. It was more direct than Old Railroad Grade, which tended to wind about the mountain.

The trail was not only sheltered from the wind but was warm and spotted with blue lilacs. I continued upward. As I wandered on and off the trail I had passed cascades, giant ferns, and small waterfalls. To the east was the Double Bowknot and ahead were the remains of Mesa Station, a simple concrete loading platform. Finally I came to the brittle red chert and soft, slick, gray-green serpentine rocks of the dry, pointed summit of East Peak.

From newspaper reports I was aware that at approximately the same time Edda was at the summit other hikers noticed a blond young man in a light-red shirt and short leather hiking pants sitting in a yoga position on the peak. His mustache was lighter than both his hair and deeply tanned skin, and witnesses placed his age at twenty-five. He had stared at them with what was later described as a long pleading look.

Within minutes of having arrived on the peak Edda must have started down. She had four choices of descent—Throckmorton, the East Park Fire Trail, Temelpa, and the Old Railroad Grade. Since the first three are difficult to climb down I reasoned Edda had chosen the Railroad Grade. I could also imagine her wanting to bird-watch on her return climb and then have lunch at the West Point Inn, which took in a panoramic view of South Marin.

I took the Tavern Trail to Old Railroad Grade, past water tanks and brush to my right until I came to West Point Inn, a former connecting point for the Bolinas stage. After a modest lunch, I sat for a while at the Inn.

On the shady veranda I glanced through the sketches of the two suspicious men who had been seen on the Sleeping Lady the day Edda was attacked. These were the men Sheriff Howenstein was the most anxious to speak with.

Other hikers had seen the blond yoga man again that day, bounding from rock to rock on the sunny south face, his long shadow racing before him, his hair flying behind. Then he had crouched periodically on boulders to look at the other visitors to Tamalpais.

The second person witnesses recalled was a man about thirty-five years old with a dark blue windbreaker pulled up over his head and chin. They thought this was odd because it was such a warm day. Sweat dripped from his face and onto the green rock.

Just as Edda had probably done, I left the Inn, took the first road right downhill, and headed down the Rock Springs Trail. The trail was remarkable for its gray and green outcroppings of serpentine and a soil that supports few common plants.

The trail would take me to Mountain Theatre and then to Bootjack and the start of the last leg back to my car. Edda had never reached the lot.

* * *

"I had in mind John Kane as a suspect in the murder of his wife, Edda," Sergeant Rich Keaton told me long afterward at the sheriff's office. "I spent above and beyond time with him using every mental gyration and psychological ploy I could think of to build up a confidence with him. John Kane and I became very close, but I never believed him and I never trusted him and I didn't know why.

"John Kane is a man who sits home all day and watches cartoons, sits in front of their TV in their front window in Mill Valley on Miller Avenue drinking his beer. Edda, on the other hand, was twenty years his junior, very vibrant, very well educated, speaks both German and English. John was just like the poor old soul sitting there vegetating away after his wife was gone. His wife was everything to him. There was speculation from some points that Edda was having an affair with a younger man, and as a result her jealous husband killed her and blamed it on this younger man.

"I found out from John himself probably why I was, in my gut, uncomfortable with him. He had confessed to me that he considered himself an ex-convict. It seems some forty years earlier he had taken something out of a railroad yard back in the Midwest, probably for sustenance, something to eat, and as a result was arrested and went to jail. Because of this he considered himself an ex-con.

"I said to him, 'I'm really concerned about you and your wife and the situation—John, did you kill her?' 'No,' he said softly, 'I loved her.' And I thought it would be almost the golden goose he would be killing if John had killed Edda. After all, she was the one bringing the money in—she was a bank executive. He had no money. He supposedly sold athletic supplies, but I don't think he really did. John had an old hutch in his room, an old double-decker hutch that had come from Germany and had a history dating back into Edda's family. John walks over to it and reaches up under. He had a secret little button and boom!—this whole tray comes out and everything in there is all of the news articles about his wife from day one to that moment. Photos of her, pieces of her jewelry, portraits of the two of them, keepsakes.

"On top of that he had almost a little altar and there were some candles up on it and some flowers and he would change them daily. With all this memorabilia I started to change my attitude about him. As a matter of fact, I asked him if he had any firearms and he said yes, he did. He gave it to me without hesitation. We examined it, and it was a lower caliber weapon, a .22.

"You see what happened was the morning that Edda Kane left to go hiking on the mountain she asked Jeanne Glaser, and, by the way, an old friend of mine, to go hiking with her. Now Jeanne has a very heavy dose of guilt that she didn't go along.

"After she unsuccessfully called Jeanne, Edda called this young man she was seeing. So he knew she was leaving to go up on the mountain and what Edda's itinerary would be. Edda made that clear. Then this young man disappears until early evening of the day she is killed. Everything this suspect told us where he was was unverifiable, every place he told us he had been that was verifiable he had been the day before. When we went back to where this young man lived there were some people in the apartment complex who felt uneasy about him and his demeanor. They told me, 'We keep an eye on him because of our children and as a result we can tell you he didn't come back till late. We had a barbecue on the patio that day and we would have seen him come back earlier.'

"During the week, when Edda would go out she would go to Greek dances and she'd go over to Berkeley quite often and made a lot of friends and a lot of acquaintances. John would stay at home. Edda brought this young man home a couple of times 'cause they stopped at the Two A.M. Club near her house and had drinks. Jeanne Glaser was present on one of those occasions, and the three of them went over to John's house and woke him up at two in the morning 'cause she didn't have her key. John opened up and let them in. Glaser was feeling like a third party, and then the hubby goes back to bed. John's like twenty years Edda's senior and the relationship was strained. With John watching cartoons all day it was almost as if I was watching Norman Bates in the motel when I'd drive by Miller Avenue. I could see him sitting motionless in front of the TV—a grown man watching cartoons all day long.

"After Edda's death John Kane just withered away without her and eventually died. As for the young man, and I don't think his relatives were really surprised, he killed himself while we were investigating him. Strange things, strange things," said Keaton with a sigh.

6

Carpenter

On August 20, 1979, the day after Edda Kane was shot, David Carpenter went to his speech-therapy program in Oakland, arriving at 5:30 in the evening. His speech evaluations had continued from May through July, and now D. Wayne Smith, his therapist, was putting the final touches on a detailed history of Carpenter's vocal impediment. Carpenter gave no reason for not attending his printing class on Tuesday, August 21, unless it was to celebrate his impending release from the halfway house.

Carpenter had achieved a "live-out status" at Reality House West by demonstrating his need for less supervision to his counselor and assigned parole officer.

On the occasion of Carpenter's authorized discharge from the halfway house on Thursday, September 6, 1979, his counselor wrote a laudatory letter to the federal parole office saying how commendably David Carpenter had comported himself while a member of the facility. Carpenter, wrote the counselor, "had made great strides in his rehabilitation and was a good risk to be returned to society." The letter concluded with the remark that "Mr.

Carpenter's days of criminality appear to be over.'' It was noted in his file* that David Joseph Carpenter was now listed as living at 38 Sussex Street, his elderly parents' home.

On September 21, the purser's sister, Anne, called from Big Springs, Texas, where she was living with her husband and told him she had a gift for him. Anne had a 1969 Chevrolet station wagon that had previously been owned by their father and she wanted to transfer the title** over to him.

Carpenter had to be in class each day, but he had Thursdays and Fridays off. Under the conditions of his federal parole he was directed to remain within the boundaries of Northern California. All the same he told his sister he would be in Texas the next day to pick up the car. He had, after all, until Monday to return to the school, since that day was a Wednesday. Probation officer Wood granted him permission to go.

The purser was back from Texas by Sunday and applied to register the station wagon. Assigned California license 978 YRO, he then applied to the DMV on October 18 for personalized plates spelling his name: D J CARP.

''I flew to Big Springs, Texas, on 22 of S-S-S-September 1979. She gave me the car at that time. I drove back to San Francisco in it,'' said Carpenter. ''I had to get a smog certificate, which I did, and then had it transferred into my name.''

On Sunday, October 21, 1979, Mary Frances Bennett, twenty-three, was attacked while jogging in Lincoln Park near Land's End in San Francisco. She was stabbed over twenty-five times and buried in a dirt- and twig-covered shallow grave behind the golf course near the Palace of the Legion of Honor. The killer had escaped unseen. That same Sunday evening, several hours after the attack, Carpenter was treated in the emergency room of Marin General for a deep cut on his left thumb and various cuts on both hands—multiple lacerations with ground-in dirt. When asked by the doctor how it had happened, Carpen-

*#28796-136.
**1969 Chevrolet, VIN #132359 Z 35311, Texas license SLA 866.

ter said he was bitten by a dog while hiking. He was
given a tetanus shot and capsules of antibiotics. He gave
the doctor his real name and current address.

On Monday Carpenter phoned his federal parole agent,
Richard Wood, and told him about the wound and then
called his instructor at the printing school in Hayward
and told him he would have to miss his classes because
of a "dog bite."

Carpenter kept in touch with his former pen pal, Mollie Jo Purnell.

"I used to talk to M-M-Mollie by telephone because I
was usually at my parents' house," recalled Carpenter,
who usually spoke on the main phone in the kitchen.
There was a living room extension. "She would call from
Santa Rosa. I met Mollie three or four times at the place
where she worked—Sansome Street between California
and Bush in San Francisco." Carpenter would meet her
while he was on his way to school, and she would drive
him the five and a half blocks to the Fifth Street BART
station and drop him off so he could get to Hayward, in
the East Bay.

"I had a very good relationship with my bosses, Joe
Elia and Lane Thomsen," Carpenter said. "They were
very good friends. I attended their annual Christmas party
toward the end of 1979. I distinctly recall it because I
got a picture taken of me s-s-s-sitting on Santa's lap,
which is something I always wanted."

On February 22, 1980, Carpenter completed his printing course at the Hayward school and had a graduation
party. He immediately started looking for a job. The following week he was taking his father shopping at the
Diamond Heights Safeway grocery store when he bumped
into Florence Neuman, who was wearing one of the wide-
brimmed hats she favored. She had been a friend of the
Carpenter family for forty years, had known the purser
since he was eighteen, and was aware of his prison background.

Florence and her husband, Jack, owned Gems of the
Golden West,* a firm that assembled key chains and other
novelty items and sold them to gift shops, automotive

_____
*2275 Revere Street, San Francisco.

stores, and other large merchandisers. Florence was looking for a warehouseman and wanted to give Carpenter a chance to start fresh. "You're looking for a job?" asked Florence. "I'm looking for someone in our key-chain warehouse."

Carpenter stated later, "I said OK and I had myself a job. I had turned down other jobs because I didn't like the m-m-money offered. And so I was route man, general handyman. You name it, that's what I did." Carpenter was also used as a driver, office helper, and factory worker by Florence and Jack.

Carpenter had mastered typing as a clerk. He noticed there were from four to five old typewriters in the little room where Jack's son sometimes worked. The purser was introduced to his co-workers: Sophie Ortega, Rosa Perez, Shirley Yeh, and Anita Ng. They were sorting broken key chains into three-foot by one-foot boxes.

"On March 3," said Carpenter, "I took a sales trip on behalf of the firm to Fairfield, Vacaville, Napa, and Vallejo. I was servicing accounts—key-chain racks of fifty-one dozen apiece. They were placed at Long's, Pay n' Save, and so on. I had to inventory the old ones by counting and subtracting."

Shortly after Carpenter was hired, Florence Neuman discovered a duplicate set of keys that he had made to the warehouse and had hidden in his battered Chevy. She was puzzled. "Frequently," she recalled, "he asked Jack for the key to the warehouse when he needed to do weekly chores in the building. But I never mentioned the duplicates to anyone because it just never bothered me."

7

Wood

Few people knew David Carpenter as he really was. Florence Neuman was one; Richard Wood was another.

"I can't remember what year it was, 1978, maybe 1979," federal probation officer Richard Wood said later of his first meeting with Carpenter. "I was on a trip down to the correctional facility at Lompoc. We'd travel around and do prerelease meetings where we'd explain to guys in the joint what parole is like, what conditions are, the best way to find jobs, help them to prepare a little bit to get out.

"Until the funds dried up we used to do that quite a bit. So four or five of us drove down to Lompoc Camp and we did a parolee seminar and then they gave us a tour of the joint the next day. We were wandering around this very, very secure institution when this guy comes up to me stuttering away and says, 'I understand y-y-you guys are from San Francisco.' We said, 'Yeah,' and I started talking to him. He introduced himself and said that he was going to be hitting the halfway house in a couple of months and would I mind if he corresponded with me. He just sort of picked me out. I said, 'No, not at all.' I used to correspond with a lot of the inmates. I felt these guys needed as much help as they could get.

"I felt he was no different, so he and I started corresponding, not a lot though. He had some questions about the halfway house and on this and that and I answered what questions I could.

"When he came out to the halfway house," said Wood, "my name was in the file, and since I was the only one in the office to have had any contact with him . . . they gave him to me, which was fine. From all I knew here was a guy who was forty-five, forty-six years old and serious. The reports we had from the state prison said that he didn't have any write-up in all the time he was there; he didn't have any write-up in federal prison.

"Hey, next to most of the people we talk with this guy was ideal. As you can see it didn't turn out that way, but there was no way we could know at that point. . . . In many ways he's a very nice man, in many ways he was a very likeable guy. I liked him a lot, see, and this takes some talent. If you met him under different circumstances you could have a very good conversation with him. The only thing he wouldn't talk about is what happened to him in the past because even when I attempted to talk with him about that he was really reluctant to discuss it.

" 'I've done this therapy, I've d-d-done that. I don't want to talk about it,' he would say. In hindsight, the system has to realize with guys like this, group therapy doesn't do it because in group it is easier to get by than in individual therapy. A good hard-nosed individual therapist could have done a little confronting with this guy and could have dealt with him a little more effectively. Whether or not this would have changed the cards in this case who knows. A lot of us caseworkers ask ourselves, Jesus, what could we have done differently? and the answer is, Nothing.

"On many levels, he was doing exactly what he needed to do to get by, and he was also talking about things. Like he was just panicked because of his age and he didn't have any particular retirement planned. He was panicked about what he was going to do when he got too old to work. I still believe to this day those were real issues to him.

"This guy, from his background, should have not been

working around women. But again, how do you gauge how far a guy has come in therapy and changed over the years? Who would have thought those two guys at the printing school would put him to work teaching younger students? I didn't know that. Nevesny didn't know that.

"Realistically there's no way that sex offenders can be kept away from women, and that was what I explained in the 'duty to warn' letter that he passed on to the school, though the school later denied that. . . . Yes, he [Neil Nevesny] told the people at the school. I have no doubt in the world he told them.

"In August of 1979," Wood recalled, "I visited the printing school in Hayward. I was given a guided tour. Nancy, Nancy Morrison, was there. She was having some problems because she wasn't really prompt in getting to school. She tried to shake Carpenter down. She told her husband—her husband is a painter *and* a second-story man—that she wanted him to help her take down the two guys that ran the school, but I don't think she told him about Carpenter. Then she sleeps with my client and then tries to hold it over his head. I found out about it later. Nancy was a real handful, a fairly attractive, fairly promiscuous girl who was very easily used."

"It's hard to believe," I told him afterward, "that she was shaking him down over sexual favors. Carpenter seemed to have no trouble getting what he wanted."

"Yeah," agreed Wood. "What was she going to do? Tell his mother?"

"There must have been another reason," I said.

"You just opened up a really interesting subject. One that I don't think that's been examined by anybody and that is this guy's sexual deviance. And you might want to take a look at his relationship with the two guys who owned the school. He used to take off with them for weekends in their motor home. In fact, there was one incident of them having a gun [a .38] and going up to Lake County and doing some target shooting with him.

"One of the things you do when you are a p.o. is develop an innate sense about people. You learn how to read people fast. It's sort of a survival mechanism. Carpenter, to all appearances, seemed to be a hardworking guy who was trying to get his life together. He was very bright, not average bright, this guy was smart. When I look back at the numbers I realize I spent more time with him than any of my other clients.''

Wood sometimes dropped in at the homes of his clients. ''If a guy's screwing up you make surprise visits. With Carpenter you had to pretty much make an appointment, because you wanted him to be home when you got there. You didn't want to waste your time running around.

''He was reporting regularly, he was working, he had a job, he was living with his parents. On the surface he was doing everything right. I met him fifty-two times over a two-year period. A couple of times a month. Most of the time it was at his home and sometimes we met at his employers' and sometimes we met on a street corner for a couple of minutes. Whenever you supervise somebody you don't want them to lose time at work, 'cause time is money. Most guys on parole are real picky about having their employers meet the p.o. anyway.

''He was doing well. When a guy is doing this well maybe you don't see him as often because with probation and parole you are always dealing with the guys who are screwing up. The guys who screw up are the guys who get all the attention. Those guys are using drugs or alcohol or are not showing up and you have to go out looking for them.''

Wood thought for a moment, gave a sigh and said, ''Carpenter's many different things to many different people. This guy has a feeling for a situation and he just picks up what is needed in that situation to gain confidence. In the old days you'd call him a confidence man.''

When Wood first visited the purser's parents' home he was struck by the steep stairs and the narrowness of the street. The steps led directly into the living room, off to the left. ''In the older homes,'' he told me, ''they had this skylighting. Off to the right was the kitchen and a dining room and the bedroom was behind it. My client's bedroom was in a separate studio apartment downstairs. I never got out of the living room. There were no antiques. No valuable pieces of furniture. It was paneled, clean, rug on the floor. Sort of like Ma and Pa's home—nothing extraordinary about it.

"I never discussed Carpenter's childhood with his parents. His childhood problems—it was primarily his mother was my understanding. She was one of the most charming people one could ever meet. She was a cultured and urbane woman conversant in many different subjects. We both shared a love of opera." Wood wondered if Carpenter's return to living with his retired parents had brought him back in touch with his troubled past.

"I'd gone over to the house a number of times before he got home from work. I talked to the parents to see how he was doing. Very, very nice people. His father had some problems, but his mother was just a real nice bright woman. Bad eyes. One of her frustrations is that she couldn't read."

Wood saw Mrs. Carpenter studying her son through the large magnifying glass she used to compensate for her fading vision. He saw her eye enlarged to mammoth proportions staring back at him.

"I think the speech impediment figured very significantly in his development. As far as I know, he never received any therapy. That's the one thing I don't understand. She was a seemingly sensitive woman. So I never saw any of the occasions when she was abusive. You couldn't help but sense though that this woman, at a certain level, was hard. She had something about her that was strong.

"One of the things I don't understand about stutterers is how stress plays a part," continued Wood. "Now, Carpenter was the best jive talker you ever heard . . . This guy was the most charming guy when he was jive talking. He was being someone else.

"His father was a heavy drinker, would retire early and rise early so they all ate early. He had one messenger service in the financial district, and did well at it. However, the parents didn't get along real well. One time I was sitting in the living room with my client when his dad starts taking a swing at Mom in the kitchen. His dad was drunk, and this guy laughed about it and thought it was funny. I thought it was one of the most pathetic things I'd ever seen. Here's this three-quarters blind woman and Dad who's in his eighties. It was sad, and Carpenter thought it was funny and light."

8

Mill Valley:
Barbara, 1980

Barbara Schwartz, a young organic-bread maker, had been looking for a small home to buy. Since the median price for a home at this time was around $150,000, too much for her, she finally settled on one of two cabins just a few miles from Muir Beach.

Barbara loved to hike on the mountain with her Labrador retriever, even though dogs are expressly forbidden on the hiking trails. After Edda's death she became afraid, like everyone else, but as 1980 approached she began taking to the trails again with regularity.

For Barbara the best time to take to the mountain was now in late winter—when the runoff was at its zenith and the falls were "a roaring." At three in the afternoon on Saturday, March 8, 1980, she and her dog started for a brisk hike on the slopes of the Sleeping Lady, leaving the lot near Bootjack Camp, about two and one-third miles from Mountain Home Inn. The twenty-three-year-old woman descended into the redwood canyon, which was a very thick forest. She had a dark shock of tight curly hair, thick eyebrows, and a determined set to her lean mouth.

The trail was too steep to ascend and in the rainy season more than slightly dangerous because the heavy umbrella formed by the trees holds in the moisture and keeps the earth wet. Barbara went around Mountain Theatre, up Rock Springs Trail, past Rattlesnake Creek #1 and past Colier Rock to her right. She passed a second creek and finally came to West Point, where she strode onto the short Nora Trail.

Eventually she crossed four streams, the last of which intersected the looping, claylike Matt Davis Trail beneath Old Railroad Grade. She took this, intending to follow it back to the beginning of her hike. She crossed various canyons of brush and oak, some with streams and stone runoff channels, keeping an eye out for poison oak. She made her way over an embankment that had been reinforced with old railroad ties. In steeper sections of the trail, saplings had been fashioned into handrails.

Barbara bent and examined a yellow poppy, part of the mid-February explosion of wildflowers created by the mild but wet winter. Her dog explored the underbrush. Then she continued hiking for another two and one-half hours. The rocks that crunched beneath her tiny feet were stones not normally found within a thousand miles of each other. The mountain had been heaped together, in a formation called the Franciscan Jumble, from limestone, serpentine, brittle chert, shale, quartz-tourmaline, and yellow sandstone.

Just ahead of Barbara on the trail were two hikers, a thirty-five-year-old toxicologist and her male hiking companion. Walking briskly they soon left her behind. Pat Jennings, the toxicologist, and Peter Walters* approached a point where the Matt Davis Trail was intersected by a shallow gulch. Standing in the twilight, Pat and Peter saw an older man. He had thick glasses and a stern countenance, and he struck them as looking like an accountant. "I think," Pat said afterward, "he had on a raincoat, but I remember more than anything his stare. He seemed to be thirty-five to forty years old.

"But I can't remember his face. It's the strangest sensation. It's as though his face dissolved. Maybe he turned

*These names have been changed.

his face away; he must have turned his face away. I've tried very hard to remember . . . I just can't.''

As Pat and Peter completed their hike Barbara Schwartz sat down in a redwood grove near the gulch where the stern man with glasses had been seen. She rubbed her legs as the dim evening light came down among the trees and shone on the bare gray rock and fine bark of the trees.

Barbara gazed upward at the pyramid-shaped crowns of the Douglas firs and then looked at the reddish bark of the tall madrones and white-flowered chamisa shrubs nearby.

Instinctively she became conscious of someone watching her. Barbara got to her feet and looked warily around the gulch. Among the ten-foot-high manzanita bushes that ringed the clearing, there was the glint of glasses and the shadow of a man. She did not see them at first. Barbara listened and waited in the heavy silence. Finally, another hiker, a strange man in spectacles, stepped from the brush and moved toward Barbara. Her dog began to bark.

It was now 5:30 and Jan Christie,* a lone woman hiker, balancing on the uneven terrain of the path, drew near. Twilight cast deep blue shadows under the trees. In the dusk Jan saw what she thought was the figure of a slim, athletic man, attractive in some ways, possibly as young as twenty-five, approaching Barbara Schwartz. His lean figure shimmered and danced before her eyes. The strange man's hair was black, combed straight like a helmet or eagle's crest. Even his sharp nose was birdlike. He was clean-shaven, and Jan thought she could make out that he was wearing a dark plaid jacket that came down over the outside of his pants.

The strange man was to Jan's left, fully visible, some sixty-five feet away. He was looking down on Barbara, who was in a clearing in a gully and partially hidden from Jan by a stand of thin-trunked trees. Suddenly Jan's breath caught in her throat as the slim-figured young man raised his left arm—a reflection of what little light was left was caught in the shining surface of a long, thin blade. The knife was thrust at Barbara a number of times, and Jan

*This name has been changed.

could see glimpses of Barbara and the man struggling between the trees, portions of figures going back and forth. Barbara's dog frantically barked. Although the actual time that Jan witnessed the attack was forty-five seconds at most, the battle seemed to go on forever. Finally Barbara staggered a step forward and then dropped silently on her left side to the forest floor.

During the attack Jan had called out for the man to stop, waving and shouting to distract him. In another second or two the man whirled and plunged into the deep brush. Jan Christie could hear the thud of the attacker's hiking boots beating down the path. For another moment Jan heard Barbara's coughing and the dog's barking, and in a few moments—silence. Jan rushed down the mountainside for help.

The trail had been deserted only a short time before, but now there was activity, confusion, panic. Dark shadows flickered onto the trail, set there by brilliant lights. For a while Barbara's dog would not let the rangers near. As a deputy bent over Barbara's lifeless form, in the gully right off the trail behind some trees, he could see that most of the stab marks were in the upper part of her body, in her throat and breasts. "She was repeatedly stabbed," recalled Sergeant Keaton. "When the investigator turned her over her whole blouse was bright red, so red that he thought she was wearing a red blouse. The red was from the blood that she had lost. But she put up a helluva fight."

"The killer may have been wounded," said one detective. "She defended herself, and possibly he received some injuries."

Barbara had instinctively thrown up her hands to fend off the thrusts, had grasped the blade in her hand only to have it pulled away leaving behind deep gashes on the undersides of her fingers. Similar cuts were on her forearms. Bloodstains were everywhere, glistening in the pine needles, but something else glittered near her foot. It was a pair of black framed glasses. Investigators lifted the spectacles from the dirt by the nosepiece in case there were prints. The bifocals could be the victim's or they *could* be the attacker's.

A search was made for the knife. None was found.

Casts of any footprints in the area would be made. Meanwhile, the turned earth was scrutinized for clues.

Investigators continued to arrive, some puffing from the exertion of the slope, and boxes and cameras were piled on the woodland floor. Yellow plastic strips reading CRIME SCENE—DO NOT ENTER were draped over the bushes and tied between trees, ribbons festooning the path. A fingerprint and identification team took photos, notes about the placement of each object in the photos, and measured with their steel tapes the distance of the objects from the camera lens. Searches were made for witnesses.

The coroner, Dr. Ervin Jindrich, arrived, conducted his own investigation, and then Barbara was lifted onto a stretcher, covered in a green blanket, and carried down to the coroner's van.

At 7:10 P.M. Carpenter drove to the emergency room of the Peninsula Hospital in San Mateo, two counties and thirty-five miles away from where Barbara Schwartz had been murdered only hours before. Dr. James Tuzinski treated him for a deep wound on his right hand. "Severe cut on the thumb," he wrote. "How did this happen, Mr. Carpenter?" he asked.

"There was an attempted robbery at a 7-Eleven store in Burlingame. I w-w-w-was attacked and injured by the holdup man."

"I'll have to report this," said Tuzinski. "Hospital policy in any stabbing."

The police arrived, and Carpenter was questioned in a small waiting room away from the staff. He was kept until 11:05 P.M., but eventually the police accepted his story. Their interview with him was written up and filed away. In Burlingame no formal report of any 7-Eleven robbery was filed with the police department, and no all-points bulletin about the stabbing and the possibility the suspect had cut himself was received. The computerized machine through which Burlingame received reports from other law enforcement agencies was not capable of receiving an all-points bulletin sent by the equipment used by the Marin sheriff's department.

The day after the murder, March 9, Dr. Ervin Jindrich

filed his own report, "MARIN COUNTY SHERIFF'S DEPARTMENT. Mt. Tam Station. Date: March 8, 1980. 4:00 P.M. to 6:15 P.M." Barbara was D.O.S. [Dead on the Scene], and a potential witness, Jan Christie, was being questioned in greater depth. Christie was also working with an artist in preparing a composite drawing of the man she saw. Barbara had been photographed from every conceivable angle, and a map showing the relationship of the body to the crime site had been drawn. Their best clue, Jindrich noted, was "a pair of blood-stained glasses found at the victim's side."

Determining what the missing murder weapon looked like was not impossible. Various portions of the body are more elastic than others, and there are cleavage planes in which the fibers of the body run parallel, much like the grain in wood. A knife wound that penetrates parallel to the cleavage plane and then is withdrawn leaves behind a closed wound as opposed to a gaping wound left by a penetrating blade that cuts across the cleavage plane.

The wounds themselves could hold the answer to what kind of knife the police were looking for. Every blade has its own characteristics—its sharpness of edge, its double- or single-edgedness. Unless the blade is inserted at a perfect right angle and pulled straight out again, the stabbing wound is always a grim marriage of cutting and stabbing, the wound at entry being wider than the actual width of the blade.

One of Jindrich's first priorities was to find the one wound among the twelve in the victim's body best representing the true width of the blade—where the blade had entered and exited at as close to a right angle as possible. One technique was to fill the wound with a semiliquid X-ray-opaque material and then have X-rays taken at right angels to it giving an approximation of the type of knife used.

Jindrich examined the dermal layer of the victim's skin to see how sharp the blade had been. It seemed sharp enough to have been brand-new. Finally the doctor determined that the murderer's knife was a ten-inch-long, one-inch-wide boning knife.

One of Barbara Schwartz's friends, Ron Barcroft, who had often seen her at the Marin Flea Market, told me later, "She was so spiritual and innocent I can't fear but that she drew it to herself. She projected an aura of real vulnerability. Even though she was afraid, she thought everyone should get out and hike to make it safe on the trails if only through sheer numbers."

"There's a little gal," one policeman told me, "she works down in the DA's office now, but she was in the sheriff's office at the time of Barbara Schwartz's stabbing. She worked as a photo tech, somebody who developed film and whatnot of crime scenes. As you know, color film, when you develop it, green is red. It's one of those opposite spectrum things. She said for the longest time she couldn't look at anything *green* without feeling she wanted to throw up."

Sergeant Keaton had an idea. "Barbara Schwartz's dog was with her. I suggested that when they got a viable suspect and had a lineup they let Barbara's dog walk the lineup. Just put six or eight guys in the lineup and let the dog go and see if anything happens."

Many investigators were linking the murder of Schwartz with that of Edda Kane over a year earlier, but Keaton had his doubts, because he had handled the Kane case. If, he argued, the same man who killed Edda stabbed Barbara then why had he used a knife this time? Was it because the .44 was too loud? For a fleeting moment an image of the .44-caliber Bulldog gun flashed through his mind. He could almost feel it dropping into the dark water beneath the Golden Gate Bridge. If the killer had thrown the gun away, then why had he found it difficult to find a new gun? From this point on the .44 was known among the investigators as the "mystery gun."

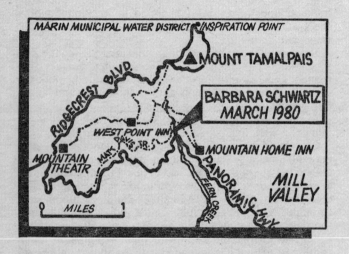

MARIN MUNICIPAL WATER DISTRICT INSPIRATION POINT

▲ MOUNT TAMALPAIS

RIDGECREST BLVD.

WEST POINT INN

DAVIS TR.

MATT.

MOUNTAIN THEATR

BARBARA SCHWARTZ
MARCH 1980

MOUNTAIN HOME INN

PANORAMIC HWY.

FERN CREEK

MILL VALLEY

0   MILES   1

9

Gaddini

On Monday morning, March 10, two days after Barbara's murder on the mountain, David Carpenter selected Dr. Donald Wright, an optometrist, out of the yellow pages and, as a "drop-in customer," entered his office at 720 Market Street. "I definitely remember the guy," Wright said later. "He seemed slightly strange to me, maybe too quiet. He said he needed a pair of glasses quick. He indicated he had lost his."

Wright checked his prescription for a new pair of bifocals, and in examining him discovered that Carpenter's left eye was so different from his right that "he'd be definitely uncomfortable" without the corrective glasses. As was usual for an older person, he needed slightly less power in the new prescription. Carpenter ordered a pair with dark frames and left. Wright, who, ironically, was Barbara Schwartz's optometrist as well, noted how unique Carpenter's prescription was.

Across the Golden Gate Bridge in San Rafael, a handsome, athletic police officer, Robert Gaddini, closed his desk drawer with a bang and laid out the files on the

Schwartz slaying. His office was housed in the most unusual administration building in the world, Frank Lloyd Wright's 770th building. Wright's Civic Center had been described by the people of Marin County variously as a "pink and blue monument to the harmony of man and nature," "an ocean liner at sea with soft lights aglow in portholes," and a "futuristically designed pink-stucco palace." One wing was as long as a forty-story building. The building, as it blends into the greenery of the surrounding countryside, is topped by a shining golden spire. Gaddini's office was in the Hall of Justice, a mate to the 858-foot-long Administration Building.

Tall, trim, rugged, Captain Robert Gaddini was the strong right arm of the sheriff of Marin County and the highest-ranking detective in the department. He was a private man, hard at work in his office after the second murder on the Sleeping Lady. He knew and kept many secrets.

Gaddini's second wife, Marsha, who was also in law enforcement and whom he had married ten months after his divorce in 1974, probably knew him better than anyone.

"Bob really liked challenges, but he never wanted to be sheriff or a chief of police. He wanted always to be behind the scenes controlling things, making the chief either look good or beholden to him. He was diplomatic and knew how to use words well. Howenstein, the sheriff who worked with him, had a knack for putting his foot in his mouth, but Bob was real smooth.

"Bob was a secretive man. He had a fear of ever allowing himself to be emotionally dependent on someone. He fought loving me . . . and it bothered him that he felt very vulnerable to me. He had a charm and an aura and I went bonkers over him. Just totally. I know I never felt such passion for anyone. Could not believe I could live without him. I can remember those first few years I thought, If I'm not with this man I know I'll die, and I know I'm not the only one who felt that way. His first wife never remarried."

Bob Gaddini was the son of a San Francisco police officer, Frank Louis Gaddini, now in his eighties, who had been head of the police garage, drove the chief around, and held a rank the equivalent of today's inspector.

"Bob was an only child," Marsha told me, "on his father's side Italian. Of course he said he was a 100 percent Italian. One his mother's side it was Scandinavian-Irish-German. She was a model, about five foot ten inches, a very good-looking woman. Her father had been a multimillionaire. The name was Gebford, and he developed Sparks, Nevada. When I saw a picture of his grandfather I said, 'My God, what a good-looking man.' Like Bob. Bob was about six foot four and so was his grandfather. Both of them had a mustache, hazel eyes, black hair. His grandmother on his mother's side lived to ninety-nine, one hundred years of age—everyone in his family lived long.

"There were a lot of things I didn't want to know about his work and he wasn't going to tell. He got his secretiveness from his childhood. His mother was an alcoholic and was in and out of his home from what I understand. His dad was the stable one and his dad was old Italian. He believed you shouldn't gush, you didn't tell people you loved them."

Martha, Gaddini's first wife, said, "He probably had always been interested in becoming a policeman, but I didn't know it when we were first married, that was 1961. He was a carpenter, went to school, and then one day when he was about twenty-seven he surprised me and said he was going to apply at the sheriff's office in San Rafael. He had graduated from Drake High School in San Anselmo and had some college before he started: afterward he attended the criminology program at the College of Marin and then later, when he was in his late thirties, he went on to get his master's in public administration at Golden Gate. This was around 1975 to 76.

"The police work was dreadful," she told me. "It was in the late sixties, when all the race problems and everything were happening. There was quite a bit of danger involved at that time."

When Gaddini was in his twenties he was an army airborne special forces paratrooper from 1957 to 1961, and he did some boxing in the military. "He was always looking for the challenge," said Marsha. "It was a personal thing. He didn't care about other people knowing. I guess he was in his late thirties when he went down to some FBI thing at Fort Ord related to the SWAT stuff. The thing he was really getting off on was how much better he did than these guys in their early twenties."

Bob and Marsha met in 1972 when he was the commander of a substation and she was working for Youth Authority in Marin City, where she had been assigned. Marsha had grown up in Los Angeles, gone to UCLA, married a medical student, and followed him to Northern California, where he did his residency in orthopedic surgery. Her job as a state parole agent was tough. "A correctional officer has a harder position. It's a terrible, difficult job. But I feel safer in prisons than on the streets going to see guys. You have more backup, obviously more structure. On the streets you don't know where the person's friends are."

Marsha recalled meeting Gaddini on her first day at work. "See Robert Gaddini, he's a doll. He'll help you out," she was told. Marsha walked in and saw him. "He looked like McCloud to me, who was on TV, what's-his-name, Dennis Weaver. Here's this tall, good-looking man coming at you. I had to find out who the hell is this. And then he invited me in and one of the things I liked about him was—you know how men are always coming on to women. I've had that experience so much in my life. And his was a different approach. Not the 'How could such a nice-looking woman become a parole officer,' you know, all of that kind of stupid comment I was used to hearing. He didn't do any of that. It was just, 'How can I help you?' "

Six months after Marsha was divorced they were married. They had known each other a year and a half. Their first house was in San Rafael. "Bob was an extremely interesting man," said Marsha. "Part of him was macho and authoritarian and yet he had also a real feminine side to his nature. He was a fabulous cook. In some ways he was more feminine than I was and I was the more masculine of the two, and yet I'm physically very feminine, blue eyes, dark hair, petite.

"The type of courage Bob had. Say he was going to deal with a criminal and the guy had a gun. Bob was willing to walk up to the guy with a gun and basically say, 'OK, fucker—go ahead: Pull the trigger, because before I get it, if I go, you're going too.' He would try to reason with the person, but he had absolutely no fear of death. There was one time a guy had escaped up into the ceiling of the jail and Bob could have told someone else to go up but he was the one who went up. There was a bomb one time at Marin General in 1969 and he could have been blown up. He would constantly place himself in those situations. But if he wasn't in law enforcement he would have wanted to be a college professor.''

Joe, Marsha's nine-year-old son by her first marriage, idolized him. Joe and Gaddini had season tickets together for the 49ers games. Once he overheard Joe say, ''Mom, I know why you married him, but why did *he* marry you?'' Marsha told me, ''Joe just thought Bob was the most handsome man in the world. This is the kind of feeling Bob evoked from people. Joe has still never met anyone as strong as Bob. Naturally strong. Bob was just naturally hard as a rock.''

Bob and Marsha did argue over one thing consistently—Gaddini's complete and unwavering loyalty to his commanding officer, Sheriff Al Howenstein. Gaddini was almost in the position of being the sheriff's press secretary.

''He kept referring to him as The Sheriff,'' said Marsha. ''What is this—The Sheriff? He's Al Howenstein.'' Marsha had known Howenstein since she was a twenty-year-old with the Youth Authority and Al was doing juvenile work. ''Bob would do things to save him,'' she told me, ''and Howenstein would acknowledge it to me, but then would go in front of a group of people and totally act like either he did it or not give Bob the recognition of all he was doing.''

''He's The Sheriff, Marsha,'' Gaddini would say.

''I was just trying to say, Why are you giving him so much respect?''

''When you're in a military system then you have to do that to have the discipline and the order and so that you carry out things and do them right.''

''But the guy, at times, treats people like a piece of

dirt," said Marsha. "Why are you giving him so much respect?"

"I don't care what you think," said Gaddini, getting angry with her for not understanding what he considered a "higher level of belief."

"I don't want to understand that," Marsha said later, "and I guess that's a problem of how men are raised."

Bob Gaddini picked up the reports on the mountain stabbing and walked them to the office of his boss, Marin County Sheriff Al Howenstein.

"Bob Gaddini and I grew up in the department," Lieutenant Don Besse, the highest-ranking officer in the department after Howenstein and Gaddini, told me later. "He'd been in the sheriff's department about three years, and then he left the office to become a Southern Pacific investigator and he did that for a year or two and decided he'd made a mistake. Meanwhile I came on the department in 1968 from the Oakland Police Department. Just before I got here Bob came back in May of 1968. In 1968 the Marin City substation was a volatile place like Dodge City.

"Gaddini had those couple of years in the department—he was a go-getter and wasn't the kind of guy to sit back and take any shit. He was a terrific guy, a little taller than me, real black hair, real Italian. He had his office in the administration wing next to the sheriff's office. Investigation was kinda on the other side of building. I always went through Gaddini. I never really felt comfortable with Howenstein.

"Howenstein loved to show his chest. The sheriff would wear the most outrageous clothes you ever saw, green plaid jacket, open-necked shirts with jewelry. He was just outlandish. It was his custom to wear his shoulder harness and his gun at his desk. We had trouble understanding him but we did understand the most important thing about him . . . he was involved with himself and his prima donna attitude. We did things his way."

Born in East St. Louis, Illinois, the forty-two-year-old sheriff had been a Marin resident for twenty-two years. He and Gaddini were the same age. Howenstein's father was an auto dealer in the Midwest, which fit the sheriff perfectly, since in spite of his commanding voice, well-

coiffed hair, sideburns, and good grooming he reminded
some of a smiling used-car dealer. His penchant for loud
sports coats only served to enhance this image.

Howenstein grew up in Omaha, moved to Alaska, then
came to Marin County as part owner of a San Anselmo
service station. He began as a street cop in 1959 with San
Anselmo as his beat, and within the space of four years
he had become sergeant. During this time his speciality
was juvenile crime, and by studying nights at the College
of Marin and San Francisco State University he was
quickly promoted to be the tiny department's only captain.

Howenstein was president of the Northern California
Juvenile Officers Association, the California JOA, chair-
man of the state Juvenile Justice Delinquency Prevention
Commission, member of the Governor's Advisory Group
on Juvenile Justice, winner of the Kiwanis Club Awards
for community service, and president of the Parents-
Teachers Association.

In 1978 he took on the sheriff of Marin, Louis Moun-
tanos, and defeated the twenty-year incumbent. In effect
Howenstein was not only sheriff of a county of over two
hundred thousand people but the chief law enforcer for
five hundred miles of unincorporated county territory.

"The sheriff's department," Don Besse told me later,
"handles the unincorporated area, we handle crime—the
highway patrol handles traffic. The sheriff runs the only
jail in the county. We work out of the administration
building, run a central warrant bureau for all of the departments."

Howenstein was at his best with juveniles. I spoke with
a young woman, Carolyn, who as a teenager had been in
trouble with the law and her parents. She told me more
than once that Howenstein was the only reason that she
was alive today. However, if the sheriff had one fatal
flaw, it was his hunger for the limelight, and if he lacked
one quality it was the ability to communicate with the
lower echelon of officers and deputies. "Howenstein,"
recalled Marin County Supervisor Gary Giacomini, "to
the cops was too esoteric, perceived as too sensitive, and
too touchy-feely. He'd say 'I can't relate to that,' and 'I
want to talk to this psychiatrist.' He wasn't a hands-on
kind of cop . . . he would talk like a shrink too much,

weird out the cops. They'd have some squad room meeting and he'd use some of these buzz words. The guys would come out scratching their heads, 'I don't know what he said,' He was, in a way, too sophisticated . . . to retain the confidence of rank-and-file law enforcement.''

Gaddini entered the sheriff's office, sat down, and passed around copies of police reports. Jan Christie, working with a police artist, had prepared a composite sketch of the suspect and was trying to produce more, including a full-length drawing of the assailant. The description provided by Christie read:

> WMA, possibly 25 to 40 year old, 5′ 10″, 170 pounds, slim in appearance, clean shaven, black moderate length hair combed straight back.
>
> Prominent beak-like nose, wearing dark pants and dark colored plaid shirt-jacket worn on the outside of pants.

Gaddini listened intently as the events of Barbara's death were rehashed. He knew that with this second death on the mountain there was intense political pressure on Howenstein to come up with a solution to the case. Though the five-man council of supervisors did not have the power to tell the sheriff how to conduct the investigation, they did hold the purse strings.

Though the murder weapon had not been located, the police did have a valuable clue—the bifocals found next to Barbara's body. The unique prescription, while not quite as good as a fingerprint, could go a long way toward finding the man the police were looking for. As a rule individual prescriptions are kept on file and many times glasses are contoured to fit the shape of a particular wearer's head.

Most important, the identifying code number and style of frames marked the lost glasses as institutional bifocals: they had been prescribed for someone in prison. This, Gaddini knew, pointed directly to a man on parole. The police report read: ''Both glasses and prescription are exceedingly unusual. They are bifocals with American optical frames. They are Stadium Brown Fade. Code: 46 0 22, 5¾ sk. The left hinge has been repaired. The suspect's right ear is slightly lower than the left and closer to the front of his face. The prescription for the right lens was:—0.50 0—.25 × 1.75 and for the left:—1.25 DS. Bifocal: Add R plus 2.00. Add L plus 1.75.''

Howenstein ordered two thousand circulars printed showing the glasses and listing the prescription and assigned a team of deputies to distribute the flyers. ''We followed through with hundreds of optometrists,'' he stated later, ''but it was kind of voluntary on the part of the optometrists to get back to us.'' Some optometrists failed to receive a bulletin on the glasses, and Barbara's doctor was one of these.*

In an effort to trace the bifocals Gaddini mailed a copy of the optical prescription to the state prison optometrists. He also included a copy of the detailed description Jan Christie had made of the young man she had seen on the trail. They were looking for a young parolee with that lens prescription.

Although Gaddini was informed that trying to match that odd lens prescription was ''like trying to track down an individual Ford carburetor,'' Marin lawmen conducted a personal search of Vacaville state prison archives to see if they could match the frames and if such frames had been issued to a recently released prisoner. No such match was found.

On Tuesday, March 11, two high school students were playing on the Matt Davis Trail on the upper slopes of the Sleeping Lady along the killer's flight path. Attracted by a flash of bright metal in the weeds they discovered the killer's blood-encrusted knife, which had lain overnight in the cool foggy air 220 yards from the site of the slaying. Stamped into the Forge boning knife, discarded or lost by the man during his race down the mountainside, were the letters ''E C K O.'' A Safeway label was still on the handle.

The students knew enough not to touch the knife, but

*On April 12, David Carpenter came back into Dr. Wright's office on Market and picked up some sunglasses. After Barbara's death investigators from Marin contacted Dr. Wright about her prescription but failed to mention the flyer listing the suspect's optical prescription.

when they saw an Oakland television crew they waved their arms and gave out a shout. The news team stopped filming, came over, and as the boys watched, open-mouthed, one man picked up the blade and held it up to the cameras to be filmed. What prints not destroyed by the cold night fog were now obliterated. "If there were prints," Gaddini said, "we'll never know."

Police learned that the knife was sold at the Mill Valley Safeway as a special promotional item available at only a few of the grocery chain's stores. The same knife was also available at the Safeway in the Diamond Heights district of San Francisco.

The suspect's description was released to Northern California papers, and on television screens that night the suspect's composite sketch was shown. It showed a tall, lean, young and hawklike male with a shock of thick, black hair and a pointed chin. He looked the classic hiker dressed in a green plaid shirt or jacket, his backpack cinched securely high on his broad shoulders. The rugged suspect's feet were drawn planted firmly apart, his hands defiantly, confidently thrust deep within his pockets. The narrow collar was buttoned up to the last button close under his strong chin. Penetrating eyes stared out from under dark and thick brows. The skin was tanned and stretched tauntly over high cheekbones. However, to one viewer watching the sketch on her television it did not remotely resemble the killer.

On March 13, five days after the stabbing, Pat Jennings notified Marin County detectives to tell them she may have seen the killer on the trail. "My friend, Peter Walters, and I think we may have been close to the murder site at the time of the attack." Jennings and her friend had been the last ones on the trail ahead of Barbara, who had been hiking just behind the couple.

The detectives showed Jennings the composite sketch and asked her if she thought it looked like the man she had seen standing motionless in the twilight on the Matt Davis Trail. "No, I didn't see *him*," she said gesturing toward the drawing. "He seemed more like an accountant." The officers' faces fell. They were not looking for an accountant.

10

Mollie

Mollie Purnell often wondered about the package containing the large gun she had received from New York in her name, which David Carpenter had picked up from her while he was at the halfway house. Could Carpenter have ordered the gun himself from New York, from inside Lompoc Federal Penitentiary, using Mollie's name and had it sent to her house? Because of his stock transactions Carpenter did have the opportunity to make money and call in special favors from the other inmates she knew.

After Carpenter's release from prison in May of 1979, the friendship between Mollie and Carpenter blossomed, affection flourished, and the ex-con visited with her from time-to-time over several months. "He was such a help to me after my husband's death," she recalled. In spite of Carpenter's penchant for far-out fantasies involving organized crime, Mollie thought him "bright and highly supportive." He was mailing her two to four cards a day which he bought at Courtino's in Stonestown. In fact, they got along so well that a business arrangement between the two was set up that would outlast the romance.

The purser agreed, in exchange for a moderate amount of money, to transport flea-market goods, mostly figurines, for her throughout the Central Valley. She owed him back wages.

On January 9, 1980, Mollie left a message for Carpenter to call her at a friend's home in Modesto where she was thinking of moving. "Mollie was excited," Carpenter said later. "She s-s-s-said it was urgent to see me. I met her at a freeway off-ramp. We talked about just a few subjects. She wanted to borrow $200 to make a trip to Canada to pick up some silver her brother had and bring it back." Carpenter had been interested in commodities in prison and particularly interested in silver and the selling of it, at least until the silver market began to drop.

Near the end of January Mollie loaned the ex-convict the .22-caliber Ruger revolver which she had, since 1976, kept hidden under the front seat of her car. "I need the gun for target practice," Carpenter claimed. Though when Mollie offered to go with him to the firing range he refused.

Two weeks later Carpenter told Mollie that someone had stolen the .22 and offered to pay her $150 to replace it. The purser wrote her out a $200 check drawn on an account at the Union Bank. He dated it February 3. Casually he asked Mollie if she wanted a job transporting money and she declined.

By February Mollie was living in Modesto. "Mollie," recalled Carpenter, "m-m-m-mentioned it would take a week or so before she could go get the silver. She told me she had to get herself fired from her job so she could collect unemployment and applied the same day she was fired [February 14]. On March 11, 1980, she called me collect from a Modesto telephone booth and we spoke for twenty-one minutes. The price of silver was dropping and she asked my advice. I told her, 'Sell a third. That's money in the bank. If you don't sell and something happens to the market, you might not get anything at all.' She was very excited. She had expected to see two to three hundred thousand for the silver."

Mollie called collect again on April 7. She had not sold any of her silver. "At that stage of the game nobody wanted it for a good price—it was worth seven, eight dollars per ounce—in that range. Mollie was broke at the time. She asked me to get her some money, perhaps in a partnership. She was asking for help from me." Carpenter later claimed this involved the selling of marijuana. In reality, Mollie didn't even like pot and would wrinkle her nose at the word.

Mollie never had an involvement in the selling of pot, although the calls and meetings between the two did take place. It was only much later that Carpenter invented a cover story to explain them away and hide his true purpose for the relationship. His constant manipulation of Mollie had only one real objective—he wanted her to buy him a gun, something his status as a convicted felon prevented him from doing himself.

"I had any number of people who I knew who sold marijuana. Mollie and I discussed a 70–30 arrangement—I would get 30 percent of the profit. I picked up a half pound of marijuana and took it up to her the following Sunday, April 13. I drove up to Modesto to her El Greco address and we talked for three hours. I remember specifically because she showed me her silver."

Both David Carpenter's social life and home life were full at this time. On April 20, Florence Neuman, his boss, held the first of her nostalgia parties in her remodeled San Francisco house. "I was dressed as a Keystone Kop," Carpenter recollected. "Florence asked me to help her out and answer the door. I phoned up to order the costume on Friday, picked it up Saturday, wore it Sunday at the party, and returned it Monday.

"On April 24, I took my m-m-mother and father to the Health Fair for free blood tests. I told them I had read about it in the *San Francisco Progress*. Mother couldn't read the paper herself. She had a g-g-great big magnifying glass. If she held the glass up she could read it a little bit." Carpenter was constantly on the lookout for free medical care for his mother.

At the beginning of June 1980, Carpenter's parole officer, Richard Wood, was invited to Gems of the Golden West to see his client at work and to meet Jack and Florence Neuman. Carpenter seemed to be beaming with pleasure. Later Carpenter contacted Wood by phone to tell him how satisfied with his job he was. "This job," he said with excitement, "could develop into something big for me." Wood knew Carpenter was putting in from ten to fourteen hours a day for the Neumans. The purser often used the phone by the T.O.P. Department Store across from Gems.

On Saturday, June 14, Carpenter took his father shopping for groceries. He often drove his elderly parents. At home Mrs. Carpenter scanned the *Progress* for ads with her large magnifying glass, took her medication for her progressive glaucoma, took a bath, dressed, and waited in her pink bedroom for her son to take her shopping.

"Where did I take my m-m-mother shopping?" he said. "I took my mother shopping where my mother *wanted* to go shopping. Shopping with mother took considerable time because she had to pick up each item and examine it . . . touch it."

Carpenter took his mother to a foot clinic* for half an hour that day—a way for her to have her blood pressure and other tests done for free as part of the foot examination." Carpenter carefully retrieved the screening questionnaire and took it with him. After having cake and strawberries at Woolworth's across from the Emporium he bought a baby scale gift set and baby carriage at Consumer's Distributing for his youngest daughter, who was having a baby shower that afternoon in Sebastopol.

For some time Jack and Florence Neuman had been trying to get Carpenter used to dealing with people and decided to put him in a situation where he could gain some confidence. Jack suggested to him: "Why don't you go over to the flea market so you can practice selling to people?"

"That's a good idea," said Carpenter uncertainly.

"For the first time," Carpenter said subsequently, "Jack and Florence sent me to the Alameda Flea Market to sell outmoded key chains. The Alameda Flea Market is located at an old outdated motion picture drive-in."

Carpenter recalled it as a horrifying day. "I was scared to death because of my speech problem. But it was the

*California Podiatry Clinic at 1835 Ellis Street.

best thing Jack ever had me do. That was the thing that got me started. I started to develop self-confidence.

"But I didn't s-s-s-sell many key chains. Jack wanted fifty cents apiece for them, but I sold them for twenty-five cents. They wanted to sell *racks* of key chains. However, I did bump into a guy I knew from prison who was selling stolen radios."

Carpenter called his parole officer on July 28 and told him that his friend, Mollie Jo Purnell, who had been born in Jamaica, British West Indies, had inherited property in Jamaica and needed his help to settle the estate. "Her family came from there," Carpenter told Wood. "Her grandfather had been the governor of Jamaica. Their land was quite valuable. When she told me she was going to go down there I asked her to look into any good financial possibilities in regard to importing things from Jamaica to the United States. Can I have permission to go?"

Mollie claimed her estate in the West Indies was worth millions. She was desperately trying to gain control over a company which she had once run and was part of her father's estate, Berry Hill Farms.

She was frustrated because her four Jamaican attorneys had allegedly sold her property four different times. A bank in Jamaica also had control of the estate and Mollie had no way to get the money out of Jamaica. A small amount of estate money, silver, and heirlooms were out of the bank's reach and so trickled down to Mollie. She paid taxes on this in Jamaica, Canada, and the U.S.

Carpenter told Wood how Mollie had laid out the situation in a series of calls between July 20 and July 24. Because this was the probation officer's first contact with Mollie, he told his client he would need something in writing. "A letter's already on the way to you," said the purser brightly.

After he hung up, Carpenter called Mollie and spoke for fifteen minutes explaining about the letter. But by August 7 Wood was still waiting for the letter. After a forty-four-minute conversation, during which the purser coached Mollie on what to say to Wood, she phoned the probation officer and in a brief call made reference to the letter and her offer of employment for David Carpenter to handle her Jamaican affairs. Later in the day Mollie's letter, dated July 25, but marked "received this office August 5" was handed to Wood.

Carpenter left for a key-chain replacement trip to Modesto, stopping in Visalia first, and checked into a Motel 6. As usual he dropped the receipt in his receipt box, which he maintained in case he should ever need an alibi for his parole officer. "It was a sales drop to replace key chains. After I checked into the motel I went over to see Mollie. I brought one-half pound of marijuana and the first shipment of key chains. I thought the key chains would be a good way to cover her marijuana sales. I created a cover because if Mollie was caught, I would be caught and sent back to prison. 'Use the key chains as front to cover what you're doing,' " Carpenter claimed he told her. "I brought three dozen out-of-date key chains out of the attic. I figured they'd be ideal cover."

Carpenter's *own* cover story was the fabrication of drug sales to and by Mollie to explain away their frequent communications.

Mollie called Wood again on August 11 to say she was ill and would speak with him again soon, perhaps later in the week. Carpenter called her on the fifteenth, spoke for almost an hour about Jamaica, and then called throughout the day of August 17, a Sunday, telling her exactly how to handle Wood. By August 21 Mollie had worked up enough courage to finally call the probation officer. Carpenter had spoken with her at 9:39 for eleven minutes, then again at 10:00 for a longer time, compelling her to speak with Wood.

"She was very distressed," Wood told me later, "but she represented it exactly the same as in her letter—she was going to set up a company to employ him. Mollie explained her father had died in Jamaica and she had been left a good amount of property and she wanted this guy to go down and help her straighten the legal morass out. David was to purchase lumber, ship rice and flour, and arrange freight from Florida to California. I suggested she should get an attorney, but she said no, explaining David had helped her with her finances before. So, I said what the hell and drafted a letter to the parole commission telling what the situation was. Still, I thought it was a classic case of somebody using somebody else.

Carpenter had introduced Mollie as his fiancée or something like that. It's not unusual for people in jail to develop relationships by mail. A lot of women are homely,
older, lonely, really looking for something. I think they
are really used and abused by the people in custody.''

Mollie used the key chains as flea market items at the
Turlock Market south of Modesto. When she was slow
in paying Carpenter for the items he demanded a percentage of her profits.

On Sunday, August 24, 1980, Carpenter saw Mollie Purnell. "I gave her more key chains," he recalled, "and I
also gave her some boxes of rocks. This took place in
the Gems warehouse. Just Mollie and m-m-m-myself
were there.''

Two days later Richard Wood visited Gems of the
Golden West to see how Carpenter was doing. He was
excited.

"Going to Jamaica could be, for me, a multimillion-
dollar deal," he said.

"What are you going to get out of the trip?" asked the
parole officer.

"Well," said Carpenter evasively, "there could be
some real business possibilities for me.''

"I understand," said Wood, and when he got back to
his desk he wrote the parole board, recommending Carpenter be allowed to go to Jamaica. Wood could see the
trip was terribly important to his client. It was so important to Carpenter that he had made a total of fourteen
calls to Mollie, from August 7 through August 26, concerning her letter and what she should say to Wood about
the trip.

For some time Carpenter had been trying to get Mollie
to buy him a gun. She had gotten cold feet.

Mollie Purnell was a woman who couldn't set limits,
and Carpenter knew this. Beginning with a forty-minute
call at 5:45 P.M. on September 2, he called nearly every
day until September 12, when the one-, two-, and four-
minute calls were only minutes apart. The following day,
September 13, 1980, Carpenter went shopping with his
mother in the Mission District in the early morning. "I
remember this because I bought a twelve-year-old bottle

of brandy for my brother's birthday party," recalled Carpenter. He was excited about the possibilities of Mollie's holdings in Jamaica. "I could see all of the opportunity there was in Jamaica to make a lot of m-m-m-money. I could see a lot of money if those things came through down the road."

When Carpenter returned home he got a message from Wood—his request to the parole board to allow Carpenter to travel to Jamaica had been turned down. Rage and frustration began to build within the ex-con, and he drove immediately to Mollie's home.

Mollie opened her door to see Carpenter dressed in drab, baggy pants, stocking cap, shirt, vest, and white tennis shoes. He rummaged in his pockets until he found a tattered ad, on pink newsprint, which he unfolded and handed to her. "I have a request," said Carpenter. Mollie looked down at the ad, which showed a gun—a .38 Rossi revolver—which was on sale for $199. Carpenter had been using his bosses' .38 when they went target shooting in Mendocino and was familiar with it.

"I w-w-want you to buy it for me. In exchange I will forgive some of the m-m-m-money you owe me."

Once again Mollie refused, and the purser asked why. "I don't want to have the gun in my name," she replied. She had never mentioned she had seen the gun in the package to him.

"If there's a problem in the future," he said, "just say the gun was stolen from you."

"Why do you want the gun anyway?" After all, she thought, he had lost one already.

"Well, I'm thinking of going to work for the Mafia in Las Vegas."

Carpenter persisted and pressed two hundred and thirty dollars in cash on her. That afternoon Mollie found herself walking into a local sporting goods store, The Trader Gun Shop in San Leandro, where she made an application with part-time clerk Sergio Fanucchi to buy Carpenter his gun. Mollie had taken the money partially because she was behind on her utility payments, but she felt angry with herself for allowing the purser to intimidate her into buying the weapon.

Carefully she wrote her birthdate. Mollie was one year

older than the purser. She filled in her address, 2620 El Greco Drive, Modesto, California, and was told by Fanucchi to come back on Thursday, October 2. "Fine," snapped Mollie. State law prohibited an ex-convict from buying a gun or ammunition and also required a buyer of any gun to wait fifteen days before picking up the weapon. Fanucchi offered her two boxes of ammo. "Why," she said, "would I want to buy ammunition when I haven't even passed the test yet?" But she bought the shells.

That evening, Carpenter recalled, "I loaded the van for the flea market the next day. . . . Mollie owed me money for the marijuana transaction." Carpenter would later claim that all of his calls to Mollie Purnell involved marijuana sales and not a gun. This was not true. "There were always two topics—one was Jamaica, the other was the m-m-marijuana. The day after my brother Bill's birthday party, September 20, Mollie called me at 6:43 P.M. and we spoke for almost an hour. I had told her I would be at her home after the Sunday flea market. I called and then hung up. The idea was there were no phone charges on the Gems' bill.

"The following Sunday Mollie called me again. She told me one of her customers needed to buy two pounds of marijuana. I only dealt in small amounts—I would only touch half pounds. I told her I would look into it. The evening of September 29 I took off from school."

Richard Wood had canceled the probation meeting for September with Carpenter and contacted him on September 29 to arrange an early October meeting. That night at 9:17 Carpenter called Mollie collect and one minute later she called him back and they spoke for fifty-eight minutes. Carpenter later said the long call concerned two pounds of marijuana. "The gun is ready," she told him. The next day he called at the same time and they spoke for another twenty-two minutes.

On September 30, Tuesday, Carpenter's boss, Florence Neuman, told him they would probably work Friday night and Saturday. "I told Mollie," he said later, "I didn't know when I could get the marijuana to her. 'Call me at lunchtime,' I said." For over a month he had been taking a bookkeeping course at the San Francisco Community College Adult Evening Program in Chinatown.

On October 2, 1980, while Mollie was entering the Trader Gun Shop to pick up the cheap Rossi revolver the purser was on the phone canceling his lunch meeting with Wood for the next day. "Jack is ill," the purser said. "I have to s-s-s-stay here." Meanwhile, Mollie carefully filled in the serial number of the .38-caliber pistol—#D 484341—and returned home.* At 12:23 P.M. she called Carpenter during his lunch hour. They talked one minute. "Call me early the next morning," he said. She put the gun in the closet where she had kept Carpenter's packages.

Mollie was terribly upset about the gun and called Carpenter the next morning at 6:12, but because the purser was in the shower she got his father instead. Carpenter called her back at 6:25 and again at 10:32 A.M.

Later, Carpenter recalled, "I explained to Mollie I was going to have to make a sales trip. Jack Neuman, my boss, came down with a bad case of the flu. On October 3 I made the Concord, Walnut Creek, and Oakland trip. I called Mollie to set up a new time to meet. On Saturday, October 4, 1980, I worked with Florence at Gems."

Friday or Saturday afternoon, Mollie was uncertain in her memory, Carpenter, driving the Gems of the Golden West truck, showed up unannounced at Mollie's to pick up the new gun. Mollie said later she watched while he stowed the weapon and ammunition away in a blackish case similar to the ones used by jewelry salesmen. "He wasn't supposed to come around anymore and that ended it as far as I was concerned," recalled Mollie angrily. "This terminated our relationship because it settled the money owed him and I didn't want any more to do with him." Another reason for the breakup was that Carpenter

---

*The .38-caliber gun was made by Amadeo Rossi, Sao Leopoldo, Brazil, and was a Rossi model 68. It had a three-and-a-half-inch-long barrel, held five shots, and had a solid frame with a swing-out cylinder. The serial number was located on the frame above the trigger guard. No record was ever found of Mollie Purnell purchasing two boxes of ammunition although ammunition purchases are required by law to be recorded.

had mixed up envelopes and sent Mollie a letter intended for another woman. Mollie, additionally, had once had to fight off Carpenter's sexual advances by grabbing an ax and threatening him with it. At 10:58 P.M., Friday night, Mollie got a call from Carpenter at Gems. Now, she thought, what was he doing there so late?

"On Sunday," said Carpenter, "I called Mollie and we talked for thirty minutes. I told her she could come down Tuesday to pick up the two pounds of marijuana and made her understand she was to bring the m-m-money with her. Bring the money first. On Tuesday, October 7, she did, that evening." Again, Carpenter used the drug cover to explain their meeting.

Jack Neuman was always on the lookout for good deals, and he got one on a shipment of rubber plants. Carpenter brought one home to his mother, intending to build a box for it. Mrs. Carpenter decided she wanted to put it in a clay pot, and mother and son began the first of many arguments over the plant and took the first of several trips to find just the right pot. At this time the purser's mother and father were fighting often, and the friction between the two was getting to Carpenter.

11

Rick and Cindy

Rick Stowers, nineteen, a coastguardsman at Two Rock Station west of Petaluma, had fallen in love. Afterward, his mother, Joyce, told me how Rick and Cindy Moreland had met. "I imagine they had known each other several months. She was working in some civilian capacity at the station and he met her there. It was sort of funny when he called to tell me about her on the eighth of October. Rick was very, very thrilled with her, and one of the things he told me was her mother has a 'Motherhood Manual' too, which was a joke because I was always quoting to him according to my 'Motherhood Manual,' saying you couldn't do such and such a thing. He felt very good about that. Rick wouldn't always follow our advice, but he was very good about calling in.

"Rick was the only person I know that enjoyed basic training. He needed regimentation. I think he had planned on the coast guard being his life's work. My son-in-law, Jay, who's about two years older than Rick, had made it his career."

Joyce had seen her son change in his four years at Te-hachapi High, had seen him through Little League, attended all the games, seen him through football and basketball. But Rick had never lettered. In his junior and senior years he dropped out of all sports. "The last two years," Joyce said, "were a little aimless for him, and then Rick decided right after school he needed to do something with his life. The jobs he had in a small town were dead ends. Tehachapi is about forty miles east of Bakersfield, and we had lived there for ages in a little valley in the mountains. The town itself is a valley. We are noted for prisons—for years it had a women's prison.

"My son-in-law sat down with Rick and explained all the advantages of the coast guard to him. He was a friend of Rick's as well as of my daughter. They grew up together. 'The coast guard saves lives, not destroys them,' he said. Rick enlisted at Thanksgiving, 1979, after he got out of school in June.

"After basic training Rick went into communications. His biggest problem was trying to get over ten words per minute on the Morse code. Rick would type me notes on paper towels, or whatever he happened to have, because he was having a hard time and he was stuck at Two Rock.

"On October 8, 1980, Rick told me Cindy had agreed to marry him, he got his orders to be stationed at Point Reyes Station, and they were going to go up on the coming holiday weekend to look at it.''

On October 11 Rick's fiancée, Cindy, was at her sister Alice's house. Alice's husband was also in the coast guard, and since Alice was about to have a baby, dark-haired, eighteen-year-old Cindy was staying at their Pacifica home for a few weeks to help out. Saturday was the best day for the sisters. "It was our day together," said Alice, who looked remarkably like her younger sister. However, Cindy had planned to spend this Saturday with Rick.

"My daughter," said Mrs. Stowers, "had talked to Cindy and her sister Alice, but I never had. But I knew Rick spent quite a bit of time at her house." Rick showed up at 9:15 A.M. in his family's small, chocolate-brown Toyota Corolla. Alice watched the young couple leave— Cindy in jeans, an off-white sweater, and a quilted jacket she had made; blondish Rick in his blue jeans, black coast guard-issued jacket, which zipped up the front and had a large emblem over the breast. Both wore tennis shoes.

"They left," Rick's mother told me later, "to go to Point Reyes Station, where Rick was being transferred. And of course Cindy was very excited. She was familiar with the area and had wanted to show Rick. She had done quite a bit of hiking there."*

Coastguardsman Jim Davis, stationed at Two Rock Station, knew both Rick and Cindy. He had worked with Stowers and had seen Cindy when she worked the galley there. At noon he ran into them at the bookstore in the three-block-long, one-street town of Point Reyes Station. They had a short conversation about Rick and Cindy's engagement plans and arrangements for living out at Point Reyes. "We came to check out the town," said Rick, "since we're going to be stationed here together." Davis said later, "They promised they would stop by my house and visit with my wife, who took a class with Cindy." Davis saw the couple an hour later eating lunch at the Palace Market, directly across from the bookstore, and Rick repeated his promise to come over to his house later.

Earlier that morning two hikers, Sharon Melnyk and Larry Drapkin, had left Berkeley for Point Reyes and arrived while Rick and Cindy were at the bookstore. Somewhere between noon and half-past they had assembled their gear in the parking lot and within fifteen minutes they had started out on Bear Valley Trail and then on to Sky Trail. Sky Trail was unpleasantly steep. "I am not a rapid hiker," said Sharon later, "uphill people pass me." On flat areas, however, she walked quite briskly, and the couple soon made a loop and went to the coast. Between 1:15 and 1:45 Sharon heard noises. "They sounded like noises in rapid succession from a backfiring motorcycle. They seemed to be off to my left, the west,

*Between 9:15 and 9:30 A.M., David Carpenter cashed a personal check for fifty dollars, #204, with the memo, "expenses," at the Continental Savings and Loan in his Glen Park neighborhood. All of the bank's checks were bulked together and time-stamped after 1:00 P.M., which later made it appear that he had cashed the check in the afternoon.

to the right of the parking lot. They were close enough to hear distinctly and loudly, but far away.''

Cindy and Rick were due back for dinner between 5:30 and 6:00, and her sister, Alice, was worried when they didn't come back on time. At 9:00 P.M. she called her brother, who said, ''Perhaps you should wait until Sunday to see if Cindy comes home from work.'' Alice said afterward, ''Cindy was supposed to work at her job on Sunday morning. I was a little overprotective, I think, and I didn't want to needlessly worry anyone. So the next day, when they still hadn't shown up, I called my parents and casually asked if they had dropped by, but they hadn't.''

''They disappeared on a holiday weekend,'' Mrs. Stowers told me afterward, ''and we didn't know Rick and Cindy were missing until Alice called me up on the fifteenth. She said she didn't want to upset anyone. She had called the coast guard station and the police and couldn't think of any place else to call. She got me on the phone. It was a strange conversation because, well, I'm sure I was a little defensive. I said, 'What if they went off . . .' In the back of everyone's mind was the thought that the couple had eloped to Reno on the long weekend.

''But then Rick had told me they were so excited about Point Reyes, so nothing would fit about them running away. We couldn't think of anything. There was no reason for them to run off just before a pay day.

''When we had gotten over to Petaluma, the police kept saying you've got to go to the coast guard, and they would say we can't do anything *yet*. And I told them I'd been up to San Francisco the last time I'd seen Rick in July. He'd spent a night with us in a hotel near Pier 39. The police wanted to know if Rick had made the arrangements for the hotel—I guess they were going drug related or whatever. They wanted to know any of Rick's acquaintances.

''And then it was the timing. I felt kind of bad because they had just had that helicopter crash that had killed several deputies that very day and they really weren't too sympathetic toward someone who was looking for their adult child. The coast guard told us we'd have to wait for thirty days and in the meantime they marked Rick as AWOL. Officially they couldn't do anything, but they did agree the disappearance was out of character. They sent a warrant for his arrest to me. They sent one up to Alaska, where my daughter and son-in-law were, also in the coast guard. That was just overwhelming to Jay.

"Later, after we learned all that had happened, Jay, my son-in-law, just took everything to heart and just thought everything was his fault. My husband, Jerry, spent hours just talking to him. 'Rick,' Jerry told him, 'joined the coast guard because that's what he wanted to do.' But it was almost more than Jay could handle."

Dissatisfied, the Stowers and Moreland families began their own investigations. "We did work together," said Mrs. Stowers. "We talked to Cindy's dad several times and checked in to see if either of us had heard anything. We were more inclined to believe there had been some kind of accident rather than their running off. Nothing prepared us for what actually happened. It wasn't even in our imagination.

"Everyone would say it was out of character—that was the thing that kept going over and over. It was very frustrating because you really don't know what to do. I called friends of his down south that he had gone to school with. We tried to do anything we could think of."

Joyce Stowers worked in Kern County as a librarian, and Jerry, who had retired from working for the county, was laboring as a temporary maintenance worker at a nearby resort. Their work began to suffer. "We couldn't think of where else to go, so we had a little flyer made up. On October 28 we drove toward Reno and left them with highway patrol and police stations along the way. We felt we had to do something—anything. We first went to Carson City, then to Reno, to see all the marriage records on the off chance they had run off to get married. While we were doing that Mr. Moreland was driving hiking trails looking for them."

News of Rick and Cindy's disappearance reached Tehachapi: "A small town is nosy until you need them," said Joyce, "and they were really terrific to us. Just lots of people we didn't even realize knew Rick."

In the meantime, Mollie Purnell had continued to receive calls from Carpenter. He had called her on October 5, 8, 9, 10, and 12, but strangely had remained silent on October 11, 1980, the day Rick and Cindy had vanished.

Carpenter was growing dissatisfied with his job at Gems, he was not being granted enough responsibility by the Neumans, and he was frustrated because the parole board would not allow him to take his money-making trip to Jamaica. Carpenter's prison friend Shane Williams had been at Lompoc since May 26, 1977, and was being released to a halfway house in Los Angeles. Like Carpenter, Williams had been corresponding with a woman through a prisoner pen pal club. When his parole was up he had promised to join her in Arizona, and then the two of them could move to San Francisco to look up his friend Carpenter.

The doors of federal prison closed behind Shane Williams just as the winds at Point Reyes, to the north of San Francisco, were at their strongest and Cindy Moreland and her fiancé, Rick Stowers, started up the Sky Trail, never to be seen alive again.

12

Mill Valley: Anne, 1980

The Columbus Day holiday was being celebrated on Monday, October 13, and on that day at the West Point Inn on Mount Tamalpais, the greeter and live-in caretaker, John Henry, noticed a man about a hundred feet away from the inn. "He was just hanging around. He was in his late forties or early fifties," Henry recalled, "but there was something different about him. He was simply standing there, all but motionless with his hands hanging limply at his sides and wearing street clothing, slacks, a Hawaiian-like shirt. Most people who frequented the mountain were seasoned hikers and looked the part." The stranger was standing on a horseshoe-shaped trail sometime after noon.

Because of the heavy morning rain, which had forced his friends to cancel a visit to the inn, Henry remembered the day clearly. As for Carpenter he had arrived at work at the Gems warehouse at 9:00 A.M. and in the morning had the beginnings of what was to be a horrible day. "It was Jack's first day back," recalled Carpenter, "after a long illness. When Jack came back he was angry at everyone. He spent the day screaming at me. On that specific day I stayed at the warehouse, because I had not laid out the key chains. Doing it resulted in box loads of garbage for that evening. Since the garbage w-w-w-went out on Tuesday [for weekly collection] I had to get everything together by Monday night.'' Carpenter felt anger and stress growing within him.

At 5:00 P.M. Henry closed up the inn, laced up his running shoes, and began his usual one-hour jog on the mountain. Within the first twenty minutes of his run on the south slope he saw a young, blonde woman at Mountain Theatre, a five-thousand-seat amphitheatre. Mesmerized by the sunset, she was seated alone on one of the massive four-thousand-pound serpentine rocks that formed the seats of the forty, three-hundred-foot-long rows. She was gazing at the stage where plays celebrating the legend of the Sleeping Lady, Tamalpa, were held.

''John Henry,'' Sergeant Keaton told me later,'' came through the amphitheatre jogging, and he's a single male, good-looking guy, living up there alone, and says to himself, Whoa, get out! This is too easy. Henry considered for a moment warning her about what had been happening on the mountain, but she was so deep in introspection that he didn't want to bother her.''

''She had her legs crossed, her elbow on her knee and her chin in her palm looking down into the amphitheatre,'' said Henry. ''I was concerned about startling her so I tried to make sure she heard me coming by stamping and shuffling my feat, but she didn't budge. She was apparently consumed in her own thoughts.'' Henry would remember her because of her brown leather dress boots, which were unsuitable for the mountain. He looked back at her as he jogged away; water was puddled in the stone seats set in the ground next to her.

On Tuesday, October 14, some rangers were out looking for muscular ridgeback hogs that had been tearing up the Bolinas Ridge and wallowing in the watershed area. By afternoon they had joined other rangers in responding to an all-points bulletin for a missing woman. They had 6,000 acres of oak- and madrone-studded mountainside to cover. Her white Toyota had been ticketed at 8:00 P.M. in the Mountain Theatre lot when the park closed. When the car had remained there through the morning and into the afternoon, Ranger Michael Fitzsimmons reported the license number to the Department of Motor Vehicles. It was listed as belonging to Dr. Robert Alderson of 710 Bamboo Terrace, San Rafael. Dr. Alderson had reported his daughter, Anne Evelyn Alderson, missing the previous night. Dr. Alderson was in practice with his brother Joseph at the Ross Valley Clinic in Greenbrae and had been for years.

Anne, twenty-six years old, was a beautiful, sturdy blonde. She was also a runner and a world traveler, and had been a Peace Corps volunteer in Colombia and Peru for a year. Most recently, she had been out of state working as a research scientist with livestock in Montana. A Marin County native, Anne had attended Athenian High in Danville and U.C. Davis, graduated from Evergreen College in Washington with a master's degree in animal husbandry, and usually spent her summers as an assistant to veterinarians.

Dr. Alderson had last seen Anne at 3:00 P.M. on October 13 just before she had gone to a convalescent home in Hayward to visit her eighty-year-old grandmother. She had been expected home by 6:00 P.M. for dinner. Dr. Alderson told the police, ''It's not at all like her to do this, just disappear.''

Howenstein drove to Mount Tamalpais to take a look at Anne's car and arranged for deputies to meet him at the Mountain Theatre lot. As was her practice, Anne came to the Sleeping Lady to meditate. Her mother, Evelyn, said Anne was ''big on sunsets.'' Together the officers calculated that the earliest the car could have been parked in the lot was 3:30 P.M. on Monday. The trunk of the abandoned auto was pried open, and on top of the spare tire and some tools were the missing woman's red leather purse and a pair of hiking boots with her white socks. When the purse was opened Anne's driver's license was found inside.

Howenstein designated Mountain Theatre as headquarters and immediately put together a search party of eighty people. The sheriff then ordered the deputies to begin to canvas the north side of the mountain where the vegetation is denser, the slope steeper, and the sun weaker this time of year, and to work their way south.

Within an hour deputies had come up with three witnesses who had seen the missing woman on October 13. One was John Henry. A second witness had seen Anne shortly before Henry, when there had been as many as twenty people in the Greek theatre. Anne had been laughing and enjoying herself. The third witness had seen her after Henry, while she was walking less than one-half mile from where Edda Kane had been found. This news filled the sheriff with dread.

Later in the day Captain Gaddini distractedly walked up the slope of the amphitheatre, passed Pohli Rock, and sat down on one of the vast, cool stones approximately where Anne had been seen by John Henry. From his place among the grasses growing between the stone seats, which curved like Jerusalem's town wall, Gaddini could see Richardson Bay, Alcatraz, and Angel Island in the San Francisco Bay. He looked upward. About a mile away, framed against the sky, were two white domes, radar installations and computers manned by the 666th Radar Squadron where 125 military and civilian personnel worked and lived—people who must be checked out.

Gaddini knew the attacks would go on until either the killer was stopped or was a suicide. Sadistic types usually burn out as they age, but from the detailed description given of Barbara Schwartz's attacker this man was young. A gun. Then a knife. Wondered Gaddini, If Anne was the third victim of this man, what weapon would it be this time?

By dawn, October 15, under Deputy Ray Maynard, the army of searchers was back on the slopes. Morning came and went and still there was no sign of Anne. At 2:50 P.M. Melvin ''Moose'' Muzinich, a veteran employee of the Marin Municipal Water District, picked his way along a seldom-used path, Telephone Line Trail, where a line of decaying telephone poles stood—a row of lifeless trees in a forest of living trees. Fighting his way through weeds and crickets to a point where the trail intersected Rock Springs Trail, less than a quarter mile from the Green amphitheatre, he discovered Anne. She was just off the

path and had been shot only once, like Edda Kane, but
in the right side of her head instead of the back. None of
Anne's jewelry had been taken.

Deputies raced to the scene. Maynard was just east of
Anne's body and twenty yards off Rock Springs Trail. He
was led by a deputy through brambles and shrubbery to
where they found the woman's body, face up, propped
against a blood-stained gray-green rock, her upper body
half-turned. Anne was still clothed, wearing a purple
print blouse, a blue jumper of rough fabric, a necklace,
and calf-high brown leather boots. She almost appeared
to be sleeping. Her right gold earring was gone.

There was a metal fragment from a bullet, twelve
inches from her right foot. Blood stains on the rock had
run like syrup to the grass. As more people gathered at
the scene, tears welled up in the eyes of some, and many
hardened cops had to turn away. Howenstein was notified
by radio and he made arrangements to inform the Alderson family.

Pubic hair combings, the victim's semen-stained panties, and a vaginal swab would be sent to Dr. Richard
Waller, the criminalist at the state department of justice
crime lab in Santa Rosa along with the bullet recovered
by Dr. Jindrich.

Howenstein was positive that the attacker on the trails
was back. He picked up his phone and in a tight voice
ordered the trails above the Panoramic Highway, from
Mountain Home to Pan Toll Camp and Ridgecrest,
closed.

Once again Detective Sergeant Rich Keaton of the
Marin County sheriff's department was struck by the site
of the murder—another heavily canopied area. "When I
set a purple smoke grenade off out there some weeks
later," he told me afterward, "when we were trying to
pinpoint the site for aerial photography, the smoke didn't
penetrate the umbrella of trees. Christ, it just drifted
slowly right over the top of the ground and down back
into the amphitheatre. You could see how it showed the
incredible canopy effect of the murder site. It was so well
canopied there was not enough updraft for the smoke to
be seen."

Keaton noticed something else in common with the

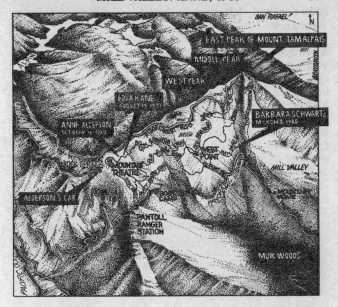

Kane and Schwartz slayings—"You had to go by foot in each and every one of the killings because the killer never was in an area where you could park close by, pull off the shoulder, and get out by the side of the road. We always had to hike more than a mile into the area.

"When I went up there," Sergeant Keaton told me, "I could just imagine Anne sitting in the amphitheatre. Now I'm trying, in my own unobjective way, to determine just how the bad guy got her from here to there. When I talked to her boyfriends and girlfriends I asked them if she would fight him, would she try to sweet-talk him, would she go along with it until she got to the point where she could punch out his lights and then run like hell.

"But I really think no one knows what they'll do until they're faced with that situation. She may very well have been terrified, felt it was easier to submit and be alive. Who knows?

"There was a shortcut from that theatre over a little service road to where Anne was killed, and the only way you would know that is if you had surveyed it before, checked it out, scouted it. I found myself always looking up because I envisioned him, whoever he was, sitting high in the rocks like some sort of vulture.

"Why was Anne dressed again? I've never figured that out. No one else ever has either. We have all sorts of speculation. I picked up on this right away. Some of the streams of blood on Anne run vertically straight down and some also run to the side, horizontally. You don't know why—he kills her. Boom! And then pulls her back over to the side to be sure she is dead. Otherwise why would you roll her over. It's all hypothesis.

"We've contemplated on several occasions using some of our undercover female officers as bait and we had some say, point blank, 'no.' Some said, 'yes' provided they could sit there with a gun inside their purse. We never went to that point. I think it would have been obvious no matter how we did it."

13

Mike Waller

$\mathbf{D}$r. Richard Waller, ballistics and serology analyst for the state crime lab in Santa Rosa, was known to just about everybody as Mike Waller. He had been with the California Department of Justice since 1972, initially specializing in drug and drunk-driving cases.

Genetic markers, a series of complex energy-releasing molecules and enzymes present within the fluids of each individual's body, can be lifted from stains. These genetic markers can be identified by microscopic scrutiny of their electrical charges and analyzed by various high-tech serological tests—the ABO and PGM systems. ABO deals with long-lasting, stable molecules, while PGM deals with more perishable enzymes.

In 1976, Waller had drawn up the testing procedures and serology guidelines for secretor samples in ABO found in semen, saliva, and blood. He had kept these guides flexible because of the variability in each case. Waller's tests were unlike fingerprints in that one specific individual could not be pinpointed. However, since certain combinations of marker characteristics occur only in limited percentages of the population, investigators could use his findings to narrow the field of suspects.

Identifying properties of genetic markers break down at varying rates, depending upon time, concentration of the sample, humidity, temperature, and especially moisture. Alderson's ABO-PGM was complicated because of the number of samples—semen stains, vaginal swabs, and pubic hair combings.

On October 22, 1980, Waller performed two intricate tests—absorption and electrophoresis. The first, *absorption inhabition,* is a test for ABO substance in water-soluable form, such as is found in semen and saliva, and would demonstrate if the attacker was a secretor.

Taking careful bench notes Waller began an examination of a copious semen stain on the left side of the victim's panties. As usual Waller tested an unstained portion of the cloth because the underlying material the stain is on, the substrate, sometimes reacts with the stain in such a way as to mimic ABO characteristics. All tests indicated that the victim and rapist were both Type-A secretors.

Dr. Waller now turned to the second type of test for genetic markers, *electrophoresis.* Begun in the 1930s, the procedure traced the movement of charged particles through a liquid medium in response to changes in an electrical field. First he made a starch agarose gel in something like a large Jell-O mold in which he deposited his sample. When current is run through the gel the particles, depending upon their charge, migrate in predictable directions and at a characteristic speed toward the plus or minus poles on either side of the horizontal "origin" line. Conventional PGM is what is seen on the glass after development by staining—a series of bands.

The maximum number of bands one person could have would be two. Any more, and the analyst would know there was a mixture of fluids from both victim and donor. Alderson's chart showed a PGM subtype with a third band—a mixture of two people. PGM showed $2-1+1-$ and since Alderson was a $2-1-$ this meant the killer had contributed a $1+$. However, this band was weak.

Dr. Waller began work on the physical process involved in the PGM subtype. At 10:00 A.M., October 23, he checked on the progress of the subtype and decided to incubate the sample to develop it further. At 2:45 P.M. he checked the readings on the electrophoretic plate.* The enhanced subtype had given him his answer. Waller could now tell Keaton and Maynard that the killer was a Type-A secretor, with a PGM of $1+1-$. He had narrowed the list of possible suspects to 6 percent of the population.

Serology completed, Waller turned to the ballistics. Though he had no weapon Waller could still determine the class characteristics of the bullet. The slug was a .38. Its weight, 158 grains, told him it was manufactured by Winchester. It was contaminated by blood.

Marin County coroner Ervin Jindrich had noted that the slug had exploded through the back of the victim's head. He wrote, "The bullet tore through the part of the victim's brain that controls heart rate, blood pressure, and respiration."

Waller placed the round-nosed slug in the electron microscope. Weather conditions such as excessive moisture could do as much damage to a slug as to the fragile enzymes he had just been studying. In fact, as Waller told me later, "Body fluids themselves can react with a fired bullet and thereby cause loss of fine striations and detail needed for subsequent comparison and identification."

Through the magnification, Waller's eyes followed the grooves. When a gun is manufactured a brooch is twisted through the barrel to carve channels, which cause the bullet to twist, usually to the right, and to give it flight stability. These lands, the high points, and grooves also mark each bullet and link it to the barrel it was fired through. Mike Waller could plainly see through the microscope six lands and six twisting grooves, all with a right-hand clockwise twist.

In his office Howenstein shut the door, poured a cup of coffee, and sat down behind his desk to think. The Sleeping Lady was visible in the oval window to his left; the officer's reports, Dr. Jindrich's autopsy results, and Waller's ballistics and serology conclusions were in front of him. Because of the high caliber of the weapon used in Edda Kane's murder

---

*PGM conventional on the electrophoretic plate read: (1) $2-1212-1$. PGM subtype read: $2+1+2-1-1+1-2-1+1-2+2-$.

and the lesser power of the gun used in the Anne Alderson attack, a .38, the sheriff knew he could not make a link between the two by virtue of ballistics.

However, there were links, both in the position of the bodies and in indications that both women had been forced to plead for their lives before being executed. Howenstein had to wonder if this was some sort of ritual for the killer. There was always the possibility the murderer could be a member of some sect or cult, but the sheriff felt that the crimes were the work of a loner.

As far as he could determine, after talking with Keaton, Anne had been meditating, the killer had taken her off at gunpoint, raped her, let her get dressed again, and *then* killed her. He had been cool-headed enough to immaculately sweep the area clean of the shell casing and footprints. Howenstein pushed his chair back and studied the calendar. Anne had been killed and raped on the Columbus Day holiday. This might point to a man who had a steady job and was only free on holidays and weekends.

MOUNT TAMALPAIS GREEK AMPHI-THEATRE

14

Gaddini

Under the pressure of the search for the seemingly unstoppable rapist on the mountain, Bob Gaddini had begun to feel deep stress and had become withdrawn. His health began to suffer. He was smoking too much and tired all the time. Immediately after Barbara Schwartz's stabbing he had called the state Department of Justice and requested a list of all recently released men with a history of sex crimes and violence toward women. After Anne's murder he repeated the request. Oddly enough, David Carpenter, with his terrible history of violence to women, was not listed either time.

"People get lost in the system all the time," an official told me later, "a system that seems to have great big holes. One of the reasons why Carpenter didn't show up is that Marin investigators were looking for someone on parole. You see, when Carpenter was released from the state prison at Vacaville in early 1977 he was taken into *federal* custody by marshals to serve out a thirty-month term for parole violations related to his 1960 Presidio attack. Now, the state prison's attitude is: we turn a man over to the feds, he's their problem, not ours. If he's put on the streets it's not going to be under our authority.

"Carpenter was at McNeil Island, then at the Federal Correctional Institute at Lompoc. When he came out in May of 1979 he was under federal supervision, not state authority. The feds have an attitude similar to the state's. They say: we have no jurisdiction over state laws and we don't give former inmates instructions on how to comply with those laws—laws such as registering as a sex offender.

"Carpenter was in a re-entry halfway house—officially still assigned to federal prison. Sure he was out there on the streets, but he technically was not a parolee. He had slipped between the cracks of the system."

In June of 1980, Gaddini had checked the state sex registry for a list of the 58,000 sex offenders in California.* Though California does not require the registration of armed robbers or mass murderers it does, under Penal Code 290, enacted in 1947, require the registration of known sex offenders, whose names are stored in the registry's computer and are available only to law enforcement groups.

Gaddini knew that although the registry was supposed to provide information within twenty-four hours, a week's time was the usual wait. The overworked, three-person sex registry staff, with a budget of $128,000, is expected to handle 150 new registrants per week and a list of 30,000 narcotics offenders as well.

If a convict is paroled under state jurisdiction, he is advised to register at the time of release in the jurisdiction in which he is moving and bring back a copy of the registration slip to his state parole officer. The Department of Corrections also sends out notices to pertinent police departments.

---

*In California a person convicted of oral copulation on an unconscious victim must register, while a person convicted of sexual intercourse with an unconscious female does not have to. Registration is required for a person convicted of performing sodomy but not for committing bestiality. Registration is required for "exciting the lust of a child," but not for giving pornography to children. Registration is mandatory for loitering in public toilets for lewd purposes, but not for Peeping Toms.

Richard Wood, Carpenter's federal probation officer, aware of the inadequacies of the system, told me later, "The sex registry doesn't work. You send them down to the police department, but the department isn't terribly receptive to these people coming down and registering . . . a lot of times the clerk would tell them to come back later. No one seems to comply with the sex registry because no one enforces it."

Thus, registration is almost completely voluntary, and a 1977 study showed 94 percent of the local police agencies failed to prosecute a single sex offender for failing to register or notify them within ten days of an address change during that year. A prisoner released from state custody into the community would be on record, but not one released from federal authorities. The requirement that Carpenter register as a sex offender was overlooked because he was still technically in federal prison when he was released to the halfway house.

15

Mill Valley:
Mark, 1980

"**Y**ou can shoot at me. Throw snakes at me. Knife me," said Mark McDermand, a pallid, six-foot-four, two-hundred-pound writer who lived with his elderly mother and demented older brother on the slopes of the Sleeping Lady, and who became a prime suspect in the Trailside case. "Throw snakes at me, knife me, go 'Boo!' in the night—and I won't bat an eye. Put a potato bug within a block of me and I fold right up."

Because within Mark's family there existed a history of hereditary schizophrenia and biological depression and because the rest of his family had gone insane, McDermand's greatest apprehension was of becoming mad himself. The agitated, awkward, and sepulchral young man with the sandy-blond ponytail lit one Chesterfield after another and looked at his watch. It was 11:00 P.M., the evening of October 13, 1980. Anne Anderson had been shot on Mount Tamalpais less than five hours earlier. Mark was now in the midst of his grueling shift as a fry cook at a Denny's restaurant, working the graveyard slot.

* * *

"Oddly," Mark told me after the Trailside case was re-solved, "much of the period in question is difficult for me to remember in any reliable detail, particularly those aspects directly related to the killings themselves.

"I *know* I did the deed, but I'll be double-damned if I can *recall* it. I *do* remember it—but I can remember several mutually exclusive 'versions' of it. Oddly enough, while intellectually I am fully convinced of what I did, emotionally the whole bloody thing fails to fully regis-ter."

Mark, a diabetic, had been working at Denny's, a low, tan and brown building in Corte Madera, quite a lot dur-ing September and October—four to five shifts per week, spread out to double shifts as needed. Though he couldn't recall just how much work he had done prior to the kill-ings, he did remember being "damn tired." Fry cooking was, he told me later, "a horrible job for any human being unless one happens to be suited to it, in which case it can be a remarkably interesting and satisfying way to spend time."

Mark had started fry cooking in the mid-1970s and had worked in eleven Denny's in six states during that period. "All good fry cooks," he told me, "are animals. With a fast turnover you are faced with forty-five tickets and perhaps 150 different orders between them, and in any given minute ten of the tickets will 'sell,' and fifteen more will appear that you must enter into your short-term memory. You simply haven't the time to act rationally. The animal can do it—the guy concerned with trivia such as burns, cuts, and the practical impossibility of *thinking* about how to erase twenty items of memory and instantly replace them with twenty others, simply is out of his league."

Mark was also an alcoholic. "I coped with drink," he said. "I don't think I've cooked a total of more than ten shifts sober, and my drinking got in the way of my cook-ing on less than half that number. In fact, the job is so stressful that I can honestly state that of the perhaps fifty fry cooks I've worked lines with—the fifty or so who were good fry cooks, fast, effective, put up good food no matter how bad a rush, only ten cooked 'straight.'

Sober. On neither pot, drugs, or booze, and of the ten, five went home and *then* got bombed.''

Severely depressed, Mark was hurting all over and drank from a pint to a quart of vodka per day. At the end of September he had been struck temporarily blind at work.

For most of his life Mark had suffered from vision problems and severe headaches and in the last six months had begun to have difficulty walking. Frequently he hobbled and had trouble rising to his feet after sitting for a time. Pain was etched on his ashen face when he made various movements, and Mark was aware of a loss of sensation in his hands and feet. His epileptic tendencies were exacerbated by both alcohol and insulin abuse, and insulin shock often caused McDermand to be confused and disoriented. John French, Mark's friend of seventeen years, said of him, ''Mark was always a little drunk or wobbly when his insulin level was off balance.''

Mark's father, the naturalist Charles McDermand, had written a brace of books in the forties that popularized golden trout fishing in the Sierras, and for this a lake was named after him in King's Canyon. The happiest days Mark and his older brother, Edwin, ever spent were hiking with their father through the High Sierras. In emulation of his father Mark tried to complete a book. He tried six in all and burned all but one.

After a series of strokes Charles McDermand, himself a borderline schizophrenic, died in 1966. Mark's unpredictable, erratic, and intractable mother, Helen, then began a decade-long decline into schizophrenia and religious mania.

Mark, Edwin, and his mother all shared the same ramshackle, unheated, two-bedroom house that clung perilously to a wooded shelf on Shoreline Road just over a mile from Tam Junction. The family had moved into the isolated home in 1944. It had been built in the thirties as a ''weekender'' and partially renovated so that it could be used as a year-round house. Mark felt it had never been intended to be occupied by more than ''two very compact people.'' In 1949 Mark's father had expanded the one bedroom to become the brothers' room and remodeled the porch so it could be used as a bedroom for the parents.

"It was a goddamn small place," Mark told me, "a *tiny* place. I remember visiting other kids and wondering how they coped with so damn much space. It was a common thread throughout my life there—no *room*. There was no such thing as privacy. I wonder how people live in apartments without going quietly mad."

Mark's job, his past, all of these were elements that created the powder keg that was the exhausted Mark McDermand of 1980.

"Mark is one of the nicest, most tolerant, and decent persons I have ever known," said Marion Irving, a long-time friend of Mark's, "yet, when he was fifteen, he held two teenagers at gunpoint after they had spray painted, in brilliant orange paint in several places in our neighborhood, signs that read, 'Mark is a Queer.' Mark was so different—so quiet, so tolerant, and he would not fight, not even to protect himself—that they felt it was fun to torment him. I personally painted out those signs with black paint, but not until they had been there overnight and well into the next morning for all of the neighborhood and his friends to see."

Mark's religious fundamentalist mother thought it was sinful to feel anger, so she prayed for the perpetrators of the cruel prank. "Mark," Marion told me later, "tried to suppress his deep hurt and anger, but two days later, his efforts for control shattered." Mark reached for his father's shotgun.

The bookish daydreamer threatened the two boys with the gun and was taken to Juvenile Hall, where he was held in detention for two and one-half months. There he was raped by two older boys. The shy, hurt boy was given no counseling to deal with this traumatic experience. On the basis of an abnormal electroencephalogram, Marion told me, a diagnosis of petit mal epilepsy was made, and Mark was placed on medications of Dilantin and phenobarbital for three years. Mark was diagnosed as having had encephalitis between the ages of seven and ten and had suffered seizures and blackouts since the age of thirteen. Because of the graffiti and the

gun incident Mark dropped out of Tamalpais High in 1960
in his sophomore year.

Years later, Dr. Cress, a psychiatrist, in reviewing
Mark's files, felt that the rapes had completely alienated
the boy from people from that time on. "Henceforth
Mark felt that he was an outsider and 'the lowest of the
low,' viewing himself as both physically ill and morally
and sexually defective." Cress also believed that Mark's
paranoia included a morbid jealousy over his mother and
brother. Mark saw his brother as a distorted mirror image
of himself.

"At age nineteen," Marion told me, "Mark attempted
suicide from the Golden Gate Bridge [in January of 1965],
but was pulled back from the catwalk by bridge workers
and taken to Langley-Porter Neuropsychiatric Institute
where psychiatrists diagnosed him as mentally disordered and a schizoid personality, a borderline condition
that often precedes breakdown to full schizophrenia."

"It was a personal crisis," said Mark, in referring to
his suicide attempt, "coupled with the social and political pressures of the time."

Mark's brother, Edwin, left the army in 1968 and immediately began falling into the pattern of his mother's
schizophrenia. He sat staring at the wall, was unable to
touch certain objects or cross specific streets. In attacks
of indecision he would wheel about on the sidewalk in
circles. As for Mark, his happiest times were when he
played guitar in the sixties—"Odd gigs," he said, "such
as backup for the Coasters and Round Robin, backing
singers, strippers, and some wonderfully crummy acts.
Had a hell of a good time for a while. . . . Vietnam was
cranking up at the time, and for some unfathomable reason I volunteered for the draft in 1966. Figure this—I
volunteered for the infantry and was made a medic; I
volunteered for Vietnam, so they sent me to Korea." In
Korea Mark developed diabetes and was discharged in
1968.

As more mental problems beseiged Mark he tried to
take his life four more times between 1969 and 1972. He
entered Mendocino State Hospital on April 28, 1971, and
was discharged on January 21, 1972.

In 1980 Helen McDermand was almost seventy-five

years old and had been bedridden for several years. As a 1965 report showed, she was "highly anxious, neurotic and a schizophrenic." Still, Helen was able to exercise a strange control over both her sons, especially forty-year-old Edwin. He assumed the mother's symptoms and grew progressively more ill. Edwin left scattered notes around the house pleading for psychiatric care—"God above, protect me. I need his help desperately" and "There is no God. My mother is insane."

During her moody periods, when lubricious Helen surrounded herself in her bed with a sea of religious tracts, her personality became bipolar, swinging dramatically and without warning from agreeable to tempestuous, confounding Mark. "No one ever knew," he said later, "what response an action would generate in that household . . . especially with my mom. What earned a hug Friday, got yelled at Saturday, ignored Sunday, and caused tears Monday. I do not ever recall a single, unambiguous, clear, or unmistakable signal from her."

In the remarkably compact house on the side of Mount Tamalpais, unpredictable Helen in her room, Edwin and Mark sharing the remaining bedroom, the relationship between Helen and her two sons had many of the same qualities as that of Frances Carpenter to her son David—an extraordinarily intense but highly ambivalent relationship, a capricious giving or rejecting of feelings.

Over a fifteen-year period, beginning in 1959, mental health experts and social workers had analyzed the unique case of the McDermands. Both sons were in and out of various institutions separately—Mark in a total of six hospitals, and in 1970 both brothers shared the same ward at Mendocino State Hospital. Edwin, diagnosed as having chronic (undifferentiated) schizophrenia, became so psychotic that the heavy doses of drugs failed to temper his bizarre behavior, still the sounds of inner voices, or dispel his delusions. Mark and Edwin's mercurial mother often visited the boys at the facility, where Mark had assumed a protective role in regard to his more seriously ill older brother.

William Simmons, a psychiatric social worker at Mendocino State Hospital, was aware of Mrs. McDermand's domination over Edwin. He had never seen Edwin relaxed. "His face was very wooden," he said later, "and the only emotion that I saw him express was disgust. When Mrs. McDermand came to visit Edwin, he would focus his eyesight on her, relate with her to the exclusion of everyone else, make eye contact with her face and keep it. Edwin showed pupil dilation almost as if entranced. She wasn't doing anything to break that focus, she was maintaining it."

Simmons believed her to be a "schizophrenigenic" person—an individual who has a way of using words and suggestions mesmerically to cause schizophrenic symptoms in other people such as hallucinations, rituals, false beliefs, dependency, and delusions.

After nine months of pacing the L-shaped halls, Edwin was discharged from Mendocino. He promptly abandoned his medication and then—although he could still converse intelligently on history and astronomy—collapsed into madness. Mark's ears were filled with an unceasing racket as Edwin trooped around their room, howling and periodically dropping to the floor, an odd strangling noise in his throat. Each morning the shingled house shook from Edwin's stereo, which pumped a throbbing beat into the clear mountain air.

In 1974 Mark had another breakdown, this time at work, and began pounding his head and fists against a bathroom wall. His fists were huge. He was forced to undergo treatment at the Veterans Administration Hospital in Menlo Park, where they noted his alcoholism, entered a new diagnosis showing him to be a schizoid personality with strong antisocial and manipulative behavior, and became aware of his passion for guns.

After 1974 the experts had ceased studying the tortured family, and rudderless, muttering, and unwashed Edwin began compulsively consuming gigantic portions of food and drink in single gluttonous binges, littering the floor with food scraps. Away from the troubled home, Edwin would order several complete breakfasts, wolfing them down one after the other. Unsated, he would then drink each beverage on the menu in order of its listing. Often he would buy every paper on a newsstand, turning all the pages as rapidly as possible. Edwin would make a moaning noise each time he sat down or got up.

After Edwin's release he developed a fixation. A family friend remembered, "He thought his mother was a witch or a sorceress. [Witches sometimes held rites in the open forest of Mount Tamalpais.] Edwin would put a paper bag over his head whenever his mother came into the room so he wouldn't have to see her." So severe was deluded Edwin's fear of bewitchment that he took a room elsewhere for a while. On weekends Mark drove his brother home, but Edwin refused to enter for fear of being entranced. Mrs. McDermand put his food on a tray and Mark took it out to Edwin to eat under a tree.

"My brother was flaky," said Mark, "and my mom was really out of it—she was hiding from him, sleeping a lot. I was just tired, exhausted." While his mother hid in her small bedroom Mark kept his distance. Mark's feeling was that murder would occur, he just didn't know when or who would do it. An aunt remembered that even as a child Mark had wanted to die, and as soon as he could talk he told her so.

Often Mark's bosses at the restaurant, Larry Norris and manager Tony Benson, toiled as fry cooks dressed in their suits alongside him. In Mark's estimation Norris wasn't really used to the business and occasionally got in the way in the kitchen. "But he was a pretty good guy," Mark said. Norris felt the same about Mark but was sorry for him as well. "He had so much trouble dealing with others he could only work for a few days at a time," he explained. Mark was soft-spoken, but there was a barely contained tension about him, an irony and bitterness in his tone that was not lost on his co-workers.

"Benson was an able manager, did his job well, had a good sense of humor and almost all of the employees at Denny's felt they could talk to him and not walk away feeling slighted. I enjoyed working for Tony very much," Mark told me. "Some restaurant bosses are so nasty one often wonders why they've managed to live as long as they have . . ."

Benson knew that Mark had been more depressed than usual lately, so tense his long legs jiggled up and down when he was sitting. When he was in a bad mood nobody approached Mark.

As he worked, a picture of Edwin at home with a bag pulled over his head kept running through Mark's mind: Edwin pacing round and round to his music, faster and faster, a whirlwind of pain. Clockwise went the tread of his feet, his shrieking audible even in Mark's cramped basement hideaway.

His Monday-night shift on October 13 completed, Mark left Denny's. ''I had come directly home from Denny's somewhere between midnight and 1:30 or so. I had made a drink and sat on the couch, had turned on the light and had read a—I believe it was the newspaper. I had looked into the hall just as I sat, and I saw nothing there, *then*. I was tired, and kind of lazing around, and I feel like I napped, but I don't recall actually napping or sleeping. But the rest was a blank, everything after this was a blank.''

Early on the afternoon of October 16, Mark went directly to Denny's and insisted on being ''cash-paid,'' which was against the restaurant's policy. He wanted an advance of one hundred dollars. ''I have to leave town,'' he told Larry Norris, the assistant manager. Mark was so distraught that Norris advanced him fifty in cash. With tobacco-stained fingers Mark nervously lit a nonfilter Chesterfield and left.

In the Tamalpais fog, sheriff's officer Lieutenant Gerald Miklos found it difficult to navigate, especially on a mountainside. He was accompanied by a partner, Elana Gulbransen, and Cooper, a deputy trainee. It was Thursday, October 16. The cruiser's wipers swept away the dampness but not the shadows cast by the roiling clouds and tall redwoods. The lawmen were dodging potholes on the way to the old McDermand house at 564 Shoreline. The rundown home was perched high on the south slope of the Sleeping Lady above Highway 1 where the road pulls away from the mountain.

For several days now the neighbors had been fearful for the safety of the McDermands. Late Monday night, or more precisely at 1:45 A.M., the same day Anne Alderson had been slain, the neighbors heard what they thought were gunshots. There had been one shot, followed by a long silence, another shot and a shorter period of silence, then, abruptly, a volley of seven shots.

Since then no one had seen any of the McDermands around the house. No one had answered the door, and the 1969 yellow Chevrolet coupe, California plates 427 HVW, had vanished from the driveway. Miklos knew Mark McDermand. "I knew him from being on the beat when I spent nine years in the Marin substation. I had known Mark for years. I had dealt with him and we had developed, if not a friendship, an acquaintanceship."

Earlier in the evening, June Berry, a Mill Valley friend of Mark's mother, concerned over the fact that Helen had not called during the week,* phoned the sheriff's office and then drove to the McDermand home. She found Helen's auto in the carport but noticed Mark's was nowhere in sight. After banging on the door and calling out Mrs. McDermand's name, June returned home and phoned the sheriff's department a second time. Miklos had been sent in response.

The landscape the deputies rode through was as dull, dark, somber, and wet as a sea cave. The only selection of color available to them were variations on the theme of gray—yellow-gray, blue-gray, green-gray, and brown-gray, the last being the color of the McDermand house, which loomed up in front of their headlights at the end of a curved seventy-five-foot driveway. Miklos could see a short, crooked, redwood staircase. He consulted his watch—9:10 P.M.

The deputies got out of the patrol car. As the wind intensified so did the moan through the trees and hillocks. All three officers buttoned up the clasps of their car coats over their sheriff's uniforms, but the damp fog still crept down their collars. They brought up their flashlights and played them about. Monterey pines scraped forlornly against the old house.

Where the back of the house faced the highway Miklos and Gulbransen could see an overhanging deck. The slid-

---

*Helen McDermand's sister, Edna, in Berkeley, had also called the sheriff, expressing her concern over the McDermands.

ing glass double doors of a small room were visible above
it. They walked uphill around the house, passed stone
steps on the side leading downward to a garage, and
climbed a steep bank covered with rose bushes, trees,
and blackberry bushes until they reached the front of the
building. Here at the top was a patio and beyond that
they found double French doors leading into the living
room. The doors were locked.

Down farther was the kitchen window, out of which
billowed a yellow flowered curtain made damp by the fog.
Miklos put his hand up to his eyes to blot out the wind
and looked upward to the square and flat top of the
house. Multitextured shingles ran down the side of the
building and onto the top of a peaked redwood section of
the roof. Against this was leaning a painter's ladder.

No lights shone through the half-open window, so they
returned to the French doors. Miklos said, "We're going
in." He told me later, "The cumulative facts—nobody
had seen the family, inactivity in the house, mother's car
sitting alone, the house shut tight—it was just a feeling.
The house was dark, very dark. I decided to go in, and
as we made entry we used cover and concealment."
Miklos and Gulbransen found themselves in the living
room. To the left of the entry doors was an undersized
kitchen with a small space heater and a chair. Across the
room, past the built-in bookcases and fireplace, which
made up an entire wall, was another chair. "We made a
scan of the room and didn't see anything," recalled Miklos and so they proceeded farther into the house. They
were jittery.

They could smell the faint odor of unwashed dishes or
spoiled food. Their flashlights illuminated a floor cluttered with papers and discarded clothes. The people who
lived here seemed to have rarely left home. A quick
glance in the kitchen revealed a sink filled with dishes,
some trash at least three days old, an old washing machine next to the patio door, and an open cabinet filled
with linen over the stove.

Guardedly they left the kitchenette and returned to the
disarray of the living room, moving slowly across the
room toward a small bathroom. Its door was partially
open, completely blocking a narrow carpeted hallway.

The fog had made the house damp and the walls glistened from the outside light. On the other side of the open door the double windows of the bathroom down the hall facing the highway allowed the flashing lights of the patrol car and the shadows from the moving trees to enter the darkened passageway. It was by this light the officers first saw the dark stains on the floor and wall. Blood.

The closing of the bathroom door revealed more stains on its outside surface and, sprawled just outside the bedroom door, half in the hall, half in the living room, feet protruding toward the highway, the body of a man. "He had been there a day or two," Miklos told me afterward, "and had a few holes in him." The man, clad only in trousers, had as many as eight wounds in his upper torso and head.

They turned him over to see his face. Obviously it was one of the McDermand brothers. The settling of the blood had given a bruised and beaten appearance to his face. Miklos knew Mark, and this wasn't him. It had to be his brother, Edwin.

Deputy Cooper observed post mortem lividity, which indicated to him that the man had been killed, at the very least, twelve hours earlier. One bullet had entered behind the man's right ear and four others were visible in the area of the right forehead and temple. There were three wounds in the right chest. They could see no sign of powder burns.

Miklos decided to call for backup before trying to enter the other bedroom. He circled around to the cruiser and informed Captain Gaddini of the situation and requested a code-three backup. He returned to the house. Gulbransen and Miklos now turned their attention to the remaining bedroom, which opened into the living room. It was locked, but a set of keys were lying on the living room floor and Miklos found that these fit the lock. "While we had backup coming," Miklos told me later, "we made entry to the room, again not knowing if there was someone alive or barracaded in there."

Miklos turned the key and slowly twisted the handle, opening the door gingerly with his foot, stepping to the side—at this point he really didn't know what he was going to find. The door opened soundlessly an inch at a time, but before it was open the officers knew the pale, crumpled old lady under the quilts in the double bed was dead.

There was a note tacked up near her, and both Miklos and Gulbransen focused the beams of their flashlights onto the scrap of paper and peered into the room. It was not unlike the multitude of other similar scraps throughout the house. Neither officer spoke. The officers gingerly crossed the tidy room to read what it said:

Hi shitheads, if you can read this you're way too late. Catch me on the news or on the slab. I'll look the same either way: ugly.

Mr. Hate

16

Manhunt

Miklos carefully pulled a lamp back from where it had fallen and stood it upright on the marble-topped table next to the woman's bed, where sat a vase of dried or dead flowers. There were few signs of a struggle—"The room was neat, orderly," noted Miklos. "She was just lying in bed. The mother wasn't that bloody. He had shot her in the ear, so it looked like she was just asleep with a trickle of blood coming out of her ear. She had been there a while, lost in slumber." He could tell from the powder burns that she had been shot at close range, a single shot fired into her left ear, probably with a low-caliber pistol, such as a semiautomatic .22. In all likelihood the dead man in the hall had been killed with the same gun and also at close range. They shone their lights around the rest of the room. One bullet casing was found on the floor.

Three buttercup-style lights hung from the ceiling. The two chairs in the room had elaborate lace coverings that duplicated the stripe and floral wallpaper and echoed the intricate design of the rug. In the far corner of the room was the old woman's dressing table, topped with a small triptych mirror that reflected the deputies own lights back into their eyes. To their extreme left were an old black piano and two large closets built into the wall.

After a fruitless search for Mark, Miklos and his partner left the house. Outside, the veteran officer's eyes wandered to the steps leading to the open doorway of the garage below—another place where Mark might be holed up. They started down the stone steps, which were slippery with green moss, some covered completely by lichen. Miklos and Gulbransen carefully felt for each step as they descended in the mist. In minutes the policemen, flashlights extended, made their way into the damp, cold, windowless garage. In the fog their lights seemed exceedingly dim and dry. The garage had no door because years before it had been removed and never replaced.

Silently they crept up to a door inside the garage. The grease puddle where the Chevy Malibu had been parked had mixed with rain water and made little rainbow islands around the rubber of the deputies' boots. A larger adjacent puddle reflected them and their flashlights full length. Cautiously they pushed open the door located right where the driver's side of the Chevy would have rested and looked into an adjoining room twice as large as the garage.

A black furnace sat almost in the center of the dank chamber and there were crude wooden shelves scattered about. An earthen bank, the base of the wild hill above, filled the front side of the room. Water was puddling in front of the furnace. The officers continued past the shelves until they came to a second door. The door was padlocked with a hasp lock. Miklos forced this and a tiny room sectioned off with plywood was revealed. The boards had been pieced together with small nails and reinforced with tape that had begun to buckle and peel away. A large bowl of cigarette butts and a bag of dirty napkins lay on the floor. Miklos discovered two boxes of .306 ammunition, two shotgun shells, nineteen spent .38-caliber casings, three live rounds of .22-caliber ammunition, gun cleaning equipment, and an ankle holster for a handgun and one for a knife.

A mattress lay on the floor next to a table scarred with cigarette burns, both floated on a sea of paper—notebooks, magazines, science-fiction books, and paper scraps cluttered the floor in the spots where dusty boxes weren't piled. The two partners assumed it was the missing son's bedroom.

The room had been fiberglass insulated, but there was no Sheetrock. At the far end they could see a small table and a radio. A gooseneck lamp was attached to the wall, six wire coat hangers hung from a rod, and these were stirred by the wind from the open garage door.

Some of the papers were novels in progress. It was later obvious that the writer had been unable to combine these fragments into a coherent piece. Because of the trash and clutter the room seemed uninhabitable to the deputies. To choose to live in this lonely environment was unthinkable to them and, feeling uncomfortable, they went back up to wait in the night air.

The backup team was shown the mother's body and her son's. The dead man's wallet was found in the living room fireplace along with a savings book and a bank statement in the name of Edwin McDermand.

There were bloodstains on the door, the hall, and the ceiling. Five shell casings were found on the floor and one was found on the bookcase between the mother's room and the hall, one in the living room, and one in Edwin's bedroom. Eight shells in all. The deputies theorized the mother had been killed first and Edwin had been roused, then shot.

Deputy Coroner Ken Holmes at the coroner's office was notified and a hunt for a photo of Mark was begun. One of Edwin was found first—a young man in a coonskin cap and buckskins, clutching an old frontier rifle in his right hand, a fixed look in his faded eyes, and an odd smirk on his lips. Then they found one of Mark. It showed another tall, thin man in his thirties. One look at the photograph and each deputy had the same thought— in this photo Mark bore an incredible likeness to the composite sketch made of a thirty-five-year-old man in a dark blue windbreaker seen on Mount Tamalpais the day Edda Kane was killed.

All three murders on the Sleeping Lady had happened close to the McDermand home; now it appeared that the mother and her son had been shot the same day as Anne

Alderson. Captain Gaddini was contacted by radio, and since it was agreed that it was possible there was a correlation between the two acts of violence Gaddini pulled the file on Mark Venters McDermand, thirty-five, and carefully went through it. This active file on the missing son existed because Mark had been involved in an investigation three years earlier concerning a Tamalpais Valley store, the Tam Valley 7-Eleven. Allegations of embezzlement had been made, a no-bail warrant was issued, but it was never served.

Beginning with Edwin's mental collapse in 1968 and 1969, Mark had been arrested for possession of stolen property, the thefts of a car, cash, and a gun in February of 1971, and then encyclopedias and other property. Mark fled the state, returned, and used his history of blackouts as a defense for his actions. Rather than go to jail he had himself voluntarily committed to Mendocino State Hospital.

The file had a six-year-old Polaroid photograph of Mark clipped to the inside of the manila folder. In the picture the missing son's face was framed by sandy-blond hair worn in a ponytail and set off by the horn-rimmed glasses he only occasionally wore. The glasses dropped near Barbara Schwartz's body were like these. Behind his glasses Mark McDermand's intelligent pale blue eyes peered out over a lantern jaw, below a broad forehead. A smile played about the corners of his mouth.

On the possibility Mark might try to pick up any money owed to him, officers were dispatched to Denny's restaurant. By this time it was already too late. Mark had picked up fifty dollars on Thursday, before the murders had been discovered. Tony Benson told them this about Mark: "He's highly intelligent, given to depression, and very unstable. I do know that Mark did not like his brother at all."

They also learned that on October 15, Mark had bought one hundred hypodermic syringes from a Tam Valley pharmacist and told him in passing, "I'm movin' on to Montana." Mark then drove three miles away and bought another hundred syringes. After news of the homicides reached the media, one of McDermand's co-workers at Denny's, Kevin West, recalled that Mark had borrowed his 12-gauge shotgun in July and on September 22 had borrowed a .22-caliber pistol. West also remembered that he had loaned Mark the keys to his apartment and discovered that two clips of ammunition were missing from his home.

Immediately after the discovery of the murders on Shoreline a friend of Mark's, John French, told the police that "Mark called his brother 'it' or 'the thing.' He told me that someday he was going to put 'it' out of his misery."

Dr. Jindrich performed autopsies on Mrs. McDermand and her son on October 17. The presence of powder burns in the single bullet wound behind Helen's left ear indicated to the coroner that the gun was only several inches from her head when the bullet was discharged. One of the bullets in Edwin's head had entered behind his right ear and had lodged in the bone at the base of his skull. Jindrich could not determine the exact time of the death of the mother and son, but samples of vitreous humor fluid taken from their eyes at 3:30 and 3:46 P.M. suggested to the coroner that both were killed from sixty-five to ninety-five hours earlier—early Tuesday morning.

Jindrich felt that Mrs. McDermand had lost consciousness almost immediately, and that any one of Edwin's wounds would have been fatal. He could not determine the order in which the bullets were fired. Two of the bullets in Edwin's body came from the same .22-caliber gun, but the other slugs were so badly damaged that it couldn't ballistically be proven they had been fired from the same gun.

Mark had written several dozen letters to Guy Wright of the *San Francisco Examiner* over the last three years under the pen name Wallace Bing. Wright found them wry, perceptive, concerned about the world's injustices. "Well, son," began one, "it's almost that season again. The politicos are sniffing the breezes and each other, issues are being fabricated out of nothing and real problems are being ignored into oblivion."

As a fugitive, Mark wrote to Wright. "Unmasked! Curses!" he began. "This is a certified scoop, ol' son." His first letter, postmarked Corte Madera was to Wright:

Dateline Sitting Duck, Ca. [Sunday Oct. 19, 1980] Go
with grace. I saw the crime scene. I sat there studying
it—I know "who dunnit" . . . I'll take care of it my
own way . . . No one would believe it if I told them.
But (you were ready for that I trust)—Seein's how I've
been deemed "guilty," if you think I'm not going to
act guilty you're not thinking. Ever been locked up? I
have . . . and never shall be again. I may get killed.
I may "elude" pursuit, I may kill to escape. But I
ain't having my "rights" read to me again.
Macho? Hardly. Scared shitless? Decidedly. As soon
as I finish my business I'm shaggin' ass for parts unknown. Till then, I'm as dangerous as a coral snake
in a sleeping bag. "Never corner a frightened man."
You can quote me. Well, I gotta find a tree to sleep
under. Ciao, son.

"In the basement," Marion Irving told me, "Mark
had built a room to escape, to some degree, the noise
made by his brother in the house above. Mark's room
had no windows to let in light and no door to the outside.
It was dark and gloomy—also damp and cold. This was
not condusive to good physical or mental health, especially to someone like Mark who was suffering from diabetes, arthritis, lung disease, and borderline
schizophrenia. There was no heat, and the sound of Edwin's shrieking filtered down through the air vent and
into Mark's room."

Mark told me that his mother had bought the lumber
herself for his basement room. But there was no refuge
for him even there.

"The house was *tiny*. Even after a small addition,
turning the large porch into a master, if unheated, bedroom and doubling the size of the bedroom Edwin and I
shared, if we'd added anything bigger than a carton of
cigarettes you couldn't have taken a deep breath. After
things went to hell, people kept asking me why I didn't
stay away if things were so bad. Well, I tried. The problem was, however, that my mom, Edwin, and I were too
closely knit. Even while we grated on each other.

"Beyond that I just don't know. I eventually threw up
a boxlike room in the basement, used variously for sleep-

ing and storage. Tacky, but more or less of use. A few months prior to the killings, I moved back upstairs. You can shoot at me, throw snakes at me, knife me, go 'Boo!' in the night—and I won't bat an eye. Put a cricket or a potato bug within a block of me and I fold right up. A potato bug got into the room and I got the hell *out*. Don't know why.''

The sight of the potato bug had thrown Mark back into the maelstrom above, adding to his tension. At night he struggled to sleep on the couch in the living room near the French doors. ''A pressure like a heavy load began to exert itself on the base of my neck. I could feel it building and could feel myself being forced over some invisible line inch-by-inch,'' he told me.

''I arrived home from Denny's on the night of the murders [October 13, 1980] around 1:30 A.M., and after a drink or two I must have drifted off. I got up after what seemed like a passage of virtually no time and I went outside, walked around for a few minutes, and came back in, went into the kitchen and made another drink, came back out, and as I was sitting down, I glanced to the hall again, and I saw my brother, and I put the drink down and went over and just looked at him.''

A flash of memory came to Mark of his brother, Edwin, being hit by a bullet fired into his head behind the right ear, and of the slug not penetrating beneath the lower edge of the cranium, but lodging in the bone instead, of his brother turning slowly around to look directly at him, ''horror and amazement etched on his face.'' Dimly Mark recalled shooting his brother six to seven times more to keep him from ''being alive anymore . . . 'cause he was hurting, and killing's one thing, hurting's another. And I don't want anybody to hurt.

''There was no shock involved. It was kind of a 'Oh, boy, look at that—' feeling, I can't think of the word. It was—it was acceptance, you know, 'There it is,' you know, 'My brother is laying there dead. I saw the wounds in his chest. I thought I saw wounds in his head. I mean, with the blood that was there, I was sure he had wounds in his forehead, and there was a lot of blood under his head.

"And I reached under his head and felt the back of his skull, and I felt a wound, the bullet wound, and went out and washed my hands outside. The kitchen sink was full of dishes, and I just didn't go that way. I went outside again, and I came back in, and my mother's door was shut, which it hadn't been when I came home.

"So I unlocked it. I had a key in my possession; I always had a key because it is the same key as for the front door. And I went in, and she was laying there with the blanket below her head, and I could see the wound in her ear and some blood on her upper mouth. And again, no shock, no stunned feeling; just a final feeling— a finality. It was like, 'Well, this is it. Well, there it is.' And I pulled the blanket up over her head and I went back out and sat for a while, and then I left."

Mark had blanked out the details, but he was certain he was the killer, "I've thought about it. There's no possibility it was anyone but me . . . I finally decided I had three options: turn myself in, get killed, or run . . . I ran. I drove to 7-Eleven and bought some cigarettes and then I went to Denny's and talked with a friend, Don, for a while.

"I can't write about the actual murders," said Mark. "They're tucked away in my memory, beyond recall."

Don had talked with Mark on Sunday, October 12, and on Monday afternoon, so he was surprised to see Mark again at Denny's close to 2:00 early Tuesday morning. McDermand took Don away from his group of friends so they could talk privately. He noticed Mark was acting more "loose" than normal and later would say his memory of what McDermand told him was incomplete. "I did not want to hear it, and I blocked most of it. I did recall Mark mentioning that the toes of one of the victims had curled. He told me that they had died as they lived."

Don talked with Mark again on the evening of October 15. Late Thursday morning they met again at Denny's and agreed to meet the next day, October 17, at the International House of Pancakes in El Cerrito. Afterward Mark and Don went to a park in the Berkeley hills where they considered his options. On Sunday, October 19, McDermand gave Don some letters to mail to the papers, and he did so.

The police learned Mark McDermand had three guns, a nine-shot .22-caliber pistol and two .38-caliber guns. The police knew a .38-caliber had been used in two of the killings on the side of Mount Tamalpais. Because of Mark's resemblance to one of the composite drawings and his proximity to the attacks, McDermand became their chief suspect. The deputies interviewed the neighbors and learned that the McDermands were reputed to be odd. "They're sort of like the *Beverly Hillbillies*," said one. "Very, very, very unsophisticated to say the least." The police knew they would have to recover the guns to determine if they were the ones used in the killings.

Mark had taken out an ad in *Soldier of Fortune* magazine to obtain weapons, according to the police, and had used two aliases: Wallace Bing and Gloria Washington.

In a letter to Carol Pogash, a reporter for the *San Francisco Examiner* who had commented that his life between Denny's and home seemed dreary, Mark wrote:

Oct. 19, 1980

My Dear Ms. Pogash:
Why did I trundle back and forth, hang out, sit around and generally do zilch? Easy, Ma'am—1) I hurt too much to ramble about, 2) the relative anonymity suits me, 3) The atmosphere was conducive to thought, Crazy, Si—Unstable, No.

The letters from Mark flowed on, and in one to the *Oakland Tribune* he said:

Oct. 19, 1980

I lose my temper for the same reasons anyone does—I just lose it easier: intentionally. I've simply decided that social "acceptance" is not worth putting up with idiocy. There is nothing to connect me with the "Tam killings" because I am not connected period. I know only a little more than the police about the shootings in my home—but that little is enough, and I'll take care of it in my fashion . . . I shall never again be

imprisoned, and this means that I must—in the eyes
of the law—be shot on sight.

On October 20 Mark mailed a letter to Gaddini explaining he had nothing to do with the killings on the
trails of Mount Tamalpais. Through the papers Gaddini
requested Mark call him at 479-7233.

Another letter from Mark ran in the morning *Chronicle,* addressed to staff reporter Paul Liberatore and date-
lined "Sitting Duck—CA."

I must confess to a few chuckles (a rarity, of late)
while reading your article of this date (page 5). I realize that a story can be no better than the available
information, but I've gotta make a comment or two of
clarification:
1) I used *no* drugs of *any* nature prior to 1970—and
the total since has been 2 (count 'em: two) hits of
LSD, 10 benzedrine tablets and 3 joints. I'm a drunk,
not a "user."
2) The *Soldier of Fortune* was *not* directed toward the
procurement of weapons: Rather, it was to provide
chemical, explosive and "blackbag" data to the
whacko right (as opposed to the whacko *left,* which
wants to blow up nuclear plants to show how dangerous they are. You figure it—I gave up trying). My
experience with the law, by the way, tells me that—
having been accused—I am thereby guilty, accusations
being in and of themselves proof to the veracity *of* the
charge. Well, *being* thereby "guilty" I guess I have
little option other than *acting* as though guilty. Mean-
ing? . . . Well, let's just say I'm not going back to
jail. Ever.
(Hell, that's going to sound "contemptuous," ain't it?
You ever have "one of those days"?) Thank you for
not furthering that "Gloria Washington" joke—*that*
one threw me.
CIAO.

At 10:15 A.M. the police operator at the Marin sheriff's
office picked up the phone and heard these words: "Mr.
Mark McDermand will be in a phone booth at the Civic

Center today at 11:00 A.M. He will be armed. Mr. McDermand will be in the Civic Center to kill somebody or himself.'' The caller then hung up without giving his name.

But *which* Civic Center?

The Marin County sheriff's office was located at the San Rafael Civic Center, so they alerted San Francisco's police department to cover the Civic Center in their own city. Police scattered throughout the area of both centers and placed the few phone booths under surveillance. A man answering Mark's description went into a booth in an open area to use the phone at the San Francisco Civic Center. Officers radioed: ''We're ninety-nine percent certain this is McDermand.'' The suspect was arrested immediately, cuffed, and taken to the Hall of Justice for questioning.

However he was two inches taller and had lighter hair than McDermand. It took only a moment for the investigators to become less positive. They radioed other officers to fan out and continue their search of the Civic Center. They found no trace of the fugitive and released the first man.

On October 23, 1980, Sheriff Howenstein contacted Dr. R. William Mathis, the psychologist who had been assisting on the Tamalpais investigation as a consultant. Since it was obvious that Mark was following the newspaper coverage of the search for him, Mathis thought that the papers would be a good way to ''defuse'' Mark by printing that the fugitive would be treated fairly if he surrendered. Howenstein made a plea through the next afternoon's *San Francisco Examiner*—''We know that you're frightened, Mark, and we want to help. . . . We have what we think is a portrait of the scene at your family home and understand why it happened. We also know that you are the only one who can fill in the whole picture. . . . Please call me at 479-5736.'' Mark called the sheriff's office at 9:00 P.M., October 24, and Captain Gaddini answered.

Because Mark was the major suspect in the Trailside investigation, Dr. Mathis had coached Gaddini on how to talk Mark in. Mathis later told me that he was impressed by how well and how quickly Gaddini thought on his feet. Often the doctor prepared scripts for the police detailing the proper approach to use in convincing a man on the run to surrender. Gaddini, however, expressed himself so superbly that he was more effective in his wording than any script could ever hope to be.

Mark identified himself by giving Gaddini his driver's license number, which he had marked on his letters to the police, and mentioned that he was considering giving himself up. "But I've still got some things to do first." Mark called Gaddini again on the evening of October 26, Sunday, called him twice and spoke about the murder on Shoreline. "I fired the first bullet into my mother's ear because it's probably the quickest guaranteed kill in this existence . . . and I just didn't want her to have to see what I was going to be doing . . . or know it, even." Mark haltingly told Gaddini the same story of his discovery of the bodies of his mother and brother as he later told me. The act itself was blocked from his mind. "We are better off dead," said Mark later. "They are better off dead." Mark was asked if he would rather die than live out his life, and he replied in anguish, "Oh, Christ, yes."

"During the hunt for Mark McDermand," Sergeant Keaton recalled, "there was a round-the-clock phone surveillance waiting for Mark to call in. I remember a couple of times at 6:00 or 7:00 P.M. somebody in here would notify the brass that Mark was on the line and was going to call back. The sheriff was in walking distance. Gaddini was right across from the sheriff." Officers gathered at the long table where the phones to monitor Mark were set up, and in the evenings would step out onto the balcony to grab a smoke and gaze at the Sleeping Lady in the distance. "We had a fine view of the Sleeping Lady," Keaton told me, "in the old wing. Behind the sheriff's office where the building ends and goes into the hillside, directly above is the jail. The barbed-wire area above is an exercise area for the prisoners that is actually sunken into the hill. We'd come out on the deck to think about the case."

McDermand was able to elude the police for eleven days. He later wrote me, telling me the story in his own words:

"Spend a few weeks in any jail or prison, with your ears open and your mouth shut, and you'll discover something not commonly realized by Joe Citizen, weaned on the idiot box: in most cases criminals are *not* 'caught' by the police. Criminals, by and large, wind up in the clink due to stupidity, design, or incredibly bad luck. If the cops don't catch a guy during or immediately following the commission of a crime, they're very hard pressed to catch the 'perp.'

"Why? First, they're too busy playing traffic cop, settling family squabbles, or dealing with paperwork, or sitting around either snoozing or sucking up coffee. In short, they're just like everybody else. Second, *very* few cops care for the thought of being hurt. Sensible. They don't mind being in the thick of a set-piece battle—a hostage situation, an ambush, or any action involving a large number of officers—since the odds of getting hurt are lengthened. A random search or traffic stop is goddamn dangerous for a cop and he knows it. As a rule, he's *aching* to have the citizen he's checking out have a good story. If the guy can even maintain a good facade, the cop will be delighted to have the encounter over and done with.

"How do crooks get caught? Bluntly, they fuck up, virtually saying, 'Here I am—take me in.' They sweat bullets and stand around looking guilty. The prisons are full, *not* with dangerous crooks but with damn fools.

"The cops who were looking for me were no more or less competent than any others. As in any profession, you have a few extremely good cops, a few extremely bad cops, and a hell of a lot of people taking up space. No insult—that's just the way it is. When you get right down to it, I was able to 'elude' the police before surrender simply because I tried to use my head and to act as *innocent* as I could. Guilty people tend to avoid contact with police, for instance, even going to the idiot extent of not even looking at a cruising cop car. Now, cop cars are *obvious*, and cops know this. If a citizen 'doesn't see' or obviously ignores a cop car, a cop thinks, 'Why?' Might as well wear a red beanie with a patch reading, 'Crook! Crook!' on the visor. Dumb.

"I picked a 'game face'—con talk for a mask—that

reflected, as well as possible, the citizens around me. If a coffee shop had only one open stool and that next to a cop, I didn't hem and haw and walk out. I sat down with a paper, nodded if the guy happened to look at me, and drank my coffee and did the crossword puzzle. I was usually sweating blood on the inside, and had my weapon cleared for access, but I didn't *look* like I felt guilty. When a cop cruised by, I reacted as much as possible as the citizens around me.

"I spent most of the time on the run in Vallejo, Corte Madera, Oakland, and Richmond, staying with friends. Apart from a very few bad—and one real nerve-racking—moments, I don't think three people even looked at me hard. Once, driving to Oakland a few hours before my name hit the news, I passed a highway patrol car as it pulled a car over. I was about two hundred yards behind as he came to a halt and was in the slow lane, and I made a point of briefly glancing at the cars as I passed. Watching the rearview mirror after I passed, I spotted the cop stare hard after me, then wheel and head for his car. I took a Richmond exit and made myself scarce, getting as far from the freeway as rapidly as was safe." Mark stayed with friends, shuttling between Sonoma and Vallejo.

"While staying with an acquaintance in Vallejo, I walked to a store to get some food, and when I returned found the area around the house, and the car, to be hip-deep in Vallejo cop cars. Scared the hell out of me. I kept walking and got scarce. I made my way to a motel and checked in for the night. I needed a TV, to see if I'd been made or if it was just coincidence that led the cops there. I found out the next morning that a neighbor had kind of nutted up and, as usual, the local cops *all* showed up. . . . One cop, in fact, had arrived so zealously that he'd gently matched bumpers with my hot-as-a-two-dollar-pistol car.

"All in all, avoiding arrest is a matter of thinking before acting and making a practice of mirroring your surroundings. Too, it's a very good idea to carefully scout out your surroundings when you first make a move into an area. You just never know when you're going to have to cut and run—and it's an even better idea to *never* return to a specific area once you've left it for more than a few hours. You never know when or if some nosy Parker has in some sense or way made you. I stuck to busy freeways as much as possible. Road cops are busy enough keeping traffic sorted out without looking for one of a few dozen cars on their hotsheets, provided the hot car's driver has the brains to obey the traffic laws—and always parked with the rear of the car, where I had a license plate, up against a wall or such. It's legit to have no plate on the front, and that was the first thing I removed when I went bad.

"When I had mostly made up my mind to surrender (I truly had no real idea what had gone so wrong, and hoped, foolishly, that some effort might be made by 'the authorities' to help me figure things out) I started calling the Marin County sheriff's office. We made our arrangements over a period of a few days. Captain Bob Gaddini spoke for them, and scrupulously avoided making promises he couldn't keep or telling me lies, a practice honored far more in the breach than the observance by cops, I have since learned."

"I just wanted to resolve it," Mark said later. "I just wanted to get it straight. If I was ever going to be free of what happened to my mother and brother, I wanted to know as much as I could about why it happened and what happened. I don't think there is anyone who wants to know more than I do."

At exactly 3:00 P.M., Monday, October 27, Mark McDermand stepped into a phone booth and dialed the Marin County sheriff's office. This was his fourth call to Gaddini, and they talked for only nine minutes, mostly about the stream of letters he had written the press. "I tried to write everybody, every day," Mark joked. "McDermand," Gaddini said later, "was vague about the exact location of his surrender site. He mentioned the possibility of giving up at Denny's or in the parking lot of the International House of Pancakes in Vallejo, but was not definite." To Gaddini, Mark seemed to be suggesting most strongly the pancake house in Vallejo.

"Mark called us from Vallejo," Sergeant Keaton told me afterward, "so one of our investigators, Linda

Schmid, went up there and she goes in and, 'Whoops! It's Mark!' She called us from the coffee shop on the same pay phone he had been calling us on.''

Howenstein and Gaddini sprinted for their cruiser and raced to Vallejo, where the sheriff had arranged for backup, five additional policemen. Vallejo was asked to keep its patrol cars out of the area so McDermand wouldn't be scared off.

''I had a 'last meal' with a friend in the International House of Pancakes in Vallejo,'' McDermand told me later. ''I could feel police presence but didn't bother to figure out who was who. I was saying good-bye to my friend, and if anybody had gone nuts at the time it wouldn't have really mattered.''

At about 4:00 P.M., two blocks from the restaurant, Howenstein shut off the lights and siren, and as they reached the lot he shifted into a slow crawl.

Mark McDermand told me afterward, ''I went out and sat on the hood of my car, as agreed. Smoked a smoke and wished I had a bottle of vodka with me. A beer. Anything. I briefly thought about how much hell would erupt if I tried to take off at that point—I figured it would be great theatre but extremely bad judgment—and ever-so-briefly considered what my reaction would be if Gaddini's scenerio wasn't what was tried. We'd agreed that in exchange for my peaceful surrender the bust itself would be quick and clean. No crazy stuff on either side, no sirens, marked cars, bullhorns, or pages from that *terrible* show *SWAT,* and that I would be cuffed in front— I hate cuffs—pending any dumb stunt on my end.

''I was simultaneously very relaxed and wired tight as the takeup drum on a fifty-ton crane. I really didn't know how I'd react if five green cop cars blew in with three guys in each car, everybody playing L.A. cop. I really wasn't too keen on going to jail, and in spite of myself had cleared the .38 for rapid access.

''Yes, I believe if I had decided to *not* be busted, I would likely still be 'free.' On the run more accurately. 'The guilty flee where no man pursueth' is valid. Being on the run, while *never* boring, kind of sucks.''

Howenstein and Gaddini caught sight of Mark almost

immediately, passed him, and parked some feet away. They got out carefully.

"At the time of my arrest," McDermand told me, "I was in possession of a 12-gauge pump shotgun, a .22-caliber semiautomatic pistol, and a Smith & Wesson snub-nosed .38 revolver. I'd borrowed the shotgun and .22 from a friend earlier, the .22 being needed for what may seem a nasty purpose—my family has always had cats as something-more-than pets, and when one became painfully, incurably ill, or severely injured, my pop fed it a big slice of liver, scratched its neck, and put a bullet in the back of its head.

"The one cat we still had, a black, brown, and purple Persian named Gladys, had become ill, a very painful tumor in her gut, and my mom asked me to 'help Gladys leave,' and I'd borrowed the pistol . . . she died painlessly and instantly.

"The .38? I'd had the damn thing for about three years and hadn't the slightest notion of where or how I'd obtained it. Yes, I have a *highly* selective memory. During my trial, the DA came up with a witness from Arizona who said I'd taken it from him. Made as much sense as anything else . . . didn't remember him, either. In a way I was relieved, since I didn't know where I'd gotten the thing. I could have gotten it anywhere. Could have killed some guy for it. Was glad I hadn't."

Howenstein could see the fugitive, his hands in plain sight, as agreed over the phone, sitting on the hood of his yellow Malibu. His hair was pulled back and he was dressed in a blue plaid Pendleton shirt, brown slacks, tan boots, and a holster with a .38-caliber pistol outfitted with two speed-loading clips in it. In addition Mark wore a belt with twelve more bullets and had another speed loader and a set of thumb cuffs in his pocket. A wicked-looking 12-gauge shotgun and another .38 were propped up on the front seat beside a metal box containing hypodermic syringes and insulin vials.

"When Gaddini's car pulled up ten yards away," Mark related to me, "with a blocker next to it, and a third unmarked car pulling in to block the other parking lot entrance, and when Gaddini and Howenstein came out, weapons drawn but pointed at the ground, I slid off the car, my back to them, and raised my hands.

"Gaddini took the .38, turned me around, put my hands on the hood, and shook me down, then put the handcuffs on, from the front. My glasses not being worth a damn, I didn't have a good image of the four or six other cops involved. Nobody raised their voice. Nobody got out of line—they were a well-disciplined crew." Mark waived his Miranda rights and signed a written consent to search his car.

Howenstein walked around the car and was amazed to see there was no plate on the front of the car. A car with a missing plate is usually the kind of vehicle that attracts the attention of the highway patrol. The sheriff was relieved to find that the lanky suspect offered no resistance and, as the press put it later, was "calm, lucid, amenable, and cooperative." Howenstein seconded this to the media afterward: "He was very cooperative. He said he'd do exactly what he agreed to do and he did."

"The bust went down very cleanly," Mark McDermand wrote me later, "and Gaddini kept his word in detail—no silliness or hardcore, big-time cop stuff. Three cars, unmarked, Gaddini and Sheriff Howenstein in one, no yank and push, a measure of politeness between them and I. Pretty decent, as arrests go."

"The ride back to jail was fairly quiet but not tense," said Mark later. "It was simply over with. . . . Sheriff Howenstein was a good dude, progressive, intelligent, a very logical thinker, fairly humane."

Mark had been keeping notebooks on his life and his wanderings while he was at large. As the sheriff and the dirty and tired suspect talked on the way back to Marin County Howenstein remarked, "You know, the papers said you were a good writer."

"Well," said McDermand, "tell them to hold a job for me."

I asked Mark how he had been treated. "As I mentioned," he replied, "Captain Gaddini was honest and straightforward. Over the following months, he stayed that way. He never took a cheap shot, was always friendly, and to be honest made the behavior of a lot of other cops look pretty crummy—I thought he made the Marin sheriff's office look better than it really was."

"If there was a case in Bob's career he was really proud of it was the McDermand case," said Marsha Gaddini. "He talked McDermand in. He was so good with words he could convince you black was white. He was very intrigued with Mark, and Mark was intrigued with him. McDermand respected him so much because he knew when not to say anything. I know he had many conversations with McDermand. As far as all of Mark's artillery, Bob would walk into anything. He had this fatalistic worldview. He did not feel he was going to be here forever."

On Tuesday, October 28, Mark's impounded Chevy was searched and another pistol was located. Then the car was towed back to San Rafael. As to Mark's involvement with the killings of the three women on the Sleeping Lady, Howenstein was keeping his lips tight. Mark had requested a cell by himself and this was granted.

Gaddini finally called a conference with the media and stated firmly, "We have no evidence linking McDermand with the Mount Tamalpais murders, but obviously we're looking at everything we can to evaluate everything and then make a connection if there is one."

While Mark was in jail awaiting trial his mother and brother were cremated and the lonely Shoreline house was unencumbered of the family possessions, stacks of books primarily, which were given to charity. Howenstein had hoped, during his eleven days of negotiations with Mark, to assure psychological treatment for the disturbed man. A wave of shock ran through the community, stunning Mark's friends at Denny's when the DA's office asked for and got the death penalty.

"I have yet to meet *anybody*," said Mark's friend, Marion, "who believes that Mark coldly deliberated the killing of his mother and brother. Support for him, after his crime, was strong among his friends, neighbors, and co-workers at Denny's. Mark's fellow workers at Denny's hung signs from the restaurant's roof in support of Mark—saying "Mark, we love you," and "Please don't jump."

Mark's death sentence was reduced to life imprisonment without possibility of parole in the summer of 1981, and he sent me a series of neatly typed letters from San Quentin's East Block, where he had become a twelve-cent-an-hour clerk.

"Parole? I don't expect it," Mark wrote. "My health being what it is, I really don't expect to live the fifteen to twenty-five years it will likely take to decide I'm worthy of release. If I were paroled, I'd dig a hole, crawl in, and pull in the dirt. I'm not too fond of the real world anymore, and figure it would be best for both sides to keep a low profile. Not crazy, I just like privacy—which does not exist in any way, shape, or form in the pen. I've had enough people wander past my face in the last five years to be quite enough, thank you very much.

"Besides, it's easier to write in quiet and privacy, and writing is about all I know anymore."

Mark's copy of the book his father, Charles, had dedicated to him lay on the bunk in his cell. It had fallen open to the dedication page—"To Mark, I hope your sturdy legs will carry you to the peace and contentment of the far mountains."*

With the murders that were to come after Mark's arrest it would soon become obvious to the police that McDermand was not the Trailside killer. Mark's .38 was also not the Trailside gun. The frightening crimes of the stalking rapist of the parklands continued in the months ahead, leaving the police at a loss.

---

*Mark had entered prison with diabetes, arthritis, and a fifteen-year-old dose of Valley Fever. He was stabbed by an inmate in January of 1982, developed pneumonia, and suffered twin heart attacks in March of 1986, followed by congestive heart failure. In April of 1987 he had pneumonia and congestive heart failure again. Just after finishing his prison novel he died of a heart attack and various complications on January 16, 1988, just before his forty-first birthday.

17

Kenny and Tina

Friday, October 24, 1980, was one of those rare days when Mollie Purnell received no phone calls from the former purser. It was just three days before Mark McDermand's arrest, fourteen days after the disappearance of Rick Stowers and Cindy Moreland, and only twelve days after Anne Alderson had been slain.

Down in the south bay area of California, in Lawndale near Torrance, fourteen-year-old Tina Vance learned her boss, forty-five-year-old James Wolfe, had no reservation about loaning her his brand-new Toyota Tercel. In fact he had done so previously. The lithe, raven-haired, fast-talking, and raspy-voiced girl had requested the car for the night though "I had no intention of returning it on time." The attractive teenager, who had been working local flea markets selling belts and belt buckles since she was twelve, waved as she drove away from Wolfe's. "Just me and my purse," she recalled. "I was going with Kenny to see Adam."

Kenny was Kenneth Alan Baughman, her tall, blond, and lean nineteen-year-old boyfriend. Adam was Adam "Thumper" Purnell, Mollie's youngest son, who had gone to school with Kenny and lived in Modesto with his mother. Tina drove to Freeman Avenue and picked up Kenny at his mother's home. Baughman had a minor drug problem at the time, "coke and pot." He said, "I felt a need to get away from it for a while." At 8:30 P.M. Tina and Kenny began a drive to Modesto in Northern California to see Adam. It was Tina's first trip to that part of the state.

Kenny had lived with Mollie and Adam from January 2 until August 2 of 1980 and actually accompanied Molly and Adam to Jamaica in late June and early July to see a dairy farm left to Mollie by her father. Mollie was thinking of getting involved in the lumber industry there. Adam had been speaking to a Hayward lumber company and they were interested. "There were big profits to be made," she said. For the two boys it was a vacation. "Morning we'd wake up and she'd be gone, back at 6:00 P.M." Kenny had met the purser on a couple of occasions. "Mollie said she was going to do important business with him as general manager. Mollie referred to Carpenter as the connection." Both Kenny and Adam had stayed around the hotel.

It was Saturday, October 25, about 3:00 A.M. by the time the couple arrived in Modesto. Mollie's house was an impressive house, with cheap rent—$350 a month. Tina noticed as they entered the ground floor of the house on El Greco that there was a bathroom and a bedroom to their right, Mollie's, and a kitchen at the back. To her left was a flight of stairs going to the second floor. Beneath the stairs was a living room area that looked into the kitchen. They went to sleep on the floor in Adam's room and awoke at 10:00 A.M. to see a smiling Adam standing over them.

Meanwhile, between October 15 and 21, a series of phone calls transpired between Mollie and David Carpenter. They focused, he claimed, on only two topics. "Probably the two most important subjects we discussed were that Mollie was trying to replace me in the marijuana business and that Mollie was going to move from Modesto to Sacramento." There was, of course, no marijuana business, but in his recollection of the events it was an alibi that Carpenter would cling to with fierce determination. His visit to Mollie's had to be explained and the events that transpired there cast into doubt.

"Mollie was so enthralled with the two-pound s-s-s-sales she wanted to become a big-time dope dealer. I was very concerned because she was moving up to an area where she didn't know anyone. I told her, 'Mollie, I'm going to have to bow out.' I didn't want to go back to prison. She asked instead for a half-pound bag of marijuana because she needed moving money.

"I went to Mollie's on Saturday afternoon, October 25. It was about a two-hour d-d-drive to Modesto. I took the Bay Bridge, then 580 to 5 to 132 and on into Modesto bringing with me a one-half-pound bag of marijuana. I arrived at 1:30 and found Trudy Preston [Mollie's foster child], Tina Vance, and Kenny Baughman there. Mollie was expecting me and she and Adam Purnell arrived at 6:00 P.M. I went down to Kentucky Fried Chicken, brought some back and we had supper."

Tina saw Carpenter for the first time sitting in a chair in the living room. "He just showed up. . . . He was wearing a multi-colored vest-sweater, metal frame glasses," said Tina. "He talked about the perfect robbery. Told me he was a professional thief and burglar in every single conversation we had. I recall being in a downstairs room with him, about forty-five minutes after he arrived, when he showed me a gun he had and began talking about burglary and thieving and things like that. A big handgun is all I remember."

Saturday night there was a party, though everyone described it differently. Tina recalled it as being "dull. No radio, no records, no pot smoking." Mollie recalled a "mad party going on" with drinking, drugs, and Tina in the kitchen in a bra and a slip, the teenagers playing Cardinal Puff, a drinking game. Mollie saw a whiskey bottle on the kitchen table. Kenny said later, "There was some drinking. Lucky beers. I smoked a little pot, but that was it."

Carpenter remembered that "We smoked pot and drank bourbon and 7-Up. I knew Trudy Preston, a foster child. I knew Kenny because he had been living there. I'd never seen Tina Vance before. Tina both smoked and drank—I thought she was about eighteen or nineteen."

Mollie took her for twenty-five, but said she wouldn't have cared if she was fourteen.

"My mother," Adam said later, "was tolerant of the marijuana smoking me and my friends did at the home. . . . There was no illegal drug dealing [as Carpenter has claimed]."

Later on Saturday night Adam, Tina, and Kenny went to a party at a park. While they were away a collect call was placed from Lawndale from Kenny's mother, Betty. She spoke with Mollie for six minutes and said she would try and reach her son tomorrow morning. "David was too drunk to drive," said Mollie. "There was liquor all over our house."

Early Sunday morning, October 26, Betty called again. Tina's mother had relayed a message to her from Tina's boss—"The car must be back within two hours or I'm reporting it stolen!" Wolfe had also called Betty. Kenny was still asleep on Adam's floor and Betty was asked to call back.

Carpenter recalled the Sunday morning call and described it this way:

"Mollie Purnell answered. I was there. I was in the kitchen and talking to Mollie when the phone rang . . . all the kids were upstairs, sound a-a-asleep. 'Kenny Baughman's mother is saying you and Tina stole the car,' Mollie told them. Both Kenny and Tina said Jim Wolfe had loaned them the car. Mollie turned to me.

"I figured the kids were telling the truth . . . must be some sort of misunderstanding. Mollie spoke to Mrs. Baughman. Mrs. Baughman to Mollie . . . Mother to kids . . . I said, 'Call Mr. Wolfe to see if we can't get this whole thing straightened out.' Then we all discussed the situation . . . Kenny kept saying, 'I've got the keys.' Everyone w-w-was waiting for Mrs. Baughman to call back with the information.

"Jim Wolfe said the car was taken without permission. After the call Kenny and Adam were smoking pot. Kenny didn't care if he ever went back . . . the selling of marijuana [Carpenter claimed] was going on. The evening before Mollie and I had sat around and bagged the marijuana. We divided it up according to who would get it. Sunday morning the kids were out selling it.''

While Kenny was standing with his back to the living room area facing toward Adam in the kitchen, Carpenter took out a black lawyer's briefcase. Inside was a leather case and inside this was a ''bright blue Crown Royal Whiskey velvet bag about eight-inches long with gold and blue imprints and a gold pull string.'' From this blue bag the purser extracted a gun and said, ''You should have one of these for protection.'' Although Kenny knew there was a .22-caliber rifle in the house, he was ''not fond of guns.'' After the bag was opened ''I was only in the room three to four minutes and then went upstairs to shower.'' Kenny was in the shower for half an hour.

While he was there the purser ''was running in and out of the house all of the time,'' remembered Tina. After his shower Kenny did Tina's laundry and then went swimming at the park three-quarters of a block away. ''El Greco Park,'' said Kenny, ''nine houses to the right as you exit Mollie's.'' While Kenny was swimming with Adam and then playing Frisbee Betty called again. It was 1:16 P.M., and she talked to Mollie for seven minutes and was told to call back.

Kenny was at the park for an hour. Tina was in the kitchen eating breakfast. Carpenter and Mollie came in and sat down.

''Ken's mom's said the car may have been reported stolen,'' said Mollie.

''You're in a l-l-l-lot of trouble,'' said the purser. ''This is grand theft auto. Now this is the best way out— you ditch the car, go to San Francisco and lay low with me for a couple of weeks and then fly back. Hey, you're in school. You're going back to school, back to L.A.'' Carpenter then told Tina he could get her a modeling job.

Tina offered, ''I'll call Wolfe to make him feel better.''

''That wouldn't be a good idea,'' said Mollie.

''They led me to believe I was going to be arrested for the theft of Jim Wolfe's car,'' Tina remembered. ''They made it look a lot worse than it was.''

At 2:07 the phone rang again. Kenny had by now returned and spoke with his mother for four minutes.

"Get your ass home!" she said.

"After the 2:07 P.M. phone call," Carpenter said in retrospect, "I had by now found out that Tina was only fourteen. I told Mollie, 'I don't like the way the whole thing is c-c-c-coming down. We got a car that's stolen here in Modesto. I'll take the little girl to San Francisco and if Kenny's not in San Francisco by seven I'm putting her on a bus for home. I'm looking out for the kid and I'm l-l-l-looking out for me. You're not going to get into trouble and get me sent back to prison.' "

"I told her not to go," said Kenny later. " 'You're fuckin' crazy,' I told her. 'Stay here while I go say good-bye to my friends.' I went to the park for half an hour or so and it was after 2:00 P.M. when I returned. When I came back she was gone . . . I freaked!" Mollie told him she had left with Carpenter. "Mollie said we should stash the car and get us back where it was safe. My intentions were just to get the car back to L.A. and take whatever I had coming."

After Mollie had given him directions to Carpenter's home, Kenny sprinted three blocks to Wolfe's Toyota, which was parked behind a liquor store, and left for San Francisco. It was 3:00. Kenny was concerned. "I was going as fast as I could go." However, he soon became lost.

"I went with Carpenter toward San Francisco, alone," said Tina afterward. "I left the residence with him. Mollie and he strongly suggested I do this. I was in a lot of trouble and this was the best way out." Carpenter and Tina took the green Chevy station wagon. "It was loaded in back. Things in it. We could only sit in the front. We were on the way to his parents' house."

As the purser drove, Tina listened to the older man's stories, not really believing any of them. Tina later said that on the trip from Modesto Carpenter suggested that she become a prostitute as an easy way to "make some m-m-m-money. You only need to sit on some laps performing a daddy's little girl thing."

Tina would never be able to recall precisely the route. "The freeway was alongside, to the left, a curving road went through a park . . . there was a big sign as though a major park. There was no information booth. We did not pay. He was driving. It had horses, no stables, mountains, full of trees . . . I don't recall seeing water," Tina said in retrospect.

"Past the park entrance were two parking lots and eight minutes away was a Charbroiled Burger place, a stand where they had pastrami and steak sandwiches. We picked up lunch there and he parked away from all the other cars. It was then he showed me what I call his Thief Kit."

Abruptly Carpenter had reached over on the seat, popped open the lid of the case, and showed the teenager the contents.

"I was scared," recalled Tina. "I looked around to see if people were nearby." The case contained ropes, wires, and a type of gag. Laying on top was a black pistol with a three-and-a-half-inch barrel and a brown handle. Tina saw no bullets. "He had what I've always referred to as a Thief Kit—a small handgun, in a brown- or black-handled briefcase. Gun, strips of nylon or cloth, lengths of cut cord, and light wire rope, things of that nature. He said the strips of cloth were what he used to gag people with.

"Then he pulled out the ball of wire and said that was what he used to tie people up with. The wire was like you hang pictures with." The purser pressed the gun toward her thin hands. "Here, hold this . . . take it," he said. Wide-eyed Tina just looked at it until Carpenter closed the "little suitcase" with a hollow snap.

"There were some dirt trails," Tina remembered. "We walked up to a dirt clearing. The trails allowed us to look down a cliff and I could see a mountainside. I remember we walked up a dirt path. Going off to the right were a lot of trees. The clearing was there and a horseback rider."

Tina thought it odd Carpenter had brought his briefcase into the woods for the picnic, and while she was eating lunch the purser got up and walked away into the bushes. "He excused himself to go to the bathroom. He didn't have his pants on when he came back," Tina recalled. He asked her to give him a blow job. Tina refused and they immediately left the area. The young girl was frightened; she had only five dollars in her purse and was having her period. Blood had soaked through her dress, but she was afraid to go to the rest room.

Tina drove the car back to Modesto while Carpenter apologized effusively. "I wanted to see if the car was there. I was getting scared. I wanted to see Kenny," said Tina. "We reached Modesto before dark. We went back to see if the car was still there. Carpenter called Mollie from a phone booth to see if Kenny was there, but Kenny was on his way to San Francisco."

The purser called his parents collect and spoke for two minutes. Then they drove to San Francisco. "It was dark by then," said Tina, "and we went to his parents' house. Kenny wasn't there. He had gotten lost."

While Tina was left to have tea, salad, and vegetables with the old folks the purser went in and out. At 8:30, Kenny called. "I got into San Francisco at 7:00 P.M. and I'm lost," he said.

"I'll m-m-meet you at the bottom of the hill," said Carpenter, "just around the corner next to the pizza place."

When he saw Kenny they ordered pizza, waited, and brought the pizza home for Tina. "After Tina had finished her pizza," said Kenny, "we left and went straight back to Lawndale. . . . Tina did not mention the gun. . . . We didn't talk much on the way home. We went home and returned the car on Monday."

After Mollie's move to Sacramento Carpenter's relationship with her continued. "We would talk about Jamaica," he recalled, "but there was no further key-chain dealing or [he alleged] marijuana dealing with her." Carpenter ordered a new black attache case at Ward's. On the second Saturday of the month, November 8, 1980, Carpenter took his father shopping and afterward took his mother to the foot clinic. In the afternoon he took his mother to Sears to see a vacuum cleaner he had read about that was on sale. He saved the salesman's card and the forms from the clinic and put them in his receipt box. He might need them if he were questioned by Richard Wood.

PART TWO

THE PENINSULA

Life is a long Dardanelles . . . the shores whereof are bright with flowers, which we want to pluck, but the bank is too high: & so we float on & on, hoping to come to a landing-place at last—but swoop: we launch into the great sea!

—Melville, 1852

GRAKSMITH-1987

POINT REYES LIGHT

1

The Floating
Island

Hook-shaped and isolated, a prisoner of continental drift, dislocated and ever active, Point Reyes juts twelve miles into the ocean, stretched toward the Farallon Islands. They may once have all been part of the same land mass. It is a lonely place, seemingly at rest. As part of the Pacific floor, Point Reyes peninsula has drifted, scraping along the San Andreas Fault, only pausing near Drake's Bay in a momentary respite on its northwestern voyage to the bottom of the Gulf of Alaska.

Before and after a lighthouse was erected, there have been roughly one hundred shipwrecks along the chilly, windblown coast, most of them vessels that have mistaken Drake's Bay for the entrance to San Francisco Bay. The most fog-shrouded station between Mexico and Canada, it is one of the most hazardous sections on the Pacific Coast, a graveyard of ships.

It was to Point Reyes that the Trailside Killer came next.

To reach 70,000-acre Point Reyes National Seashore from San Francisco entails a drive north on 101 to Sir Francis Drake Boulevard to the town of Fairfax, then fifteen more miles to Olema on State Highway 1, which abruptly swerves inland and into a valley that effectively conceals the 145 miles of wilderness trails just over the ridge to the west. After Olema, a quick turn on Bear Valley Road brings you within a mile west of the park headquarters, the gateway to the park. As you turn out of the entrance road you cross the mile-wide swath of the San Andreas Fault, which slashes southwest separating Point Reyes from the rest of Marin County. Nearby is a large red barn where an operational blacksmith shop and Morgan horse stable are kept. A half-mile farther on is a dirt-floored parking lot in the meadow.

"Some of those back-ridge trails are dark and weird," a Point Reyes hiker told me afterward. "When that fog came in it was blowin' forty-five, fifty-five miles per hour. It was howlin' and it was cold. Same as on Tamalpais."

Later, re-creating the movements of the Trailside Killer on Friday, November 28, 1980, the police theorized he would have come by car, parked in the lot, and may have begun stalking his victims there or later on the trails.

He would have had the choice of two trails—Sky Trail or Bear Valley Trail. Sky Trail is two miles long, steep, strenuous, and straight uphill through the dense black forest of spider-limbed Douglas firs of Inverness Ridge, a high, windy, granite spine that runs parallel to the fault line, to the slopes of bald Mount Wittenberg. Not many people are fit enough for Sky Trail, and it would be difficult going without a pair of sturdy hiking shoes.

To the killer's left would have been Bear Valley Trail, an old wagon trail, the most popular, usually packed on weekends. It was the path the police felt the attacker took, for it is level for almost the entire four and one-half miles to Arch Rock.

The killer would have passed a small stream flowing north, Olema Creek draining into Tomales Bay, that runs parallel with the trail to the Divide Meadow. At the trail's high point a quarter-mile away is a second stream, but running south, Pine Gulch Creek, which drains into Bolinas Lagoon. The two streams follow cracks created by earthquakes.

At the south end of the broad meadow he would have

come to a giant Douglas fir where he would have had to take the Old Pine Trail leading into the forest, the first real uphill climb. Traveling upward for one and one-half miles the trail becomes the Sky Trail at the crest of a ridge. At Sky Trail Junction he would have passed a giant, double-trunked laurel.

Unlike the Sleeping Lady, the mountain forest thickens on 1,407-foot-high Mount Wittenberg above the Sky Trail. Wittenberg is the tallest of Reyes's three mountains and grows denser as you climb. Eventually the treetops grow together and create an umbrella of darkness through which little shafts of light come from every direction. Here the forest is at its deepest and most silent.

At Sky Camp where the trail winds around the mountain the Trailside Killer would have seen the hills run right to chaparral-covered bluffs and the brittle, eroding cliffs at the shore. Beyond that he could see surf breaking against the towering stone stacks. Along the shore are cave tunnels, flattened shale formations, and a cascade spilling down the rugged hillside onto the beach.

As the stranger continued on the trail it would have dropped suddenly, steeply, and he would have left behind the dense forest and exchanged the coast live oak for a series of sunny and sometimes dry grasslands. Even in November, the wet season, the area can be quite hot—all types of weather exist at Point Reyes. Pity to the poor hiker without a hat. The descent is rapid here, and he would have picked a spot by the trail to hide, scouted the area, then returned to wait. He was waiting on what geologists call the Salinian Block, which is entwined with roads and horse trails and composed of granite bedrock, which is alien to the rest of Marin.

From this point, as I later discovered when I hiked the area, you can hear voices from far off, but the narrow switchbacks fifty-yards apart make it difficult, if not impossible, to see people approaching and avoid being surprised.

Diane Marie O'Connell, a petite, long-haired blonde from San Jose who had just graduated from Cornell University, was visiting friends in Oakland on the day after Thanksgiving. One friend of Diane's had suggested, ''It's

such a nice day, we should go hiking at Point Reyes.''
And so Diane, Nancy Dagle, and Sharon Raymond had
driven to the federal wilderness area.

Moving along Meadow Trail the three women stopped
and had lunch at 11:45 A.M. and then began the easy
climb to Sky Camp. Just as they started down Sky Trail
on their way back to the Trailhead, a woman hiker, Professor Holloway, passed a man near the upper switchbacks. He was standing near the side of the trail wearing
a green baseball cap and carrying something blue. ''He
was about fifty, wearing glasses, and had an angry expression on his face,'' Holloway recalled. The older man
passed Diane, Nancy, and Sharon and moved quickly
ahead of them down Sky Trail. It was 1:30 P.M.

As the women wove their way through the series of
switchbacks they each hiked at their own pace on Sky
Trail. Sharon took up the lead, and the distance between
the three friends lengthened to about one hundred yards.
''We were descending several minutes apart,'' remembered Sharon. ''I was at the front, our other friend,
Nancy, was at the rear, and Diane was in the middle. We
agreed as we started down to wait at the Bear Valley
Trailhead. I would look back over my shoulder every
couple of minutes to make sure Diane was there.''

The trail was crowded. Michael and Ann Craycraft,
hikers, estimated that at least every five minutes another
hiker would pass them on Sky Trail. Although they passed
Diane and her friends, they saw no single male hikers.
It was 2:40 P.M.

Sharon soon came to the last of the switchbacks and a
number of open meadows as the trail became woodsy,
the trees heavily canopied over. Just as she moved into
the treeline she caught a glimpse of a figure. ''I suddenly
saw a man,'' she said later, ''in the bushes just off the
trail. I can only remember that he really alarmed me. I
cam tripping down the trail and there he was with his
back toward me.'' Sharon didn't want to look in his direction, but thought that he was ''a white male with dark
hair, a young man with average height and build. I
thought I had taken him unaware. I startled him. He was
to my right. The man had gone into the bushes to urinate
and he spoke to me in a clear adult voice, but for a mo-

ment there I thought he was going to expose himself. Anyway, he alarmed me and I instinctively quickened my pace.''

Farther on down the trail, just as she came to the last switchback, Sharon passed another hiker, who was going uptrail. Shauna K. May, a former Idaho resident now living in San Francisco, a legal secretary and a strapping no-nonsense hiker, cried out a cheery hello. Sharon came to the end of the two-and-one-half-mile-downward hike on Sky Trail and sat on a fence post to wait for Diane and Nancy. When she heard steps she looked up, expecting to see Diane, but was startled to see Nancy, who had been in the rear. Nancy had stopped to take a rock out of her shoe.

''Where's Diane?'' asked Sharon. ''Did you pass her?''

''No,'' said Nancy. ''She was ahead of me the whole way. I never passed her.''

The women were mystified and looked back up the trail. Diane had been in the middle. How had she vanished from between them? Most astonishing of all, the woman in the rear had not passed Shauna May, who had been heading up the trail. They went back up the trail looking and then returned to the Trailhead. Both decided to wait until 5:00 P.M. before going to the park rangers.

2

The Gully

The brittle and hollow weeds in which the man crouched rustled when he made any movement. The thistles and stems of the dry weeds teemed with insects. He looked up. The sky above was blue and cloudless. Everything about was calm and empty except for the warm caress of a light breeze and the man's short breaths. The weeds were crowded as well with barbed wire from the dairy ranchers who used the mountain. As adrenaline pumped into his bloodstream, his palms grew sweaty, his respiration increased, his pupils dilated, and a sourness filled his stomach.

The man continued waiting, just one and one-half miles from the base of the trail. It was unlikely he heard the slow steps, accompanied by sounds of exertion, of someone climbing the mountain's toughest trail. Hidden by the switchbacks, someone was coming up the path from the Trailhead, but the killer's ears heard only another sound—more steps, but these steps were moving rapidly, joyously, as if some light-footed person were racing down the path. The man listened intently. Possibly it was the attractive blonde woman he had passed on Old Pine Trail after walking behind her and her two friends.

The descending hiker approached the man's hiding spot and he stood up, stepping into the path. With his gun he motioned the woman into the bushes with him, but suddenly a second hiker appeared unexpectedly to his left, and, furious, he was forced to stop her as well. Now he held two women at gunpoint, Shauna May and Diane O'Connell.

He marched them off the trail. Thick branches caught at their hair and the knapsacks on their backs. They climbed down off the ridge, through the thick undergrowth, over a rise, into a ravine, and then a larger gully two hundred and fifty yards from Sky Trail. In the gully was a small clearing through which ran a leaf-crowded stream. In the gully's center was a low-limbed bay tree, its branches touching the ground, its roots exposed by the winter rains which had previously swollen the now-tiny stream.

At a few minutes past 3:00 P.M. he forced the two women to strip, fold each article of their clothing carefully in front of them, and then place the pile on top of their knapsacks. As he made them kneel the man took something out of his blue backpack that appeared to be a roll of ordinary picture frame wire.

At 3:10 P.M. some hikers, a party of stockbrokers and engineers, only somewhere between fifty and a hundred yards away from the women but out of sight on Sky Trail, heard two shots. One of the hikers, a man named Vincent Kalishes, looked at his watch and noted the exact time. Precisely fifty seconds later the sound was repeated, another two shots. The hikers made no effort to investigate.

Compulsively, the killer erased his own tracks and searched for any objects that he may have dropped. Police, by now, were aware that the stalking rapist would scout out a scene weeks in advance and theorized that he may even have taken the precaution of hiding a duffel bag with maps, binoculars, and a change of clothes at the murder site before finding a victim and forcing her to return with him to the prearranged spot.

Finally at 5:00 P.M. Diane O'Connell's friends reported her missing to the rangers and soon afterward

Shauna May's friend, Margaret Johnson, did the same. By then nine two-man teams of rangers and Marin and Sonoma County deputies were searching the lengthening shadows. At 11:00 P.M. drifting fog and darkness forced the men to quit.

At dawn, November 29, a larger group of searchers began combing the trails and by 9:00 A.M. anxious rangers were asking the coast guard, California highway patrol, and the Marin sheriff's office for help. For almost forty-five minutes a coast guard helicopter darted over the trails while a flock of sparrow hawks echoed its movements, wheeling high above Inverness Ridge.

At precisely 9:00 A.M., at Marin sheriff's headquarters, police sergeant Anthony Russo heard about the missing female hikers. With Detective Linda Schmid he went directly to the Bear Valley ranger station where he interviewed Diane O'Connell's and Shauna May's hiking companions. "Then," recalled Russo, "I went to the hiking area, drove the paved road to the fire trail to Sky Trail and then down. It was about noon."

At noon, a volunteer searcher, Reno Taini, a Wilderness teacher at Jefferson High in Daly City, met at the Point Reyes ranger station with eleven other searchers and was given a briefing. The men were divided into two eight-man teams, issued radios, and by 1:30 P.M., within earshot of one another, they were sweeping across the smooth terrain where the two women had last been seen.

"On the day you went out there," I asked Taini later, "were you ready for anything but a simple search?"

"I had no idea it was a police action, any foul play, or anything like that. Basically I figured we'd find these people before dark. No problem. The atmosphere was very casual, it was one of those wonderful fall days. It hadn't rained really that much. The sun was out and it probably got up to seventy degrees, eighty degrees maybe on the coast side. It got dreary when the fog rolled in in the late afternoon, toward the end.

"We had a call out. Two women were reported missing. We showed up, got a little briefing, and there we were. It hadn't even been twenty-four hours. I always assume that they're alive. I'm not going out there as a coroner: that's not my deal. I deal with the living, always have, and always will.'' Only a year earlier he had helped in a successful five-day search on the back side of Yosemite for a hard-of-hearing, elderly man with a heart condition. ''It was one of the best experiences I ever had. It tells me let's walk that extra mile to make sure this person's really alive. Let's really pay attention to detail.

''I was out there five minutes. I had guys on each side of me. We were pretty well trained, you know, it was a grid-search type of thing. We had about eight or nine in my unit, I guess. We were going to cover this one area on the ridge.''

In the far distance at the base of a dense grove he thought he caught a glimpse of something dull white and he began to wriggle through the shrubs until he reached the clearing. For a moment he stood, unable to determine what the object could be. He took a hesitant step forward and then another. As the wind turned he was suddenly assailed by what he later called an ''ungodly stench.''

''I just saw a little bit of white. I'm out in the woods a lot so I knew something was a little off there. Previous to this I was thinking of how nice and beautiful it was. The contrast was so dramatic. It went from the absolute, pure, serene beauty of nature to horror in a couple of instants.''

Taini was able to see now what the piece of white was. ''Jesus,'' he thought, ''that looks like a shoe, a foot, a white tennis shoe with blue stripes. I just got a little bit closer in the underbrush and there were two folks there and they had been there a while.'' The two bodies were so badly decomposed that he could not tell the sex of the victims, only that they were fully clothed in the remains of T-shirts and Levi's and were lying facedown.

Taini looked around but did not see their knapsacks anywhere. The searcher had set out to locate and rescue two women, and the discovery of two long-dead people completely disoriented him. Where had they come from? He stood stock-still for what seemed a long time, his lips parted, his hand over the lower part of his face. These people had been here possibly for many months. He could see that a cursory attempt at a shallow grave for the two bodies had been made. The next thing he was aware of was running.

"We kept in contact by walkie-talkie. I had to get to one of the guys in our unit . . . I had to run, I'd say, about fifty yards. Not that far. We were in a pretty tight pattern. 'I found two individuals,' I shouted over the static 'and they're *not* the people we're looking for!' "

Taini sent his colleagues back to guide the authorities to the scene while he remained behind to flag off and guard the site. "It was the longest, strangest period of time I've ever had in the woods. I just didn't understand it. What transpired was a lot of soul searching."

At Sky Camp detective Russo had gone down Sky Trail into the middle of a large meadow when he suddenly received a radio call about Taini's discoveries and walked south to the site.

"There was a canopy effect," said Russo, "trees so heavy they blot out the sky. There was a strong odor. It became obvious they had been there a long time—two bodies facedown. One face turned looking at the second by a large tree. There was a jagged hole in the top of one body's head."

The stocky Russo, admittedly not much of a photographer, took a series of pictures which would develop too dark, but would show a large tree at the head of each body. Russo could tell one was a man and the other a woman. "There was no wound visible in the man's body, which was facing toward the woman, who was clad in a white sweater. There was a real wound in the top of the skull of the female body." This was easily visible to Russo because the hair and skin had disappeared. He noticed the woman was wearing blue tennis shoes with yellow stripes.

Meanwhile, after being questioned by deputies, Taini began to walk around the area to "unscramble" his head. After a brisk three minutes he came upon the murder site of the two women victims in the drainage gully. Searchers had found them at the bottom of the trail only a half mile away from the bodies of the pair who had been killed months earlier. The two missing women were lying facedown, side by side, the arm of one draped pathetically over the other. They were naked and doll-like. Placed at

the top of their heads were their clothes and their knapsacks, eerily piled in neat stacks. There were odd, razor-
thin bruises visible on Diane O'Connell's neck, which
the coroner would later determine were consistent with
strangulation by something like piano wire. Because
blood vessels had burst in her face it was determined she
was strangled first. A pair of panties was stuffed in her
mouth. Abrasions on May's left wrist had also been
caused by this kind of wire. One shot had been fired into
the back of O'Connell's head, two shots into the back of
Shauna May's head, one shot into her right eye. A pair
of panties lay in front of her head, blown out of her mouth
by the gun blast. Her head was turned to the right, her
legs were spread.

There was something else odd at the scene. A hole had
been carefully dug into the earth eighteen inches below
the area of Shauna May's crotch. One foot away another
hole, two-inches wide, had been carved out of the earth
above O'Connell's head. Police could only guess at what
significance this held for the killer.

Shaken, Taini said later concerning the discovery of
the four bodies, "It was grim. There might be more out
there. That's what we were worried about.

"Basically Point Reyes is a cathedral, and to me it was
a strange, bizarre crime. It was almost like someone
coming in and shooting this couple that had gone to
church. I use Point Reyes as a classroom. To me it was
a shocking, turnaround experience for me. After all these
years to be out there and all of a sudden, whoom!, here's
an urban city-type crime way out here. It just hadn't been
in my realm."

"At 5:30 that evening," Marin County Sheriff's Sergeant Rich Keaton told me afterward, "Chuck Prandi
and I go walking over the top of the hill and it's starting
to get dark. We see these two girls side by side and there's
nothing around but darkness and these little piles of
clothing. We knew they had to be sitting on the ground
at one point. They're facedown when they're shot.

"Chuck and I were the ones who had to sit with Shauna
May and Diane O'Connell while the authorities spent
four or five hours deciding who was going to take the
case—the FBI or the sheriff's department. We were sit-

ting on that hillside with two bodies and I noticed our
flashlights were growing dimmer and dimmer. I turned
to Prandi and I said, 'Why don't we turn our flashlights
off for a while, Chuck?' He said, 'I don't care if the
flashlights go dead, I just can't do that.'

"So about four hours later the FBI shows up and gives
us the case. Well, thanks a lot. We thought with all the
publicity of a multiple murder, four bodies on the same
day in the park, what better agency to have than the FBI
with all the research and resources at their hand.''

As he sat in the night Keaton reconstructed in his mind
the sequence of events that led to the deaths of May and
O'Connell, something he would do often over the years
ahead. "So what happens," he told me in retrospect,
"after the killer has taken O'Connell off the trail. He has
the first girl. She's a little tiny, blonde girl and all of a
sudden here comes May, charging through. Now Shauna
May is a much bigger gal than O'Connell, five foot nine
inches, not muscular but well proportioned, could really
take care of herself.

"The killer takes out a garrote. There are garrote
marks around her throat according to the coroner, enough
to cause unconsciousness, not enough to cause death."
Police theorized that the Trailside Killer's intended victim that day was O'Connell, his chosen and stalked victim, but his plan went awry when May stumbled onto the
abduction scene. That's why two women who didn't know
each other were taken together.

"Later crime photographs are significant," Keaton told
me, "because it shows the girls had dirt on their hands,
dirt on the bottoms of their feet, and dirt on their but-
tocks. They were sitting on dirt with nothing underneath
them, apparently propped up with their hands. I could
see where they had been digging their hands into the dirt.
It's under their nails. At one point they sat with their
hands cradled in the small of their back. The most obvious part of this is to see the dirt, and you know that
before that happened they were naked on the ground.

"The sequence of shots is interesting as described by
one of the witnesses. They were within one hundred yards
of the murder site. At 3:10 in the afternoon, according
to Kalishes's fancy watch, a chronometer, they hear

'Bang! Bang!' Holy shit! your first reaction. The killer has fired a gun and now thinks, Now, let's get the hell out of here before someone starts looking for me. But seconds later, fifty seconds later, the witnesses hear: 'Bang! Bang!' May had three, the other girl one. What did the killer do first? One girl, one each, I think. Then because he's angry at May, back to her for two more.''

Some policemen believed the killer focused his anger on May because of her interruption of his stalking of O'Connell. In order to rape May, O'Connell had to be strangled because the killer didn't want to attract attention at that point with gunfire. May was forced to watch. He left May alive, some believed, while he strangled Diane O'Connell. Can you imagine, they asked, the terror that woman felt knowing what the killer was doing and knowing that she would be next. "I can't get out of my mind," one investigator told me, "the thought of the two women, both facedown, O'Connell bound with a ligation around the hands and the neck. Raped. Strangled. The other still living, knowing she will be next.''

"There were people," Keaton told me, "who were telling us the bodies of the man and the woman, rapidly decomposed, could have been there six months. The sad part was we just didn't know how long we were talking about as opposed to the amount of time O'Connell and May had been there. Jindrich was able to give us an estimate, but we had something better—we had the automobile.''

A small chocolate-brown Toyota Corolla, license number 559-LMC, had been sitting forlornly in the parking lot at Point Reyes, a distance of one and four-tenths of a mile from the male and female bodies. On November 30, 1980, two days after the murders of O'Connell and May, Lieutenant Don Besse of the sheriff's office dispatched Ray Maynard to process this car.

The brown Toyota was parked in front of a white log and facing toward Bear Valley Trail. A yellow truck was parked alongside. There was puddling and streaking along the car from the moisture. "We had vivid photographs," recalled Sergeant Keaton, "of the waterline, the drip line around the auto where it had sat. The keys

MOUNT WITTENBERG

SKY TRAIL
PARK HEADQUARTERS
BEAR VALLEY TRAIL

MOUNT WITTENBERG
SKY TRAIL
TRAILHEAD
PARK HEADQUARTERS
MEADOW TRAIL
BEAR VALLEY TRAIL
SKY TRAIL
OLD PINE TRAIL
DIVIDE MEADOW
MILES

PT. REYES NATIONAL SEASHORE
PARK HDQTS
DRAKES BAY
MILL VALLEY

PACIFIC
OCEAN
N
SF
GRAYSMITH

MT. WITTENBERG
OLDER MAN SIGHTED 1:30 P.M.
SWITCHBACKS
TRAILHEAD
SKY TRAIL
SKY CAMP
NANCY
DIANE
SHARON
MAN IN BUSHES
3:10 P.M.
PARK HEADQUARTERS

to the car—it turned and there was only one set—were in the murdered boy's pocket. So the car didn't move. It had been there for six weeks, since October 11, 1980, unnoticed, which is hard to believe.* And when Maynard tried the keys from the boy's pocket in the door, they fit, and when he placed them in the ignition they fit. The battery was dead. Maynard felt under the seat and found a purse and a wallet. ID cards inside were those of a missing couple, Cindy Moreland and Rick Stowers.

"When you back up to six weeks," said Keaton, "that was the weekend before Anne Alderson was killed. When we did that we said, 'Oh, my God, what have we got here. We have somebody on the prowl who did the kids on the weekend and for whatever reason did Anne Alderson on Monday.' The hypothesis was that they didn't provide the sex fulfillment that the killer sought. That morning Maynard had the car towed to a garage at Point Reyes Station."

Since Ray Maynard had participated in the Alderson slaying investigation on Mount Tamalpais he was put in charge of the Point Reyes investigation, while Keaton, the department's homicide detective, was to bring in outside agencies, like the FBI, to assist. Maynard went up in an FBI copter and took aerial photos. "We had an aerial view of Point Reyes National Seashore," Rich Keaton told me, "which showed all these dense, dark trees and then you'd see what looks like cigarette smoke— smoke grenades to mark the sites of the killings. And one was here and one was right here—out of this whole massive, breathtaking area they were side by side." The park was sealed and a hands-and-knees search of the sites of both attacks was begun. Next came metal detectors in an inch-by-inch search for clues. Casts of any footprints in the area were made.

Sergeant Keaton began to organize the related and known facts in the Trailside case. "I made up this little file just for guys who were coming in to work the case and I'd say, 'Here, this is for you. Take a look at this.

*Point Reyes rangers claimed the car had been driven and returned prior to the discovery of the bodies. The waterline and dead battery disproved this.

Because of the investigation we have going on, this is confidential. Keep it under your hat. This is all we have—beyond this we don't know anything. We're looking for a common denominator, a common clue.' ''

On December 1 at 9:30 A.M. Ray Maynard had to act as witness at the autopsy of the four bodies found in the park. O'Connell and May positively identified, Stowers and Moreland tentatively identified. The autopsy would be performed by Marin County Coroner Ervin Jindrich, and Maynard, as custodian of evidence, would receive the recovered bullets and fragments.

There was a slender but unique bruise on O'Connell's neck that led Dr. Jindrich to believe she had been tethered and may have died from strangulation before being shot. "The ligature marks on the victim's neck," he later stated, "were consistent with markings that would be left by a cord or wire like you would use to hang pictures."

Maynard kept careful notes as the bullets were removed:

> *CAO-A-1 13625 11/30/80 O'Connell, metalic fragment removed from brain. 9:30 A.M.*
> *CAO-13625 May #9MM. Metalic fragment recovered from left cheek at 10:31 A.M. Placed on a white paper towel, wrapped up and placed in a vial.*

Each bullet or fragment was placed by Maynard in a plastic vial with a red screw top, numbered on a red property tag, and then stored in brown paper sacks. May's autopsy was the most difficult since she had been shot three times in the head.

> *May #10MM. Recovered right forehead of May at 10:37 A.M.*
> *May #11MM. Recovered from right occipital of the brain, 10:47 A.M.*
> *May #12MM. Recovered from right sinus area, 11:05 A.M.*
> *May #13MM. "Flick" portion of metal from right temple area, 11:16 A.M.*
> *Moreland #6MS. A metal fragment in the head. 12:47 P.M. Bullet marked 174 B, bag marked 174 B-1.*
> *Stowers #7MS. A bullet in the head. 1:03 P.M. Bullet marked 174 A-1. Bag marked 174 A.*

Maynard took all of the evidence to Dr. Richard Waller at the state crime lab. Waller studied the bullet that had killed Cynthia Moreland. "It was without the fine lines or characteristics that I could use for identification. Exposure or many other things could cause that type of reaction," said Waller afterward. "The slug's outer metal shell had been degraded through a process similar to the rusting of iron." The size, weight, and shape of the damaged bullet corresponded to the other slugs Maynard had brought him, but Waller knew he could not link it to the fatal weapon.

This was not true of the bullets used to kill Stowers, May, and O'Connell. "I found correspondence in . . . individual characteristics among all three bullets and between those and the Alderson bullet. That showed me the bullets that came from May and O'Connell were fired from the same weapon as the bullet that came from Miss Alderson."

Waller studied a vaginal swab and an anal swab from May. If the spermatozoa were from the same attacker who had raped Alderson then he expected to find a $1+1-$ on the electrophoretic plate. There was less semen than in the Alderson attack. It was present in May's vagina and anus. Waller discovered an almost invisible semen stain in the center of the crotch of May's panties, developed it, and saw under the microscope that the few spermatozoa that were present were tailless. He noted that May had a strong positive for AP. May's vaginal swab was marked $1 C-1$, her pubic hair classified $1-C$. Waller also did a PGM subtype for the panty stain, which showed up as $1+1+$.

Waller then did a test on O'Connell's vaginal swab. There were no sperm in her vagina, but some on her pubic hair. The results obtained showed both victim and donor shared the same PGM. Anyone could have been the semen donor. However, the one thing Alderson, May, and O'Connell all showed in common in their tests was a PGM reading of $1+$.

3

A Killer's Mind, 1980

What conclusions could be reached concerning the new atrocities on the trails of Marin County, I wondered. My guess was that the killer, in addition to the rush the violent and brutal subjugation of his blameless young victims obviously gave him, had begun to crave attention in the media. In some ways the crimes had become a cerebral chess match between himself and the authorities. Perhaps, police wondered, it was a way for the unknown man to even the score for some past abuse.

After the discovery of the bodies at Point Reyes, "that horrible day when all hell broke loose," as Rich Keaton put it, the detectives began to develop some theories. "Some of us," Keaton told me, "believed that the killer's sexual drive operated on a thirty-day basis. At one point we were doing a lot of charting or plotting. It was almost like he was going through a cycle every thirty days when he had to have sex."

Lieutenant Besse had a theory that the killer had been forced to kill Moreland and Stowers. Perhaps he had come onto the woman alone, approached her, and then was confronted by Stowers. "He ends up killing them both," he told me, "and doesn't get laid and three days later he's out looking for Alderson. We know he was patrolling the area."

The most cynical and depressing theory of all was that the killer murdered Moreland and Stowers in order to test fire a new weapon, a dry run for the murder of Anne Alderson.

When the Trailside Killer had struck in October he had done it so skillfully and expertly it had gone undetected, and the maniac had used the signposts of the new victims, O'Connell and May, to point the way to the earlier deaths. The killer must have known that when the search parties started looking for the missing women on November 28 the earlier male and female victims would finally be discovered. Or had he killed at Point Reyes because he considered it safe because the bodies had not been discovered.

Because of his extensive knowledge of the criminal mind and his work within the prison system, Napa psychologist R. William Mathis, the thirty-eight-year-old head of a consulting firm, had been called in as early as March 8, 1980, to look at the crime scenes. Mathis was shocked by the brutality of the murders and began to work closely with Howenstein and Gaddini.

At each murder site Dr. Mathis had been able to point out the ritualistic aspects of the attacks. He told me later that his analysis of the unknown man had not been influenced by the composite sketch of Barbara Schwartz's killer. One of his suggestions to Howenstein was that when they did find a prime suspect they follow him for at least a week before any arrest. These types, the psychologist noted, had a tendency to keep souvenirs of their crimes and might lead surveillance teams to the location of clothes and perhaps even the .38-caliber gun used in the murders.

Dr. Mathis, Howenstein, and Gaddini had hit on several traps for the attacker on the mountain trails. One involved male rangers dressed as female hikers; this was tried without success.

Sheriff Howenstein was interviewed by the press on Sunday, November 30, and said, "We're not disclosing anything about the crime scene at the moment. The killer carefully and deliberately plans the acts, lies in wait for vulnerable victims, takes them to remote locations, and executes them. . . . We don't perceive we have seen the last action of this person. I have a very strong personal apprehension." Discussing the Point Reyes murders Howenstein sat in front of microphones emblazoned with the numbers of the five leading television stations. To his left were the sketches of the hawk-nosed man on the trail and an even younger-looking full-face composite of the suspect. Behind the sheriff, tacked to the bulletin board, was a full-length illustration of the same man in hiking gear.

"The thread of similarity is in the ritualistic aspect of the killings," an exhausted Howenstein told the press. "He puts his victims through some sort of discomfort and personal trauma before killing them. He puts the victims at a point of pleading for their lives. The killings are his effort to give himself some sort of psychological release. But this won't solve his problems. His problems will be getting worse. . . . He obviously has problems with women. Without question I feel this individual is capable of striking again. Danger does today lurk around us."

Howenstein stated that the killer was a "murder-holic," a runaway train, and concurred with the theory the killer had called attention to his earlier murders. Dr. Mathis added that "The killer's thrills are necessarily sexual," and then painted a detailed portrait of the suspect: "The killer is handsome, with a winning personality. We believe his maximum excitement is mentally terrifying his victims. He probably has a minor prison record . . . is very much a loner . . . he would suffer hypertension, hot flashes, small anxiety attacks, general physical tiredness, tremors of the hand, would find his ability to work deteriorating. He would become disorganized, a clock watcher, and suffer hyperventilation. He will feel very dirty, experience personal anger, and will be easily upset." Mathis concluded sadly, "I think we are dealing with a community tragedy that has no parallel."

"This is a terrible intrusion on the beauty and sanctity

of Mother Nature,'' said the embattled sheriff. ''Previously, I suggested that women not hike alone. Now, I must caution women of even traveling in pairs. This shows what the killer is capable of doing. I would say he is capable of taking even a small group. There is no way I can tell people that. I used to say 'There's safety in numbers.' I'm not sure of that now. All I can do is issue the strongest warnings to people—that is, to be well-guarded whenever going into areas of any remoteness.''

Later, Joyce Sutton, a psychiatrist at the Parole Outpatient Clinic of the State Department of Corrections, put it best it seemed to me: ''This person has trouble with women, with his mother, or grandmother, or a lover who rejected him. He hates women, and the ultimate expression of hatred is to kill. For him it's just another lousy woman. With killers like him, between the first and second killings, it's hard to say whether a pattern will be set up. But once the killings have been repeated, then the more you have had, the more there probably will be. The killing doesn't solve the problem or relieve the torment. The delusions don't go away.''

The police also consulted a San Francisco psychiatrist, Dr. Edward Shev, who later told me, ''One of the things I suggested is they go back over the releases from prison of people with this kind of behavior and see if there was anybody let out of prison recently who had a history of this kind of violence, somebody who had a feeling of destruction about certain kinds of women. The killer, usually it's a young person, is probably quite intellectually cunning.'' Shev told the police, ''The killer probably selects his victims by picking up girls and questioning them and talking to them before he decides to act. . . . But you're both guessing and not guessing. The whole picture has to be examined. Does the person steal panties? Does he mutilate? Does he make them kneel? Knowing all the findings of the police at the scene there is a 90 to 95 percent chance of outlining what the suspect's behavioral pattern might be in general.''

Finally, Dr. Donald Lunde of Stanford commented on the accuracy of a profile: ''You can say some fairly specific things about a person when there is a pattern in the victims selected and in the manner of killings and simi-

larities between the area where the crimes take place, and
age, hair color, or physique of the victims. Especially in
certain kinds of sex murders you can quite accurately
narrow the age range, background, educational level,
marital history, and intellectual level of the suspect. . . .
It is most difficult when a seriously mentally ill person
is committing the killings. An example is a killer who is
hearing voices and selecting victims on what looks like
a random basis.''

''The families assumed it was them the whole time,''
said Cindy Moreland's sister Alice, after Cindy and Rick
Stowers had been positively identified through dental
records. ''But it was December 4 when they told us for
sure.'' When Rick's mother, Joyce, was asked by the
press, ''How do you feel?'' She snapped back, ''To begin with, you don't feel—and then you just fall apart.''
She told me later, ''I wasn't overly impressed with the
newspapers and TV, but we were lucky enough to be at
a distance. We did have a TV station north of Tehachapi
who called us after the sheriff had called and I can remember saying to the TV person, 'Just how did he die?'
because I was very confused and so when she started
telling me how, it was really more than I had asked for.
I didn't really need to get the details.

''It wasn't until they found the bodies that they really
got into it, no one was really interested—'They've gone
AWOL,' was all we heard. It was our first encounter with
police—I guess they were doing their job, but . . . as
long as I could stay detached it was certainly interesting.
I was most upset by the detective magazines calling the
killer a 'human murder machine.' They were dramatizing
the murderer. After it was all over Rick did get his honorable discharge.''

Use of the Point Reyes National Seashore Park dropped
to one-third of normal attendance and even Point Reyes
station was gripped by the same fear that affected the
hikers. Ordinarily the little resort area was crowded, so
much so you couldn't get a parking place on the main
street, but now, even on weekends, two to three cars at
the most would be parked there.

For a time permits for overnight camping had been

refused and park police and sheriff's deputies had stood stern watch at the trailheads, stopping all hikers from entering, questioning all those leaving.

In early December 1980, rangers and deputies patrolled the paths lockstep, crossing one another on the mountain, stopping to methodically post Day-Glo orange signs that read:

WARNING FOR HIKERS:

BECAUSE OF THE TRAGIC DISCOVERY OF FOUR BODIES IN THE PARK ON NOV. 29, 1980, PLEASE DO NOT HIKE ALONE. EVERYONE SHOULD HIKE/CAMP WITH AT LEAST ONE OTHER PERSON AND THEY SHOULD STAY TO-GETHER AS MUCH AS POSSIBLE. WOMEN SHOULD BE ESPECIALLY CAUTIOUS, AND UNDER NO CIRCUM-STANCES TRAVEL ALONE.

Keaton and his detectives prepared a color photo composite of Moreland and Stowers showing them dressed in the clothes they were wearing when they were last seen. "We made this poster up and sent it out in December literally all over the world," Keaton said.

"You see, Robert, there were hundreds in the park that day including some Europeans who were thoughtful enough to sign the register at Point Reyes Park Headquarters. We wrote them overseas to have them send us their photos. What we did was we took the witnesses' names and then plotted on a wall-sized, color-coded map the places where they had observed lone male hikers. Ones marked in black were identified eventually, the ones in red weren't. We were able to rule some out because they couldn't conceivably reach the area from where they were witnessed to the crime scene in the amount of time allowed. We paced it off ourselves. We did mark some possibles along the shoreline."

Supervisor Giacomini would go down to the sheriff's office from time to time to keep tabs on the investigation. The open bay near Howenstein's office was filled with long tables and telephones. Sergeant Keaton told him they had no idea where they were going to put all the new investigators—"All these FBI agents." "They had these

little photos up like you have on your driver's license,"
Giacomini later told me, "thousands of suspects, arrows
and lines, strings of yarn from one photograph to another. They were investigating everybody in the world."

Giacomini strode to the lone male hiker chart. It had
an accompanying map with corresponding numbers. In
the last column of the lower left corner was a mention,
overlooked by everyone at the time, lost in the forest
of names, that would prove important. A woman hiker
had witnessed a man in his fifties near Sky Camp at
1:30 P.M., one and four-tenths of a mile from the site of
the May-O'Connell slayings, one and one-half hours before the November 28 attack. He appeared "antisocial,
angry, wore glasses, a baseball cap, jeans and backpack," the witness said.

4

The Caller

The sheriff's department had spent $41,000 on overtime so far and Howenstein was forced to go to the board for the $52,000 that would be needed for the next ninety-day period. The supervisors decided to offer a $25,000 reward, the largest ever offered in Marin County, for the capture and conviction of the killer who had struck on the Sleeping Lady and at Point Reyes along the trails. The reward was quickly enlarged to $37,000 by an anonymous donor.

"It's really an example of my and everybody else's frustration," supervisor Giacomini said. "The county has a tight budget and twenty-five grand is not nothing, but is a small price to pay. . . . I think the people of Marin frankly feel about the land—I hope this isn't sexist—like a woman.

"It affected the people horribly," he told me later. "They were killing my people in my parks, my district. That sonofabitch was killing everyone in the great parks, national and state and county parks, and terrorizing the people of West Marin, who had always looked to the parks as an extension of their backyards. The people of Inverness, Point Reyes, they flew in and out of the parks. It's their whole life-style, so they were in abject terror.

"There was a sick feeling, a scared feeling. Fear always translates in very strange ways. There's usually a great warmth when you're in the parks, but, believe me, in those days there wasn't. There were a lot of community meetings in those days where people tried to figure out what to do, self-defense classes. Other people started carrying guns. Very mild people who never would use violence. They brought guns and learned how to use them. I remember one of the old ranchers of West Marin said, 'I'm going to dress up like a woman. Use me as bait. We'll get this s.o.b. and we'll shoot him. When he comes out into a clearing, we'll just gun him down.' Generally the people of West Marin are quite peaceful.

"Listen, the worst thing about it, in addition to the horrible murders, was the unbelievable affect on the psyche of the people of Marin. People suspected neighbors and friends. That deep psychological terror and anger was so pervasive and ugly. I've been here all my life and so I could really sense that feeling . . . I'm so amazed there weren't tragedies caused by these weird suspicions."

Howenstein made a plea for the killer to turn himself in and gave a phone number for him to call. In reaction to this entreaty the sheriff received two letters, handwritten and handprinted, postmarked San Francisco. "Both writers claimed to be the murderer and each said he would be tough to catch," said Howenstein. Of course both couldn't be valid and in fact both letters contained numerous inaccuracies. Howenstein turned the letters over to Dr. Mathis's team of psychological consultants, Barry Dollar and David Corey.

In Bolinas, on December 2, a man at a bar began bragging to a girlfriend that he had committed the Point Reyes's killings. Police questioned and released him. They felt that he was simply trying to impress the woman.

Because there existed the possibility that more bodies may have been discarded in the woods Howenstein ordered infrared aerial photographic searches be made of both Point Reyes and the Sleeping Lady. Decomposing matter gives off heat that shows up on infrared film. But this could not be done until the weather cleared up. The sheriff also began plans for a re-enactment of the Point Reyes's murders to be staged on the actual murder sites and arranged for the ten hikers who were on Sky Trail between 2:00 and 4:30 P.M. to be there.

Since Mark McDermand was in custody when the latest killings took place, Howenstein announced that he was cleared. "He was certainly accounted for. It puts us in an entirely different ballpark. Yes, Mark is off the hook." Mark's reaction to the twist of events was mixed. He was both "elated and appalled" by the new murders. "I can understand why the police said I resembled the composite drawing of the Trailside Killer," he said. "Both my photo and the composite each had a nose, two eyes, and two ears, but the composite showed a suspect with black hair. My hair is blond.

"Obviously they would have had to assume at the very outset that I had something to do with it. The proximity was too much. I'm glad to realize that justice does tend to get done even though it does use its dogged slow fashion."

One of Diane O'Connell's hiking companions, Sharon Raymond, had been questioned and hypnotized. She explained to investigators in the presence of Diane's father that the three friends were hiking down Sky Trail a couple of hundred yards apart, and that she was the leader with Diane in the middle and the third companion taking up the rear.

"Did you see anyone at all on the trail?" she was asked.

"Yes. A man. In the bushes just off the trail," she answered.

The sheriff's investigator tensed. "Do you remember what the man looked like?"

Sharon described an average young man with dark hair.

"Did he speak to you at all?"

"Well, the man told me he had gone into the bushes to . . . gotten off the trail to, uh . . . urinate."

Diane's father asked the witness, "Why didn't you think to go back uptrail, stop, and go back and warn my daughter, walk with my daughter after you saw this

man?'' Diane's companion just looked at the floor help-
lessly. It had all been so fast.

The sheriff's department had received over 1,500 calls
about the killings, but the call they got at 11:00 P.M.,
Thursday, December 4, on the special Trailside hotline
had a macabre sense to it. To the deputy on duty the
petulant, anonymous voice on the other end of the line
had the qualities and phrasing of a spoiled child or very
young adult male. Over and over the caller alleged he
knew much more than the police about the murders.
"What are you getting at?'' asked the officer.
    "I'm the killer.''
    Alarmed, the deputy felt it would be better if one of
the appointed psychologists shared in the conversation,
but all attempts to transfer the calls to Mathis's Napa
home proved unsuccessful. The mystery caller was put
on hold, but he disconnected. Finally, at 11:11, the unknown man called back. "I know this call is being taped,
analyzed, and traced, but it won't do you any good.''
    "In that case,'' suggested the deputy, "tell me about
yourself and save us some time.''
    "It's not pleasant,'' the caller said after a pause. "I'm
tortured by voices from the inside. I'm a haunted person
and the voices tell me to do terrible things. I'm so plagued
that I have a dream of victims every night and then I
can't sleep.''
    Dr. Mathis had pointed out that sexual sadists view
their victims as objects, existing only to give them pleasure. Not only do they not suffer remorse, but they relive
their acts as a form of enjoyment. Dreams would not have
kept the Trailside rapist awake.
    "Have you seen anyone, you know, a doctor?'' Scripts
were available for the deputy, and seven other answering
officers, prepared by Dr. Mathis for a situation such as
this.
    "How do you expect me to get any help?'' moaned
the stranger. "I tried. But when you tell somebody that
you've killed someone they aren't going to help.''
    "There are people,'' said the deputy.
    "Not for me.''
    The last call from the unknown man was at 11:24.

Only a minute long, it consisted mostly of a sulking silence from the caller. He hung up and left the deputy staring at the phone. After this Dr. Mathis took to waiting by the hotline in hopes that the man would call again. "I will wait as long as necessary," he said.

After Howenstein's afternoon press conference on December 6, the same man called KRON-TV four times and told them he was going to surrender, which created an incredible stir at the station. Arrangements were made during a series of four phone calls for a meeting in Berkeley near the university campus.

"I'll be at the telephone booth on the corner of Telegraph and Durant in Berkeley at exactly 9:30 P.M. I want you to bring a TV crew to ensure my safety and to witness the surrender," ordered the stranger. "Oh, and one more thing . . ."

"What's that?"

"Bring over a pint of brandy."

By instruction KRON contacted Howenstein and the area was sealed off. By 9:30 P.M. there was no sign of movement at the chosen booth. Since it was obvious they were going to be stood up, the sheriff returned to his office. There the hotline rang and the anonymous voice stated, "It's me. I'm not far away, but I won't be coming in tonight. I have no comment for the 11:00 news on my nonsurrender. As a reward, though, if you have one of your men look under the phone ledge you'll find a package taped to the bottom. It's wrapped in brown paper and masking tape."

When the package was retrieved the police saw that on the outside the caller had written—"This will prove I am the Trailside Killer and no one else." Inside was an item of common domestic use, nothing to prove he was the killer. Gaddini told the press, "It's not a weapon of any sort but I can't tell you what the object is at this time."

Dr. Mathis, who by this time had spoken twice to the unknown caller, told the reporters, "He really does need us. He's obviously not doing very well. We can give him some specific ways of relieving stress." Over fifteen brief, pained calls had been made to the hotline by the unknown man.

The next day, Sunday, the anonymous man rang the hotline at 10:30 P.M. Though he offered to surrender again, the man vacillated constantly between where and when, pausing in silence for as long as thirty seconds in some of the calls before continuing in his fairly distinctive, odd, and forced voice.

Earlier in the day, at 2:50 P.M., the sheriff had received a call that seemed to hold more promise. Two nurses at St. Mary's Hospital in San Francisco phoned to say a visitor to the city had just been admitted to the emergency room for a minor wound, and a doctor felt the patient bore a resemblance to the composite sketches of the hawk-nosed young man on the trail. "He's a man in his midtwenties with dark black hair and a prominent beaklike nose," said one of the nurses.

Police raced to the hospital and to a small room on the main floor where the man was questioned. On the basis of the interview the police decided to take him to the Hall of Justice to check his story.

The suspect called his attorney and his parents, all of whom were able to establish that he had an alibi. By the time he was released, the tight-lipped young man and his attorney had to literally fight their way to the lawyer's car through hoards of newspapermen and television cameras. "It's just a case of mistaken identity. We're all going home now," said the attorney, slamming the car door.

5

The Man with
a Dog

Richard Wood went directly to the Gems of
the Golden West warehouse to see Carpenter for their
probation meeting on December 12, 1980.* "He was
having problems then at work," Wood recalled. "His
employers, he complained, were not sharing responsibility. The Neumans had a mom-and-pop type of business.
He wanted them to share responsibilities with him. He
had ideas of different ways to do things."

Carpenter had loaned Joe Elia and Lane Thomsen, his
former bosses at the printing school, $2,000 for their
company, Moon Tide. He was growing dissatisfied with
the rate of repayment which was supposed to be monthly.
He sat down at one of the typewriters at Gems on November 16 and wrote them a vaguely threatening letter.
"If I turned on the vigourish clock it would go up to
$10,000." They instead came to him with another get-
rich-quick scheme. They wanted to print free TV guides
with ads to pass out at supermarkets.

---

*Wood had also visited Carpenter at Gems on November 3 and 21,
1980.

   After Wood left, Carpenter wrote out a check for
$45.50 for the San Francisco Ballet spring season tickets.
He had renewed his acquaintance with an old friend, Jef-
fery Kent Jackl, who shared his love of ballet. The check
was made out to him.

On hilly Sussex Street in Glen Park in the southern part
of San Francisco, Bobby Sue Klemke looked out on the
narrow hillside street of light-colored homes. On the high
ridge behind and above her was a ring of dark windswept
trees and condominiums, which gave the area a terraced
look. Bobby Sue remembered her first day here two
months ago, in October of 1980, when she and her two
sons, Joshua and Jason, had driven from Waterloo, Iowa,
and pulled up a battered rented truck in front of her Aunt
Verna's three-story house. It had been two weeks before
the murder of Anne Alderson on the Sleeping Lady.
   A bespectacled, soft-spoken man with a stutter had
come up to her and explained how and where to park so
she wouldn't block the driveways and traffic on the per-
pendicular street. Indicating to Bobby Sue that he lived
just three houses down from her aunt's, he introduced
himself as David Carpenter. He told her he was divorced.
Bobby Sue especially recalled him because he was the
first neighbor she had met on Sussex Street.
   Over the next two weeks the lonely man continued to
show kindness to the new family on the block, loaning
the thirtyish, red-haired Bobby Sue a new drill so she
could install hanging plants and offering to fix the chil-
drens' record player. Joshua and Jason liked to play with
the older man's dog, Herman, or to visit the balding man's
aged parents, who were described by the other neighbors
as "very quiet, reserved, dignified, and aloof."
   People in the neighborhood spoke to Bobby Sue of
Carpenter's father, Elwood, whom they considered strict
and demanding, a man whom the boy could never satisfy,
more like a career soldier; and they told her of a kindly
mother, Frances, who was affectionate, though others
said she was domineering. She was often seen hugging
David. Both parents were known as political activists.
   "David was always very nice, very neat, very polite.
Nicest people you would ever find anywhere," remarked

the Carpenters' next-door neighbor Helen Lindt. "They're like you and like me. They're very nice, law-abiding people."

Bobby Sue told her aunt, "He's very quiet. His only problem seems to be his speech impediment. He stutters terribly. He doesn't seem embarrassed by it. He just keeps working at it until he gets out whatever word he's trying to say." She knew he was a printer and had once been a ship's purser. "To all appearances he looked like a good guy. He showed us pictures of his daughter, his granddaughter, and a baby niece," she said.

In the days ahead he took her to the humane society and got a dog for her children, a dachshund. Later he found a second dachshund, and he brought this to her as well. He took the kids on walks and brought them toys.

In the evenings as the fog was crawling in off the ocean, Carpenter would walk his dog over the arduous, steep Glen Park hills, over the cracked sidewalks and patched, twisting streets. His father would sit in the open front window reading while his mother with her failing eyesight gardened below in the front yard.

One afternoon the purser came over to Bobby Sue's for a game of pinochle with her aunt and a third woman. Bobby Sue's aunt was Verna Rees, a retired nightclub singer. The four played on into the night. They all had highballs, and Bobby Sue could see that the stuttering man was getting too much to drink.

Although he didn't become mean or violent in any way, "He seemed to be getting pushy," said Bobby Sue. When he asked the women if he could come again, they all said no. "He seems to want friends very badly. He tried so hard to be friendly," said the aunt. Another neighbor said, "I always thought it was very nice of him to come take care of his parents."

As she had gotten to know him, Bobby Sue had noticed he seemed nervous and was not a stable individual. Never for a moment did she think he was violent.

The times Bobby Sue would see the purser walking his little dog grew rarer, but when she returned home from her job she would find him waiting at the door. "I didn't want to encourage him," she said later, I just said 'Hello,' and 'I have to get going.' I didn't mean to encourage him. There's no sense in encouraging someone you're not interested in." When he invited her to dinner she refused. "He just didn't appeal to me," she said.

At Christmas of 1980 he had given her a small onyx stand with three white and blue plaster dachshunds, look-alikes for his dog, Herman. Included with the present was a box filled with key rings. Each was decorated with a replica of a gun.

As December 1980 drew to an end, Edward Nation Meyer, an old friend of David Carpenter and Jeff Jackl, called the purser to introduce the older man to his girlfriend, Rebecca "Reba" Lehman, who was also known as Rachel Goodman. "I want you to have a friend," Nation told Reba.

"On December 19," recalled Carpenter, "Nation c-c-c-called me and asked me to meet him at the Delancy Street Restaurant. We'd sit there and drink coffee and at that time he introduced me to Reba Lehman. I used to see her once a month or every six weeks at the restaurant. Nation Meyer asked me if I could help his girlfriend recover $70,000 worth of rugs that had been stolen from her."

Carpenter had been lonely since his girlfriend at the printing school, Nancy Morrison, had been sent back to the federal prison at Pleasanton on December 4 for parole violations. He readily agreed to act as a go-between and said, "Let's see w-w-w-what I can do to solve some of these difficulties."

Reba Lehman would be one of those, in the months ahead, to whom David Carpenter would show his .38-caliber gun. The list was growing. He had already shown it to Mollie Purnell, Tina Vance, Kenny Baughman, as well as to Mollie's son, Adam. Three days after his meeting with Reba and Nation, Carpenter was driving through the intersection of Chenery and Castro at 6:00 P.M. when he almost hit Dale Watts. Watts, young, tattooed, streetwise, got into a fight with Carpenter. As the argument escalated the purser brandished a .38 revolver at Watts, who spit at him and shouted back, "Why don't you stick that gun up your ass!" Carpenter fled the scene as Watts jotted down his license plate, D J CARP, and reported it to the police.

Just as Diamond Street levels off and intersects expansive Bosworth Street is the Glen Park Continental Savings and Loan, a white, two-story building with Greek columns. It was December 20 and Carpenter was shading his eyes, looking in through the glass where the tellers were at work. He could see Anna Kelly Menjivar, a part-time teller whom he often talked with. Carpenter had met her a year and a half ago and, claiming to be a book-keeper at Gems of the Golden West, had offered her bookkeeping lessons.

After her shift was finished Kelly met the purser and stood chatting outside the bank as her mother, Juanita, drove up to collect her daughter. Because of his severe stutter, she knew her daughter was especially kind and sympathetic to the balding, clean-shaven man in glasses. Kelly, seventeen, was a beautiful brown-eyed girl with shoulder-length black hair and thick well-formed eyebrows. She was a senior at Mercy High School.

Carpenter offered to take the mother and daughter to the Gems warehouse to give them some trinkets to use as Christmas gifts. They agreed, and he got into his light-green station wagon to lead them there, Kelly and Juanita following in their car to Revere Street. They passed the Pan Pacific Building on an industrial street with light-colored low buildings, then came to Gems of the Golden West. They parked pointed toward the hill parallel to the curb. Carpenter produced a key for the warehouse. The thud of the older man's shoes and the light clack of the women's heels echoed in the gloom. Carpenter turned off the alarm, got down a crow bar, and began prying open two large crates just inside the entryway of the cluttered warehouse.

"Go ahead and h-h-h-help yourself," he told Kelly. "Take anything you want. You might want to give these to your co-workers." The first crate held small ceramic dolls, and Kelly smilingly took three of these. One was a short, blonde doll with a wide-brimmed hat covered with roses like Florence Neuman wore. In the second box were little key chains with plastic charms attached, and the older man gave her an entire carton of these.

Kelly had told her mother, a chemical factory worker, and another relative, Ana Intriago, this about the man:

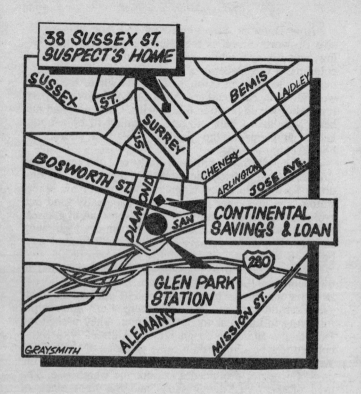

"He's very kind and he loves me as a daughter." Ana was Kelly's cousin, and it worried her that Kelly liked him so much.

On December 28, between 6:00 and 9:00 in the morning, Kelly disappeared from her own bed. Her mother and fourteen-year-old brother slept nearby and heard nothing. At 9:00 Juanita found Kelly's purse left behind on her dresser. It contained all of her IDs, all of her money, and even her uncashed paycheck. Her mother, after a search, decided the only clothing Kelly could have taken was a white wool sweater, a skirt, and her gold necklace with a one-inch gold crucifix.

Mrs. Menjivar tried to recall all that Kelly had said the night before. Most puzzling was a remark her daughter had made to her just before they had all gone to sleep. She had promised her mother a really big surprise.

The rugged terrain along winding Crocker Avenue with its lots of shoulder-high vegetation was searched because Kelly often jogged in the area. However, because of a mother-daughter quarrel over a pet rabbit that one of Kelly's boyfriends had given her for Christmas and an argument over keeping her room clean, the police suspected Kelly was a runaway.

A description was circulated and Kelly's picture was put up in the bank where she worked. "Her hair would probably be tied back," said her mother.

On January 8, 1981, Sister Mary Pyke, one of Kelly's teachers at Mercy High, was riding a bus in San Francisco. She looked out of the window as the bus approached the corner of Masonic and Fell streets and thought she saw Kelly. She waved and called out, but the girl did not stop.

On January 10 and again on January 17, a horse owner, Chuck Jones, at the Daly City horse stables thought he saw the missing teenager. He swore to police he had let her ride his horse and identified her from a police photo. She was dressed in her Catholic school outfit and he knew her only as Kelly.

To the Daly City police this proved Kelly was a runaway. However, when her mother looked in the back of her daughter's closet, she found Kelly's school uniform.

6

Candy

On December 31, the last day of 1980, Carpenter had worked with Florence Neuman all day, and on January 4, 1981, he had made his final trip to the Alameda Flea Market: "I realized I was going to stutter whenever I met a strange person. I got to thinking: I could use that as a sales technique . . . turn a speech handicap into an advantage so I could become successful in business as 'the stuttering salesman.' I made up my mind to be the only stuttering salesman around. The culmination of the trips is something I could take with me—use further on down the line. I tended to relax more. I still stuttered, I just didn't let it destroy me.

"On Monday, January 19, I had a change in attitude. I s-s-s-started to sell, racks of fifty-one key chains . . . going in with the rack, setting the rack on the counter and *selling!* Yes, sir, I had more confidence in selling than servicing. In doing something I've always w-w-wanted to do and that was to sell."

Jack Neuman sent Carpenter down to Fisherman's Wharf to check out the latest key chains being sold to tourists. This set the purser to thinking. "I came up with a m-m-million-dollar idea. Mr. Neuman, my boss, had produced a beautiful, pastel-colored key chain, but it was more expensive than the rest and he would have trouble selling it. I had an idea on how to improve it. On the reverse side he could p-p-print on it, 'San Francisco, The Gay Capitol of the U.S.'—a golden idea to make money! The perfect gay key chain! It would fill a void.

"Although I had any number of gay friends, *I* am not gay. However, I didn't tell Jack about *my* idea because if I did tell him I might get a pat on the head from him and that's all. I wanted a piece of the action!" In the days ahead Carpenter would continue to work on his adult key-chain idea, "I had some ideas on different styles . . . with two or three movable figures." The purser, however, did not have the expertise to put his ideas on paper, and then other things began to happen in his life.

"I was so happy about selling s-s-some key chains that on January 21, 1981, I called my parole officer to tell him. He said come in around 3:00 P.M., and on my w-w-way to Wood's I met Candy."

The woman Carpenter encountered at the intersection of Golden Gate and Van Ness Avenue in San Francisco, Candace Dawn Townsend, was passing through the city from L.A. and Riverside traveling to Guerneville and was planning on staying at a friend's home in Sonoma County. For three weeks she had tried to get into heavy equipment school in L.A.

"What drew me to her," recalled Carpenter, "was s-s-she had two black eyes. I don't think I've ever seen a women with two. One maybe." Candy's driving companion, Bud, had given her the black eyes in L.A. "She had her hood up. She looked as if she could use some help. Her car had broken down a block or so off the freeway and a cop had pushed her there. I have an AAA card and I offered to have her car towed to a service station. I told her I had some business and I'd be back in an hour, and if she was still there I'd be glad to have her car towed."

David Carpenter went on to his monthly meeting with his probation officer, Richard Wood. "He was dressed nicely," Wood said afterward. "Shirt and tie and sports jacket. He was happy with his job, but stressed to me he just considered it a stepping stone to greater things.'' Carpenter left Wood's office at the Federal Building on Golden Gate Avenue and started for his car. Candy was still sitting on the curb. It was 3:50 P.M.

"It was an hour later and she was s-s-still there,'' recalled Carpenter. " 'I don't have any money to have it repaired,' she told me. In the run of the conversation she made it very obvious she would do ANYTHING to get up to Guerneville. I went back to Gems of the Golden West and we met again at 6:00 to 6:15 P.M. after work.

"After I m-m-met her back on Golden Gate Avenue the first thing I did was have her cover up everything in the back of her Datsun: all of her personal things were exposed. I drove in my Chevy station wagon up Highway 101 north to Petaluma on route to Guerneville. . . . She had made it really obvious she was willing to exchange sexual favors if I was to drive her up to Guerneville. Around Petaluma, 7:15 to 7:30 P.M., somewhere in there . . . I suggested we stop and get something to eat.'' Candy had only $8.

As they drove Carpenter promised to have her 1966 Datsun towed to a garage just as soon as they had dinner in Marin County. She told him about her days as a cocktail waitress and a truck driver for Griff Davies in Montana. "Candy had taken a course at a school to be a bartender,'' said Carpenter in retrospect, "and she w-w-wanted to work as a waitress in San Francisco. She was only going up to Guerneville because that was the only place she had to stay. Before we got something to eat we engaged in sex in the back of my Chevy.''

"He stopped the car in an isolated spot near Sausalito,'' Candy said later. "It was actually very near to Mount Tamalpais. It was dark. Hilly. Lots of trees. No one else was around. It was frightening. I felt very uneasy about the whole thing. He asked me to marry him [after talking about prostitution] and have sex with him and offered me money. We had sex in the backseat. . . . He showed me a turn-off where people hiked up the mountain. I remember he mentioned the death of a woman on Tamalpais as we drove by the state park. He didn't stutter much at all.'' Candy noticed a royal blue backpack with black straps on the rear seat.

Carpenter drove Candy to Sebastopol, where they ate at Johnnie's Restaurant. During the multicourse dinner Carpenter leaned across the table and told her, "I have very strong romantic feelings toward you. I want to marry you." Although Candy could feel he was serious, she could not countenance the idea of marriage with this man. However, she agreed to move in with Carpenter at his parents' house in San Francisco.

"I enjoyed her company so much," said Carpenter. "I invited her to s-s-stay at my place for a few days. She was agreeable . . . We returned to San Francisco by 101 somewhere around where her car was parked. I called AAA at 9:44 P.M. and they arrived at 9:57 P.M. I rode inside the truck, Candy drove my station wagon to the garage, and went with me to my parents' house on Sussex.

"She brought a whole carful of clothes with her. She had a red jacket, a blue one, and one particular yellow jacket, a Western Bar jacket. It had a shirt collar, black nylon cuffs, no stripes on the sleeves and when you opened it up, it had black buttons, it had a nice black lining. On the front it said, 'Oly' "

Candy's unusual yellow-gold jacket was to prove to be a distinctive and ultimately crucial article of clothing to everyone engaged in the Trailside investigation.

At the time the jacket was made there were over 175,000 people living in Billings, Montana, and many bars, but there was only one Western Bar and this was in the roughest section of town. On the morning of December 19, 1979, the owner of the Western Bar drew his own artwork and took it over to Nancy Alice Hill's printing shop at 6612 South Frontage Road. She added two small beer mugs on either side of the curved lettering and photographically enlarged the design before light-etching it onto the silk screen.

She screened the stenciled illustration onto the backs of twenty Hilton jackets with gold draw strings—ten of blue and ten of yellow-gold. Carefully she sewed OLY GOLD or OLY LIGHT emblems onto the front of the finished jackets. When she had finished, Mrs. Hill held up the completed garments with the full design on the back.

"Yeah," said Candy in her soft-spoken manner, looking back over her shoulder at the purser, "that's the bar I was telling you about where I used to work. It was a promotional item there and one of the customers bought it for me. It never really fit me well." Candy tossed the jacket on a sack of oil cans in the basement and the purser eventually started wearing it himself, leaving it in the back of his station wagon when he wasn't using it. When he did wear it, it was often with a green baseball cap. The very last time she actually saw the jacket was in the back of Carpenter's Chevy in the blue backpack.

"Most of the baseball caps in the house," Carpenter later related, "were up in my father's closet. I personally remember buying five or six of them—one was an Oakland A's cap. I remember it particularly because that's the one I used to wear most of the time, a white A's symbol on the brim, green mesh on the back." Carpenter often wore a black watch cap pulled down over his ears.

Carpenter told Candy that he was a member of the Sierra Club and Aububon Society, explaining he often hiked on Mount Tamalpais. Though he asked her frequently to accompany him she had never gotten around to it. Candy lived upstairs in her own room on the second floor, Carpenter told everyone, but others said she shared quarters in the older man's downstairs studio apartment, a single room to the left of the stairs. Under the stairs was a small room where the purser kept filing cabinets, receipts, and personal papers.

During this time Candy had several different jobs and could sense Carpenter was growing more serious about her. She was feeling just the opposite. He told his probation officer about Candy immediately, telling him how they had met and that she was now living in his home. Wood was anxious to meet Candy and caught his first glimpse of her on January 26.

Candy took a refresher course at bartender's school and soon started tending bar at Clancy's on Powell and at El Grecho's at the Cannery. Candy was so accepted by the Carpenter family that a regular plate was set for her at the dinner table next to David's even though she often worked nights and rarely ate with them. Elwood continued his practice of going to bed early and this dictated the time that they ate. From time to time Candy would call Frank, her son, in Montana.

In February 1981 the San Francisco Gift Show at Brooks Hall was held so all the buyers could see the latest products, and Carpenter and his bosses, Jack and Florence Neuman, attended.

"I helped get the merchandise together," Carpenter recalled, "loaded, unloaded, set displays up. Jack and Florence were there, and I m-m-met Kris Frank and Buff Alexander, who purchased some of our key chains. We agreed that I would deliver them to Kris in Elk Grove where she lived.

"On Valentine's Day I bought Candy an engagement ring. I became officially engaged that day. I took my father shopping, got a haircut, and then we came home.

"From February 23 through February 26, 1981, I was on a s-s-sales trip in the Fresno and Sacramento region." He had made similar trips in May, August, and December. "On February 22, when I had returned home, my father told me that I had received a phone call from a young lady and I was requested to call the number. It was an answering service." Reba Lehman had phoned trying to get in touch with the purser at 6:39 and 8:05 P.M. "She had called about my help in getting her stolen rugs back. I told her I had to be out of town most of the week.

"I saw Kris Frank on the second day of my sales trip, on the twenty-fourth, since I had the key chains she had ordered at the gift show and I was delivering them to her. She wasn't home, so I delivered the key chains to her partner, Buff Alexander. I returned to Motel 6 where I was staying to place a call from a phone booth to the ex-convict I had met at the Gift Show."

Carpenter later claimed he was a victim of a robbery around 8:00 P.M. on February 25. "A man stuck a gun in my back while I was in the most well-lit place outside in a phone booth. I lost thirty dollars, a watch. I lost all the change in my pocket. I had a little suitcase filled with shoes and my blue jacket. I lost that."

Carpenter was angry enough about the holdup to make a police report telling them, "The guy had a .38-caliber handgun," and giving a nebulous description of the robber. Kris Frank later said that the purser called her immediately after the holdup and told her, "I habitually carry a gun in the Gems van and if I had had that I would never have been held up." Kris made a mental note to tell Florence Neuman about the gun.

"On February 26," recalled Carpenter, "I returned to Gems and c-c-called Nation Meyer, who was attending cooking school in Denver, Colorado. I wanted to know if Reba actually knew where the stolen rugs were being held and I made plans to call Reba. The next day while I was typing up invoices on the trip I thought I overheard Kris Frank calling from Sacramento and telling Florence Neuman about the holdup.

"I got a traffic ticket on March 7, 1981," remembered the purser, "while I w-w-w-was taking Candy out to see a telescope out by the Cliff House and was pulling across the road to a space. I said, 'Ah, ha. There's no cops.' "

Carpenter crossed the double-yellow line. "No sooner had I pulled in than this cop pulls up. 'I told you so,' scolded Candy."

Officer McCann approached the vehicle and noticed a gold jacket on Carpenter with an *oly* label on the breast pocket. "I normally drink Olympia," said McCann as the two men momentarily discussed beer.

At approximately the same time Carpenter was getting a traffic ticket, hikers up on Mount Tamalpais were startled to hear an ear-piercing series of shrieks near the spot where Edda Kane had been shot. A dozen deputies, highway patrolmen, and rangers swarmed over the paths and searched for four hours until it began to get dark. Just before the sun went down a woman deputy walked in the area where the screams had originated. "Help me!" she shouted from ten different spots on the trail. Two deputies listened below and tried to pinpoint the spot of the original shrieks. Later they theorized the screams were those of someone practicing the martial arts.

7

Howenstein

Each hour the crimes on the trails remained unsolved added to the building public pressure for results. With the approaching election of 1982 there was a possibility that Howenstein might be replaced as sheriff of Marin County. On the wall of the San Rafael Civic Center briefly appeared black and orange posters that read: DUMP HOWENSTEIN. MAKE MARIN SAFE AGAIN. In addition, the sheriff's relationship with the press continued to worsen.

Precisely one year after the murder of Barbara Schwartz, a $2,500 reward was offered for information leading to the arrest and conviction of her killer. "We wanted to publicize the reward for a long time," said a spokesperson for Barbara's friends, "But the sheriff's department said no. Then finally they said to go ahead because they thought it might shake up the killer."

An intricate plan was conceived that entailed the sealing off of all traffic in and out of Marin County in ever widening circles the instant word was received of another Trailside attack. Gaddini, as spearhead of the task force, dubbed it Plan 555.

213

"Plan 555 was both Giddini's idea and a joint idea," Sergeant Rich Keaton told me. "We have had in Marin County a plan, 777, which is a system of roadblocks which would be initiated when there was an escape from San Quentin. Then they'd block off all the key arteries. We just changed the numbers and said why don't we umbrella that and make it even larger."

On September 30, 1980, Lieutenant Don Besse had been in a motorcycle accident which laid him up for sometime. When he returned to work he was amazed at the change in the sheriff's office. Before his accident he had been in charge of fourteen people. With the discovery that the same gun that had killed four people at Point Reyes had taken the life of Anne Alderson on the Sleeping Lady he was put in charge of thirty-two people in the search for what was now officially a serial killer. Besse was to oversee the investigation. Drawing upon his background in narcotics and intelligence divisions and his eleven years of management skills, he divided his officers into three groups: one to work witnesses, one to work suspects, and a third to work evidence.

Through sheer numbers the officers had overflowed into the other side of the records room and into a windowless, yellow room which they made their nerve center and named the *Barney Miller* room. Keaton told Besse that working there was like "living in a smoke-filled tunnel. So we had someone paint a picture of a window with an outside scene, which we hung on the wall." They placed boards across the desks to make more room, filled the hallway so that people coming to report crimes found only investigators looking for the Trailside Killer.

Around the corner and down the hall from the nerve center was a small coffee room, next to that an interview room, a conference room, and then Lieutenant Besse's office, which offered some privacy. Across from this was the get-together room where conferences were held and exhibits, such as the lone male hiker chart, were shown. These charts were constantly photographed and brought up-to-date.

"In November of 1980," Besse said to me in retrospect, "when we found the four bodies at Point Reyes and realized they had all been killed by the same gun, one that matched Alderson—that's when we knew for certain we had a serial killer. And because the four bodies were found on federal property that was concurrent with the jurisdiction of the FBI. But they didn't want any part of it. They told us, 'We'll give you anything you want as long as you take the case.' We dealt with the Santa Rosa office of the FBI, Mike Dooher, special agent in charge, and a fellow named Bob Tucker was our direct liaison.

"The FBI sent out a guy named Douglas from Quantico, Virginia, who was a specialist in serial murders. We had him a couple of times for several days each time. He'd come out and look over our reports and profiles. We also had four retired FBI agents working for us. Graham Dezvernine was one of the four. He had worked undercover for the FBI. We had something like thirty-two people at its peak. They sent me ten rookie FBI agents and they were the best ten agents sent by far because they were so hot to work homicide that they really did a good job. Along with rangers and volunteers we brought back some retired people with the department. One was a retired assistant coroner, Dick Fontaine, whose organization of the files had an impact on the case.

"We had around three hundred official suspects during the course of the investigations and there were several we really focused on. I've never been big on composites that are the result of a momentary glimpse. The killer was in a darkened area and the witness was coming out of a lighted area. She was horrified by what she saw, and from this they did their composite. Howenstein hung onto that composite like it was the best piece of evidence they ever had even though he was told many times by Rich Keaton, by me, others, that we shouldn't be depending on it.''

"We had all the call-ins being made,'' said Sergeant Keaton. "Husbands being reported by their wives, boyfriends by girlfriends—we had a little over four thousand male subjects identified to us as possibles for one reason or another. The only description we had which we really played down after the four people were killed was the Schwartz composite. At that time we still didn't know whether they [the Schwartz stabbing and the Point Reyes

murders] were tied in. I would say to some of the men,
'How do we know? How do *you* know who we're looking
for? What if we're looking for a woman or a black guy.
Don't get tunnel vision in thinking that this twenty-nine-
year-old male with a plaid shirt and a backpack is the
guy. And if in fact it is him, don't you think he's intelligent enough to change his clothing, his appearance?' I
tried to play down the original composite from the stabbing. It was unfortunate that of all the people calling in
the majority were calling based on this composite.''

In 1980 there had been an increase in the murder rate
in California of over 17 percent. A governor's spokesman
said, ''People think they can get away with murder. And
with other crime. And very often they do. There is a
wantonness about the crimes that are occurring. Some of
these are the most vicious cases you can imagine. They'd
turn your stomach. These smaller, rural areas may show
a great increase in crime, too.'' Santa Clara County
Sheriff Bob Winter agreed. ''What was a stable, rural
population is now seeing the impact of urbanization,'' he
said.

The sheriff's office collected, analyzed, and indexed all
the available information and, against a backdrop of pes-
simism, on March 14, 1981, Sheriff Howenstein unveiled
for the press his ''Mount Tam/Point Reyes Homicide Investigation Decision Model.'' It was an elaborate management system, it wasn't computerized. An investigator
told me later, ''It was all manual, index cards, flow
charts, file folders by the drawerful. Conceptually it was
good, but it caused us endless grief as we went along
because we had a good way to get all the stuff in but
there was no way to get the stuff out.''

The next step was a ''decision model system'' for
Phase II, which would process their names. Phase III
was to be a series of interviews, and Phase IV was to be
an investigation of the suspects, which would produce a
prime list of suspects—the distant Phase V. David Carpenter, with one of the worst records on the books, was
not in Howenstein's ''system management plan.''

''The essence of this investigation is collection and
retrieval capability,'' said Howenstein. ''It's broken down
into five phases—Phase I has been completed . . . a list

of 2,200 potential suspects have been prioritized into a prime list of 168 and a secondary list of 800." Each step of the program would bring the detectives to the next plateau, he said.

Though on relatively good terms with the electronic media, Howenstein was concerned about his "interface with the press." In 1980 the coroner of Marin County, Dr. Ervin Jindrich, at the request of the sheriff, had initiated a policy of sealing all autopsy data about any victim of an unsolved homicide, information that previously had been public and available to the press. Local papers went to court to gain access to the records, but on December 29, 1980, a Marin Superior Court judge ruled Dr. Jindrich has acted within the law. Was there something in the official reports that the sheriff was hiding? Had some blunder or blunders been made by the department? Howenstein felt that disclosing details could hamper his investigation.

The animosity between the sheriff and the journalist had dated back to the time the sheriff had told them *some* of Edda Kane's clothing had been taken by her attacker; he meant the killer had taken *all* of her clothing with the exception of one sock. The journalists had felt lied to. They believed that Howenstein had delayed crime reports, used bureaucratic language and computerese to dam the flow of information, and courted the electronic media to the exclusion of print reporters.

"The sheriff's trouble with the print media," Supervisor Gary Giacomini explained to me, "was his own doing, 'cause he'd now and then have these press conferences. It was like Nixon or Kissinger saying 'I can see the light at the end of the tunnel.' Howenstein made that mistake . . . 'In the next few days we'll have something good.' 'Next Wednesday, we're going to have a link.' Then the press was going crazy because he wasn't able to deliver on his promises. I don't blame him. The killer was a very brilliant madman, very brilliant, and he was operating on 200,000 acres. He could be behind any tree. What's Howenstein going to do? It's easy for those on the outside to fault those who are carrying on the investigation. I don't do that. I don't see any percentage in it . . .

unless there is some demonstrated incompetence, which I never felt.''

"The killer's much more clever, more manipulative than any one has ever suspected," I said.

"That's what I concluded," said Giacomini, "and that's why I'm not doing a number on Howenstein. My recollection is that as time went on he got absolutely hounded by the press.''

Immediately after the four bodies had been discovered in November of 1980 at Point Reyes the Trailside detective force had grown to thirty-two members, but by mid-March 1981, it had been reduced to nine. Howenstein, who had already received $40,834 in addition to his annual budget of $6.1 million, requested enough money to carry on the search for the killer another three months. The Board of Supervisors overwhelmingly approved $50,024 for this purpose.

"The supervisors don't control the investigations. We fund them. And we, of course, open the county treasury to them—whatever it is you need.'' Giacomini told me, "The budget grew a lot during the case. . . . We weren't about to say this cost too much. When Howenstein came to us we always said yes to resources. This killer was a very smart guy. They didn't have much to go on.''

Isolated, the sheriff continued to fight a losing battle against not only the media but an almost invisible killer who seemed unstoppable, uncatchable. Howenstein still placed a tremendous amount of faith in the five-phase program.*

---

*Campaigning as a ''new-era lawman'' Howenstein maintained that his long, frustrating search for the Trailside Killer was ''one of the most comprehensive, multijurisdictional investigations'' in law enforcement history. He was defeated in the Marin County election of November 2, 1982, by political unknown Charles ''Chuck'' Prandi by 45,713 votes to Howenstein's 42,938.

"The fact he was retired as sheriff didn't have anything to do with his handling of the Trailside Killer,'' Giacomini told me. ''He was, in a way, too sophisticated to be retained as an elected sheriff, too esoteric to retain the confidence of the rank-and-file law enforcement . . . I don't remember a hint about Trailside. No law enforcement guys around here were saying he should have done this or that 'cause *they* didn't know what to do.''

* * *

On March 11, 1981, Carpenter offered to help his friend Jeff Jackl move to a new apartment in San Leandro and set a date of March 29 for this although Jackl said he didn't need his help. The following day he quit his job at Gems of the Golden West and four days later started as a full-time employee at Econo Quick Print at 25673 Nickle Place, a new facility of the trade school where he had been trained in printing by computer.

One of the reasons for Carpenter's job change was that he had ideas for key chains that he considered million-dollar properties and he felt that if he developed them at Gems of the Golden West he would have to share profits with his bosses, Jack and Florence Neuman. "That particular one, the gay key-chain idea, I wanted to develop on my own," recalled Carpenter.

When Carpenter took the job at Gems he changed the conditions of his parole. This was a job *he* had arranged, and it loosened the reins of the federal probation office. Without warning, Carpenter was back at the printing school around young women and under fewer restrictions than before.

"After I quit, Jack and Florence asked specifically if I would s-s-s-still help them out—if I would come in and load the van for their first trip up to Yosemite. I also said I would come in to help with the accounting and things of that nature from time to time." He would help train Anita Ng as the new bookkeeper.

"Carpenter lent his bosses at the printing school some money," an official told me later, "two thousand to five thousand, to start some business on the side. Carpenter wrote them a letter that was very threatening, not in a necessarily physical way—he talks about the loan shark business and says if he doesn't get his money back by a certain day the clock gets turned on."

Carpenter was officially supposed to start his new job at the printing school on Monday, March 16, but came in on March 13, 14, and 15 to help on the construction of new office space and a new print shop. When he got off work the night of the 15th, Sunday, he called Reba twice concerning her stolen rugs. Carpenter went over to visit Reba.

Reba had been living in a home on Shelley Road in Mill Valley for the past two months doing light house-keeping in exchange for rent. Reba owned Tekke Carpets in Novato with a partner, Peter Saunders, who was also known as Peter Ware, where she cleaned, restored, and sold antique Oriental and Persian rugs. When Carpenter got there Reba was sitting in the living room. They had drinks. Victor St. Martin, an attorney and owner of the house, was in the adjoining dining room.

"Reba knew who had s-s-stolen her rugs," remembered Carpenter, "and wondered if I knew someone who could help her. I asked her, 'How much are you willing to pay to get them back?' That's where we ran into a difficulty. She didn't want to pay anything. I explained things don't work that way."

While the purser was in front of the fireplace, Reba said later, he took out a brown jeweler's-type briefcase with latches and buckles and displayed a gun. Because she was seeing the gun from a distance it seemed fore-shortened, she recalled. "Put it away!" snapped Reba. "I don't like guns. I really hate guns." She ran from the room. However, she later decided not to say anything to the police because Carpenter was on parole and she didn't want to get him in trouble.

Printing school records showed that on March 19 Carpenter had punched in at 8:27 A.M. and had lunch between 12:02 and 12:30 P.M. A checkout time of 2:15 P.M. was written in in pen. "I was working on the building," he claimed later, but almost a hundred miles away near Santa Cruz, at 4:15 in a redwoods park, a suspicious-looking man in a gold jacket was seen and remembered by a ranger.

As far as Carpenter was concerned his relationship with Candy Townsend was serious and she did nothing to dis-suade him from this view. They had a joint checking and savings accounts, but by the latter part of March Candy was beginning to have serious doubts about being able to stay with the older man.

Carpenter's old Chevy was burning gas. On March 25, a Wednesday, using a thousand dollars he had borrowed from his father, Elwood, the purser purchased a 1974

Fiat 124 four-door red sedan* from a man on Seventh Avenue for a total price of $1,175. Carpenter's niece's husband, Louie Bonfiglio, helped him look it over. Carpenter bought the car "as is" and found, he claimed, that the smog equipment had been removed and that there was a leak in the transmission. Carpenter left work early on March 27, 4:00 P.M. was written in by his boss on the time card. It was marked F.R., which meant Friday.

"On Saturday, March 28, I got out of bed at 6:30 A.M. and took the car out to Montgomery Ward in Daly City to get a s-s-smog certificate." Carpenter knew the garage opened at 7:30—first come, first served. "I got there at 7:15 and was number six in line. I came home," he recalled, "at 10:30 A.M. and took my father shopping. Then I went to Abbe's Clothing Store where I bought $49.45 of clothes and ended up at Gemco about the time the Fiat was ready."

While waiting for the smog equipment to be installed Carpenter and Candy, who had accompanied him on the return trip to Daly City, went to the Gemco Store in Colma to buy shoes.

Tammy Brinkley, who had been working in the Gemco sporting-goods section for over six years, noticed the woman with the long, dirty-blonde hair and the man wearing the green A's baseball cap because he was so much older-looking than his companion. The man picked a pair of Nike shoes, Electra-style, royal blue at the heel and with the trademark swoosh, gray at the back and white in the front. They had a distinctive Corsair-pattern tread, a "6-W" pattern. The blonde woman was holding a pair of Adidas with three gold diagonal stripes.

"Candy s-s-specifically wanted to buy a pair of running shoes," remembered Carpenter. "She was looking at a pair of Adidas. While we were there I noticed some Nike's on sale for $19.95. I thought that was a real good deal, so I purchased a pair for myself."

Candy and Carpenter brought their running shoes to the desk and Tammy added up the purchases. The Adidas shoes were $24.97, the men's size nine-and-one-half Nike's were $19.97. With the 6 percent sales tax the total

---

*VIN # 124 B 01494826, California license # 682 LYJ.

was $47.42. Later, this would be important. As Tammy checked the man's driver's license and initialed the check, number 613, she noticed it was a joint account for a man and a woman. Tammy handed the man in the green baseball cap the stapled bag containing both pairs of shoes and put the check into the bottom of the register.

Carpenter and Candy picked up the Fiat at 2:15 P.M., the purser later claimed. He put his new shoes in his blue backpack and left for Sussex Street. In the early evening, out at Henry Cowell Redwood Park near Santa Cruz, the Wilkinson family noticed a man in a gold jacket smoking. He was at the Felton Gas Station and 7-Eleven at the intersection of Graham Hill Road and Highway 9 to the north of the park.

The next day, Sunday, March 29, 1981, would be a fateful one.

PART THREE

THE FOREST

Mother is Nature
And I am just her child,
A sister of all her creatures.

My bed is a field
And its grasses my cousins,
I hear their flowers' Lullabies.

Love is in Nature
And I'm nestled in love,
For nature's my life and my soul.

Ellen Hansen
April 29, 1975

CARPENTER FAMILY HOME AT 38 SUSSEX STREET   1988 GRAYSMITH

1

Santa Cruz: Ellen and Steve

Ellen Marie Hansen had wanted to be a writer since age ten and had written enough poems to fill several volumes. The twenty-year-old sophomore at U.C. Davis often mentioned her philosophy of life to her mother, Marilyn, "Do *now*, what you want to in life." Ellen had been in the Outward Bound program, climbed in the High Sierras, and skydived during her freshman year at Berkeley. She had recently transferred to Davis, near Sacramento, where her father, Robert, was a professor of veterinary medicine. Ellen was majoring in sociology.

"But, at heart, Ellen wanted to be a writer," Marilyn Hansen told me later. "For a time she considered becoming an electrician because she heard they made money. She figured she could work twenty hours a week and then write the rest of the time.

"Ellen was very, very human, an open, loving individual. At the beginning of February 1981 I was between jobs, and while I was looking through the want ads I noticed a $269 budget flight to Hawaii. I said, 'Why, not.' As high-spirited and adventurous as my daughter was, she decided to go along with me on vacation. 'Take me along, Mom,' she said. 'I'm getting A's in everything. I'd rather go to Hawaii with you and get B's.' So Ellen studied on the beach in Hawaii and *still* aced her finals.''

At the time, Steven Russell Haertle, Ellen's boyfriend, couldn't go with Marilyn and Ellen because of his studies and work. Steve was a junior at Davis majoring in agricultural resources and managerial economics. Both he and Ellen had attended Davis High and both had been editors of the school paper. Always close friends, the couple had begun dating in the fall of 1980. "Steve," recalled Marilyn, "would just sit in our living room and grin from ear to ear. 'Stop smiling, Steve,' I would tell him. 'I can't help it,' he would tell me, 'I'm just so happy.' ''

Because Steve had missed out on the trip to Hawaii, he and Ellen made plans to go hiking at Henry Cowell Redwoods State Park in Santa Cruz at the end of March. Steve had to be back at work by Monday in time to register for the new quarter, and so the weekend of March 28 and March 29 would serve as his entire vacation.

"I had suggested Santa Cruz," Marilyn told me, "and I was even going to go along. But whereas I could only point out various plants and trees and shrubs, Ellen knew the scientific names for each. She was going to be Steve's guide on his first camping trip ever. In the end, though, I was unable to go.''

On March 28, 1981, during the college quarter break, Ellen and Steve drove from Davis down Highway 17, through the mountains just north of Santa Cruz and eighty miles to the south of San Francisco. Because Ellen was driving her father's car—he had been on sabbatical leave in West Germany—she was being, as her mother put it, "super careful about driving it." They passed through Scotts Valley and the thirty-three-acre wooded community of Santa's Village. Santa's workshop was open for kids, as it was most of the year.

In an eighty-mile swath, neatly sliced by the San Andreas Fault, from San Bruno Mountain to the Pajaro River, is the low-lying Santa Cruz mountain range. At the southwest tip of the range, a few miles from Santa Cruz, is Henry Cowell Redwoods State Park, which is made up of two units, the steep, rough Fall Creek unit, northwest of the Felton-Empire Road, and a more gentle section of river, redwoods, ridges, and canyons just south of Felton, where Ellen and Steve were headed.

Although it was technically the rainy season and would be until May, it was a beautiful day, "a clear, cool, sunny day," as Steve recalled. They followed Mt. Hermon Road, turned left onto Highway 9 at the northwest end of the 1,800-acre park, and went directly to the ranger station to get maps and make arrangements for an overnight campsite. It was 11:00 A.M. Just south of the park's concession area were the oldest and largest redwoods: The Neckbreaker, The Fremont, and The Giant, 285 feet high and over 51 feet in circumference. They pitched a tent at the campgrounds.

Afterward Ellen and Steve drove into seaside Santa Cruz itself at the north end of Monterey Bay to see the boardwalk. From far off, they could see the 1923 "Giant Dipper" roller coaster, which dominates the boardwalk. Far across the lot where they parked their car was an ancient penny arcade: shooting galleries, claw machines, quick draw and air hockey games, and the newer electronic video games.

Outside was a Ferris wheel, and several booths away, a beautifully constructed antique merry-go-round with sixty-two hand-carved horses and two Roman chariots. About twenty steps down from the boardwalk was a mile-long beach that ran the length of the boardwalk and on to the mouth of the San Lorenzo River. In the distance Steve could see the Municipal Wharf that stretched one-half mile seaward to a bandstand.

Steve put a quarter in a telescope and for a while the couple watched the trim sailboats and orderly rows of waves. The sky above them was of the most biting cerulean blue and the colored cars of the overhead tramway—acid yellow, bright pink, pale greens, and sparkling whites moved unendingly across it. Carnival flags stood straight out in the wind.

Ellen and Steve took another look at the rides and ultimately decided against them, returned to Ellen's car, and discovered they were locked out. The keys were still in the ignition. Steve called a locksmith from Dave's Lock and Key, and the man arrived and quickly opened their door. They then drove out Pacific Avenue, in bumper-to-bumper traffic, looking at the tree-shrouded malls of restaurants and craft shops, the white Victorians on hilly streets and the glitzy neon of the beach motels. They arrived back at their campsite at 5:00 P.M.

That night Steve and Ellen slept on the ground of Graham Hill, which can accommodate twenty-four-foot trailers and thirty-one-foot motor homes and is enclosed in a stand of ponderosa pines on the extreme edge of the fifteen miles of hiking and riding trails in Henry Cowell Park.

The next morning, Sunday, March 29, they got up at 9:00 A.M., and after Steve took a walk by himself on Ridge Trail they drove to Monterey to check out the wharf, leaving at 11:05 A.M., and then stopped at Aptos. By the pier Steve took a snapshot of Ellen in her purple sweatshirt. But because Ellen was having her period and feeling ill, they started back to the campsite, arriving at 2:00 P.M. Steven and Ellen looked around the Graham Hill campground. There were almost ninety campers spread out in the pleasant meadow. The couple decided to take a leisurely nap and lay down on the cool green grass.

2

The Golden Man

When the couple awoke later, about 4:15 P.M.,
the site was almost deserted and a blue mist had begun
to seep into the hollow. Roaring Camp Railroad runs
alongside the park, and in the distance Ellen could hear
a plaintive train whistle. In the beclouded atmosphere
everything seemed dreamlike to them. Whether they were
drowsy from their short afternoon nap or from the meal
they had eaten in Monterey—they were having trouble
waking up. Ellen and Steve agreed to take one last walk
before packing their belongings for the homeward trip.
Steve put on his blue down vest and red Stanford sweatshirt. They left the sheltered grove by way of Pine Trail
and walked south to where it intersected the popular
Ridge Trail.

Ellen and her friend climbed to the redwood observation deck on a water tank at the highest point of Ridge
Trail, an elevation of seven hundred feet, overlooking not
only the park, but Santa Cruz Beach, where they had
been the day before. In the distance was Monterey. They
consulted their map.

Ellen's spirits lifted when she saw the scenery, and

things began to seem a little less unreal. Fueled by the invigorating sea air, the pair decided to go for a walk to Cathedral Grove, a ring of trees growing from a solitary base. Ellen was a seasoned hiker, and found the narrow trail easy going. The center of the path was filled with sand in most places, so Ellen and Steve trudged opposite each other and on the extreme edges of the trail, where the ground was firmer.

As they reached a point where the trail began to slope downward, about one-eighth of a mile from the observation deck, the walking became easier. Cowell Park was, on the whole, an easy area to hike. Far off Steve and Ellen could hear faint shuffling steps, and then heavy breathing and cursing. Finally over the crest of a hill came another hiker. He was wearing a green cap like the ones tractor companies or ballplayers wear. His mouth was open and he was perspiring a little. From the black straps visible Steve made out the stranger had a backpack. The glasses he wore were dark glasses.

Steve could see right away that the man wasn't an experienced hiker, for he was out of breath. The man was wearing a gold jacket, reading a map while he was walking, and passed between the students. Momentarily the three exchanged glances, smiled, and then broke eye contact. They were five hundred yards from the observation deck. No words were spoken as the older stranger passed on his way in the direction of the deck.

Ellen and Steve looked up at the thick umbrella of foliage. This canopy reduced the direct sun to darting and transitory shafts of light that penetrated to the moist, dark woodland floor and permitted only a thin undergrowth of fern at the base of each tree.

Ellen and Steve pressed on and at the intersection with the Pipeline Road met a woman in curlers accompanied by a bald man eccentrically dressed in a woman's blood-red housecoat. As they reached the end of the path they laughed at what they had seen.

The length of Ridge Trail, from dark forest to sunny ridges, took two hours as a rule to hike, but the young people were only going as far as Rincon Trail, which would take them to Cathedral Grove. It had taken them twenty-five minutes from the observation deck to the

(RIGHT) *Roberta Patterson (left) and her children, Shelby Lynne and Robert Dwayne, February 15, 1955, preparing to leave for Japan on the freighter* Fleetwood. (COURTESY OF DOUGLAS AND SHELBY LYNNE SMITH)

(BELOW) *David Carpenter recovering from bullet wounds at Letterman Hospital on San Francisco's Presidio after his arrest. July 25, 1960.* (UNPUBLISHED *SAN FRANCISCO CHRONICLE* PHOTO)

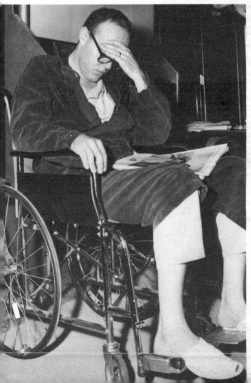

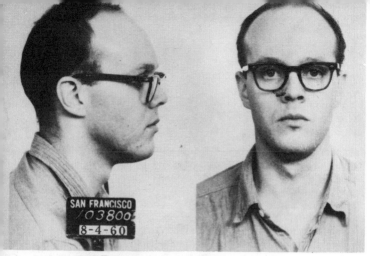

(ABOVE) *David Carpenter August 4, 1960, police photos.*

(OPPOSITE) *David Carpenter August 30, 1976, police photos.*

(BELOW) Fleetwood *purser David J. Carpenter's autograph in Roberta Patterson's daughter's scrapbook.*

(ABOVE) *Marin County
Sheriff Al Howenstein.*
(RIGHT) *Captain Bob
Gaddini.* (COURTESY OF
MARTHA GADDINI AND
FAMILY)

(LEFT) *Police composite of the Trailside Killer. November 30, 1980.*

(ABOVE) *Trailside suspect Mark McDermand.*

(CLOCKWISE FROM BELOW) *Marin County investigators and coroner's department bringing the body of Anne Alderson down from The Sleeping Lady. October 15, 1980.* (FRED LARSON/SAN FRANCISCO CHRONICLE) *Rick Stowers, Point Reyes victim.* (COURTESY OF JOYCE AND JERRY STOWERS) *Cindy Moreland, Point Reyes victim. Anne Alderson, Mount Tamalpais victim.*

(LEFT) *Diane O'Connell, Point Reyes victim.*

(RIGHT) *Ellen Hansen, Santa Cruz/Henry Cowell State Park victim.* (BELOW) *The last photograph taken of Ellen Hansen. It was in her camera, undeveloped, at the time of her death.* (PHOTOS COURTESY OF MARILYN HANSEN)

MISSING PERSON

DATE: Reported missing Sunday 12-28-80
Daly City case # 80-11911

MISSING
PERSON: MENJIVAR, Anna, Kelly, Latin Female Juvenile, DOB 06-19-63
5'-2" 110 lbs, very slim, Black shoulder length hair, Brown
eyes, has a mole on right arm, where it joins the shoulder,
26" waist, bra size 34B, shoe size 6½, no identification
in possession.

CLOTHING: White sweater, white blouse, blue jeans, white Converse tennis
shoes: Also missing from residence: Blue "farmer type" overalls
and a small brown leather-like purse.

JEWELRY: Gold colored Crucifix type cross, approximatley 1" in size, with
a gold colored chain.

OTHER
INFORMATION: NO marks, scars or tattoo's, no missing organs, has never broken
any bones. Blood type and fingerprint classification unknown.
Dental records available

Anna Kelly Menjivar, Santa Cruz/Castle Rock Park victim.

(ABOVE) *Heather Scaggs, Santa Cruz/Big Basin Redwoods Park victim.* (RIGHT) *Shane Williams*

(ABOVE) *(left to right) Sergeant Ken Womack, San Jose Police Department, Inspector Stoney Brook of the Santa Cruz District Attorney's Office, and Detective Walt Robinson, San Jose Police Department, at the San Diego Trial, 1988.* (BELOW) *The home of David, Elwood, and Frances Carpenter at 38 Sussex Street, San Francisco.*

(ABOVE) *May 15, 1981, 7:11 A.M. In the first of a series of FBI surveillance photos, published here for the first time, the exact moments of David Carpenter's arrest are captured. Carpenter, on his way to work, leaves his first-floor studio and starts for his car.* (BELOW) *Santa Cruz detective Stoney Brook extends his hand toward Carpenter as he introduces himself. "Mr. Carpenter, my name is Stoney Brook and I've been waiting to meet you." Brook's aim was to keep the suspect's hands away from the plastic shopping bag, which he suspected contained a gun. "What's in the bag, Mr. Carpenter?" Brook asked.*

(ABOVE) *Marin County Police Sergeant Rich Keaton attempts to develop communication with Carpenter, and in the course of the conversation the suspect says, "That sounds a lot like m-m-m-murder, a capital case."* (BELOW) *After shaking his finger at the detectives, Carpenter folds his arms and says, "I'm not talking to you anymore. I have nothing more to say."*

(OPPOSITE TOP) *As Keaton moves Carpenter against the wall to frisk him, the purser whispers to him, "Please don't hurt me. I've always been a model inmate." Brook now has the bag, which contains only Wagner records.* (OPPOSITE) *Carpenter turns as the other members of the Trailside task force leave their cars. The plastic shoebag now rests against the left of the garage door at 36 Sussex Street.* (ABOVE) *Other members of the task force pass as Keaton prepares to cuff Carpenter. Carpenter is subdued, his legs spread wide.*

Cuffed, Carpenter, as he turns to be led away, fixes his gaze on the hidden camera, now revealed, in the white van across the street.
(EXCLUSIVE FBI PHOTOS COURTESY OF THE MARIN COUNTY SHERIFF'S DEPARTMENT)

grove. On arrival they played for a while in the shady clearing and then looked around Cathedral Grove proper and at the six-hundred-year-old redwoods, firescarred, moist-cored, heavily armored, huddling closely together, each massive trunk shielding the other from winter's fierce rains and gales. The grove was given its name because the redwood trees gave it the feeling of a Gothic church. Point Reyes has a similar cathedral-like peacefulness.

Back at the observation deck forty-five-year-old Leland Fritz, a Fresno florist, and his sixteen-year-old son, Ken, were looking out over the trails after hiking and spending the night at the campground. They noticed a man in a bright gold-yellow jacket wandering around the deck aimlessly. The stranger plopped down, looked over the railing from the top of the stairs, and began to scan the trails. While the other campers and hikers were viewing Monterey Bay this man was searching the paths for something else. Ken talked to the stranger about how beautiful the park was for about ten minutes. The boy later described the man on the deck "like someone who was ready to go to sleep, dreamy. He weighed about a hundred and seventy-five pounds, was between fifty and sixty years of age, balding, and wearing glasses with dark frames."

The elder Fritz also spoke to the man. "How about joining my son and me in a hike down to the river?" The San Lorenzo River cut through the park.

"No thanks. I'm getting too old for this and my bones ache," joked the stranger, and then to Ken: "I'm feeling a little stiff, getting too old." Leland Fritz noticed the stranger spoke slowly and carefully. It reminded him of a young stutterer he had known.

The man now seemed suddenly alert and, ignoring Ken, went to the edge of the deck where he could see Ridge Trail to the southwest. Its length was easily visible because it was lined with low, thick pines growing no more than six to eight feet high. There were widely spread gaps between the clusters of trees, and a clearing covered with a canopy of tree branches revealed portions of the trail over three hundred yards in the distance. From

where he stood the stranger had a completely unob-
structed view of a large section of Ridge Trail, could
effortlessly see left and right on the path, and hear the
slightest sounds, which carried easily over the sandy path.

Steve and Ellen, after only ten to fifteen minutes at the
grove itself, retraced their steps toward the observation
deck. About four hundred yards from the deck uptrail
they were at the levelest portion of Ridge Trail, at a turn
in the path. After this came a slight rise and then a dip,
which would hide anyone approaching them from the
east. From a point behind them they could see both the
roller coaster and the city of Santa Cruz. They stopped
at two points to see the boardwalk in the distance. It was
when they looked uptrail again that they saw, near a dead
pine, an apparition on the path.

Coming down the trail was a man: gold gleamed and
glinted from his figure. A gust of wind preceded him, a
tiny breath that rolled and tumbled along the narrow path
and caressed Ellen's cheek. The man hadn't seemed to
be standing or waiting for them. He was just there, Steve
recalled.

It was as if a little piece of the sun had come to earth
and been gathered up in the folds and metal snaps of the
man's jacket. It was not so much that the man himself
was bright, but that the background around him was an
amalgam of contrasting dimness and blue twilight. The
strange individual was in such a position that he caught
the sunlight and like a mirror reflected it back into their
eyes.

Fascinated, they watched the figure walking down the
center of the path, moving between the tall weeds that
lined the trail. The hotness and stillness of the approaching evening oppressed Steve and Ellen.

All this time the students and the yellow-gold figure
had continued to approach one another. Ellen on the right
side of the trail, Steve on the left. Details of the man's
face had been momentarily burned out by the glare, but
now the students recognized the phantasmal image as the
out-of-shape man in the golden jacket who had passed
them fifty minutes earlier.

"Oh, I see we run into each other again," said the man.

Ellen and Steve laughed at this.

But as they watched, the stranger reached under his golden jacket and into the left waistband of his bell-bottomed Levi's. His hands, Steven noted, were extraordinarily white and clean. No jewelry. Now, why did they seem so clean? Of course, he realized, it could have been the light, but it seemed they had not a single hair upon them. Abruptly the clean, white hand reappeared, but now the tapering fingers were holding a black-barreled revolver with a brown handle. A cheap gun. Steve could actually see the bullets in the weapon. They were gray bullets.

Steve noticed something odd about the way the stranger held the gun in his right hand. He had placed his thumb between the cocked hammer and the firing pin so that if it did fall the hammer would strike his thumb and not the cartridge case, a method known as single-action procedure and something most professionals avoid when handling weapons.

"If you don't want to get hurt," said the man in gold, "do what I say—put your hands on your head and you won't get hurt."

Steve put his hands up saying, "Stay away, Ellen, he's got a gun."

"I want you to come into the bushes," said the man.

Steve was later asked why he continued to walk toward the stranger after he pulled a gun. "It wasn't believable. You didn't know what to make of it. . . . I was thinking I was going to die. I was thinking I had to remember what this man looked like if I didn't die. I made notes in my head. . . . I thought I was going to die but I wanted to remember as much about him as possible. . . . I noticed his bottom teeth were yellow and they were crooked."

"I don't want to have to get nasty," warned the stranger.

Steve's hand moved to his back pocket, felt for his billfold and came up without the wallet. It was back at the tent. The stranger waved the weapon downward in a quick gesture. "I thought we were being robbed," recalled Steve, "and I had put up my hands but then he told us to put them down."

"I don't want any money. I want something else. You know what I mean. All I want to do is rape her," said the man. He gestured with his gun to his right.

Steve was thinking. "I saw the man's face. I remember his eyes were wide open, his eyebrows really arched. . . . He was fair-skinned, his hair short and jagged at the back. His nostrils were flared. His speech was terse and angry—just orders and commands. They were never very long sentences."

The couple and the stranger had reached a distance of about four and one-half feet from each other. Now the choreography started to change. The gunman was trying to get them off the trail back in the direction from which they had just come. Ellen began to move from side to side, bobbing like a lightweight. She was defiant. Her perky face followed the movements of the gun's muzzle, which followed her own motion. Steve and Ellen were touching. Steve began to back up and for a second so did the golden man. While motioning for them to follow him into the bushes the stranger gestured not only with his gun and body but with his eyes.

"No, I won't let you," Ellen cried out. "Don't listen to him, Steve, because he's going to shoot us anyway. Don't listen to him!" Ellen approached the gunman, hands outstretched as if to grab the gun.

"Go down the trail," said the man. "Do what I say. Do what I say. I just want to rape her." The man kept looking back at the observation deck and back uptrail.

"I begged with the man to let us go," Steve told the police later. "That we would not say anything if he'd just let us go."

Steve was back-pedaling now, turning his head to look behind him over his left shoulder and then looking back at the gun. Now he was walking backward and looking forward and abruptly he felt the edge of the narrow path crumbling under his foot. "I looked over my left shoulder to see what was behind me," Steve recalled. "I looked back at Ellen [as she stepped between Steve and the gun]. I looked again over my left shoulder and then

I heard the shooting." As Steve whirled he lost his balance on the trail's berm.

"I heard two shots," he told police later, "and then I felt like somebody hit my neck with a sledge hammer, just walloped me on my neck. Felt like my arm went from my side up above my head. I remember falling to the ground with a buzzing sensation in my arm and everything was slowing down."

What had happened was that the stranger in the gold jacket had fired two shots at Ellen and then a single shot at Steve. The bullet tore through Steve's neck, cut the main artery in his right arm, and ended up in the sternum, two inches from his heart. As he felt the blow to his neck Steve dropped to the ground and briefly lost consciousness. Far, far away he could hear what he thought were other shots, but spaced apart. One of them may have been a shot fired at Steve that went wild. The people back on the observation deck could hear them too because sound traveled so easily along Ridge Trail. Altogether the hikers on the deck heard four shots. Then perhaps came a fifth, or it may have been only an echo.

Steve was unconscious for under a minute. When came to he felt himself bleeding and fought to lift his head. When he had succeeded at this, he opened his eyes and looked over at Ellen some inches away to see if she was all right.

"I was lying on the ground, facedown, next to Ellen. I looked down and saw Ellen there. I picked up Ellen's head and saw she was bleeding, and it looked like she had been shot in the back, and then I looked up to see the man who shot us across the trail with his back toward us," recalled Steve.

Ellen's head was floating in a pool of blood and Steve tried to move her away from the puddle, getting blood all over himself. "Then I realized she was dead," he said afterward, "and I said, 'Oh, Ellen.'" Everything was out of focus but Steve could make out some lettering on the back of the gold jacket, though his wound made it difficult to read. "And I looked across the trail, saw the man who shot us, and I got to my feet and started walking and then running up the trail as fast as I could."

Swaying dizzily, Steve forced himself to his feet and

careened uptrail toward the observation deck, stumbling
through clumps of chaparral until he reached two hikers,
Lee Fritz and his son, Ken. Five to eight minutes after
the man in the bright yellow-gold jacket had left the deck
and started downtrail they had heard what they thought
were four or five shots and had gone to investigate. With
open mouths they surveyed the bleeding, shambling figure holding his neck lurching toward them. Fritz moved
to place himself between his son and the horrifying figure. The wounded man spoke:

"I've been shot. My girlfriend's been shot. There's a
man down there and now he's raping another woman,"
Steve said hysterically. He had begun to hallucinate from
his terror and his pain. Finally Lee Fritz was able to calm
Steve down enough for him to be able to explain about
the attack.

"He told us," recalled Fritz, "that he and his girlfriend had been shot and that he thought that she was
dead. He told us the gunman was wearing a gold jacket."
Fritz sent his son for help at the front of the park and
headed with Steve, who was staggering, uptrail to the
observation deck.

Bob Rearden, who lived on the campground, saw Steve
next. "I was just sitting here around four o'clock when
I heard four or five shots. Then I seen two guys come
running down the hill. They were yelling about some guy
getting shot and calling the police. Then the guy that got
shot came running. He said, 'Help me!,' and I thought
he was kidding until I saw the blood everywhere. I'll
never forget what he said after that. He said, 'I've been
shot and he killed my girlfriend.' "

Rearden ran to scatter the other campers out of the area
to safety. He started up the trail to see if the girl was
really dead, but he stopped short after realizing the killer
might still be up there.

Steve weaved on with Fritz toward the deck. On the
way he met a man and a woman, Fred Morse and Maureen Thorpe, who steadied the young man and helped
him to a redwood picnic table. Morse lay Steve down on
the table and then went to see how Ellen was. As he ran
downtrail he passed a nondescript man in a gold jacket.
Maureen, a certified emergency room nurse began look-

ing after Steve's wound, which was in his right shoulder near his neck.

"The wound," Maureen recalled, "was just a hole with a little blood. I always thought that if you got shot there would be a hole with blood spurting all over, but it wasn't like that. He kept saying that his girlfriend, 'his dear Ellen,' had been shot farther up the trail and that he just knew she was dead."

After a minute or so Maureen heard the sound of footsteps as they crushed against dry weeds. Steve, with great effort, turned his head to look over his left shoulder. His eyes widened.

Horrified, Steve pointed at the stranger who was moving casually toward him, looking straight ahead, toward the picnic table across from the observation deck. "I stood on my feet," recalled Steve later. "I said, 'Lady, that's the man that shot me. Run! Get the hell out of here!'" Mrs. Thorpe saw a man walk calmly by the table. Later she would not remember any yellow-gold jacket on the older man.

Fred Morse had found Ellen in the bushes by the trail, and Maureen joined him to help her. Maureen felt a very weak pulse in the girl, but was probably feeling her own heartbeat from the run up the hill. Fred and Maureen placed their jackets over Ellen. "I checked for a pulse a couple of minutes later," recalled Maureen, "and there wasn't one." Shaken, Thorpe and Morse waited for help to arrive.

Steve ran as fast as he was able to their campground, where he collapsed. Up until this point no one had stopped his staggering run because people were so panicked they had no idea what to do. Taken to the parking lot by a man and woman, Steve was put in the back of a camper's van. Fritz and his son stopped the van for a few seconds and then Steve was rushed to the hospital. Meanwhile, as the older man barreled over Ridge Trail, his path crossed that of Lee Fritz and his son, Ken. The man in gold hesitated, then ran. As Fritz watched the man scrambling over the trail he realized it was the man from the observation deck he had spoken with earlier.

There was speculation the attacker was heading for the No-Name Trail, an almost impassable animal trail, in order to cut over to the Powder Mill Trail and get around them. Fritz had told the people in the van to get Steve to the hospital and to get the cops. Fritz rushed for the phone by the kiosk in the parking lot at the trailhead and was calling the police when he saw the man yet again, dashing for his little red car. Behind the wheel, the man ripped off his glasses, gunned the engine, and leaned into the horn. The car's wheels spun on a patch of loose gravel, gaining and losing control and traction for a moment. A cloud of dust billowed behind the escaping man. Near the entrance to the lot was the phone where Lee Fritz was dialing for help. He saw a four-door red car roaring in his direction.

"It was a foreign boxy-type red car," remembered Fritz. "Something about the rearview mirror caught my eye . . . it was extralarge for the car. The face and the mirror were all together when I saw it. . . . He had turned and we stared at each other eye to eye . . . it was like our eyes met . . . the car was in view for five to seven seconds as it drove past me. The driver was the same man I saw walk down the trail. I cried, 'There goes the person I think committed the crime.' "

The sound of the horn filled his ears, the red car's wheels spun for a second, smoke rose, pebbles and rocks shot up behind the auto, and with a blast of exhaust the car shot by Fritz and in a moment all the hiker could hear was the faint squeal of tires and the bleeting of a horn. The fleeing man was rising now toward the rock-lined road that led out of the park.

A twelve-year-old girl, Melissa, was playing in a cul-de-sac near the park and saw a red car driving right up into the cul-de-sac. The driver had apparently made a wrong turn; the driver had turned a block too soon and was trying to find his way out. Melissa could see him through the window, a balding perspiring man.

The way out was steep. Now the killer found the exit; there was no one in sight. Long shafts of the setting sun cast shadows ahead of him as he passed out of the park, spun off Graham Hill Road onto Lockwood Lane. He roared onto Highway 17, and as he sped on he passed Roberta Patterson's house.

At 5:32 P.M. Deputy Sheriff Larry Holtzclaw, patrol car no. 22, was at the intersection of Graham Hill Road and Highway 9, two miles north of the observation deck, when he heard the first radio call for help. Deputy Jim Johnson in car no. 21 was nearby and received the identical broadcast: "There's been a shooting in the park. Someone's on the way to the hospital. Another is still on the trail." Other officers from the Santa Cruz sheriff's office had already been dispatched to the hospital to meet the camper carrying Steve. Deputy Dennis Smith saw that Haertle "was in shock, trembling, and distraught." While Johnson searched along Graham Hill Road for the assailant, Holtzclaw was pulling into the little lot near the ranger shack. He saw Lee Fritz and motioned for him to get in beside him and explain what he had seen. Two minutes later the officer and witness had driven the quarter mile to the beginning of Ridge Trail, parked, and with two paramedics and three fire-rescue personnel had gone downtrail to the crime scene.

As the group moved west they met Fred Morse and Maureen Thorpe. Holtzclaw cautioned all the witnesses not to share their impressions with one another. "It was very quiet," he said later. "I didn't want anyone talking because of the way sounds carried on the trail."

When the group reached the crime scene Holtzclaw motioned all of the witnesses off the trail so they wouldn't contaminate the footprint evidence. "Stay back," the deputy hissed. He consulted his watch. The walk had taken five and a half minutes. Holtzclaw saw that Ellen was in a fetal position and bent down to check for vital signs. He felt her neck but there was no pulse, so he notified the sheriff's office by portable radio to send coroner John Mason to the scene.

Holtzclaw began taking statements from the four witnesses, pulling each aside some ten to fifteen yards away out of earshot while he wrote down all the descriptions—"gray, thin hair, five foot ten, 160 pounds, blue Levi's, yellow jacket, green cap, white Nike shoes with dark stripe, blue nylon backpack, red or green foreign car, Toyota or Datsun." It was Ken Fritz who was certain about the word MONTANA on the jacket and the type of shoes. The father, Lee, told Holtzclaw that the man on

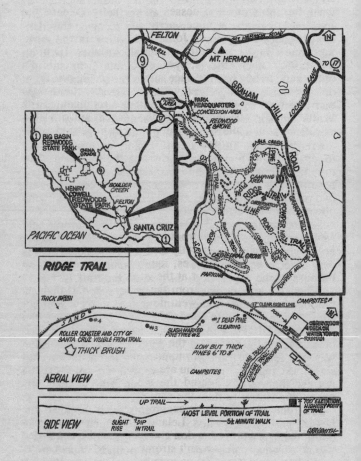

THE COULTER MAP

FELTON

MT. HERMON ROAD

CAR TRAIL

9

MT. HERMON

GRAHAM HILL ROAD

LOCKWOOD LANE

TO 17

17

YOUTH AREA

PARK HEADQUARTERS
CONCESSION AREA

REDWOOD GROVE

1

BIG BASIN REDWOODS STATE PARK

CHINA GRADE

BOULDER CREEK

HENRY COWELL REDWOODS STATE PARK

FELTON

SANTA CRUZ

1

PACIFIC OCEAN

RIVER TRAIL

SPRING CREEK

PINE TRAIL

CAMPING AREA

PINE RIDGE

OBSERVATION LINE

RIDGE FIRE TRAIL

POWDER MILL

GRAHAM HILL ROAD

OX TRAIL

S.P.R.R.

CATHEDRAL GROVE

PARKING

POWDER MILL

RIDGE TRAIL

THICK BRUSH

SAND

#4

#3

ROLLER COASTER AND CITY OF SANTA CRUZ VISIBLE FROM TRAIL

THICK BRUSH

SLASH-MARKED PINE TREE #2

#1 DEAD PINE CLEARING

LOW BUT THICK PINES 6' TO 8'

37" CLEAR SIGHT LINE

CAMPSITES

POOL

OBSERVATION DECK OR WATER TOWER FOUNTAIN

NO-NAME TRAIL (ALMOST IMPASSABLE)

PICNIC TABLE

AERIAL VIEW

CAMPSITES

SIDE VIEW

UP TRAIL

MOST LEVEL PORTION OF TRAIL

5½ MINUTE WALK

SLIGHT RISE

DIP IN TRAIL

700' ELEVATION HIGHEST POINT OF TRAIL

GEO SMITH

the observation deck seemed "weird, strange, quiet."
Holtzclaw stayed with the witnesses until 6:30 P.M. interviewing them.

At this point the witnesses were transported to the
Santa Cruz sheriff's office, arriving at 7:00. Detective
Joe Henard was asked by Johnson to go interview Mrs.
Thorpe. They worked with a Smith & Wesson ID composite kit, assorted noses, eyes, and mouths on celluloid
that could be fitted over face shapes also on celluloid.
Three other officers worked with the remaining witnesses
as Officer Stoney Brook took Lee Fritz's statement. Fritz
at first thought the lettering on the jacket said OLYMPIA
CHAMPION BEER DRINKER. He was certain it said MONTANA across the bottom.

Detective Sergeant Charles Stoney Brook, with fourteen years' experience with crimes against persons, later
told me how he began to organize the search for a suspect: "There were a number of witnesses in the park that
day. There was Leland Fritz and his son, Ken, and of
course Fred Morse and Maureen Thorpe. Morse and
Thorpe later married." Brook's investigative philosophy
was this: "I didn't go directly to the scene. My approach
is that we had the witnesses, the victim's on his way to
the hospital, the guy's not at the scene—so my idea is to
get as much as you can from the witnesses and then go
backward to the killer. I went down to the office and got
the witnesses separated and I had each officer assigned
to interview one person.

"We took them through the whole story. We had each
officer do an Identi-Kit composite after completing the
interview with them. As you are aware, Robert, everyone
sees things differently and the things that register the
strongest are not always the same. A kid sees it differently from the father, for example. So we took all the
composites and it seems Leland Fritz's was the most
solid, most committed. I don't want that to be construed
that the other people weren't strong; they were. But when
I put everything they told us together it came out looking
a lot like Fritz's man."

Dr. Richard Thomas Mason, the county coroner and forensic pathologist, a sturdy, balding, ex-army officer who had served two years as a doctor in Vietnam, was notified of the killing by John Stremitas at 7:00 P.M. and asked to view the body. At the scene Sergeant Jim Morris filled him in on what had happened. Ellen was lying on her right shoulder, where a quantity of blood had gathered, and Dr. Mason could see there was a gunshot wound on the left side as well. Deputy DA Jim Berglund stood nearby.

"Because of the cold night air," the pathologist was asked, "would it be all right to leave the victim there overnight so that the odd-patterned shoe tracks, and any other shoe tracks, would remain undisturbed?" Mason agreed, on the provision that the body be straightened out so that rigor would not lock it into a fetal position, making an autopsy difficult.

At 7:55 P.M., in San Francisco, David Carpenter drove off the freeway and went directly to Jeff Jackl's house. At the beginning of March, Carpenter had offered to help his tall, dark-bearded friend move from his Page Street address to the East Bay. At the time Jackl hadn't taken him seriously and so was surprised when the purser showed up in his battered Chevy, which the two of them often used, and offered to transport his belongings. "I didn't expect him to be there," Jackl recalled. "I insisted I didn't need his help. My friend Terry was helping me. He had a pickup."

Rebuffed by Jackl, Carpenter went directly to a telephone. At 8:00 P.M. he called Reba Lehman, Nation Meyer's girlfriend, at her home in Mill Valley. "When Carpenter called he was very excited," she said later, "very hyped up. He wanted to come over, was really insistent about it, but I told him not to. He wasn't very pleased. He had come over two or three times previously, but I never really liked him."

Reba Lehman tossed and turned in her bed that night because of Carpenter's odd call. Even though she had declined his visit, the purser showed up early at her home in his new red Fiat on the morning of March 30.

Once inside her house, Carpenter said, "I've got an idea about m-m-making some m-m-money and getting your rugs back." Though she was his friend's girl he asked her to perform oral sex on him, but Reba refused.

"I have connections I met in prison. In Sacramento," he said. "I'm going to distribute drugs, cocaine, in Sacramento. These are the same friends who can find your rugs and get them back."

"I don't believe you," said Reba.

"I tell you I'm going to make a deal with organized crime to get the rugs back all in one fell swoop." Carpenter told her his Fiat was not working and that he needed to borrow her BMW* for the day so that he could make the trip to Sacramento. Reba must have wondered at times if the purser himself were behind the thefts.

Carpenter was lying to her. He later claimed, "I was really going to Sacramento to discuss my key-chain proposal and I wanted to look as prosperous as p-p-p-possible. I really only wanted to borrow her BMW. 'Is this in relationship to getting my rugs back?' she asked me. 'Absolutely,' I lied."

Through her huge picture window Reba could see Carpenter, thirty-five feet away on the other side of the street, removing a blue gym bag, clothing, and other articles she wasn't certain of from the Fiat trunk, walking to the cream-colored BMW, and putting them in the trunk of that car. After transferring his things, Carpenter left to keep his 2:30 P.M. date with Richard Wood at the Federal Building on Golden Gate Avenue.

"I returned to San Francisco," said Carpenter, "went to the bank, dropped off my [February] parole report, and missed w-w-work." When Carpenter showed up at Wood's office, the parole agent thought this was peculiar. "It was the only time he had ever dropped off the monthly report in person."

At the same time Carpenter was delivering his report to Wood, 2:30 P.M., Monday, March 30, the day after the attack on Ridge Trail, Dr. Mason was performing an autopsy on the victim, Ellen Hansen. The pathologist noted that two of the gunshots were to the head and one to the right shoulder. "A through and through gunshot wound,"

*California license #036 XQS

said Mason into his microphone as he examined the shoulder first. The bullet had entered one and one-half inches from the top of the right shoulder, four inches from the center of the chest. It had exited twelve inches below the shoulder, four inches from the center of the back.

Mason now moved his attention to the head wounds. One slug had entered three and a quarter inches above the left ear, traveled to the right side of the skull just beneath the forehead, ricocheted, and embedded itself in the right hemisphere of the brain. Dr. Mason retrieved a gray lead slug from there, "a common garden-variety, 150 grain, .38-caliber special with residual rifling of a right-hand twist."

A bullet had also entered the top of the skull just off center to the right. The lead slug had been trapped in the skin behind the left ear. There were no powder burns or external tattooing so Mason reasoned that the muzzle of the gun was held in excess of two feet away. He looked at Ellen's "beautiful long nails. There were no marks to show she had contact with the assailant," he noted.

Mason asked himself, What was the probable sequence of the shots?

The right shoulder wound must have come first since the bullet could not have reached her in the position she had fallen in. This was "fired bullet number one" and had been fired while she was standing.

The second bullet must have come as she turned away, presenting the attacker with the left side of her head. The pellet had entered at a forty-five-degree angle just above the ear. Dr. Mason took into consideration that she was downslope to the gunman. This shot alone would have been fatal the doctor knew.

This meant the third shot, fired while Haertle was unconscious, was unneeded and deliberate, a bullet fired through the top of the head, an angle possible only after the victim was on the ground—an execution-style wound. Mason thought that this was very like the killings done on the trails to the north in Marin County.

It seemed as though the attacker, when defied, as Ellen Hansen had done, or confounded in his stalking, as Shauna May had done, reacted with extreme rage. Sergeant Keaton told me, ''I still believe if the .38 used by the killer had been a six-shot gun instead of a five-shot gun we'd still be looking for the killer. Think about that, Robert. Think about that. He confronts Haertle and Hansen and says, 'All I want to do is rape your girlfriend.' She stands up to him and gets three shots. The boy gets two. One misses, one is in his neck and the shoulder. Three for her and two for him—one more and we wouldn't have had a witness getting up and running away holding his throat.''

In the daylight the detectives on Ridge Trail had discovered four unusual shoe tracks next to Ellen's body. All had a herringbone pattern that transversed from heel to toe. In the toe portion the herringbone consisted of three wider herringbone patterns. Between the ridged chevrons at the heel and the toe of the footprint there was a series of twenty-eight narrow ridges.

The prints were circled with red paint, fixed with hairspray and covered with boxes. Plaster of paris was mixed to the consistency of pancake batter, the boxes removed and aluminum frames positioned around the tracks. The plaster batter was not poured onto the track but allowed to flow into the ridges and grooves. It was immediately recognizable to them as the tread of a running shoe.

3

The Composite

"The day of the murder, my son was in the park with me," Inspector Stoney Brook told me later. "We were near the ranger station, heading over to the area near the observation deck, but the people we were with were not feeling well so we headed home. On the way out I saw the patrol cars blocking off the roadside and I checked on what was going on.

"I used to run that trail, one of my exercise places. I don't know if you would call it bad memories or not but I don't go there anymore. It's just I've been there so many times I feel like I know every stone and stick. I must have been there a hundred times since all this happened."

Stoney Brook was an ex-marine drill instructor and looks it—ramrod straight, lean, hard, balding, and mustached. Not a tall man, he dresses impeccably and resembles the actor Alan Arkin. After four tough years in the marines he worked as a tactical officer in the police academy in the midseventies.

"One of the reasons I got the name Stoney is that I was actually considered humorless. I don't smile a lot and I'm not a real compassionate person, at least as far as the troops were concerned at the police academy." The voice was firm. "One of the things we have to do is have the people stand inspections. They were compelled to live in a little barracks while they were undergoing their ten weeks of learning to become police officers. While they were in class we would inspect the barracks and we could give them demerits. I was the least popular of all those people because I was strict. I would gig them for small infractions. The point I tried to make with them which many times was lost was I was trying to get them to pay attention to details at a scene.

"That's why I go back to the scene over and over. I do that a lot. You never see it the first time." Brook would go back to Ridge Trail almost thirty times over the coming days and three of these times he took Steve Haertle. "A lot of times," said Brook, "when I'm working a homicide case I don't get there first. I don't really see that as necessary. If you've got people who are real good at doing crime-scene work, let them get there and do their job. Take the photographs, pick up the prints. The guys who worked the scene picked up a lot of footprints and they did a pretty thorough job. What I do is keep going back and looking for the things they missed and then I go back and look for the things they missed and I missed. Then I look for the things I missed that time, to examine the physical nature of the scene and get some sense of what must have taken place.

"I spent a great deal of time going over the hillside and I had some officers get out and start knocking on doors. That's how we were able to locate a young girl who saw the killer's car leaving the scene on the day of the murder on Ridge Trail. Her name was Melissa and she was eating ice cream and playing on her bike in a cul-de-sac in a housing development near Henry Cowell Park when she saw a red car make a wrong turn while trying to get to Highway 17.

"She could see its driver was balding, perspiring, described the car and even drew a little sketch for me. Drew it on a piece of cardboard. 'You know,' she said, 'I thought it was a Fiat. Had a little plate in the middle of the thing, kinda a dirty red color.' That kind of stuff. Really a good little witness.'' Melissa was interested in cars, especially red Fiats, because at that time she wanted to buy a red Fiat.

''Fritz had seen a car leaving, which he described as a boxy-looking foreign car. So I had the little girl go with one of the detectives to a Fiat dealer, go through the Fiat book till she picked out a car that looked like it. Then I had her go through color chips and pick out the color that looked like it, the one she saw. Then we had the State Department of Justice just run every Fiat registered to Santa Cruz, Marin, San Francisco, San Mateo, and Alameda.

''The unsung hero in all this is Fred Shirasago of the CI&I [Criminal Identification and Investigation] in Sacramento—a hell of a guy, never got any credit for all his work. Running all those license plates we ended up with boxes full of computer printouts. What I hoped to do was to go through and eliminate station wagons, the convertibles. We were looking for something along the lines of the 124, a little boxy sedan or coup.

''Now the average bureaucrat would have loaded that stuff on a Greyhound bus or UPS and sent it down. Shirasago took a pool car, loaded it up in Sacramento, and drove it to me. Sat there and ran all that crap and then drove it to me. Then we had to get back to the little girl. I wanted to hypnotize the girl, to try and get the license number because she had seen it head on and her recall was so good.

''Her parents wouldn't let her do it. This girl's family are Jehovah's Witnesses, I think. And I *tried . . . everything* with those people. Told them he's killed people. He's gonna kill again. Knowing that license number could save a life. All that. They wouldn't let her do it. Of course, as it worked out, it was all for the better. It would have been thrown out of court anyway.''

Brook thought for a while about the description of the shooter. ''That faded-Levi, stonewashed look, jeans kind of flared at the bottom, and this jagged baseball cap—the man everyone was describing was an old man dressing as a young man. My experience has been you take a guy who has been in prison for ten years, he comes out—he's in a time warp. Whatever the fashion was when he went into prison is still the fashion when he comes out of prison. He still sees himself as the same age he went in.'' Possibly the attacker was someone recently released from prison he had told his men.

After Steve Haertle was operated on at Community Hospital and placed in the intensive care unit in stable condition, his parents came down from Davis. Steve's vocal cords had been badly injured so he could make himself understood only by nodding and pointing. The nerves that controlled his right eyelid and pupil had been injured as well.

"We did the original composite drawing based on Steve Haertle's word,'' Brook told me later. "He was of course severely wounded and couldn't talk. I talked with him, actually talked *at* him for a great length of time. Within the first two days of his being shot he could communicate, once he'd been through surgery. I have the greatest admiration and respect for him. Now he's with Pacific Gas and Electric. I think he works out of the city.

"Then we had the one other fellow who saw the suspect run from the park. The suspect was not wearing a hat, so we had him balding. The other people all saw him with the baseball cap. We have a kid here, locally, Dennis Diedrick, who does a lot of drawing for the police department and the sheriff's office. Works for the city out at the corporation yard or something. He's very good. He has a real sensitivity with the witnesses, doesn't try to force feed his own description into the witness. At any rate what we had him do was draw a more lifelike drawing in charcoal from the Identi-Kit composite and then I said, 'Now draw one without a hat on him. Leave off the hat and make him balding.'

"I took those drawings and went out to the hospital and sat with Steve, who we knew got a good look at him. Steve made a few minor changes. Changed the nose a little and the lips and he made the glasses a little more square.

"Dennis kept changing the picture, rubbing out charcoal lines, adding some. Finally I held up this one drawing, the one with the baseball cap and Steve went—''

Brook demonstrated visually for me with his finger excitedly hitting the paper, rap! rap! rap!

"We figured that was good enough for us. Later on I took this picture and made a slide of it and superimposed on it suspects' driver's license photos, which I blew up to the same size, dropping them one over the other to see if they matched."

In the early hours of March 31 the search on Ridge Trail spread out to encompass the rest of the park. Deputies began at the observation deck and walked up Powder Mill Trail. They found tracks consistent with those at the murder site. At first they were very slight, but as they progressed uptrail they became more frequent and more obvious.

From the area just below Pine Trail and the intersection of Powder Mill Trail the tracks descended toward Pipe Line Road. Then tracks ascending led toward the parking lot.

The farthest track on Ridge Trail was approximately seventy yards from Ellen's body, pointing in the direction of going downhill. This indicated to the detectives that the shooter had walked seventy yards toward Pipe Line Road, then stopped, and turned back. The Pipe Line Trail was ten to fifteen minutes downhill from the crime scene and this was scanned as was Pine Trail all the way up to Eagle Creek.

Deputies timed the walk from the observation deck to the attack scene over level ground and this was clocked at five and one-half minutes. At the deck a little room at the base of the tower on the west side was searched. Tracks like those found near Ellen's body, prints from a running shoe, were discovered by the water fountain next to the deck.

To ensure that investigators could find their way around the constantly changing trails, prey to both flood and storm, the landscape was mapped by surveyors who plotted the exact elevations of the Ridge Trail and deck. Four valuable reference points, trees flanking the murder site, including the dead pine the killer may have hidden behind, were scored by an ax, numbered one through four, and marked with orange fluorescent paint by Deputy Tanner. These marks remain to this day.

Attempts to photograph the area from the air were foiled by the dense canopy of foliage that covered the clearing where the killer had been. Meanwhile, at the parking lot, a 1972 Ford van was timed as it duplicated the killer's escape past the phone kiosk over and over.

Howenstein was alone in his office early on Tuesday morning, March 31, wondering if the Santa Cruz attack was the work of the Marin murderer. A killing of any kind was exceedingly rare in the Santa Cruz mountains. Before the murder of Ellen there had been only one unsolved homicide in the forest, a strangling in an isolated section of Henry Cowell State Park two years before. Of course no one knew for certain if *that* murder was not also the work of the Trailside Killer.

Howenstein read through the various descriptions from the witnesses and what so far had been learned from the surviving victim. The killer's jacket had a snap front and some sort of short, standing collar, yellow- or gold-colored nylon fabric bearing a sewn-on patch on the front with a short name. On the reverse side of the jacket were the letters saying OLYMPIC DRINKING TEAM followed by the name of a state, probably Montana. The man in gold had also been wearing a green adjustable baseball-style cap with an insignia, faded blue jeans, and a pair of white "leather-looking" tennis shoes. The killer had worn a yellow shirt over a white crew-neck T-shirt and had a blue backpack that had contained binoculars and maps.

The car had been described as a "reddish Fiat, Datsun, or Toyota."

The killer spoke in a slow and deliberate manner.

There had been a threat of sex and there had been the use of a high-caliber weapon. These two factors were blazing signals that Marin's elusive maniac was involved.

On the other hand, there were negative elements in the equation—the new attack took place about a hundred miles from the last and the detailed descriptions of the killer didn't match the composite drawing of the handsome, hawk-nosed man on Mount Tamalpais.

Ballistics could link the Marin and Santa Cruz incidents, but Howenstein knew that ballistics analysis couldn't be rushed.

Santa Cruz County Sheriff Al Noren told the press there were "dissimilarities and similarities between Sunday's killing and the Marin murders."

Sergeant Bruce Simpson, speaking for the sheriff's office in Santa Cruz, said later in the day there was officially no link between the attack on Ellen and Steve and the unsolved Marin crimes.

When Carpenter told Candy on March 31 that her gold jacket had been stolen out of the back of his Chevy she thought that odd. Habitually Carpenter was exceedingly thorough, almost ritualistic, in the locking of his car doors.

That night, at 8:05, Carpenter made a collect call to Reba Lehman from a Sacramento phone booth and afterward drove to the home of Kris Frank at Elk Grove, still using Reba's car. Kris had met him at the San Francisco Gift Show in February when Carpenter was still with Gems of the Golden West. She was also in the gift business, and Carpenter had made deliveries to her home.

"Carpenter," I was told later by an investigator, "showed up at Frank's house unannounced. He seemed different to her, dressed preppylike, a long-sleeved sweater tied over his shoulders, multicolored shirt on, driving a BMW. He had that briefcase and he started talking to her about the sexual-type of movable key chains. He was getting down on the floor and demonstrating how they worked, showing her the different sexual positions, told her how well the homosexual key chains would go over. She became uncomfortable, then frightened, because whenever she had had contact with him in the past he had stuttered and now he did not. He kept asking her about the family schedule—'Where is your husband?' 'What time is he due home?' Finally she went outside to wait until Carpenter left. He was, she said, 'acting very strange and secretively.' She was so shook that her husband had to stay home with her for three to four days afterward."

"Mrs. Frank," Carpenter said later, "was n-n-not interested in my key-chain proposal. I went up to Lake

Tahoe and gambled, winning $300, and returned to Sacramento after that. I continued to see a friend that evening.''

On Wednesday, April 1, Carpenter returned to San Francisco. ''I was stopped by my boss at work. I had gotten a neck brace conveniently and told him I had hurt my neck playing with kids and throwing them in the air. This was a lie. I lied even though my bosses really needed me because I had s-s-s-so much happening in my life. I returned to work full time the next day.'' Probation officer Wood said he had never seen Carpenter in a neck brace. ''He never had any neck problem I knew of.''

As Steve Haertle recovered, a final composite was developed. It showed the gunman as a man forty-five to fifty-five years old, five foot ten inches tall, possibly six feet, weighing 165 to 175. The killer had short, blondish hair or thinning gray hair, balding at the front crown, hazel eyes, crooked yellow lower teeth, and was clean shaven. Steve admitted he did not make out any of the special writing on the gold jacket and differed from the other witnesses in that he described the killer as having worn red-striped Adidas shoes with one broad stripe and one narrow.

The killer had been seen both with dark-framed glasses with faded stems and without these glasses. This gunman was a far cry from the Marin composite drawing of a man between twenty-eight and thirty-five years old, handsome, and with a full head of dark hair. Throughout the day Santa Cruz investigators compared evidence with Marin County sheriff's detectives Don Besse and Rich Layden.

On April 1, in a reversal, both Marin County and Santa Cruz County detectives said they now ''strongly believed'' Marin's Trailside Killer was the man responsible for Ellen's murder. They would not say what had changed their minds. But Howenstein's suspicions had been confirmed that morning—with the exception of the murder done by a .44-caliber pistol and the boning knife, every one of the shootings in Marin County was linked by ballistics to the same .38-caliber weapon used in Santa Cruz.

Still there seemed to be no way to account for the

considerable difference between the March 8, 1980, description of the Marin County attacker of Barbara Schwartz and the older man seen on the trail beneath the observation deck in Santa Cruz. There was always the possibility there were *two* Trailside Killers—a handsome, athletic young man with a full head of dark hair and the out-of-shape man who had accosted Ellen and Steven. The sheriff and Gaddini had to find out where and why they had gone wrong.

Jan Christie, the witness to the Schwartz knifing, still badly shaken, was picked up by Detective Russo and an FBI agent and driven to the Sleeping Lady. Captain Gaddini followed from the Civic Center in another car, parked at the mountain, and met with the two men and the witness. All four hiked to the gulch where Barbara had been stabbed to death over a year earlier. It was silent and close to 5:00 P.M. Jan was asked to stand where she had been the day of the attack and Gaddini re-enacted the murder, taking the part of the hawk-nosed young man. When he had finished he asked Jan what she had seen.

Gaddini was shocked to realize that she was unable to distinguish his thick dark mustache from sixty-five feet away. The shadows cast by the swaying pines created a surreal landscape. Jan had seen the attack through a line of thin trees and had only brief glimpses of struggling figures. It was understandable now to the officer why the composite picture was unreliable. Suddenly exhausted, he leaned against the tree for a moment. The sudden quickness with which everything happened, the natural hysteria of anyone witnessing such a scene, and the possibility brought to Gaddini's attention that it was rumored Jan had had a friend hypnotize her to bolster her memory before she spoke with the composite artist—all these elements had conspired to create the image of a man who never was.

Shaken, Gaddini was unable to calculate how many people must have been removed from serious consideration as suspects because of the description of a nonexistent man. Had the handsome, lean hiker come from some buried memory in Jan's past? Yet every study, every psychological evaluation had assured the police that the killer had to be a young man. Now Gaddini recalled another witness, a Point Reyes hiker who said that she had seen an older man, a man with an angry look, in a baseball cap and glasses, at around 1:30 P.M. on Sky Trail. To Gaddini it sounded much like the Santa Cruz composite of the killer of Ellen Hansen.

Now it was Gaddini's difficult job to explain to the irate press and public about the differences in the descriptions. "It is my feeling," he said, "that the eyewitness at Mount Tamalpais was traumatized and caught only a glance of the suspect's profile." Probation officer Richard Wood recalled in hindsight, "The first composite was the most damaging thing that was dreamed up. I think that the sheriff over there was in such a tough place politically he had to come up with something and so he did. He came up with a composite which threw everyone off. Threw me off."

"We've never had this kind of eyewitness capability," said Howenstein of the new composite. By now the sheriff had spent two years hunting the elusive Trailside Killer and the weight was in his eyes. "It should greatly enhance our ability to close the case." Howenstein was shown the plaster casts of the tracks found at the scene of the crime on Ridge Trail, and the joint investigation was in full swing. It was important to go back and show the new drawing of the killer to earlier witnesses to see if any of them remembered the man. It seemed now that the killer may have chosen Ridge Trail because it had enabled him to see people coming from far off and thus would not be surprised as he was at Point Reyes when Shauna May appeared on the path unexpectedly.

If the Trailside Killer was the same man who had attacked Ellen and Steve then he must have worn some sort of wig on Tamalpais. There was no other way, it seemed, to explain the full head of hair the witness had seen from sixty-five feet away. The 11:00 P.M. news came on and the new composite, one that was still in flux and would be until the middle of April, filled the screen.

A mile away from the Santa Cruz sheriff's office a middle-aged woman was watching the broadcast. She leaned forward, hearing the news anchor say, "This is how the Trailside murderer looked, or so thought Marin detectives. But tonight the sheriff of Marin County has released what they think is the most accurate portrait of the killer yet.''

For the woman, Roberta Patterson, the room grew very still. She was only dimly aware of the sound of her youngest daughter playing, a child she had had late in life. Roberta studied the drawing that appeared on camera next. It resembled someone she had long known. Though the fullness of the face was absent and the nostrils lacked the flair—the piglike quality she recalled—it looked enough like the man from her past to curl her lip. In the drawing on the television screen a green baseball cap covered the head so Roberta wasn't able to tell if the man was bald or not.

Roberta steadied herself. She was alone and in shock. Had her dislike of this particular man so distorted her thinking that everything reminded her of him? She did know that she was becoming obsessed with this man and his connections with the series of murders in Northern California.

Thursday morning, April 2, Carpenter started work at the printing school in Hayward at 8:15 and dropped by the Glen Park branch of Continental Savings and Loan to deposit the $300 he had won at Tahoe. Peter Berest, the manager of the bank, noticed the clean-shaven man in glasses from his office. He recalled that he used to come in to talk with Kelly Menjivar, the high school student who had worked as a teller until her disappearance on December 28, 1980. ''Carpenter used to come in just to see her,'' Berest remembered. ''He'd ask for crazy things like five dollars in pennies or nickels. Just any reason to talk to her.''

Between 7:30 and 8:00 P.M. Carpenter crossed the Golden Gate Bridge to return Reba Lehman's BMW and collect his red Fiat. He locked the BMW, put the keys on the front tire, and picked twenty dollars out of his wallet to make up for the gas he had used while driving the car. After returning home he called Reba to see if she had gotten the car and keys and money. ''The first thing she wanted to know,'' said Carpenter, ''was what success I had had w-w-with the rugs. I told her I had no luck.''

"When the BMW was returned," Reba recalled, "it was in the evening. It was low on gas, one quart of oil short. It had been driven hard. I could tell." Now where had the purser been, she must have wondered, to burn that much oil and get it so dirty?

During the week after Ellen's death, Cowell State Park was closely patrolled by mounted posses, dogs, and rangers on foot. "You'd have to have a death wish," one ranger told me, "to come back into Cowell Park looking anything like the description of the Trailside Killer." Carpenter left work early on April 3, at 4:16 P.M.

On April 4, an amazing thing happened on Ridge Trail. Sergeant Brook had returned over and over to the spot where Ellen had been killed to examine the physical nature of the scene and to try and make some sense of what had taken place. Joe Henard and other officers had gotten in the habit of doing the same. That afternoon a Santa Cruz officer went up to Ridge Trail to study the sealed-off area where Ellen had fallen and the killer had left four distinctive footprints. There were now many more of these prints and someone had left a large puddle of urine there. There was speculation the Trailside Killer had returned to the crime scene seven days after the attack.

Through their intensive investigation the Santa Cruz detectives now began to realize that the killer must have scouted the crime scene both before and after his attack on Ellen and Steve. In the past David Carpenter had serviced Super Auto in Santa Cruz, less than ten minutes from Henry Cowell State Park.

That evening David Carpenter did some work for Jack and Florence Neuman at the Gems of the Golden West warehouse. "I loaded the van," he said in retrospect, "and d-d-d-did bookkeeping until 7:00 to 7:30, working for free." Anita Ng was to be the new bookkeeper. Carpenter typed out some correspondence for the corporation. "I would type out in capital letters the name of the person it was going to. It's one of the things I picked up being a clerk in prison." Carpenter's eccentric style of typing business letters would, in the future, be of importance.

Zsuzanna:
Mount Tamalpais

On Mount Tamalpais, under towering and aloof trees, mild bay-cooled air slipped gently around a wood as green as the eyes of a sorcerer's cat. Moonlight illuminated the wooded floor where thirty figures, crowned with flowers, danced and chanted among lighted candles that cast their shadows into the darkness of the surrounding rocks.

There were a group, actually several covens, of witches from San Francisco and the East Bay. Their leader, Zsuzanna Budapest, of Oakland, had been a self-proclaimed witch for sixteen years and now, with the others, scanned the sky anxiously. The celestial surface of the moon touched each of the upturned and expectant faces and each of the sensuously writhing figures with silver light.

These were good witches. "I am a pagan—the religion of simple folk," Zsuzanna explained. "It simply means that I belong to a religious thought that preceded Christ . . . earth religions don't worship the devil. I believe most people are good, but when they're alienated from nature herself they're not in touch with their feelings or their bodies. When they're in touch they're kinder and hap-

pier. People can be misguided or misdirected or in anguish and do wrong.''

It was a person doing wrong that had brought her here
tonight.

''Essentially,'' she told me, ''I had just moved up from
Los Angeles and I started a new coven and we were looking for a place of worship and of course we went to the
sacred mountain—Mount Tamalpa. On Mount Tamalpa
we found leaflets tacked on redwoods and they said
'women stay away because there is a murderer stalking
here and he has already killed seven people.' It seemed
like he struck at joggers there, people who were out in
nature walking about. And we felt that was the wrong
idea. I think he should go and the women should stay.''

The white-haired woman told me of the preparations
for casting a hex on the evil spirit of the mountain.

''It was raining, Robert, somewhat like right now.
What happened was the Mount Tamalpais witches came
and brought his footsteps. From the sites where he did
the killings they gathered the earth in a brown bag. . . .
We made a voodoo doll. It was half black and half white.
The white represented what was good in him, that which
was divine. And the black represented all his evilness.
And we stuffed it with baneful herbs and we did this,
thirty of us together. We got the doll and we stuffed it
together as women.

''We put in the herbs which as you know are nettle,
nettle stings—we put in mandrake and some of us put in
rosemary—and as each woman touched it she said something to the doll. Then one of the ladies who is a very
good witch in San Francisco made an oil. Double-
crossing oil—pretty heavy stuff: It doesn't get off your
fingers so you have to anoint the doll with this bottle not
to get it on yourself. And we named him Who-so-ever-
kills-on-Mount Tamalpais. And we had Mother Nature
there. She saw it. We left the place where we prepared it
and went directly to the mountain. Around in the mud
we danced widdershins . . .''

''What is that?'' I asked.

''Widdershins means counterclockwise. Everybody
was angry about not being able to be free outdoors and
at night. Women had to stay in at night. Women had to

stay in during the day, and if you're into nature you've got to get out there. That's the whole point for witches."

The good witch had her own theory on how to catch the Trailside Killer. "You bring down his luck. Then this guy is gone. You go after his luck, and serial murderers have to be very lucky; they depend on luck. A bunch of witches take that away, honey, there's no place left for the serial murderer. So that's what we did.

"We just screamed and we became the Furies and we created a magic circle by evoking the four corners of the universe. We asked the earth to give him up. We asked the animals to give him up. We asked all living beings to turn him away. To give him out; to betray him and there would be no way to hide and that his life be gone."

During the ceremony Zsuzanna could feel the living sap of the wet forest floor even through her rubber boots. Suddenly the moon began to vanish as they recited a curse, the curse of the good witch against evil.

> By his own evil
> By his own fault
> He shall cause his own demise
> And he will be recycled into the universe.

Now in the shadow cast by the earth, only a thin ghost of a moon remained, illuminated by a tiny amount of light refracted onto the lunar surface by way of the earth's atmosphere.

"We had candles. We had one candle for each of the persons attacked. We had offerings of flowers and fruit and we dressed up the goddess in flowers and then we wore the flowers ourselves. But it was raining and we had to dance. It was the funniest thing because you have to *really* pick your foot up. It would stick in the mud. We felt like we really talked with the earth. We stamped it into her mind what to do and 'go to it, girl.' "

The chanting and dancing rose in intensity as they cast a white hex against evil, against the Trailside Killer, under the ghost of a moon on a ghostly mountain.

"And then when we had expended our energy," she told me later, "we got a little tired and we thanked the spirits we had evoked. We buried the voodoo doll in a nearby place and with dragon's blood reed we drew a triple equal-on cross over his grave. That's for the three fates who govern life, death, and beauty. A little mixture of African and European magic, but Europeans use dolls a lot too, so there are overlapping features.

"We weren't exhausted. It gets you kind of high all this outdoor dancing-in-the-rain business, and your blood is rising through and you are excited and you have a lot of oxygen. Your ears are full of the barking of seals.

"So we came home and then we said, There's no way out for this guy. He'll never get out. We've taken his luck. All that was keeping him going was his luck.

"A woman will turn him in. That's the goddesses' touch."

5

Stoney, 1981

For twenty-one chilling months the Trailside Killer had so terrified hikers that the trails were swept virtually clean. During the winter National Park Service rangers had been summoned from other states to police the trails. However, with the bright spring weather they were recalled to their own districts.

Thus the beleaguered twelve officers at Point Reyes were faced with the staggering task of providing security for 140 miles of trails and 70 miles of beach and ragged highway.

Santa Cruz fared better. They had twenty sheriff's reserve officers patrolling the four state parks in four-wheel-drive vehicles and on horseback. They also had the benefit of state police.

As the weather became beautiful again, the trails surged with hikers just as the amount of protection was being eaten away.

"Throughout April," Stoney Brook told me, "there was a consuming fear we all felt. This man was going to kill again and we could do nothing to stop it.

"We went to the state parks, all the local motels, every

gas station in Santa Cruz, and obtained the gas credit-card slips, the hotel registrations, and the people who checked into the campgrounds, and ran every single license number. Then did a background of every registered owner to see if they fit the physical description. We did a lineup of suspects right away.

"We must have had four hundred people those guys on my team looked at. They really busted their hump. We'd get people calling, 'Looks like the drawing,' and we'd ask, 'When did you see him,' 'Two days ago.' Well, we kept track of every one of those reported sightings. The way we did that, we made up a sheet, had it printed up on colored paper. It was a reporting form with standardized questions, ten of them. 'Where did you see him, Where was he going, What was he wearing, Do you know who he is, Where does he work?'

"Around the first of April, Ray Belgarde [the DA's chief investigator] gave me his office. That afternoon we got four new phone lines at Belgarde's request, big answering machine, a hotline. Belgarde had called in his favors in Sacramento. Marin County sent down a couple of guys, Rich Keaton, the case agent on the thing, and Rich Layden, his partner. I took a map and drew concentric circles on it. The circles met at Redwood City, and so the agreement was that everything north of that point we would forward to Marin for follow up, everything south went to us. This prevented duplication of effort. Twice daily we would courier all the packets and the stuff by telephone to their respective places." Brook set up a bank of dispatchers and officers who fielded tips by marking preprinted forms with colored dots: green for cleared, blue for midpriority, and orange for high priority. He also had an index system for every license plate, every name, and every address that was called in.

"I'm not a good investigator," Brook continued, "but I surround myself with people who are. I was fortunate enough to have a number of good investigators working on my task force whose judgment I trusted implicitly. I have a lot of patience and a lot of tenacity and that's about it. Nor do I suffer fools lightly. I'm a hard person to deal with. I'm very much a loner in that sense of the word.

"There's the understanding of the forensic aspects of the case and there's the understanding of the human aspects, but the real challenge that comes in an investigation is managing an investigation. How to keep all those balls in the air so that people aren't doing the same things, not duplicating, not wasting resources. The way to kill a lot of good investigations is to have a guy who believes he is such an ace investigator he's got to do everything himself. You just cannot be all those places and wear all those hats.

"I guess," Brook went on, "it's worth explaining my investigative philosophy; you'll understand me a little better. The first one is I do an investigation in reverse of what most policemen do. The tendency, unfortunately, with a lot of policemen is to create a hypothesis and then attempt to sift through the facts and find out if they fit the hypothesis. I don't do that. The parallel I draw in lectures is a lot like a public health official who is faced with an epidemic that is working through the community and killing off members of the populace.

"What I do is gather as many facts as I can and then try and figure out what fits and then doesn't fit, like putting together a picture puzzle. I'm not good at picture puzzles. I'm not a player of games. But separating the wheat from the chaff is a good way to put it, and eventually if you collect everything and then begin to shake it out, then you'll find that certain consistencies and patterns and other things like that emerge.

"I like to work a case as if I'm going to defend the man, not prosecute him. Same thing happens if you question the evidence and the motives. You come back to the point where there are just no other answers—this is the person who did it."

On Monday, April 6, 1981, Carpenter showed up at Richard Wood's office. "He was clean-shaven," said Wood, "pleasant, and wearing glasses. I gathered he was having some trouble, some difficulty, with his employers. He told me he had quit his job and was considering other opportunities. He was unsure about the printing school, considering what he wanted to do in the future. Having problems with Candy—some heavy drinking."

Near the corner where Sussex crosses Diamond in Carpenter's neighborhood one of his boyhood chums, Ray Gorrebeeck, passed Carpenter. The purser turned left by the mailbox and bus stop and started downhill; his dog Herman's legs moved double time on the descent. Later, Gorrebeeck, reading his paper and scrutinizing the composite of Ellen Hansen's killer, thought the drawing looked a lot like David Carpenter. "Then I said to myself, Put that out of your mind!" he recalled. "If I say something like that people will think I was trying to stir up stuff in the neighborhood." Delores Serrano, a former secretary at Pacific Far East Shipping Lines in San Francisco, saw the composite and said, "My God, I know that man." She had known David twenty years ago. "I looked at the composite drawing and it was exactly like his father, Elwood."

On April 4, 1981, Roberta Patterson had paced the floor in confusion at her home in Ben Lomond near Santa Cruz, then returned to the drawing she had seen in the paper. The sixty-nine-year-old woman could restrain herself no longer. Her hand shook as she dialed the number she had seen the previous night on her television screen, the Santa Cruz hotline.

Roberta waited impatiently as the phone rang. Officer Sandy Miller answered, took a report, and the call was transferred to the DA's chief investigator, Ray Belgarde, "Yes," said Belgarde: This was only one of uncountable calls he had fielded.

"My name is Roberta Patterson," she began. She had a strange story of intuition and resentment to tell the Santa Cruz police. Her throat was dry. She took a sip of tea and began—it had all started twenty-six years ago on an ocean voyage to Japan she had taken with her two children aboard the Pacific Far East liner *Fleetwood*.

PART FOUR

THE CITY

I find artificial light more appropriate for my work—man's light, not God's—man's feeble striving to understand himself, to exist for himself in the darkness.

—*Eugene O'Neill*
Mourning Becomes Electra, *Act II*

1988 GRAYSON

1

The Confidence Man

"I took an immediate dislike to him," Roberta Patterson told the Santa Cruz police. "David Carpenter was the purser on our voyage to Japan on board the *Fleetwood* in 1955. He collected passports and that sort of thing. But I just didn't like him—the way he was overly friendly with my daughter, Shelby Lynne. He didn't make any moves, but he'd put his arm around her shoulders and give her candy . . . he was just too friendly. I could not forget him.

"I noticed Carpenter again five years later in the summer of 1960 when he attacked his wife's friend in the Presidio in San Francisco. Lois, I think her name was. After that, whenever I saw my daughter's autograph album, which he had signed, I'd stop and look at that name."

"You remember the Santa Cruz DA, Peter Chang?" Doug Smith, Roberta's son-in-law, asked me. "Well, he grew up with Roberta's son, so she knew him personally. She had watched him grow up. So she called up Peter Chang and I think that Peter relayed the information to the proper authorities. She had a pipeline. She knew exactly who to go to and how to pursue her hunch. Roberta talked to me about her vehement feelings about the *Fleetwood's* purser as far back as 1968, about six years after I married Shelby Lynne. Roberta just didn't like the son of a bitch.''

''I don't remember what day we got the lead,'' Brook told me later. ''Carpenter was not the only guy we had named by name and that fit the physical. I gave him extremely high priority. Roberta Patterson told me he had made her very uncomfortable. She was the first person, I think, who called us when the picture came out, saying how much he reminded her of the purser on her trip.

''There were a number of people we talked with. Roberta Patterson's call only generated a one-page report. Marin got a copy of that report. We were getting hundreds of calls, and I arranged for all of them to be on a single-page form. We followed up on each of those. Roberta's guy looked very good, but nobody did anything about it in Marin. The representation is that they were going to get to him eventually.

''The tip was sent to Marin County because Carpenter was in San Francisco, but whoever evaluated it up there made the choice that he was *not* a good look-alike. I had even written on it that this was 'a very good look-alike.'

''At this point, in all fairness, we had not obtained all of his files. That stuff was pretty old. It was usually out in a warehouse. Carpenter had gotten filed with us back in 1970.''

''In Marin County,'' Lieutenant Besse told me afterward, ''we had Carpenter's rap sheet and photo for a period of time before we started looking at him. He was just in our pile of people to check out. Santa Cruz had done the routine thing, sent him up to us because the suspect lived in San Francisco. Here's this guy who stutters and he certainly didn't fit a lot of things we were looking for. So we put it in our pile of suspects to get to when we could.''

The thoughts of Peter Berest, the manager of Continental Savings and Loan in Glen Park, were focused on Anna Kelly Menjivar, the bank's seventeen-year-old teller who had been missing since December 28, 1980. The rumor was that she was a runaway. The Friday before she had disappeared Kelly's mood was buoyant, and she had called out a cheery "See you Monday" as she left work. What was ominous to Berest was that the money in Kelly's account had not been touched since she vanished.

In early March of 1981 "a woman of great character" had mentioned to the bank manager that she was concerned because an older man she had seen Kelly chatting with in front of the bank had once been arrested in the Presidio in 1960 for attacking a young secretary. The woman told Berest the man's name was David Carpenter, who lived only a few blocks from the Savings and Loan on Sussex Street. He sold key chains, she elaborated. Berest knew Carpenter from conversations they had had in the bank, and he now recalled that Kelly had given key chains to everyone in the office around Christmas, which was about when she had disappeared. In all probability Carpenter had been the one who gave her the key chains in the first place, since the older man had often come in specifically to speak with Kelly. However, Carpenter hadn't been in recently.

On April 16 Berest saw the balding Carpenter in the bank and realized he had begun to grow a beard and had stopped wearing his glasses. The young bank manager asked one of the tellers about the older man and her opinion was that Berest shouldn't report it to the police. "He's engaged to be married," cautioned the teller, thinking of Candy Townsend. "You'll just get him in trouble with his girl. He's been real nice to everyone here. Forget it."

Berest was reluctant to get anyone in trouble, but after a soul-searching discussion with his wife, he placed a call on April 17 to Juvenile Officer Fred Holewinske to come to the Savings and Loan to talk about Kelly's disappearance. Holewinske, of the Daly City police, would later deny that Berest had called him.

Berest said afterward, "I swear I made that phone call [to the juvenile division of Daly City police] and I swear it was Holewinske. He's six foot six, about two hundred and eighty pounds, the biggest man who ever came into this bank, and he has a very distinctive voice, youthful like a pep leader.

"I don't want to dog the guy," Berest claimed he told Holewinske about Carpenter. "He obviously has enough trouble as it is." Berest was thinking about Carpenter's speech defect.

"I told him about Carpenter, gave him information from Carpenter's bank records, including his home address, driver's license, Social Security number, parents' names. . . . I asked him to look into it.

"But I said not to get in touch with Carpenter until you've checked out to see if he does have a criminal record, and don't use my name, because if David turns out to be a pathological type I didn't want my name connected with the tip.

"Holewinske said, 'Yeah, we'll check it out, we'll check it out.' I asked him to be discreet because I didn't want him [Carpenter] to be dogged by this label of deviant—and also because he had told me he was engaged to be married. It was such good news because his stutter had made this friendly man such an ugly duckling. I thought, If his fiancée finds out through some clumsy police call or check [that I had called the police about Carpenter], it could really make it difficult for them the rest of their lives. What I tried to impress on him was that we didn't believe Kelly was the kind of person who'd stay away from home for very long even though I suppose 90 percent of missing teenagers turn out to be runaways."

Students and other instructors at the Hayward printing school had noticed that since April 7, the day after his visit to Wood's office, David Carpenter had started to grow a beard and had begun wearing contact lenses instead of glasses. "It's almost as if he were trying to change the way he looks," said one co-worker.

On Thursday, April 19, Carpenter's Fiat began acting up, and he limped into the 76 Station on Clawiter Road at 5:49 P.M. and called AAA road service. They arrived at 6:15, and he was towed to Grand Auto Company, but no one there was able to repair it. Once again the Fiat was towed, this time to Fiat Specialists in Hayward where it was eventually repaired: tuned, hood latch fixed, and smog system installed.

"I had to take the Fiat in," said Carpenter, "to have additional smog equipment installed. Sometime around the middle of April I gave the Chevy station wagon to Jeff Jackl to use." Carpenter even signed over the pink slip (certificate of ownership) to Jackl at the time. "I went through the Chevy and pulled out everything that belonged to me. I pulled out the maps. I checked the backseat area, every part. I remember, I left a blanket in the back of the car I didn't need. I had a collection of maps, fifty or sixty. I kept them all in my car. I put them in the Fiat."

During the month of April and most of May Jackl and the purser passed the "ratty worn-out Chevy" back and forth between them. Jackl distinctly recalled the first time he had seen the red Fiat in a garage in Diamond Heights.

During the four months Candy had known the purser she had seen him working with a speech instructor to correct his problem. "He told me he used an instructional cassette. I know that's one way he worked on not stuttering while I lived at the Carpenter house. He often couldn't answer the phone without stuttering. If he slowed down and took time to think and reorganized the words in a sentence, he could maybe go several sentences without stuttering. But it would be much slower speech than normal."

Before their relationship began to deteriorate in March and April, the purser had bought Candy a diamond engagement ring. The diamond was a mere chip. In April she informed him she was going to be leaving his residence. Though he tried to talk her out of it, she was firm in her decision. She had planned to leave him several weeks before she broke the news. "He was very upset that I was leaving. I don't know if he was crying, but he did have tears in his eyes." Candy began spending weekends away from the Sussex Street home.

"The final straw," said Carpenter, "occurred on April 8. She called me at 3:30 A.M., drunker than a s-s-s-skunk. Candy couldn't find her car and she wanted me to come down and find her car. When I got there she wanted to drive home. She was in no shape to drive, so

I had to physically put her in her car and drive her home. Soon after that time it was agreed she had to leave.''

On April 24 Carpenter left Candy a brief typewritten note in their bedroom directing her to vacate the premises by May 3 at the latest. "After I left her the note t-t-telling her to be out during a specific time frame, Candy asked me if she could leave some of her clothing behind. I told her I would store it in my closet.''

David Carpenter was spending more and more of his time with Jeff Jackl and the woman he lived with, Cornelia Inge Dillinger, and during frequent hours of conversation, Cornelia had arrived at the conclusion that Carpenter, at least on the evidence of these conferences, was "psychologically suppressed and was a dangerous person." She further felt he was "totally sexually frustrated, was a person who loved sex, but did not have an active sex life.''

"S-s-she was Jeff Jackl's roommate," Carpenter said later. "When I went over to Jeff Jackl's for supper Cornelia would be there, and we would have discussions. On Friday, April 24, 1981, Jeff c-c-called and told me Shane Williams, who I was in prison with, was in the San Francisco Bay Area. Jeff had contacted him and they had agreed to meet at Dario's Pizza for a little reunion. This was the same day I left the note for Candy, left it on her bed, showered, shaved. Jeff and Cornelia were already there, but we had to wait about two and a half hours for Shane and his wife, Karen. I had never met Karen before.

"We went out to the Marina Green and smoked m-m-marijuana for an hour then we decided to drive around the Fisherman's Wharf area, and we finally ended up at Coit Tower. At Coit Tower they've got those telescopes you put a quarter in and look. Later in the evening I gave Karen my name and address and told her, 'Knowing Shane, he'll get in trouble and you'll get in trouble so you should have it.' As far as I knew, Shane had gotten out of prison, was doing very well, and that was it. After Coit Tower we dropped Shane and Karen off at a concert and I drove Jeff and Cornelia home.

"On April 30 I left my car parked outside the fence and had Cornelia pick me up, and she dropped me in the

Bayfair Shopping Center. I bought three T-bone steaks for s-s-s-supper. The following Friday night, May 1, I was fixing the steaks for that evening when Karen called—Jeff had invited her and Shane for dinner. I had to go out and buy two more T-bone steaks. After dinner we just sat around and drank and smoked pot.

"Cornelia was interested in the c-c-c-criminal mind, what it was like to be inside prison. She had this idea there was a lot of romance in being a c-c-criminal. I tried to explain to her the cold hard facts . . . the philosophical nature of crime. . . . I was trying to explain from a punishment standpoint that murder was the most punishable because of the weapon used, the more serious a crime. I tried to explain to her how much time a person would have to do." Regarding the criminal personality, Carpenter indicated to Cornelia, "If you commit a crime you should have a gun—there's nothing like the power of a gun to get what you want . . . murder is the ultimate crime, and it's the ultimate thing to get away with.

"To get away with the act of m-m-murder is the ultimate challenge."

On one occasion they discussed rape, and Cornelia revealed to the purser that when she had lived in Germany a man had attempted to rape her by threatening to hit her with a large stone. Carpenter was not at all sympathetic. Cornelia expressed great abhorrence to the act, explaining that rape was very demeaning, "How do men put themselves on women like that?" she said. Carpenter replied that there were some people who had strong needs. "Strong needs that should be met. I don't have any feelings toward an individual's rights. Rape is the ultimate," he told her, taking her comments about rape as a personal affront, as an attack upon himself. "Rape is really an ultimate achievement, to do something like that." He was both angry and defensive, "It's OK, it's nothing against you. You don't need to react like this."

"I keep telling you, Jeff," she said after the purser left, "there's something odd about that guy."

Candy moved out for good on April 30 and, true to his word, Carpenter temporarily stored her clothing in his closet and in some brown shopping bags around his studio apartment.

"On Tuesday, May 5," recalled Carpenter, "I picked up the Fiat [from Fiat Specialties] and drove over to Jeff's. Cornelia got the car." The repairs had cost $255. Carpenter frequently loaned Jackl his station wagon with the personalized plates, since he was driving the Fiat most of the time. But from time to time Carpenter would return to Jackl's and temporarily take back the Chevy. It was at these times that he often suggested Cornelia go hiking with him on Mount Tamalpais, telling her how much interest he had in the outdoors.

2

San Jose:
Heather

On April 20, 1981, Joe Henard called Richard Wood from the Santa Cruz sheriff's office to ask about David Carpenter. Wood told me in retrospect that it was the first call he had gotten requesting a picture of Carpenter.

"Does Carpenter have any hair?" asked Henard.

"None," replied the parole officer. "Not much anyway."

"The guy we're looking for has hair."

"He's not your man unless he's grown some."

Wood could sense that Henard was disappointed.

"Is he a hot suspect in something?" asked Wood.

Henard said, "Well, not particularly. It's just we want a picture of him."

After Wood hung up he rested the heel of one foot against his typewriter and leaned back in his chair. What was going on? he thought. The parole officer had promised to get his client in as soon as possible for a photo and talk. He reached over to the metal file cabinet and thumbed through until he came to the purser's file, withdrew it and read:

277

Carpenter, David Joseph. 5′ 10″, 170 lbs. Brown hair, hazel eyes. CI&I #540287. Social Security 553-34-9918. D.o.B. May 6, 1930.

Wood called the Sussex Street address and Candy answered. Wood explained Henard's request to her, but he didn't know if the message was relayed to Carpenter. Wood called again over the next few days in an effort to set up a session, but he got the feeling the purser was stalling him. It wasn't until April 26 that Carpenter called him back.

Initially Carpenter had gotten his job with the California School of Offset Printing in Hayward through his probation officers. By the time of Ellen Hansen's murder in Santa Cruz he had begun a regular job with Econo Quick Print, an agency of the trade school Carpenter had helped build. His main job was to instruct students in the use of computer typesetting machines, especially the Comset 500, but he did pasteup and other duties as well.

Lane Thomsen, one of the school's directors, thought that Carpenter was "dependable, hard working . . . well mannered and well behaved." He noted that Carpenter would come early and stay late. But one co-worker, Winnie King, detested him. "I just didn't like David," she said. "He likes to tease, and I don't like to be teased. He kidded me about my age and dress. He just loved to aggravate." Another woman at the school said aloud about the ex-purser, "He thinks he is so smart . . . but he isn't."

As for most of the other students, many of whom were placed by state or county rehabilitation agencies as the ex-purser was, they were charmed by him.

Carpenter had made friends with one of the students, Heather Roxanne Scaggs, a twenty-year-old blonde with blue eyes and shoulder-length hair. Heather had grown up in Long Beach, moving to San Jose in 1979 just after she had finished high school. Carpenter offered Heather a lift home from time to time, since he sometimes had the use of the company's white, vinyl-topped Lincoln. It was known to his fellow workers that Carpenter had the use of other cars as well.

Carpenter was aware that Heather had always wanted

a car of her own and told her, "I've got a friend in Santa Cruz, Richard, who can get you a practically new used car for only $400 down—$1,400 all together."

Heather gave a toss of her hair. She was interested.

"Listen," said Carpenter. "You put down $400, I'll loan you the rest."

Throughout April, Heather's first month at Econo Print, Carpenter continued to bring up the subject of the "great car" his friend in Santa Cruz had. Still, the young woman was resistant to the idea of going off with the older man on a trip into an isolated area. Describing his friend's VW in glowing terms, Carpenter raised the ante—"My friend," he said, "owns print shops in San Jose and S-S-Santa Cruz and might be able to give you a job."

"Really?" said Heather.

"We could talk to him about it when we get the car."

Carpenter became insistent on the subject. By April 20, even though she still had misgivings, the stuttering printing instructor had almost convinced Heather to allow him to drive her to Santa Cruz.

Heather Scaggs lived with two roommates, Tammy English, who was a school friend of Heather's from Long Beach, and Dan Pingle, Heather's protective boyfriend. Pingle, who was presently a parcel service deliveryman, had met Heather when they both worked at a Santa Clara photo lab. Pingle joked with his friends that he had worked with her for six months before he got up enough nerve to talk to her.

The three youngsters shared a two-bedroom apartment, number 310, in the rambling, three-story, cream-colored stucco Glen Willow Apartments complex at 877 Willow Street. A grape latticework trellis and a red-brick ridge ran in a jagged line around the building. The residents were especially security conscious: near the front door there was a twenty-four-hour guard. The front lobby was always kept locked and could be entered only with a key, and the underground garage could only be opened with an electronic code.

Finally, Carpenter added an inducement to Heather—"I know something else we could do in Santa Cruz. We could gather some of those f-f-ferns you're always talking about." The last was the deciding factor. Heather was a passionate collector of ferns and mosses and had gathered samples at Muir Woods and Mount Tamalpais.

"Well, all right. I think I can go. But I want to bring Dan with me so he can check out the car," replied the girl.

"Heather," Carpenter explained patiently, "my friend is very nervous about strangers. This is a terrific deal on the car and I'd hate to see you miss it. I personally know a lot about cars, and if you don't like it I'll take it back for you."

On Friday, May 1, Carpenter gave Heather a lift home. "I'll see you at 7:00 A.M., tomorrow, in front of the Shop and Go Mart near your house," he told her. "Now don't tell anyone, especially your boyfriend where you're going. Tell Tammy and Dan you're going shopping on Saturday."

Anyone less trusting would have been suspicious, but, as one of her friends, Stan Howe, said later, "She's one in a million. She is so innocent and open about everything she does it's not even funny. Not telling Dan about the surprise would have been right in character for Heather."

As she left the car and was walking toward the apartment complex Carpenter called out to her. She looked back, her hair flashing in the rays of the lowering sun. "Oh, and Heather . . ." he began.

"Yes?"

"Bring the four hundred in cash."

Heather's lack of guile led her to trust her co-worker, but in the end she did tell Dan Pingle about the elaborate precautions that the printing instructor had pledged her to. "David's giving me a ride to Santa Cruz this Saturday," she told him that night. She had already told the other roommate, Tammy.

Pingle looked up. "David?"

"You know, Carpenter. The older teacher at my school. You met him at the office . . . the one with the bad stutter. Anyway, he's giving me a ride to look at his friend's car and we're going to look for some ferns to gather along the way." She paused. "I admit, though, I'm a little nervous about going with him."

"Great. I'll tag along and look it over for you."

"You can't. His friend won't hear of it. He wants me to bring cash and he doesn't want me to tell anyone where I'm going."

"Don't go," said Pingle firmly, "if you have the slightest doubt."

Tammy English, the other roommate, agreed.

"I *am* apprehensive about meeting him," said Heather. And though she decided to go, she agreed to call Tammy as soon as she bought the car.

"If I don't call by three o'clock—get worried. If I don't return home by seven o'clock, call the police."

They discussed the trip until 8:00 P.M. when Heather called her mother, Mary Joan, in Long Beach. She told her about her fears and her mother hung up under the impression her daughter was *not* going to Santa Cruz with the purser.

"She sobbed a little. Heather wasn't one to sob. She had some trepidations about the outing," her mother said later, "but she felt that she shouldn't pass up the possibility of this job."

Heather's mother called her back at 10:30 P.M. "Heather, please do not go tomorrow morning," she said. "Don't go with this man at all."

"Don't worry about it, Mom. I'll call him in the morning," said Heather and hung up. Pingle was concerned.

"I got down on my knees in front of her," Pingle said later, "and I told her I loved her. I cared about her. I don't even know why I eventually let her go."

"I won't go," Heather had told him, "if you order me not to."

"You know I won't do that, Heather, because our relationship is built on love and trust, but promise me if you do decide to go at least leave his phone number and address."

Heather could see her boyfriend was very upset and wrote down Carpenter's name and address and phone number. Before the lights were turned off she taped the piece of paper neatly to the mirror in the bedroom.

On Saturday morning, May 2, Pingle and Heather were up at six o'clock. Though half asleep, Pingle was still worried about the trip. The note on the mirror with Carpenter's phone number and address looked foreboding. He remembered her words, "If I don't return by seven o'clock, call the police because something will have happened to me." Pingle felt a chill. From his window he saw a large beige or white Lincoln "with a vinyl top and lots of chrome" drive past. David Carpenter had once been seen in a car from the printing school like that.

Heather went into the Shop and Go Mart on the corner of Willow Avenue and Kotenberg Street to buy a diet cola and a package of green pocket-size tissues. She paid for the items by breaking a twenty and then went outside to wait. She had $400 in her purse for partial payment of the used car. It was tucked in a side pocket. The clerk later noticed her pacing in front of the store and then crossing the street to where a white car was waiting. He did not see her leave or see the driver.

At 5:30 P.M. when Heather hadn't returned home, Pingle attempted to telephone Carpenter at his residence. The note with the ex-purser's address and phone number on it trembled in his hand. The phone rang for almost a minute, but finally an elderly voice answered. "Yes?"

"I want to speak with David Carpenter," said Pingle. There was a long pause, a sigh.

It was Carpenter's mother. "My son is not here," she said.

"I need to know when he'll be back from Santa Cruz."

"My son left for work this morning about 5:00 or 5:30. He will be very late. He left ten minutes ago to go to the ballet."

Pingle hung up and immediately phoned the police to report that Heather was overdue and he had reason to believe she might be in danger. He was told to wait until the next day, and if she wasn't back by then to come in and file a report.

Next Pingle called Heather's mother, in Long Beach, and told her that Heather had gotten up early and gone on the trip after all. She had not returned yet.

Then he called his friend Stan Howe for help.

At 7:55 Jeff Jackl met Carpenter at the Opera House. The two men climbed the gray steps and fought the wind whistling down Van Ness Avenue to open the heavy doors into the grand lobby. Tonight was the world premier of a new ballet by Smuin and Fox, "A Song for Dead Warriors." Jackl was puzzled that Carpenter made a show of his auto repair bill during intermission.

At 10:30 P.M., after the performance was over, Carpenter dropped Jackl off at Sacramento and Polk and started for his Sussex Street home. At this same time Pingle, after pacing the floor of his apartment for hours and driving into San Francisco with his friend Stan Howe, was parked in front of the Carpenter family home. The trip had taken less than half an hour at the speed Pingle had driven. To Pingle, the old brown house seemed unoccupied. There were no lights in the bottom portion of the house, and there were no other cars parked in front of the building.

Since Pingle had hoped to catch Carpenter either coming or going he had positioned himself on the top step of the flight of steps leading up to the shingled building. Behind Heather's boyfriend was the rustle of a curtain, and he thought for a moment he saw an elderly face peeking out from one gathered end. "Well, let them call the cops," he whispered to Stan. The grief-stricken boy could feel the cold from both the chill night air and the stone steps on which he crouched.

Pingle just wanted Heather back. "I never thought I could feel this way about a woman," he said later. "She made my whole life for me. God, I just hope she's alive. I just want my old lady back alive . . . my whole life revolves around her."

Carpenter's mother, Frances, came out peering through thick lenses and invited Pingle inside to wait. He politely declined. Finally, Carpenter pulled up and parked in front of 38 Sussex. As he got out, Pingle could see that the older man was dressed for an evening on the town. Carpenter was bounding up the steps when he caught sight of Stan and then Pingle higher up.

"Who's t-t-there?" he said, startled, pulling back from the figures silhouetted on the steps.

"It's me, Dan Pingle, Heather's boyfriend. When's the last time you saw her?"

Carpenter appeared confused. "I haven't s-s-seen her," he said.

"That's not what I was told. You were supposed to pick her up this morning."

"Oh, that," said Carpenter. "I overslept. I told her if I didn't show up by 8:15 not to wait for me. We'd do it another day. I was at a party last night where I drank a lot and smoked a lot of pot. Besides, I had to take m-m-my car in and get it fixed. It broke down and I was stuck in the city."

"There doesn't seem to be anything wrong with it now," said Pingle angrily.

"No, no, no," Carpenter stammered. "Look, I got it back at noon. Here's a receipt for it." He fumbled in his dinner jacket for it and finally produced a piece of yellow paper. Pingle could make out in the dim light that it read Tony's Service Station across the top.

At noon Carpenter had had his '69 Chevy station wagon repaired at Tony's on Mission Street in San Francisco. The repairs had been very slight, and only the points had to be replaced. By 12:30 he was on his way.

After leaving the garage he had carefully folded away the receipt, which proved his car had been incapacitated during the day. Carpenter then drove up ten blocks and appeared next at the office of Dr. J. L. Stamper, an optometrist. There he was recognized by a technician, Jacqueline Purcell, who worked for Stamper and had often seen Carpenter walking his dog, Herman, in Diamond Heights.

Carpenter handed her his glasses, and Purcell examined them. They had been subjected to trauma—the lens was half out of one frame socket and the frames were bent. Has he been in a fight? she had thought. Dr. Stein of the staff heated the frame, replaced the lens, readjusted the temple area of the frames, and refitted them to the man's face. Purcell noticed Carpenter's green baseball cap because she had to ask him to remove it to fit the glasses. While he was there Carpenter decided to get a pair of glasses drastically different from the ones he was wearing, something to change his look, he had told them. He chose the Hillside Style, paid $88, was told to pick up the new glasses on May 19, and left with his repaired glasses.

After reading the receipt from Tony's Service Station in the dim light Pingle handed it back to Carpenter and left, furious, but not before warning the older man that Heather had better be found soon. "He said he didn't know where she was," said Pingle later, "but I didn't believe him. He was too cool, cool as a cucumber, under stress. He kept his hand in his pants pocket and he kept jingling his change, and he said he hadn't met Heather that Saturday . . . never went to meet her . . . Who does he think he is?"

The following day, Sunday, May 3, Dan Pingle arrived at the San Jose police department at exactly 7:45 A.M. and filed a missing persons report on Heather. The officer marked it case number 81-123-9514 and began asking the distraught young man what kind of person his girlfriend was.

"She's the most punctual, conservative, solid citizen you can imagine, and that's why it's so out of character for her to disappear like this."

Pingle brought out a small graduation picture of Heather and then gave the officer a verbal, detailed description of the missing woman.

The officer wrote down: "Five foot three inches, 110-111 pounds, born in Long Beach, California, and has been in the San Jose area for two years."

Pingle explained he had gone by the Shop and Go Mart where Heather had last been seen and then gone home and looked in the closet to double-check what Heather had been wearing when he saw her leave. "Heather was wearing a beige windbreaker, a blue-and-white striped T-shirt, the stripes run horizontally, faded blue jeans, and Nike running shoes with yellow stripes. And, oh, yeah, I noticed her gray tweed fabric purse is missing as well." Heather had $400 in that purse.

"You've got to get hold of this old guy, Carpenter," he told the officer.

At this moment Carpenter was calling Florence Neuman at Gems of the Golden West and volunteering to work with her on the bookkeeping. It kept him there from 8:14 in the morning until 7:00 at night.

In Mill Valley at the home of David Carpenter's friend, Reba Lehman, her roommate looked up from the paper with the latest composite of the Santa Cruz murderer of Ellen Hansen. He read the description out loud. "You know, that sounds a lot like David," Reba said.

Meanwhile Heather's mother, Mary Scaggs, had flown in from Long Beach and was staying at her daughter's apartment. She remained calm and drove out to the printing school to talk to Carpenter's bosses, where she learned he had a record of sex offenses. Dissatisfied with the police investigation, Mary went to the *San Jose Mercury News*, and a story about the missing woman was run on Monday morning. Under public pressure the case was assigned to a veteran investigator, Sergeant Ken Womack. "I talked to my daughter the night before she disappeared," Mrs. Scaggs told the press. "I think she's dead. I thought that from the very first day."

3

Surveillance

Heather had still not been found and Dan Pingle could not understand why it was taking so long for the stuttering printer to be called in and interviewed. A San Jose policeman was in the process of arranging this. He called Carpenter's parole officer, Richard Wood, in San Francisco to set up a face-to-face interview with the suspect.

"By the time I got the phone call," Wood told me later, "on Monday morning, May 4, 1981, from Sergeant Castlio I was just a so-called innocent bystander. He explained to me they were looking into the disappearance of Heather Scaggs, who may have been with Carpenter on May 2.

"I was concerned. This was the second phone call I had gotten about my client. The first had been from Joe Henard with the Santa Cruz police. I told this to Castlio and suggested that he give Henard a call. Now I had no idea what this guy knew or didn't know because he didn't tell me, but what I did at this point was I called Santa Cruz and I called Marin and I said, 'I just got a phone call from this guy on a woman's disappearance and I wanted to let you know.' "

"You mentioned," I said later to Wood, "that Carpenter often went hiking on Mount Tamalpais . . ."

"Yeah, he said that. I told that to Marin County. I think Marin County had information they weren't coordinating with Santa Cruz because I told them things and I later asked Santa Cruz people, 'Hey, I told this to Marin and they never heard it.' "

Stoney Brook had expressed a similar thought when he told me, "Police agencies don't work together. They can hardly work together among themselves. The inability that exists within a case is all smoke and no heat. There's sheer chaos involved when you have agencies that don't cooperate with adjacent jurisdictions in a big case."

"In the same week that Carpenter came to light as the prime suspect," Wood told me, "another client in our office walked into a bank in Redwood City to rob it. A cop walks in and the guy turns around and blows the cop in half. So in one week I was a basket case."

As for Stoney Brook at the Santa Cruz end, he had been momentarily sidetracked. He told me later what had happened: "Heather Scaggs turned up missing, but simultaneously with that my department was supposed to host a conference at the Holiday Inn starting on May 6, one of those conferences someone had signed up for two years ahead of time. I was assigned to run it—right in the middle of this case:

"I went to George Foster [Brook's boss] and told him, 'I can't put on this conference.'

" 'Sure you can,' " he told me.

" 'I'm supposed to stop this investigation?'

" 'You're kind of in a lull at this point.'

"Joe Henard and I sat down and talked about this. He was my alter ego throughout. We picked five of the names we had given Marin. Now that we had eliminated all the other people we were going to start working these guys. Carpenter was one of the top five. But now they pulled us off the case and said go do the conference.

"I didn't have anybody to help. In one day I drove to San Jose airport twelve times. The Western States Crime Conference ran May 5, 6, and 7. I got through it, but fell asleep in the hospitality room. We're no longer a member of the conference. They never talked to us again.''

Sergeant Ken Womack and his partner, Walt Robinson, of the San Jose Police Department, were the guys Brook called "the best of the best." Since there was a whole lot on the case of the missing girl, Heather Scaggs, that just didn't get done, Womack and Robinson, who weren't originally partners, were assigned to it.

Brook later described the two officers to me with brotherly affection. "Robinson is the kind of guy you almost want your daughter to marry. You know, the boy next door, boyish look, a disarming smile. He's a dead ringer for Judge Reinhold in *Beverly Hills Cop*. Kenny Womack is your polyester-leisure-suit-with-a-western-cut kind of guy. He favors silver jewelry, turquoise, and has kind of a National Rifle Association attitude about life. Womack, in his forties, was the senior partner of the team. They're the kind of guys I don't meet very often in my career. They just instinctively knew what the other guy was going to do and that's a rare thing in this business, and it's an even rarer thing to meet two guys like that who not only work well together but work well interchangeably with me."

"When it came about," Robinson told me later, "that the Scaggs case was getting kicked around the detective division, our lieutenant decided Womack was the man to work it, so he called him in."

"I'm too busy," Womack told the lieutenant. "I can't touch it."

"Look," said the officer, "watch my lips—you're working the case. I don't care what you're doing now."

"I'll work it on one condition and that condition is I get to take a partner."

"Who do you need?"

"I want Walt Robinson." Robinson was a new man, had been a beat patrolman.

Robinson said later, "And that was the start of an interesting relationship. We were opposites in our interests, in our background, but we complemented each other in that we caught things the other missed. A couple of cases that came before the Scaggs case had caused Ken

and me to get together. I was looking for a good role
model, someone very knowledgeable in the office. I noticed how tenaciously Womack worked a case. I figured
I could learn a lot from that guy, try to emulate him. I
didn't realize the Scaggs case would be quite an initia-
tion, a trial by fire.''

"So they were teamed up to work on the missing girl,"
Brook told me, "and the reason I say without them the
case never would have gotten off the ground is that they
were savvy enough to recognize all the warning bells.
They didn't just go through the motions. They did an
investigation, and they did a good job of it.

"I came to trust their opinions. It's one of those things
where you meet the guy, and every cop is like this, and
I think I gotta wait and be shown—those guys were just
real good. What they did was they took that case and just
kept taking the steps and they got to the point where they
realized that what they had was not a missing person but
potentially a homicide and all of those warning bells went
off.''

On Tuesday David Carpenter called Jeff Jackl and told
him he had to come over for some advice. When he
arrived he told Jeff and Cornelia that an employee at
Econo Quick Print, Heather Scaggs, had been reported
missing, and he was afraid attempts would be made to
blame him for the disappearance since he was an ex-
convict.

"I've got a great idea," he told them. "I might have
to switch cars with you." Carpenter had so often loaned
them his Chevy that they agreed to the exchange.

On May 5 Ken Womack called Wood from the San
Jose Police Department.

"When is Carpenter coming in?" he asked.

Wood had talked with Carpenter, and he had agreed
to come in Friday. "The guy's coming for the picture as
requested," said Wood.

"Can you set up a meeting with me and my partner?"

Wood dialed Carpenter and said, "David, the police
in San Jose would like to talk to you about Heather
Scaggs."

"Yeah. I'm real concerned about her myself," he replied.

"Since you're coming in Friday they'd like to meet with you."

"Why don't we m-m-meet for lunch first," said Carpenter, "and I can tell you what happened."

"That's fine with me, David." Wood hung up. He thought to himself that either Carpenter was a consummate actor or he was not involved. He called Womack back.

"We're on for Friday," Wood told the San Jose officer and set the appointment for 1:30 P.M. Meanwhile in Hayward, at the printing school, a birthday party was being given for Carpenter. A banner had been stretched across the room that proclaimed: HAPPY BIRTHDAY, D-D-D-DAVID.

The following day, Thursday, May 7, Sergeant Womack and Officer Robinson began to follow up on the missing Heather Scaggs. "Her mother," Robinson told me later, "told us something about Heather going off with Carpenter. After speaking with Dan Pingle we drove to Hayward to the printing school where Carpenter worked. He wasn't there. Pingle had said that he thought he had seen Carpenter in a white sedan on the morning she had disappeared."

"What kind of car does he drive?" Womack asked Carpenter's boss, Joe Elia.

"Well," replied the printing school boss, "he has a couple of cars. One of them is parked outside." Elia had a white Lincoln.

"We went outside," recalled Robinson. "We didn't see the car at first. It was hidden in the last stall all the way down, covered with dirt and appeared to be a dull, dirty red color. It was a Fiat. This rang a bell with Womack, who had kept up on the Santa Cruz shooting. He had the presence of mind to photograph the car. This turned out to be lucky since the next time we saw it it was washed and looked a different color."

While Womack took the photos, Robinson looked inside the Fiat's window. During his interview with Mary Scaggs she had told him that Heather had a habit of dropping tissues behind her wherever she went. Robinson could see green tissues all over the floor of the passenger side. On the seat above was a *Chronicle* folded open to an advice column. "Dear Abby," it read, "I am a fifty-year-old man in love with a young, blonde, blue-eyed girl . . ." Carpenter was fifty, Heather was blonde and blue-eyed, thought Robinson. He couldn't make out any more of the paragraph. "I can't believe this," he said out loud.

Womack joined Robinson at the window. There was some detail in the back of Womack's mind that kept nagging at him, something he couldn't dredge up. Then it came to him. Several weeks earlier Brook had come to a homicide investigator's conference that San Jose was hosting and brought along with him several confidential flyers containing "hold-back" stuff, information not seen by the press about the Santa Cruz killer's car. Later, Womack had seen one of the flyers in the wastebasket near his desk and fished it out. He now recalled that when the killer had made his escape across the parking lot at Henry Cowell State Park Leland Fritz had noticed that the tail pipe of the gunman's car had been bent on the left side. Womack walked quickly to the rear of the car. Robinson followed—the tail pipe was bent.

Brook told me later what Womack and Robinson did next: "A lot of policemen would get on to this kind of thing and think, Here's my chance to make a big collar, get my name in the papers, picture on TV, get my promotion to lieutenant. What Womack did is what a real pro would do, he backed off, called me and the powers that be and said, 'Let's talk about this. I think I've got something.' "

"Robinson and Womack found out," Lieutenant Besse remembered, "that Carpenter was on federal parole so they had to talk to his federal parole officer—and a lot of stuff starts falling into place about the kind of guy David Carpenter is, his prior assaults on women. As a good investigator, Womack had kept up on other homicides in the area and he realized that a red car was seen the day of Ellen Hansen's murder in Santa Cruz. He did a series of logical steps. Womack called Santa Cruz and Stoney Brook called me. I sent investigators over."

* * *

"On Friday, May 8," Carpenter said in retrospect, "I arranged trading the Fiat with Cornelia who had the Chevy station wagon." Cornelia noticed that when Carpenter had called the previous evening about switching cars he had stopped stuttering.

At 8:00 A.M. Carpenter drove his Fiat to the parking lot where Cornelia worked, parked it, took the Chevy, and by noon was making his way to Wood's office in the Federal Building at 450 Golden Gate.

"When he walked in I was surprised," Wood later related, "because he had a beard and he had never had a beard before . . . he had grown it in-between the time I last saw him and when he came in again. I knew then he was aware the heat was on. He knew it. There was no doubt.

"It was a neat beard, trimmed, the same beard he's got today. I didn't even make a comment on it. I was just going to go and listen to the guy. At this stage of the game my attitude was real simple: if he did it you've got to get him off the streets as soon as possible; if he didn't, then you have to clear him as soon as possible, 'cause to me he was a parolee who was doing very well."

Wood and Carpenter strolled the short distance in the bright sun to Knight's, a nearby Tenderloin restaurant and catering shop. Colored flags outside Knight's flapped in the wind rushing down Golden Gate. They passed a suit of tarnished medieval armor inside the door and sat down in the deep yellow room. Carpenter reached for a menu and they ordered.

"It was always Dutch treat with David and me," Wood told me afterward. "We always paid our own way. With me it's standard. Nobody buys me lunch. Nobody. You just can't do it. There's a real ethical problem. It's like a suspect buying a cop who is investigating him lunch. It was at this lunch he told me of his change of jobs and the alibi for the day in question. I listened and didn't make too many comments. At some point in the story he looked me in the eye. I looked into this guy's eyes and I knew.

"I *knew* it was him. I didn't have the slightest doubt in the whole world. I know you've done the book on Zodiac, but I don't know if you've ever looked a cold-blooded killer in the eye before. Passion had nothing to do with this guy, Robert. When I looked into his eyes it was—you hear of people who are chilled to the bone, well, I was chilled to my *soul*.''

"Then this was the first time you really sensed this?" I asked.

"Absolutely. I looked into his eyes and it was like, 'I want to get out of here,' and I felt chills down to my very toes—it was just *'This is the guy.'* I had no doubt in my mind. I had been dealing with criminals for thirteen, fourteen years, so I'd met a lot of cold-blooded types. Nothing like this guy. I was thinking of the whole kit and kaboodle, not just Heather Scaggs. I didn't know, I still don't know, I don't think anybody's ever going to know the extent of this guy's violence. . . . I would suspect there were hundreds.''

"After Carpenter's attacks in the seventies he changed," I said.

"Absolutely. And I'll tell you what changed," Wood recalled. "Every one of those people he raped and kidnapped testified against him. This guy learned on a very basic level—*dead witnesses don't talk.*''

Carpenter ate avidly, continuing his explanation between bites, while Wood reflectively sipped his mild tea. During the walk back to his office the parole officer struggled to keep his emotions to himself. When he opened the office door the two policemen from San Jose were waiting, and for a moment no one spoke. Carpenter did manage to smile amiably. Wood could almost sense the actor in his client shifting into gear. Womack remained stoney-faced, Robinson managed one of his disarmingly boyish grins, and Wood felt like he was caught between three approaching storm fronts.

"Apparently Womack and Robinson had already done quite a bit of work on their own before the meeting," Wood recalled. "Womack is the archtypical cop. Somebody told me he's the kind of guy who goes out in his front yard and gardens with his 9-mm on his side. Nice guy, though, poker-faced. Robinson was a new cop, a temporary in homicide at the time.

"Carpenter was not a physically assuming guy. He

doesn't light up a room with his presence, but he knew how to manipulate. He expected the cops to be there.

"In a sense this guy comes on like a total schlep. Unbelievable schlep, fumbling, stuttering, and other times this guy is the voice of confidence. He really has a unique ability to ingratiate himself into a situation. It is one of the most uncanny abilities I have ever seen and I've met a lot of people in this business. He could be very much the charming man. It was something he could turn off and on, but there was a hidden side to this guy totally unknown to anybody but his victims."

When Womack and Robinson showed up in Wood's office for the appointment they had not yet seen a photo of Carpenter and didn't know the beard was new. Womack did notice that the parolee was not wearing the eyeglasses his file said he wore. He was wearing sunglasses. According to his sheet he had exceptionally poor eyesight. Womack wondered if the ex-purser was trying to alter his appearance.

"We opened," Walt Robinson said in retrospect, "by saying to Carpenter that we were working a disappearance. We didn't know where Heather Scaggs was, we're in the process of talking to her friends, fellow co-workers, and so on. We told Carpenter at that point he wasn't under arrest, he wasn't going to be, we just wanted to talk with him voluntarily. If there were any areas he didn't want to talk to us about just say so. The situation of advising him of his rights later became an issue. In reality we were just investigators looking for a missing person. It's not a crime to be a missing person and therefore you don't have a suspect. In that case you don't have to admonish a person, advise him of his rights.

"When we sat down and started talking to Carpenter, the first time he opened his mouth I thought, my God, this guy can't possibly be involved in the Santa Cruz homicide. He stutters so badly. He was struggling to get his words out and he was making all these contortions. I felt really awkward and embarrassed. I couldn't make eye contact with him. I soon got over that."

Womack asked him if he knew anything about the circumstances surrounding the disappearance of Heather.

Carpenter said no. "I hope s-s-she hasn't been killed, I hope she hasn't been r-r-r-raped," he added.

What an odd thing to say, thought Wood. Now, why would he think of rape?

Carpenter was asked how he spent the day and gave exactly the same alibi he had given Wood over lunch and in precisely the same words. "I can tell," Wood said afterward, "that someone is lying when they recite an alibi exactly the same way over and over." Wood was seated in the far north side of the office behind his desk while Carpenter sat to the south between Womack and Robinson.

The detectives watched Carpenter closely, shrewdly, listening, looking for some slip—some contradiction. Carpenter seemed so helpless, but behind the rumpled clothing and the mild, downtrodden, and put-upon manner of a man who seemed to be apologizing for living a keen brain clicked away.

"She was doing poorly in school and I only offered to help her out on jobs. I was trying to get her employment with a f-f-friend of mine who has a printing business in Santa Cruz," said the suspect.

"He was going to sell her a Volkswagen and all I did was furnish her this information." Expectantly, Carpenter looked at each face in turn.

Carpenter admitted making arrangements with Heather to meet him at 7:00 A.M. on May 2 at the market near her house.

"I was partying the night before and didn't get up in time," Carpenter told the officers. "Drinks and some good pot," he amplified, making a gesture of inhalation.

"We had a prior arrangement. If either party did not show up by eight then the other was not to wait." He told them about his car problems. There was no touch of cynicism in his voice. "I had to take my car in about 11:00, 11:30 in the morning to get it repaired. After it was fixed I took my parents shopping."

"While we were talking to him," recalled Robinson, "about Pingle confronting him, he pulled out that same piece of paper he had shown Pingle, the receipt from Tony's Service Station."

"What about your other car?" asked Womack.

"What do you m-m-mean?" asked Carpenter, adjusting his dark glasses. "I've only got the one. Just the Chevy station wagon that was repaired at the service station.

"They asked me," Carpenter said later, "what vehicle I had access to on Saturday, May 2. The only vehicle I had access to on that particular day was m-m-my Chevy station wagon. My Fiat was in the shop."

Sergeant Womack had not told Wood about the red Fiat they had observed, but the probation officer could tell the two officers felt they were on to a hot subject. "I had no knowledge of the red Fiat," Wood told me. "On the monthly reporting form he sent into me he was supposed to say what kind of car he drove. He had an old Chevy with some license plates—D J CARP I think, but he never told me about the Fiat.

"I was the third wheel there. I decided to keep my mouth shut. I watched as Carpenter manipulated the cops. So here's Womack pulling the strings and David pulling the strings and you could see what was going on. It was a fascinating situation, but it was one of the longest two hours I've ever spent."

Carpenter explained he had been to the ballet.

"A good investigator," Robinson told me afterward, "tries to establish a common ground with the person he's talking to. 'You know,' continued Carpenter, 'my mother always pressured me to take ballet. I was the only boy in my class who had to take ballet when I was nine years old.'

"I told him, and it was the truth, that when I was nine I was taking ballet, too, and I was the only boy in my class to have to. I realized I had established a meeting point. He lit up. My eyes opened up as wide as they've ever opened up before—Carpenter had stopped stuttering. He was under control. He got up out of his chair."

At this moment the balding, bearded, middle-aged man rose and, moving about the small office, carefully began dancing the different positions of ballet for the three dumbfounded men. Going through each of the steps, he named them as he executed the movements. The officers sat and watched him and then one another. Womack watched without visible feeling. Face-to-face he could sense the mind of the suspect ticking on, calculating each word.

"During the time he danced, about nine minutes," Robinson told me, "Carpenter really got into the ballet, got into himself. He was very comfortable with it. He did some of the dance he had seen on Saturday night, talked about the five basic ballet steps."

"I know you guys think I'm the number-one suspect," said Carpenter raising his arms over his head and then bending at the waist.

"We're working missing persons," Robinson told him, "not homicide."

"Hey," he brought out, "I'm the number-one suspect. I should be if I'm not." He sat down lightly.

Wood told Carpenter he was going to have to take three Polaroid pictures of him, partially because the most recent pictures they had of the ex-purser were from the seventies. "I need it to keep the records up." The bright flash lit up the small room as the probation officer took shots of Carpenter's right profile. The pictures came out with hair color darker than Carpenter's actually was, but Wood figured they would do. Wood then walked to the door with his client and saw him out. "Thanks for coming in. I'll be talking to you," Wood said.

"That was the last time I saw him for years," Wood told me afterward. "I took the pictures to the FBI to have them duplicated. That was kind of the beginning of the end. I've never been personally really a suspicious person, but, after all, all of my clients *were* criminals. Carpenter was the most fascinating person I ever met. I realized later how well he knew how to read people and manipulate them."

"After Carpenter left," Robinson said, "my partner keyed to the fact that it's almost like he's playing a game. 'This guy is really lame,' he said. 'He basically told us he did it and it's like he's daring us to try and prove it.' "

Russo and Desvernine from Marin County were suddenly there. The two policemen had been in another office out of earshot. "I didn't even know they were there," said Wood. "Carpenter left at 3:30 and we all got together afterward. Then I got the hell out of there."

"Ken and I," recalled Robinson, "were very protective at that point of our investigation, and so didn't give them our opinion, told them that due to prior communications, other leads that we had, we'd have to get back to them. But at that point it became clear that we had to speak to Santa Cruz. After the meeting Womack said in strong terms, 'This is the guy who did all those homicides. Friday night is coming up and he's going to be on the trails again.' "

Besse added to the story, "Russo and Desvernine called around 5:00 P.M. just before I left the office and said they thought they had some good information for me, so I hung around until they got back to Marin about 6:30 and Russo started running down what they had. All the stuff Russo told me about the missing girl, Heather Scaggs, the M.O., was so pat that I sent them back out that night.

"I went out with Rich Keaton to try and find the registered owner of the Fiat, and we tracked it down to a guy in San Francisco on Seventh Avenue and he had sold it to a gypsy who had sold it to Carpenter. We weren't able to find the gypsy." Besse suspected that Carpenter may have already gotten rid of any incriminating clothing by now, possibly immediately after the meeting in Wood's office.

"After seeing Richard Wood," said Carpenter later, "I went for a meeting with Shane Williams and Karen." At six in the evening the purser returned the station wagon to Cornelia Dillinger and took back the red Fiat.

Marin County sheriff's department sergeant Rich Keaton drove by that night to take a look at the station wagon. It was nowhere in sight, but, as he passed, Keaton saw a bright red foreign car parked in front of 23 Sussex Street.

Stoney Brook had been saddled with administrative work in the meantime, but that evening he got the call from Robinson and Womack and a meeting was set up in San Jose.

In San Jose Dan Pingle tossed fitfully in bed, his eyes locked on the bedside phone. There was still no word from Heather. Pingle wondered about Carpenter in the darkness of his apartment—What kind of man could kill someone in the morning and then go to the ballet that night?

"I contacted the FBI," Lieutenant Don Besse told me afterward. "I started surveillance at 5:40 A.M. on Saturday, May 9, 1981. The FBI still had to get some clearances."

As ordered, the deputies trailed Carpenter from 38 Sussex Street as he wandered. Twenty minutes later he lost the surveillance team on Spear Street. "Tailing," Besse told me, "is not an easy thing to do. Most cops are very paranoid about being seen, but in this case Carpenter acted as if he knew he had a tail." At 5:30 P.M. the deputies located Carpenter again.

On the morning of Sunday, May 10, supervising FBI agent in charge David Hines, working with his five-man team, began his surveillance at 6:30 A.M. from his post just down from 38 Sussex Street. At 11:56, Carpenter, wearing a green shirt and sleeveless sweater, climbed behind the wheel of his Fiat, which was parked directly in front of his house. Hines followed him. The suspect took 280 to Highway 101 and then took the Seventh Avenue cutoff and proceeded to Bryant, parked across the street, and went into the Hall of Justice. He returned in ten minutes and drove to the Goodman Lumber Company on Old Bayshore, where he bought a garden hose. Within fifteen minutes he was back at the family home on Sussex.

During the day the assorted investigators followed the suspect as he parked in shopping centers for extended periods of time, switched lanes, doubled back, drove in an aimless manner, or simply stared out of the window of his Fiat. Carpenter's driving was erratic, jerky, over the lane dividers and markers. The cops held back, waiting and watching.

"Sunday," Besse told me, "I took a team of people and we continued the surveillance. Carpenter was doing some weird things. One time, it was over by the big shopping center, Serramonte, he drives off the freeway into Serramonte, a pretty congested area. Two cars were trying to keep him in sight. He drives right into the shopping center, parks, gets out, and walks into one door of the place while we're trying to park. Then he walks right around and comes out another door, goes back to his car, and speeds away.

"The FBI came in with a couple of cars and an airplane. I didn't know about a beeper they put in his car later because the bureau has a special surveillance team and they don't tell anybody what they do. All I got was reports from them after they started using the van."

A milky-white van had mysteriously appeared parked across the street from the Carpenter family home, at 33 Sussex, just where the street begins to curve and drop toward Bemis Street. A federal SWAT team was inside and would stay there for the remainder of the watch on the suspect. How surveillance could be accomplished on such a narrow and short street was an amazement in itself. High above in the sunlight police planes soared over the shingled house on Sussex. A helicopter would be used in tandem with the aircraft to watch the former purser's home.

The Carpenter home was situated between Diamond Heights and Glen Park and the purser was watched as he walked his dog over these narrow streets, and steep, rolling hills, exchanging pleasantries with neighbors, sometimes reading as he strolled. Carpenter was spending several nights a week, as Robinson and Womack had learned, at a second-floor apartment in the Trinity Plaza Complex on Eighth and Market in downtown San Francisco. Carpenter headed for this apartment now.

After Carpenter had gone into the building one of the investigators checked out the names on the Trinity Plaza register and found that the two people Carpenter was visiting were listed as Jeff and Karen Williams in apartment 237. They had checked in on April 29.

Jeff Williams was a name out of Carpenter's past, though the police had no way of knowing this since the young man was registered under an alias. Jeff's real name was Shane Mitchell Williams, whom Carpenter had met when both were prisoners at Lompoc Prison. Williams had been serving a six-year sentence for bank robbery and was at Lompoc from May 26, 1977, until October 11, 1980, while Carpenter was there from May 9, 1978, until

May 21, 1979, The two men had often spent their recreation periods together.

Shane Williams was at this moment a federal fugitive
along with his wife, Karen, as suspects in the holdup of
a Southwest Savings and Loan in Tempe, Arizona, on
March 12, 1981.

At the beginning of April, when Carpenter had first
approached Heather Scaggs about going to Santa Cruz to
buy a car, to meet his friend, Richard, and to collect
ferns, Williams had walked into the tiny Bank of America on Lombard, patiently waited his turn in line, and
presented the teller at the window a note that read:

> You Bitch:
> Give me all your hundreds or else!

To emphasize the note Shane had opened his coat to
show what appeared to be a .22-caliber pistol tucked securely in his waistband. Actually he had no weapon. The
nervous teller slid $560 over the polished marble counter
and when the teller looked up again the robber was gone.

Again, seven days later, on May 8, Williams held up
the Time Savings and Loan on Polk Street. He showed
the note, opened his coat to display a ''gun,'' scooped
up $742, and dashed out the front door as a large bank
teller sprinted after him.

Shane boarded a no. 19 Polk bus and the teller began
banging on the door telling the driver, ''You've got a
bank robber on board!'' Shane pushed off the bus and
past the teller as Karen, who had been waiting for him
in a nearby laundromat where he was supposed to ditch
his disguise, waded in and began beating the bank teller
with her fists. ''Karen threw a body block,'' Stoney
Brook later told me, ''tackled the black guy who was
chasing them so Shane could make his getaway. The bank
they robbed was right down the street from the hotel they
were staying at.''

Shane escaped down an alley a half block away, cut
through the trash area of a bar, exited out the front door,
and hailed a cab back to Trinity Plaza. He stayed the
night at a motel, fearing police would trace him through
his wife. The teller held the kicking and biting Karen

until she broke free. When the cops arrived they found her hiding in a hallway where old women were making flower arrangements. Karen was arrested on suspicion of aiding a robbery suspect and at the station house gave the name Karen Black as her own.

"All I know is that I thought it was some racial thing," she told them. A computer check revealed her true name, but no mention of the Arizona robbery warrant was included in her file.

Shane Williams had seen Carpenter at Jackl's party on May 1, the day before Heather Scaggs disappeared. At the party the older man had reportedly told Shane and Karen, "In crime you have to have people around you that you can trust. I suggest using mini-storage compartments and safety deposit boxes where you can conceal any weapons and loot involved in a robbery." Shane suspected that Carpenter had just such a place where he might be keeping a gun.

Like David Carpenter, Shane Williams had been released to a halfway house, but in Los Angeles instead of San Francisco. Unlike Carpenter, Shane had some trouble in the halfway house.

While Karen was living in Akron, Ohio, she met Shane through an ad she saw in a New Wave music magazine, *Trouser Press*. Shane had billed himself as "the Rock and Roll Bank Robber." They corresponded through a prison service correspondence program. Karen enrolled in a small private university, Embry Aeronautical in Arizona, and just before her eighteenth birthday Shane was released from prison. Karen went to Shane's apartment in North Hollywood, stayed two nights, and then went back to school.

"Karen," said one fellow student, "is very nice, normal, and she can phone home for $2,000 any time she wants it." She saw Shane on Valentine's Day, 1981. "He was an awful mess," she recalled, "bruised from hitting himself with his hand, and he didn't even look like the same person. It was disgusting." Shane had used heroin in January.

Karen was furious. "Come back to Prescott," she warned, "and clean up or our relationship is over." Karen's schoolwork declined drastically after Shane joined

her. Deeply concerned about a debt in L.A. Shane
wanted to "do a bank" to repay it. "I kept trying to
keep him from doing it," said Karen, "all the way to the
last moment. But I decided I was in love with him and
had better go along with him."

Shane, using a kid's rifle and hiding the license plate
of Karen's International Scout with a bandana, robbed
the S & L, abandoned the car at Denny's restaurant, and
the pair hitched to L.A. Karen's father called the police
and the FBI was looking for the couple when Shane
robbed the bank is Studio City, California.

In April Shane and Karen went to Las Vegas and were
married, traveled to Tucson so Shane could get some
marijuana to sell, and, because the ex-con had trouble
getting a gun, went on to San Francisco and David Carpenter.

"On May 10," Carpenter said later, "Karen Williams c-
c-c-called me collect and said she had been arrested for
bank robbery, was in a San Francisco jail, and asked if
I would come down and bring her some money. . . . I
told her I would be down shortly but I went to the wrong
jail."

Karen had found the purser through Jeff Jackl.

"That evening Shane called me and asked if I had
heard from his w-w-wife. He explained to me he had
robbed a bank and had been successful in getting away.
I went over to see Shane at Trinity Plaza."

Carpenter later said that their conversation concerned
marijuana. "How come you had to rob a bank?" Carpenter asked Williams. "You were successful in selling
marijuana."

"I ran out of pot. As a case of last resort I robbed a
bank," Shane said. "Could you get me some marijuana
to sell?"

"Sure," said Carpenter.

"Be sure and go down and see my wife at the jail."
Shane gave Carpenter twenty dollars to give to Karen.

Often after spending an evening with Shane and Karen
in North Beach Carpenter would stay the night at their
apartment. The police were aware he was keeping a lot
of personal possessions in the Williams apartment and

they hoped the elusive Trailside .38-caliber gun might be among them. In order to make a case they needed the gun. Doggedly the detectives intended to follow Carpenter until he took them to his stash place. For some time the ex-purser had considered taking Shane to his personal hiding place. Shane, he later claimed, was anxious to get his hands on a gun. "If I had had a gun," Shane told Carpenter, "the fiasco on Polk Street would never have happened." "I have access to a gun," Carpenter replied, "and there's a possibility I would be able to loan it to you."

"He didn't say exactly when or how he was going to get the gun," remembered Shane. That evening Carpenter tried to reassure Shane about his attempts at a disguise and ended up giving him advice. "Shane had tried to cut his hair," said Carpenter, "and it had been a c-c-complete disaster. I told him to cut the rest off. Wear dark aviator glasses. This is San Francisco. It's the gay look. You could go back to the same bank you robbed and nobody would recognize you. Then I drove him to North Beach.

"I dropped him off at a rock concert. He was upset because he had blown all the money he had s-s-stolen. He was going down to the rock concert at The Stone to get his head together." Shane had spent $200 on heroin. UB40, a reggae group from England, was at The Stone. Shane saw a local punk-rock group, The Lloyds, starring Lulu, and the Stranglers with the Robert Williams Band.

Later that night Carpenter got two collect calls from Karen and he explained to her, "I've seen your friend. I've got twenty dollars for you. I'll be down to see you." In the second call he told her, " 'I'm concerned about what's going to happen to Shane.' I offered to pick up all her clothing which I did. I put them in my trunk and then went h-h-home."

On the thin, steep street the waiting was numbing. The job of observing while not being observed could be back-breakingly dull. One policeman told me that he'd once had an exciting twenty-minute stakeout but, "99 percent of the time surveillances are boring, eating cold burgers, cold french fries . . . a stomach gets sour, but you wait.

You wait and watch for a holdup man, a rapist, a killer, a guy who likes to cut people.''

The first meeting of the multijurisdictional Trailside task force was in San Jose at the Hyatt House on First Street. Because some of the attacks had occurred on federal property the FBI was present.* When Stoney Brook, Joe Henard, and George Foster arrived there were thirty people gathered around a huge table in the big conference room. Brook was wearing a navy blue, three-piece suit with white shirt and red-striped tie. The FBI agents were dressed identically. Brook began: "I say let's start a multiagency task force right now and centralize in San Francisco because that's where the suspect lives."

There was a brief skirmish about who would run the group. "The deputy chief from San Jose gave me the roughest time," Don Besse told me later. "I said, 'My guys made this case and now you expect us to give it to you?' Even he agreed I was probably the best choice to run the task force."

Much to Brook's anger Marin County was put in charge of the task force. "George Foster says, 'Let's let Marin County run it,' " Brook told me later, "and to this day I marvel at the fact that here we, Santa Cruz, are with the eyewitnesses, the physical evidence, the entire case, and the first lead that said this guy's name. We had the original file and we gave away the entire candy store in terms of having managerial control—you don't give away your investigation. I have little truck with that kind of incompetence.

"They put a lieutenant from Marin County in charge of the task force, Don Besse. Lieutenant Besse was not in on that case from square one. He came in much later, they brought him into it and put him in charge of it. We decided to take over a small building on the grounds of the Presidio—we were about a half mile from the scene where Lois DeAndrade was attacked by Carpenter in

*Also included were ATF agents and police from San Francisco, Marin, Santa Cruz, San Jose, and because of Anna Kelly Menjivar, Daly City. Each agency would provide at least two agents.

1960. Everybody together in one spot in one of those little wooden shacks.''

"That's right," Don Besse told me, "we worked out of the Presidio—the visiting officers' club. It was a small building with a kitchen and a couple of offices in a remote area. It was also close to where Mary Bennett was stabbed to death in 1979. Only the commander of the Presidio and the officer in charge of vacating the building knew who we were. They were the only two on the Presidio. It's not unusual for the Presidio to house a clandestine operation, so nobody bothered us.''

It was all coming together at last.

"On Monday, May 11," Carpenter said afterward, "I took a long l-l-lunch, 10:50 A.M. to 2:56 P.M., telling Joe, my boss, that my niece had gotten in trouble. I went down to see Karen but first broke the twenty into change she could use in vending machines. She thought she had a g-g-good chance of getting cut l-l-l-loose.'' Carpenter held up a note for Karen to read through the glass saying, "Jeff is bald now to look like a fag, with aviator glasses.''

As Carpenter left the Hall of Justice he was photographed from the air by a surveillance plane.

"Karen called later," said Carpenter, "and said she had gotten out. She had been released pending further investigation. I gave her my address and said, 'Take a taxi over here.' '' Karen had been released at 8:00 P.M. and her clothes, which had been in the wash, were still wet. "I drove over to Sussex, picked her up, and took her to the Trinity Plaza. 'Shane is broke,' I told her. Karen was upset Shane had spent the money on dope and they got into a fight. Finally I loaned Karen one hundred dollars." Karen noticed Carpenter was not stuttering.

FBI agent Richard Otstott, fifty feet away, wrote: "The suspect along with a white female with black and white hair, kind of punkish, was seen removing a suitcase and a dark-colored day pack and a small handbag from the vehicle and entered the complex, time: 10:05 P.M.'' Police knew that the killer during the Santa Cruz attack had been carrying a dark blue pack. Carpenter left at 10:41 P.M.

"Carpenter was followed around his own neighborhood, everywhere he went,'' Don Besse told me. He was observed at Tyger's Coffee Shop on the corner of Chenery, at Higher Grounds diagonally across the street, and at various pizza restaurants. All the stores gave the area the atmosphere of a little village. "Basically,'' Besse continued, "he didn't do anything that week that was suspicious, but the things he did led us to people that we were able to use against him. Shane Williams and his wife—they turned out to be the keys of the case and we wouldn't have known about them if it hadn't been for Carpenter.

"From the moment when he met with the Williamses, things started falling into place like building blocks. I personally was convinced by Tuesday that Carpenter was the guy. But we had to get enough evidence to get warrants.''

The Williamses went to North Beach with Carpenter and the police tailed the trio from one rock club to another, watching Shane and Karen amid the flashing lights. Carpenter usually waited in his car.

Carpenter explained that he didn't see the Williamses the next day, but did speak to them on the phone. "I went to the Trinity Plaza, but they weren't there so I returned home. Shane called me later and invited me to supper.''

May 12 was FBI agent Kathleen Puckett's first day on the Carpenter surveillance. At 4:30 P.M. the suspect left the printing school and at 4:39 was stopped by Hayward police on Clawiter Street for a traffic violation. At 4:51 Carpenter was at Keith's Body Shop and by 6:02 was leaving the Diamond Heights Safeway with a bag of groceries. He returned home, but at 7:38 Carpenter got into a "dirty red Fiat" and drove to Serramonte Center where he went into Serramonte Shoes. He left Ward's at 8:13 and Puckett followed at roughly five car lengths behind. Carpenter entered the Trinity Plaza lot and Puckett guessed his destination.

She beat him into the complex and was entering the elevator when he came into the lobby. She held the door as the suspect hurried to get in. "That's the way my whole day has been going,'' he said. Puckett noticed his speech was smooth. He got off at the second floor and knocked at the door of apartment 237. No one was home and he left the Trinity Plaza at 8:49 P.M. and drove west on Market Street. Carpenter lost the surveillance team but by 9:00 Puckett had located the Fiat parked in front of 38 Sussex Street and he was home for the night.

On the morning of May 13, Wednesday, while Carpenter was at work, Brook and Womack decided to go fishing at the suspect's house on Sussex Street and speak with his parents. By this time the ATF had located Mollie Purnell, Carpenter's pen pal who had done the actual purchasing of the gun, and were asking her general questions about the revolver she had reported stolen. The agents had started by looking for registrations on that type of gun. "Mollie Purnell," Brook had told me, "was as hard to find as an honest lawyer."

Brook told me about the Carpenter family home. "It was a very neat house. Dan Carpenter would sit by the window and drink wine. The mother is a strong lady, a powerful woman. She emasculated the kid from square one. We all go through traumatic experiences but. . . . I mentioned to Mrs. Carpenter that my glasses just got broken and asked her to recommend an optometrist. 'There's a doctor down on Mission,' she says. I said, 'OK, I'll go down there and see about this.'"

Before they left, Brook asked some more questions and she told him about Candy Townsend. Her son met Candy at an intersection, used his AAA card to give her a tow, took her up to Mount Tamalpais, and proposed on the spot. At the first of the month he had broken the engagement and asked her to leave. Carpenter's mother had no idea where she was now, only that she had once been a cocktail waitress. Her son had mentioned she was working in a bar in the financial district in San Francisco. "A little sleazy," she said, "but not a real dive."

After he left, Brook called two officers and asked them if they could try and locate Candy Townsend. "Then I went down to the optometrist and tried to see if they also had a client by the name of David Carpenter. It turned out, as we found out later, they actually had a pair of his glasses waiting there. I think he saw those pictures come out and he wanted a different pair of glasses. He got rid of all that stuff, the ball cap, the jacket, never to be seen again," Brook told me.

"Three hours later we get a call from officers Andy Balmy and Ron Kern, two of the SFPD's best street investigators, 'Candy's working down on Montgomery. Come and get her, we've got her down at the police department.' "

Carpenter left work at 5:16 P.M. and went to Southland Shopping Center, which was some ten minutes from the printing school. He went to Lucky's, exited, drove a short distance, and then got out. FBI agent Myskins observed him as he looked under the driver's seat and dashboard, went through the glove compartment and looked beneath his car and above each of the tires. He later claimed that he had heard a rattle, but police felt he must have suspected the presence of an electronic homing device. Carpenter went to the Payless Drug Store and then returned home. He went upstairs to talk with his mother.

"Some policemen were here today asking about you," she said from her bed.

"So," said her son. Visits by the police were nothing new to him. He had spoken recently with the San Jose cops.

"They said they were from Santa Cruz," continued his mother.

The purser left the house in a rush. Galvanized, he slid behind the wheel of his car and headed toward the Trinity Plaza. He appeared to have made a decision. The drive from his home to the apartment complex took twenty minutes by freeway.

The seven-story Trinity Plaza, 1169 Market, opened off a parking lot and bricked plaza adjoining a restaurant, and ate up almost half the block between Seventh and Eighth. From above it took the shape of a lazily shaped letter J.

At 6:30 P.M. Agent Hines was waiting inside the complex's glass-enclosed lobby when mobile units contacted him by radio to tell him the suspect had just parked in the apartment building lot. Within minutes, Hines saw the older man enter the ornate, red-carpeted lobby. There was an elevator under the gold clock and a smoke shop to the right of this. At the security desk within the lobby the guard gave Carpenter a quick once over and went back to his paperback. It was now approaching 6:45, and anticipating the purser's usual path, Hines started up the stairs to the second floor. Carpenter was directly behind him, taking two steps at a time, and passed the agent midway. The suspect turned right at the top of the stairs and Hines passed surveillance off to another agent, Dick Otstott, who was in the laundry room. Carpenter knocked and the door to apartment 237 opened. Otstott heard a male voice call out, "I thought I recognized that knock." The agent heard a female voice as well.

"We had man-to-man defense and zone defense around the Trinity Plaza," recalled Hines. There were, of course, the two planes on air surveillance who tailed the "distinct orange-red colored car" and a radio transmitter, a "beeper," placed in the Fiat.*

"After w-w-work I drove over to Shane's," Carpenter recollected, "I brought two figurines on a stone I had gotten for Christmas for Karen." Carpenter later claimed that neither bank robbery nor guns were discussed that night. He used his cover story of pot dealing to provide his reason for taking Karen and Shane to Gems. "During dinner Shane w-w-was talking about getting m-m-marijuana to sell. I told Shane my connection was at 20th and Mission [a man called Chuey Rodriguez], but I had been unable to locate him. I offered to let them have my marijuana. I told them I would let them have my personal stash of m-m-marijuana that I kept at Gems of the Golden West. Shane explained, 'I just want to make enough money to go to L.A. to meet my connection to buy more marijuana and then return.'"

Karen fixed steak and later, while she washed the dinner dishes, heard the conversation turn to the subject of guns. Shane was trying to nail Carpenter down about a gun. She wanted to call a girlfriend in Akron and, fearing

---

*In addition to Hines and Otstott, seventeen other FBI operatives were involved in tailing the suspect: Johnson, Buck, Lopez, Kellor, Hawks, Myskins, McKevitt, Robinson, Malone, Williams, Puckett, Hadley, Schildknecht, Gray, Newsome, Fleish, and McCann.

the apartment phone might be tapped, wanted to use a booth away from the Trinity Plaza. She made her call and returned. Shane was saying, "Hey, most of that hundred is gone just on regular expenses, and I've got to go out and do something. Help me out."

Carpenter said later he offered to buy the couple a bus ticket. Shane, Karen, and Carpenter left the Trinity Plaza and drove aimlessly.

"It came up on the spur of the moment," Karen recalled. "Carpenter said in the car, 'I've got something I want to show you. Shane should have a gun and I could get one.' His speech was just a normal excited tone of voice without stuttering. 'Let's go get it,' he said." The trio drove over to 38 Sussex and picked up the duplicate key to Gems that Carpenter had secretly made.

At approximately 9:26 P.M. Carpenter entered the Gems warehouse using the purloined key. Carpenter was unaware that the owner of the warehouse, Florence Neuman, had known for over a year he had such a key.

"We parked," recalled Carpenter, "a little way down from the doorway, fourth building up f-f-from Gems of the Golden West, parallel to the curb." Unknown to Carpenter, at that moment nine surveillance photos were silently taken by the police.

"There were two locks. The alarm went off and I turned off the alarm, clicked the light on just inside the door. I closed the door, and while Shane and Karen remained at the office w-w-which w-w-was lit I walked back to where I had my stash in the dark behind the file cabinets."

Karen remembered the visit differently, "Carpenter carried a flashlight. First there was an office area, a fairly small room with two desks. We moved into a large warehouse where two aisles went down its length on both sides. We took the aisle on the right." Their footsteps echoed in the deserted building, past key-chain racks, bins of gem stones, stock catalogues, and crated inventory.

"Two-thirds of the way was a file cabinet," said Karen, "we moved some boxes from in front and scooted around the back of the cabinet and pulled out a crumpled brown paper bag. It was bigger than a lunch bag, but not as big as a grocery sack.''

After he had gotten what he came for, Carpenter said he turned the alarm back on, locked both doors, and joined his friends standing outside. He let Karen carry the bag to the car. Shane was later to say that Carpenter showed Karen and himself ''nothing of importance.''

The police parked in the shadows outside, saw only a light through a bank of windows at the top of the door and longed to see what was going on inside the trinket and key-chain warehouse. Two minutes had passed, four, six minutes and then the trio had exited at 9:32. Silently, expectantly, the investigators continued tailing their suspect.

FBI Agent Kathleen Puckett, fifty yards away, had ''a direct view of David Carpenter exiting the warehouse'' with his friends. And although she saw them leave in the purser's car, she did not see the orange bag Williams would later claim they had retrieved and placed between the two front bucket seats.

''We drove to a service station,'' said Carpenter. ''Shane and I s-s-stood outside by the car talking while Karen made a call from a booth. We returned to the Trinity Plaza. That's when I became very paranoid. When we came in I saw a man looking at us. We went inside the lobby. A man came in and was talking to the doorman. Shane said take the elevator. I said t-t-take the stairs.'' Carpenter had Karen carry the bag into the lobby at 9:46 P.M. since he felt no one would stop her.

Shane and Carpenter entered the Trinity apartment with Karen and the purser put his blue backpack on the table. He looked around the room as if seeing it for the first time. It was light colored in every respect, from the tan drawstring curtains to the yellow walls and hanging gold light fixtures. The only exception was the dark wood paneled cabinet over the stove. Even this was offset by more gold, two gleaming square light fixtures, which were set into the cabinet over the appliance.

Carpenter rummaged in the blue backpack with black straps and, according to Shane Williams later, produced a bright bag. Inside this, wrapped in a white and yellow gingham felt cloth, was a .38-caliber Rossi revolver with a black handle. There was also an entire box of bullets in a green and goldish container. Williams said that the gun and bullets had been hidden in the Gems' warehouse. "He said he would allow me to use a gun that was on loan to him, but I had to be very careful not to lose it. It was a five-shot, .38-caliber black revolver with a black butt, and it was inside an orange bag."

"I fired it the previous weekend and it's working fine," Carpenter said.

"Great," said Williams, running his fingers over the weapon.

Carpenter looked up. He could see himself reflected in the dark square glasses the T-shirted youth was wearing. Shane said the balding man then began to give him pointers on how to use and care for the revolver, expertise picked up in his eighteen years in prison. Carpenter took a small piece of tissue paper and showed Shane how to clean the gun. He pushed it through the chambers with the plunger from Shane's water pipe.

Carpenter showed the punks two firing positions. The first was with hands clasped together with the index fingers pointing as the gun and straight out from the shoulders. The second was the same but from a crouching position, knees bent.

"Only put four bullets in the chamber," Carpenter said, according to Shane, "and then you won't shoot yourself accidentally." The purser then showed Shane how to hold the .38, placing his thumb between the hammer and the cartridge. "Hold it in the ready position," he advised. "The safety is broken so you have to hold the hammer back with a finger."

He showed Karen and did it with one hand because his fingers were large. He curled his thumb around the hammer and released it. "Because you have such small hands," he told her, "you should put the finger of the other hand in between and use that to break the pressure. Let it down slow."

"I gave Shane and Karen m-m-most of the marijuana," Carpenter said later. "I was there twenty-five minutes, then left and went home."

Unaware of the gun transfer, the surveillance team outside perked up when they saw Carpenter leaving the Trinity Plaza at about 11:00 P.M. The agent wrote in his notebook: "Carpenter observed exiting the apartment complex and carrying a gray suitcase and a green plastic bag which seems to contain several boxes which he then put into the Fiat automobile and drove away."

The agents started up their car and slowly followed the printer, hoping that if they did have the right man then he would eventually lead them to the guns used in the Trailside murders. They noticed that the suspect now drove less erratically. Carpenter arrived home and at exactly 11:16 the door to his house slammed shut.

Years later I asked Inspector Brook if he thought Carpenter was setting up the two punks by giving them the .38.

"Yeah," he replied.

"You do?" I said. "What do *they* think about that?"

"I don't know if Shane and Karen ever came to the same conclusion," said Brook. "Shane's no dummy, by the way. I put that guy right up there in the 130 to 140 percentile on the IQ list. He's an extremely bright young man and she's no fool. . . .

"They took the .38. My hunch is that David Carpenter was giving them the gun, and the idea was that Shane would go out and pull a bank job someplace and the local constabulary would blow him out of his socks and then they'd go, "Well, we'll do a ballistics check on this shooting iron,' and they'd find it matches the Trailside case.

"The other thing is I think Carpenter had designs on Karen."

"I don't know how much you know about criminals," Richard Wood said later, "but guys who are really into crime constantly use the people around them, continue to try and turn the people around them just a little bit to use them to their advantage. So I wouldn't be a bit surprised if Shane was trying to use David and David was trying to use Shane. At the same time each had his own agenda."

"In a nutshell," Shane told me afterward, "Carpenter wasn't trying to get me to lose his gun. He was far too confident for that. He was probably going to kill Karen

and me, but it wasn't that he wanted me to get busted
with his gun.''

"By Wednesday night,'' Lieutenant Besse told me,
''we had found Candy Townsend in San Francisco. She
didn't want any part of the cops. They took her down to
Seventh Street, investigations. That's where I met them
at 11:00 P.M. and around midnight or so she finally gave
us enough information to tie Carpenter in. Candy saw a
lot of things. She lived with Carpenter for four months,
so she had a lot of information which just wrapped it up.

"Candy was afraid of Carpenter, which is why she
tried to get away from him, but she was worried he might
do her in if he found her. That's why she stayed with him
for a while and was afraid to leave him because of the
way he acted and talked. Of course she wasn't the nicest
girl in the world, nor the prettiest. She wasn't ugly, but
she certainly wasn't any beauty. She was medium build.
She was a real street person, and she would have got
along just fine on her own.''

4

The Ides of May

Two interviews were held with Candy Townsend, Carpenter's former fiancée, on Thursday, May 14. The first was at the Hall of Justice and the second was at 9:30 P.M. in her flat at the Colonial Hotel near the bar where she worked. "Womack and I go to interview Candy," Brook told me. "We're just rapping and she tells us how she and Carpenter met. We haven't told her what we're there about. We're feeling the energy."

"Did he ever give you anything?" Brook asked.

Candy thought for a moment. "A ring, but the stone fell out."

"I've come to think of that as a description of David Carpenter's life," Brook told me later, "the stone just fell out of the setting."

"Did you ever give him anything?" asked Brook.

"No, he just took it."

Candy Townsend then began to describe the gold jacket.

"I don't think the jacket was very big. It disappeared in late March or early April. He told me someone had stolen it from his car while it was parked at a supermarket. I found this unusual because having ridden in an automobile with him on numerous occasions I observed that he habitually and ritualistically locks the car doors, both upon entry and exit.''

She described the jacket as a gold nylon windbreaker with black stripes and fuzzy black lining, decorated with slogans.

''Up to this point,'' Brook told me afterward, ''we had lacked the nexus—a legal term—the connection. We had him fitting the description. But we could not put him at the scene with a gun in his hand. That jacket was it—the nexus!''

''Excuse us a moment,'' said Stoney to Candy Townsend, and he and Sergeant Womack left the room. Brook was euphoric. He closed the door behind them, broke into a grin, and the two men let out a shout of joy that Candy could hear in the other room.

''Then,'' recalled Brook for me, ''we made the call to the task force.''

Laying the groundwork for the arrest and search warrants for a multijurisdictional investigation was time consuming, complicated, and exhausting. In Marin Rich Keaton had started at 5:00 P.M. working with Ernie Zunino in the DA's office. While Keaton was working, Joe Henard was obtaining the proper local papers for a search warrant with Jim Berglund, who was brought in from Santa Cruz to do the arrest warrant for that county. ''We were cross-referencing all of our information with Santa Cruz,'' Keaton told me, ''so that I could read all the reports that they had and things I had not seen up to that point.'' None of the men got much sleep that night.

As the weekend approached, the police grew increasingly nervous about the suspect eluding them once again and being loose on the hiking trails. The FBI did not share their concern and registered their objection to the net being tightened before the elusive and all-important murder gun was recovered. However, in the end, the arrest was set for the early hours of Friday morning, May 15.

At 8:15 P.M., on May 14, Carpenter drove the Fiat to the Diamond Heights Pay 'n Save drugstore and made a purchase. The surveillance team noted that it was a parcel the size of a shoebox. The suspect then returned home.

Thursday evening, near Seventh and Mission streets, Brook located a clean hotel in proximity to both the Hall of Justice and the Trinity Plaza, where the suspect and his two companions were holed up.

"I took Candy back to the hotel, the Americana Motor Lodge, along with policewoman Sandy Miller," Brook recalled. "Candy was staying with friends. She went to pick up her stuff and came back with Sandy." After arranging for the rooms for his witness and officers, Brook entered his room. Candy was complaining she couldn't move without an officer standing over her. While others had begun to show the strain of the last moments of the chase, taking advantage of the sauna and thirty-foot heated pool between the second and third floors, Brook was, as always, cool, crisp, and fresh in his tailored suit.

Brook put his briefcase with the task force notes on the coverlet of his queen-size bed. Outside, he could hear the sound of Greyhound buses departing from the nearby depot. He reached down, turned on the ebony-based lamp, adjusted the bright yellow lampshade, and pulled the amber curtain closed. Brook placed his pocket change and room keys on the round glass table before the window, carefully hung up his jacket in the closet, smoothing the lapels, and sat down in the rough gray easy chair.

For a while he looked at his notes, then at his watch, noted the time, and then stared absently at the mundane serigraph above the maple bedstead. He thought about the first composite of the Trailside Killer, done after the stabbing of Barbara Schwartz, and wondered why, if Carpenter had been the killer, it had been so far off. Brook chalked it up to the dark navy watchcaps Carpenter wore pulled down over his ears. From a distance that could be mistaken for the shaggy haircut Schwartz's killer had been described as having.

"I was impatient while waiting for the warrant," Brook told me later. "I'm a strong work-ethic person, so bureaucracy drives me up the wall. Anyway, that night Candy comes to my door. She wants to go swimming.

Wants to know if I have a swimsuit. I tell her I've only got T-shirts. She takes off her top right there and puts on the T-shirt. She goes swimming in the hotel pool. Everybody is in a good mood. Got a couple of bottles.

"I got the warrant. Plans were made to go get the magistrate to sign it. I went back to the hotel and around 2:00 A.M. I took off my clothes, showered, shaved, and lay down naked under a sheet."

Brook stared at the ceiling. "I only slept for an hour. Then I got up. Put on my best three-piece suit before going out to arrest David Carpenter.

"Remember, Robert," Brook said with a rare smile, "always look better than the crook."

At five o'clock in the morning, Friday, May 15, 1981, San Francisco Municipal Judge Albert Wollenberg, Jr., signed Brook's warrant and, at the request of the Marin sheriff's office, sealed this warrant and all supporting documents. Almost one full week had gone into the surveillance, but the suspect had still not led them to the gun, the final piece of evidence, the crucial bit of evidence.

"I was so busy managing," Lieutenant Besse told me afterward, "that I never had a chance to meet many of the actors in this story. Like the morning we were to arrest Carpenter. I had been up all night back at task force headquarters getting everything ready because Rich

Keaton and Stoney Brook were getting the warrants signed. I was putting together arrest teams and putting together a whole plan for the operation. There was a lot of logistics, serving all those search warrants—we had search warrants on both his cars and his house.

"Around 5:00 A.M. they came over with all the warrants signed and I started assigning people to do all these things. They just couldn't believe it when I said I wasn't going out to the arrest, we had decided to have a person from each agency arrest him. They asked me, 'You're not going to go out there after all this and arrest him?' 'No,' I said, 'I'm not going to arrest him, that's not my job. I'd love to be there, but that's not my job.' It takes a lot of patience and control not to do that, I'll tell you, 'cause I've been a street cop for a long time. I certainly wanted to be there.

"There was a concern Carpenter might do something, and I didn't want fifty cops jumping on him; that's why everyone wasn't there. Rich and Stoney were the actual arrest team, the FBI was backup, an FBI SWAT team hidden in the white van, the SFPD represented by Ron Kern and Andy Balmy, San Jose. Daly City sent us a guy off and on, and they only did that because they were afraid of negative publicity. I had to twist their arm because they didn't want to believe Kelly Menjivar, the teller from Carpenter's neighborhood, was anything but a missing person. There were people at the arrest site who weren't assigned but went because they wanted to be there." Ken Womack and Walt Robinson, the two San Jose officers who had solved the case, had been assigned elsewhere—Womack in San Jose for court and Robinson at the task force headquarters on the Presidio.

The looming hillsides above fog-wet Sussex Street cast deep shadows over the two dozen local, state, and federal investigators who waited, intent. During the last hour they had barely spoken. The windows of the various cars and the van were fogged up. "It was colder than a well digger's ass," remembered Rich Keaton.

At 7:10 A.M. there was still no trace of David Carpenter. He had been followed to his door the previous night. Agents of the FBI SWAT team in the white van were getting restless. Everyone knew it was well past the time the suspect normally left for work. Nerves in the waiting cars were stretched to heart-skipping tightness. Joe Henard was to the north of the suspect's home, eight houses down, while Brook watched the Carpenter home in his rearview mirror. From his earlier visit to speak with Mrs. Carpenter, Brook knew there were two exits from the ground-floor studio where Carpenter lived in the old, brown-shingled house.

"I didn't see him come out," Henard told me later. "Carpenter was just suddenly *there.*"

"There, there he is," hissed one detective. "That's him. There's the sonofabitch." Clips and metallic buttons were unsnapped, jackets rustled, zippers were unzipped, and pistols were clutched by twenty hands.

Carpenter, who was on his way to the printing school, was dressed in khaki work clothes and a tan sweater. He carried a large plastic shopping bag with the word "SHOES" on it in one hand. As the suspect descended toward his car Brook noticed he was wearing a tan watch cap pulled down over his ears to keep them warm. A cop with Rich Keaton was concerned that the missing gun might be in the plastic bag. "We don't know what's in it. If he's got the gun he could blow you away." Keaton replied then that the FBI would blow Carpenter away in exchange. Carpenter looked both ways down the street.

Brook motioned for silence, straightened his vest, adjusted his tie, and ran his hand through the sides of his dark hair to see that it was straight. Keaton said softly, "Well, Stoney, let's go sell some insurance." Brook's hand shot to the handle, the door of the car swished open, and Brook strode purposefully across the pavement toward the balding man coming down the steps. Carpenter was making a beeline for the Fiat, which was parked near the front of a garage at 36 Sussex Street. He was bending over to get out his keys to unlock the car door, the sun catching and highlighting the gray in his new beard. "He's made us," Keaton whispered to Brook. "Hi there, Mr. Carpenter, hiya, hiya, hiya . . ." Carpenter looked up, suspecting that something was up. The suspect's gaze through his rounded bifocal glasses finally rested on the ramrod straight, advancing figure of Brook.

"And what did you say to David Carpenter?" I asked Brook later.

"I said, stretching out my hand, 'Mr. Carpenter, my name is Stoney Brook and I've been waiting to meet you.' "

The Santa Cruz investigator's quiet sentence seemed to trumpet down the narrow twisted street. "How d-d-do you d-d-do . . ." said Carpenter. "W-w-what do you want?" and when they told him he said, "That sounds a lot like m-m-m-murder, a capital case."

Keaton, shivering in the cold, shoulders hunched, thought to himself, He has trouble with *murder* and *mother,* but then to him they're synonymous. I just wanted to develop a communication with him where we could legitimately get by the first step of Miranda. We didn't care about lies; lies are better than no answer."

"What's in the bag, Mr. Carpenter?" Brook asked, gesturing with his left hand, cuff pulled down against the chill. His aim was to keep the suspect's hands away from the bag that he expected contained a gun.

Carpenter was holding the bag by its drawstring with both hands. "I'm not talking to you anymore," said Carpenter, shaking his right index finger at Keaton, leaning forward and then starting to turn away. "I have nothing further to s-s-say. I'm on my way to work . . ." Keaton moved to the purser's left as Carpenter took a step backward and folded his arms across his chest defiantly.

Keaton slammed him up against the garage door, and, in a flash, clapped the cuffs on Carpenter while car doors were flung open and a torrent of men, almost the entire Trailside task force, flowed into the street and up toward the house on the steep hill. They were all drawn magnetically to the harmless-looking purser, a closing ring around a man who looked from face to face to face. Carpenter's mouth moved slowly like a fish gulping at words that wouldn't come out. The sun then began lighting up the fog-slicked pavement, burning out any shadows left on Sussex Street.

Carpenter offered no resistance and his tongue darted at his lips as Brook took away the plastic bag and gave it to George Foster.* The inspector took the keys for the Fiat from Carpenter and noticed as he did so that a Foxy Lady key ring dangled from it. The Fiat would have to be driven to the police garage to be searched. Brook carried the bag over to the left side of the garage.

Keaton was thoughtful. "When I put the cuffs on Carpenter it was somewhat strange," he told me later, "after all we had been through the last two years. As I put the cuffs on his wrists he turned to me and whispered, 'Please don't hurt me. I've always been a model inmate.' That was such a strange statement to hear after all we had gone through to catch him, hearing someone say, 'Please, don't hurt me.' " Carpenter was subdued, his legs spread wide, as he peered at other members of the Trailside task force over his shoulder.

"I let Rich arrest him, cuff him," recalled Brook. "Keaton wears about twenty pounds of jewelry, looks more like a used-car dealer, but he didn't like Carpenter and showed it. Oddly enough, Robert, I don't hate the man and I don't resent him. I try very hard not to get emotionally involved. The morning we arrested him the other cops didn't want to talk to the guy. I mean they snapped and snarled at him. Some of the guys from Marin didn't really want to have anything to do with him. But I like to think I can sit down with any guy, even like David Carpenter, and it's not my place to be judgmental and it's important to me that they understand that. I'm not judgmental about what he did . . . it's kinda like I don't care what they tell me just so long as they keep talking.

"I tried to get Carpenter to talk to us in the street. Valmy and Kern were backup and the officers were trying to get him to talk about the murders. I showed him the warrant—to arrest someone like Carpenter and hardly hear a word from him is a frustration that is hard to deal with." Carpenter's stance was so wide he lurched to the right as he turned. His eyes widened as he became aware of the now revealed camera.

"On the way to jail," Keaton recalled, "we get caught in a little bit of traffic on the way out of Diamond Heights

---

*The bag contained an album of Wagner recordings. Carpenter also had marijuana on him.

to Bryant Street, going kind of slow. I'm looking in the rearview mirror and Carpenter's looking at me. He says he wants an attorney. I knew that without his attorney present we're not going to get anything anyway."

Keaton turned and said, "Mr. Carpenter, who do you live there with? Who do you live in that residence with?"

"My m-m-m-mother. My father."

"I see. How about your parole officer. Does he know you live there?"

"Yes, he does."

"How do you get along with your mother?"

Carpenter thought a moment. "N-n-n-nice try at psychology, but it won't work."

"Mr. Carpenter," said Keaton, turning full around and reaching inside his dark suit jacket, "let me show you something." Keaton took out his bright gold badge and held it up within a few inches of Carpenter's nose. "Would you do me a favor and read that."

"M-M-M-Marin County."

"That's right. I'm a detective sergeant in Marin County. I don't need any psychology. This is my psychology. I'm just having a conversation with you."

For the first time Carpenter knew that the investigators were there not about the missing Heather Scaggs but about the Trailside murder cases.

"Y-y-y-yeah, sure," said Carpenter falling silent.

"The man," Keaton told me later, "is not stupid. He's a fox. I'm not about to downplay his ability."

Carpenter was immediately placed in secret and heavy custody as Howenstein prepared a statement for a press conference in four hours. At the same time police went with a warrant to Shane and Karen William's apartment at the Trinity Plaza on Market Street. The officers explained that they wanted to look around, and that was OK with the rockers.

5

The Search

At exactly 7:22 Rich Layden and Joe Henard climbed the two flights of steps at 38 Sussex to serve the search warrant on Mrs. Carpenter. She came down in her bathrobe and opened up the twelve-by-twelve-foot studio apartment. During the search she insisted on being present. "She wanted to see everything," Brook told me, "right when we served the search warrant." Henard added, "She's a bitch, a ball-breaker. Stoney just kind of herded her off into a corner and started romancing her." Mrs. Carpenter admitted frankly that she'd lie to save her son. She never stopped covering for him, thought Brook.

Layden and Henard's search was well organized, thorough. They had been preparing for it for twenty-four hours. Each member of the search team had a specific job to do and a place in the chain of command. Layden, the Marin officer, was the team leader, the "finder," the actual searcher who would bag and tag each item. Henard was the recorder, who listed each item in the evidence log.

Corrie Sanders and George Ito from the Sacramento

criminology section, CI&I, were the latent fingerprint
team. Melvin Peterson, also from CI&I, was the photographer and under the direction of both Henard and the
latent print team. A technician from the Department of
Justice in Santa Rosa was in charge of recovery. Arrangements had been made to pick up the Chevy station wagon
from Jackl's home in San Leandro while the Fiat was
driven to the San Francisco police garage to be searched
later in the day.

The warrant specified exactly what the officers could
look for and what they could and could not take. On the
police shopping list were the missing gun and the gold
jacket worn in the Santa Cruz attack. Brook was fairly
certain the jacket had been destroyed, but it was the recovery of the elusive .38-caliber Rossi (or the .44) that
was crucial to any sort of conviction.

The warrant listed: ''Binoculars, yellow windbreaker,
baseball hat, faded Levi's, bullets to match a .38, tennis
shoes with a 6-W pattern-type on soles, small blue day
pack, photos of young women, personal letters . . .''

Carpenter's lower-floor studio with a bath had a half-
wall that helped form a closet and was part of the structure of the main house. A small window looked out onto
Sussex Street. Although the suspect's room had a heavy
brown chest with three large drawers and two small
drawers, Layden headed directly for the makeshift closet.
There was a blue blazer there, a blue suit, and two sport
coats. Peterson was directed to take a photograph of the
sole pair of tennis shoes discovered there, a gold pair
with four stripes. They did not appear to Henard as if
they had ever been worn.

''During surveillance time,'' an official told me later,
''that guy would always go into these damn shopping
centers, this store and that store, sometimes he'd come
out with a package. Now those tennis shoes they found
in his room they're right at the front of his closet. He
deliberately put those shoes there. He bought them at Pay
n'Save on the evening before his arrest. He got those
shoes because he knew the police were going to come
and they were going to look for them. Carpenter's a size
nine and a half; it was a ten that was found in the closet
right up front.''

Peterson took several shots of the tennis shoes. Now more shoes came out of the closet—"Leather sandals with tire-tread soles," wrote Henard and then logged, "from the back of the closet, black dress shoes." There was a noticeable absence of hiking shoes.

They now turned their attention to the chest of drawers upon which a tangle of key chains lay. Layden pulled out the bottom drawer. They found a "735 Selci brand pair of binoculars, a green jacket, cloth golf hats, a watch, wire-rim sunglasses, two knit wool watch caps, underwear, nice white sweater."

Henard noticed that other than socks, underwear, and a man's herringbone jacket there was hardly any men's clothing. "Lots of ladies' though," he recalled. "There were grocery bags full of women's clothing. There was no luggage." Now the book shelves near the bed were looked over. Then Layden walked over to the top of the white shelf formed by part of the foundation of the house where he found another pair of wire-rim glasses and a two-and-a-half-foot stack of hiking maps and books.

A brochure that advertised books and magazines for sale that taught various ways to murder people was found—publications such as *Guerrilla Warfare Techniques, How to Kill,* and *Kill or Be Killed.* The brochure talked about snipers and assassins. There were no markings in it.

Henard listed:

Orange Mount Tam guide, usually purchased on the mountain. A red covered book put out by the Sierra Club, *To Walk in a Quiet Place.* [Map for Mountain Home and the East Peak were on page 94 and a map of Point Reyes was on page 164.]
A Sierra Club schedule with daily information about what was happening on the mountain on specific dates. A second schedule dated January 1–April 30, 1981.
Hiker's guide to Tam.
Motel directories.
A Murray street map of San Jose.

There were thirty-seven maps in all. Henard closed the studio noting that there were no hiking clothes. "But, witnesses," he told me afterward, "said the killer never *looked* like a hiker." Carpenter later said he hiked in army fatigues with various pockets and wore hush puppies with thick socks. The police went upstairs and searched throughout the main floor of the frame house, inside closets and behind drawers, around and above every conceivable hiding place. Layden kept an eye out for the small blue day pack that had been observed by the surveillance team and was mentioned specifically in the search warrant.

After they had searched the new storage shed in the backyard they carefully bagged the wool watch caps, various letters, and photographs of young women. Everything taken from the house was listed on an inventory sheet, "the return list," which Henard would file on May 19. After the house search Henard went with his fellow searchers to the Hall of Justice to search the Fiat.

It was now 11:30 A.M. and in Mill Valley Reba Lehman, Nation Meyer's girlfriend, who had loaned Carpenter her BMW, was answering her front door. She had not seen Carpenter since he had returned her BMW and was making plans to leave Victor St. Martin's home. Graham Desvernine of the FBI and Officer Gurinsky were at the door and Reba was "very nervous, flabbergasted," as she put it later. She had been ill and the policemen had awakened her. During the one-hour interview she gave them what amounted to a one-page report. "I told them some, but not all. I did not tell about the gun. Because St. Martin didn't say anything, I didn't say anything," she remembered. "After they left I began having nightmares. It was very disconcerting."

By noon Henard was in the basement of the SFPD. Ahead of the search team lay an exhausting two-hour examination of the red Fiat. The latent team began examining the interior. Ito and Sanders unscrewed the rearview mirror and removed the ashtray for fingerprint scrutiny while Henard continued listing the recovered items in the log one by one as they were brought to him by Layden. There were letters in the auto addressed to Carpenter and thirty assorted maps in the glove compartment. Henard wrote:

Item #33—a state map. Only marking in red ink de-
lineating county lines. In green ink the south section
from Vallejo to Del Norte County outlined. [Carpen-
ter later claimed he had outlined the boundaries of his
federal parole district here.]
A map of San Rafael with Mount Tam included.
No markings.
A map of Marin County.
A map of Tam.
A map of Point Reyes.
Map showing mileage between points.
A map of Santa Cruz.
A map showing Santa Rosa and San Francisco.
Parks in green.

Layden discovered a pair of faded brown prescription
glasses in a dark vinyl case, of higher quality than the
wire-rimmed glasses in the studio apartment and prescribed by a Dr. Wright of Market Street. Another dark
vinyl envelope, found in the backseat window, was
brought to Henard. He dumped it out and saw it contained more key chains. "Three large, eight small key
rings found in backseat window of Fiat," he wrote.
From the trunk a quantity of pine needles was recovered along with one unidentified hair. On the floorboard
of the front seat of the stammering man's new car, on the
passenger side, covered over with more dried pine needles, Layden found a crumpled minipack of green tissues. It was recalled that the missing Heather Scaggs had
brought some along with a cola from a convenience store
where she was to meet the suspect on the morning she
vanished.

6

Disclosure

Generally Shane and Karen were very cooperative, so cooperative the police commented on it afterward. She was dressing when they arrived, but let them keep pounding while she finished brushing her teeth. Since the investigators knew that Carpenter had been staying with them for some time on almost a daily basis they were amazed that the missing gun wasn't found. The police even looked for false bottoms in the table and six-drawer dresser.

After a complete search of the Trinity Plaza apartment which took about twenty minutes, the detectives cautioned the pair against mentioning the search to the press or anyone. Nodding and smiling the Williamses saw the police out the front door and practically on the heels of the departing men left the apartment complex, walked to Mission Street where they took a bus to the terminal for transportation to the East Bay. Under yet another set of assumed names they checked into a motel there.

"There were red faces over the fact our men didn't find the gun," Brook told me.

"How come they didn't? Where was the gun?"

"It was in a bag and they just didn't look in the bag," said Brook.

"You mean they went for that particular reason and they didn't look."

"I have a lot of anger about the case," said Brook in a low voice.

"I know."

"When they came to interview us after Carpenter was arrested," Shane Williams told me in retrospect, "the gun was in the apartment and we were just winging it and making up stories. We thought they were coming for us, but they were coming there about Carpenter. We started making up a story and they managed to believe it. . . . I doubt they would tell you how embarrassingly unperceptive they were. Finally after a perfunctory search they left, and this after we had just barely escaped being arrested for a bank robbery.

"When they first knocked on the door, I thought they were there for me and so I just made up a story about how we met Carpenter through an ad in a singles magazine and that he was more or less like a generous 'trick.' I told them he was paying me and my wife for sex with Karen, and because of that he got Karen out of jail as a go-between, and that's how we met. The [unloaded] gun was in a paper bag in an orange bag, which made it crinkle, completely visible, slightly under the dresser."

"Shane," Rich Keaton of the sheriff's office told me later, "I can just see him while the FBI agents and the others were in their room in the Trinity Plaza. I can just see Shane sweet-talking his way right out of the situation. He's a good con artist. He really is. He's not a very good bank robber though."

Amidst reporters and television cameras Sheriff Howenstein finally made his "long awaited disclosure." In San Rafael, at exactly 11:20 A.M., he told the press that the capture came after a number of citizens had called his office on the Trailside hotline. Search warrants were gotten, he told them, on two homes in San Francisco as well as for both of Carpenter's automobiles.

"We feel without being too speculative at this point

that evidence should be forthcoming to indicate whether Carpenter is involved in the Mount Tamalpais slayings,'' said Howenstein, indicating Carpenter's name was not on his list of 168 possible prime suspects and that it was a ballistics link that tied the Trailside murders together. Stowers, Moreland, Alderson, May, O'Connell, and Hansen were all slain with round-nosed lead .38 bullets from the same .38-caliber weapon. Although Edda Kane was killed by a .44-caliber gun police believed that she was slain by the same person who had killed the others in Marin and Santa Cruz.

To journalists' cries of ''Do you have your man? Do you have your man?'' Howenstein answered, ''It is my own very strong suspicion that we will be concluding the entire series as a result of this case.''

''We're going to be actively investigating every aspect . . . we're going to be seeking charges . . . we don't intend to sit on our heels,'' said Marin assistant DA Michael Gridley, ''but there is a lot more work to do. Charges will be filed after various searches of dwellings and vehicles are completed. We want to look at the total picture—what the searches turn up and what the Santa Cruz investigators get.''

''I can tell you this,'' Kathy Sofos, who ran the half-way house where Carpenter had stayed in 1979, told me, ''the Bureau of Prisons was a real shit when David was arrested. I called Skip Masters, who was community programs officer. 'Listen Skip,' I told him, 'they've arrested David Carpenter as the Trailside Killer. I can't say anything other than the fact that he was in the halfway house and why he was there and the dates he was there. It would be more appropriate if you, as the community programs officer, could field these phone calls from the press because I am no longer running a halfway house and he wasn't in the jurisdiction of the Bureau of Prisons.'

''Do you know,'' Kathy told me, ''those assholes closed their office and refused to accept phone calls? And when they did accept phone calls they were referring them back to me. They didn't have the balls to even talk to the press and say, 'I'm sorry. I can't give you any information.' I thought to myself, God, you little assholes. I mean you guys are supposed to be running the Bureau of Prisons and you're scared of the press.''

"The way this thing came down on the day he was arrested,'' Wood told me later, "we started getting phone calls from the press. We didn't know what to say. Then we started getting phone calls all over. I knew all the guys who worked the beat at the Federal Building. I had a good relationship with them, but not one of those guys came down and asked to talk to me. We were never informed they were going to take Carpenter down, which is just a matter of common courtesy.

"I was instructed at this point not to say anything to anybody. I also never talked to the press because a lot of the things I did were covered under confidentiality. I could only tell them what was in the public record anyway. I was instructed not to make any statements and never have until now. Carpenter's original file was locked in our attorney's safe.

"Apparently the press called up Howenstein and asked if we helped with the investigation and he says, 'No, we never had any contact with them,' which made us look foolish. At that point I was just glad it was over. I had been doing everything I could to bring this thing to a head and I had spent a pretty good amount of time with people from Marin and certainly given them everything I had, and how this guy comes off saying that I didn't I don't understand. Some people thought perhaps he was trying to protect us in a situation like that. It was, without a doubt, one of the most traumatic experiences of my life. Basically we were screwed in the press because the press sensationalized this thing. Robinson and Womack—who were to me if there were any heroes in this whole mess it's them, they did tremendous police work—never got a line in the press and missed out on the actual arrest.

"Of course, Carpenter's neighbors were shocked. I don't think anybody really had a clue. I think his parents were so concerned with their own feebleness and being elderly they just didn't have a clue either. The only people who may have suspected were the women who knew him and got 'bad vibes' from him.

"With a man like David who has a very long criminal

justice history a lot of times you don't get a lot of the information. A lot of his previous crimes in Calaveras County were just not documented very well. Ten years later it is almost impossible to document something like this because all records have been destroyed.

"Being a parole officer is difficult. You're dealing with society's losers and you're dealing with a very, very rigid system and with agents of the FBI and DEA and with judges. I'd had enough of it. It was time for different business. You do the best you can at the time and in hindsight you look back and you say, 'I did the best I could,' but it took me a long time to come back.

"You ask yourself, What could I have done? The answer is that probation officers don't have that much control over what their clients are doing. The public expects them to, but there's no way you can control another's behavior—especially the people we deal with.

"Because of this case I've got some relatively minor health problems that have not gone away, that came to light when this thing was going on and have been ongoing chronic problems of stress.

"You ask yourself, as I have asked myself ten thousand times, What could I have done to prevent one murder? All those things become ghosts that you live with. When you supervise somebody some people ask the question, 'Shouldn't he have spotted something?' 'Was he doing his job?' and those are questions I have asked myself ten, twenty, thirty thousand times 'cause you really start saying to yourself, Am I responsible for some of those deaths? and I've come to the conclusion, and it's taken me a number of years to do so, that I couldn't have known."

The AFT and the Trailside task force had tracked down Mollie Purnell, who had first learned of Carpenter's arrest while watching television. Mollie had reported her .38-caliber Rossi handgun missing shortly after a visit by the former purser. She had already spoken on May 16 with federal agents, but investigators returned now to question her for almost four hours more.

"The gun was stolen," she repeated nervously. This was the story she and Carpenter had agreed upon.

"Do you realize that you could be an accomplice to murder?" an agent asked on June 3. "You should tell us the truth." Mollie was terrified, and finally told her story. She had gotten the gun for Carpenter in exchange for money she owed him. "I broke off with him the same day I got it. I lied because I was afraid. I lied because you don't buy a gun for a felon." She got Sacramento attorney Jeanette Pearce to represent her.

"What about the 'large gun' that was delivered to Mollie Purnell?" I asked Marin County detective Rich Keaton.

"The mystery gun," laughed Keaton. "Just about the time Carpenter was getting out of prison in 1979 there was a gun delivered to Mollie, but the only description that comes back to us from Mollie was that it was a large gun. Some people would try and make that mean a large *caliber* gun, when Purnell stresses only that it was a large gun. Edda Kane, the first victim, was killed by a .44-caliber Bulldog, but in fact the Bulldog doesn't happen to be that big a gun. Its bore is big. There has always been speculation Mollie meant the .44."

"You figure she was pretty much an innocent party in all this?"

"Yeah. She was one of those people writing to inmates in prison. A really lonely woman." Though a few policemen thought there was something more to Mollie's association with Carpenter, she eventually got immunity. "I told exactly what had happened," she said, "why shouldn't I?"

Officials agreed that Mollie was not and had never been in the drug business.

"I'm not committed to the fact that Carpenter had a .44," said Keaton, "Mr. Carpenter kept that other firearm, the .38, right up to the very end. I don't know why he would have gotten rid of the other one. Jeanne Glaser, Edda Kane's friend, still believes in her heart of hearts that it was Carpenter who killed Edda. We have spent hours and hours together and I've shown her the composites. I said, 'Jean, look at this sketch. This guy was seen by one of the witnesses who was a doctor from Germany who is a plastic surgeon. What better person to describe facial characteristics—there's no little Porky Pig nose, no flared-out nostrils in the composite. I'm just trying to ease your mind.' 'No,' she says, 'I still think it's Carpenter.' Any number of my investigators do. Since we never found the .44 we're not going to charge Carpenter with the killing. I can't say he killed Edda Kane, I can't say he didn't.''

David Carpenter had been brought from his home directly to the Hall of Justice on Bryant, where he was photographed and had blood and saliva samples taken before he was conveyed to Santa Cruz. Carpenter had been moved from San Francisco's jurisdiction to that of Santa Cruz because that county's district attorney, Art Danner, felt they had the strongest case to go first. Carpenter was taken to the jail on Water Street and charged with the attack on Steve and Ellen in Henry Cowell Redwoods State Park on March 29.

Because of fears that the newspapers were going to publish photos of Carpenter, a stand-up lineup was rushed into being. In preparation for the actual lineup, photos of the individuals and of the entire group participating in the lineup were taken. As was his right, Carpenter indulged in "lineup posturing" and exchanged his glasses with those of the sixth person in the lineup. All wore gold jackets, baseball caps, and glasses purchased for them. It was an eerie sight to see so large a group of golden-coated, bespectacled, bearded men in green caps.

At 4:34 P.M. Santa Cruz deputy Steven Fitzgerald started the lineup at 259 Water Street, the county jail, by writing case #81-22KT and carefully instructing the seven witnesses on how the lineup would be conducted. These instructions were more detailed than the standard form, since they had been prepared by the DA himself. The instructions, carefully given, were taped:

"Ladies and gentlemen," began Fitzgerald, "you're about to participate in a stand-up lineup. You'll view six men numbered one through six. You will refer to them by their numbers. They will take two steps forward, turn to the left, the right, the back. They'll do this one at a time. Do not say anything as proceedings go on.

"Refer to these people only by number. Do not discuss them among yourselves. Circle their number or make a notation of a particular individual or tap me on the shoulder.'' Fitzgerald cautioned them to be aware of any changes in appearance. Danner had requested specifically that this be mentioned because of the suspect's new beard.

"Suspect's hands are too tan . . ." continued Fitzgerald, giving examples of responses, ". . . number two looks similar or five or four. Number one has the man's stature . . . same hair coloring.'' Fitzgerald told the witnesses the men could not see them. They were ushered, one at a time, into a small dark room with curtains. Fritz was first, then Haertle. The curtains were opened. "And there were six men in another room standing against the wall,'' said Steve. "They all had beards.''

Deputy Fitzgerald became aware Haertle was observing one individual specifically. He had immediately locked onto number two, Carpenter. "He became nervous and fidgeted and walked back and forth—looked straight at him,'' Fitzgerald told me later. "Haertle started the moment he saw him. He became highly agitated.''

"I knew it was him within thirty seconds,'' Steve Haertle recalled.

The twelve-year-old witness, Melissa, noticed Carpenter's hands shaking in the lineup.

Three of the witnesses, Melissa, Thorpe, and Morse, could not identify Carpenter. One of the witnesses was unsure because he had only a glimpse of a man roaring away in a red car. Another said, "That's him. He's dyed his hair and he's grown a beard, but that's him.'' However, Ken Fritz, sixteen, failed to pick Carpenter out of the lineup.

The search of the suspect's "1965 green, oxydized, poor condition'' Chevy station wagon had been delayed until the warrant could be obtained from Alameda County. The car had been taken to Gallivan's Garage, a police tow garage at 1693 Washington Boulevard in San Leandro, and placed in the last stall of the garage. The same team that had explored the Fiat and house at 38 Sussex repeated their roles. Once again Layden brought each item from the interior of the garage to Henard, who was sitting at a counter inside the gas station office.

"Case #81-2118," wrote Henard, entering "ski goggles, blue and white plastic." Sanders and Ito worked on latent fingerprints inside the auto, removing the chrome rearview mirror and ashtray to take away with them.

A small, "brown paper bag, crumpled up" was brought to Henard and placed on the counter. Henard reached in, withdrew a fistful of key chains from Gems of the Golden West, and eyed them with disgust—he had seen them all over Carpenter's house. He let them fall back into the tattered bag. Layden took the bag back. The spare tire was taken out, disclosing nothing. The searchers departed, however Layden had to return later to retrieve the bag from a workbench where it had been forgotten. The Chevy was placed in a locked storage area and then taken to the task force headquarters at the Presidio.

A week after the search in San Leandro Layden logged the collected evidence at the task force center, tagging each item with a salmon-colored tag and putting them in evidence envelopes. He came to the tattered bag, and had begun to count each of the fifteen novelty key rings when out rolled a silver-colored Winchester .38-caliber lead-nosed bullet that had been in the bottom of the sack. Layden leaped up to show Henard and the rest. The bullet was logged and taken to the lab at the Department of Justice in Santa Rosa on June 6 along with the key chains. George Ito, the fingerprint analyst, would later not recall seeing any key chains in the bag but did recall checking the bag for prints in his lab and finding none.

Sergeant Womack got back from San Jose at 10:00 A.M. the day of Carpenter's arrest, picked up his partner, Walt Robinson, and drove to the Hayward printing school in an attempt to track the missing .38 and to question the suspect's bosses. "Lane and Joe were starting to put the pieces together about Carpenter," Robinson told me later, "and we asked them if they had a gun. We thought the murder weapon might be an Astro, Ruger, Taurus, or Rossi. 'Yes, we've got a gun,' they told us, 'a .38.' My jaw hit the floor. It was the gun Carpenter had used to go target shooting with, but ballistics proved it wasn't the murder weapon the next day. However, what was interesting was their ammunition—.38-caliber Winchester with that special head, the same distinctive nose.'' Since police had been unable to find any record of Mollie Purnell buying ammunition for the .38 she had purchased for Carpenter, there was the possibility the suspect had taken some of his bosses' ammunition.

Though the weather was cloudy and cool, hikers, joggers, and bikers swarmed to the trails again. ''People are walking around with definitely a greater sense of relief,'' said a ranger. ''Now we see more individuals and couples walking around instead of being in larger groups. They are also venturing into the more isolated areas.'' ''This natural resource,'' said a hiker, ''is finally back for the people.''

And now a second search began, but not for a man— for the elusive murder weapon. Without that gun any case against David Carpenter would be flawed.

7

End of the Chase

Both Karen and Shane Williams were terrified the police might link them with the considerable trouble Carpenter was in. On top of that they were running low on cash. In the early afternoon of Monday, May 18, they took a bus from Oakland to Berkeley and got out in front of the Twin Pines Federal Savings and Loan office. While Karen, wearing her hair punk-rock style, blonde and black, cased the small bank, Shane put on a plaid jacket, donned a wig and light-colored watchcap, and held up the bank. "The holdup was another fiasco," he told me later. "It seemed I did just one stupid thing after another. I went off and left Karen's student ID and our hotel receipt from the previous night on the counter." The holdup took less than five minutes, and on the way out Williams tossed his makeshift disguise into the trash bin.

"I used the gun Carpenter gave us for the holdup," said Shane, "tucked in my waistband," the same gun the police of Northern California were breaking their backs to find.

Shane and Karen caught the next bus back to Oakland. Shane was later asked, "Let me get this straight. You made your getaway by bus. Why did you do this?" Williams replied, "I don't drive."

By this time the police knew that the Williamses were wanted on a federal warrant and raided their apartment in San Francisco. They were too late and feared the punks would disappear across America, taking with them the gun needed as evidence in the Trailside murders.

Gaddini told the press, "Leads could produce the .38 anywhere between today and six months. We're concerned with agile, hostile, and mobile witnesses at this time. Agile and mobile indicates elusive people who had to be contacted. Hostile means people we want to question who are likely to evade or avoid investigators."

Carpenter appeared before Municipal Judge Richard McAddams in Santa Cruz's top-security courtroom. He was ordered to return to court on June 8 to enter a plea. Judge McAddams sealed the affidavits and warrants in the case.

While both state and federal prison authorities were close-mouthed and evasive about the arrest of Carpenter, including the state sex registry and parole boards, police were theorizing that if their suspect was the Trailside Killer then there might be other possible victims along the route he took selling his key chains for Gems of the Golden West. In addition to Mary Bennett, Kelly Menjivar, and Heather Scaggs detectives rechecked the homicides and suspected homicides of several women Carpenter might have come in contact with. Carol Laughlin, for example, had disappeared in September of 1979. Her skeletal remains were found in April 1980 at the bottom of an air shaft near El Portal at the west end of the Yosemite Valley. The Village Store in Yosemite National Park where Laughlin had worked had bought trinkets from Gems for twenty years. Jennifer McDowell, nineteen, had last been seen outside the Santa Cruz Hospital waiting for a bus on May 27, 1980, and her body was discovered on October 19. Diane Steffy was found strangled on Thanksgiving Day, 1979, just off the bridal path at the entrance to Cowell State Park.

"His job took him all over," said Gaddini, "and it's taking us all over, too." But so far there seemed to be no link between Carpenter and these women.

Kelly Menjivar's mother, cousin, and aunt held an urgent talk with Daly City police and Officer Holewinske. Afterward Holewinske said, "We haven't gotten anything to change our minds that she isn't a runaway," but promised to visit Carpenter in his Santa Cruz jail cell and look into any connection.

Peter Berest, Kelly's boss at the Savings and Loan, still maintained he spoken with the Daly City police about her friendship with David Carpenter. Officer Holewinske admitted the bank manager had called him many times but said, "I don't remember any mention of Carpenter."

On Tuesday, May 19, Daly City police visited Berest at the Continental Savings and Loan "to apologize generally," said the bank manager, "and to say they were subpoenaing bank records and checks to see what Carpenter had purchased." Daly City Lieutenant Jim Doran said there was no record of the calls Berest claimed to have made. "At this time we have no record of Mr. Berest having phoned here about Carpenter," he said.

Carpenter's former attorney, James Jackson, in Santa Cruz told the press what he thought should be done with mass murderers. "You thrown them in a cage. That's all. You can spend hundreds of millions of dollars trying to rehabilitate them, but it seems to me that people rehabilitate themselves. However," he added, "I found Carpenter a pleasant man who could easily carry on an intelligent conversation."

On May 21, 1981, Graham Desvernine, accompanied by detective Russo, paid a second visit to Reba Lehman to get an additional statement. "The first time I was flabbergasted by the news," she said. However, this time they talked for two hours and a four-page report was the result. Reba said she could not recall articles switched from the trunk of her BMW to Carpenter's Fiat because she was distracted. In July she was leaving the Mill Valley home because she had met Tom Beechey and become engaged.

Reba had no memory of seeing Carpenter in the yellow-gold jacket. As late as May 17, 1984, in a deposition to Brook, she still had not mentioned the gun.

The day of Carpenter's arrest two detectives had visited Tammy Brinkley at the Gemco Store. She had not heard of the arrest but provided them with various sample shoes. In an interview with Joe Henard, Candy Townsend had mentioned the purchase of the two pairs of running shoes, and in the course of the 8:00 A.M. Trailside task force meetings they had exhaustively discussed the shoe track evidence from Santa Cruz with Deputies Tanner and Morris. The "6-W" style of tread of running feet was entrenched in Henard's mind, portions of a diamondlike or, more accurately, a herringbone pattern. There had not been enough to give them an indication of foot size, so Henard had made up his mind to go out to Gemco and get the size he knew the suspect wore, nine and one-half.

When Henard spoke with Tammy on May 22, he had in hand the canceled check used to pay for the shoes. He knew the total of the transaction, the cost of Candy's shoes, and the amount of sales tax, 6 percent. Tammy Brinkley explained that only two pairs of shoes sold by the store went for that price—the Nike "Electra" in blue with a matching swoosh, and the "Trend II's." Henard, to be safe, "borrowed" both pairs, drove them to Santa Cruz, and turned them over to Chief Foster. Later he took the "Trend II's" back and paid for the "Electra's," which would be kept for evidence. The tread matched perfectly the plaster casts of the tracks left by the stalking rapist.

The DA's chief investigator, Ray Belgarde, announced that Roberta Patterson, sixty-nine, a horsewoman from Ben Lomond in Santa Cruz County who had met Carpenter twenty-six years earlier on the freighter *Fleetwood* on a trip to Japan, would be in line for the $25,000 reward for her tip to the Santa Cruz police that he might be the Trailside Killer.

Severe limitations were placed by the court on publicity in the Trailside murder case as Carpenter's attorneys won an order tightening pretrial flow of information, arguing that press reports had damaged Carpenter's chances for a fair trial.

Carpenter's lawyers, public defenders Larry Biggam and Jerry Christiansen, asked that cameras be barred from the court. Biggam argued that his client was being shown in a poor light. "The image that the public has is that of my client in custody, brought into this court with three uniformed and armed guards at his side, and in an orange jumpsuit, which is a neon sign that my client is guilty. The first impression is lasting and impossible to shake despite instructions and admonitions to a jury. No admonition to a jury can unscramble this egg.''

Santa Cruz Judge Richard McAddams turned down the camera ban. ''Cameras help give a more realistic picture of how the law works. I don't think government proceedings should be handled in the dark,'' he said. McAddams made no order prohibiting officials from commenting on the investigation of Carpenter and his possible involvement in the murders of seven other people in Marin County. Carpenter had refused to answer questions from authorities since the day of his arrest. He communicated with nods of his head and whispers. Releases about the suspect's arrest, the identity of police officers involved, the length of the investigation, and the nature of the charges were also allowed.

There were now two full rooms of evidence in the case.

It was Heather Scaggs who had focused attention on David Carpenter, and at last, on Sunday, May 24, she was found. Almost twenty miles northwest of the spot where Ellen and Steven were shot, two hikers passed a logging operation near Boulder Creek where Carpenter had run amok in 1970. This rugged spot was in Big Basin Redwoods Park. The hikers made their way into the semi-wilderness where there were three miles of trails. They were just one hundred and fifty yards from the intersection of State Highway 236 and upper China Grade Road when they found the badly decomposed body of a woman.

''Heather Scaggs had been hidden well,'' Brook told me. ''The killer never expected her to be found. He had covered her over with brush, but animals dragged her out. I guess he hadn't counted on that.''

Heather had been stripped of her clothing with the exception of one earring. The hikers could see no sign of identification or a purse. They could see that a hasty attempt at a grave had been made behind the heavy, moss-encrusted log where she lay, a certain amount of digging, and that some brush had been pulled over her. Because of the dampness and the recent spell of hot weather decomposition had been especially severe. The hikers could see that the woman had been shot through the eye. They blanched, drew back, and ran to call the police.

When the detectives arrived they surmised that the woman had been shot elsewhere and then dragged to the log. The bullet that had killed her had lodged in her skull. She had been killed by a .38, the same caliber gun that had killed Ellen Hansen on the hiking trail. The police were almost certain that this was the missing Heather Scaggs, and dental records eventually proved them correct. It also appeared that she had been raped.

Investigators were struck by the Scaggs's crime scene. It was identical to the Alderson crime site—a heavily canopied area, one hundred and fifty yards from a trail, both women raped and both missing one earring. "He covered Heather up because he was ashamed of what he did," Keaton later told me. "Also she may have told him before she was shot below the right eye, in the cheek, that she had told others where she would be. It seemed that he always killed someone he knew after a lot of publicity, someone he knew well." It was pointed out to me that Shauna May and Anne Alderson looked similar to Cheryl Smith, one of Carpenter's 1970 Santa Cruz victims, and that Diane O'Connell, Cindy Moreland, and Ellen Hansen looked alike.

Police drove Mary Scaggs to the scene. She saw strands of her daughter's long blonde hair hanging from the trees in the clearing and collapsed in tears.

Dr. Mason conducted the autopsy on Heather and determined that the victim had "engaged in sexual intercourse right at or about the time of her death." Mason based his findings on the discovery of a pool of semen. "The discovery of seminal fluid was extraordinarily unusual," said Mason, considering the animal activity and state of decomposition. "Had the victim stood up the fluid would not have remained in a pool."

Richard Waller found a blood-type of B in the semen, which did not match the suspect. "The blood type was B and Carpenter's is A," he said. [Carpenter is an ABO Type-A secretor, PGM $1+1-$.] "However that doesn't necessarily exclude him. Miss Scaggs's blood type was

B and her fluids mixed with the semen and could have distorted the test results.''

In San Jose Sergeant Castlio was not surprised that Heather had been murdered. ''I didn't have any thought of finding her alive from day one. Nobody did, including her mother. What's amazing is that she went with him at all. Her mother said she was an extremely careful person, more so than others. Maybe she just didn't want to believe that anyone she worked with would be capable of that sort of thing.

''To this day,'' Castlio continued, ''it amazes me, but apparently he had this ability to con a lot of people. . . . It's too bad they didn't pick him up before.'' The discovery of Heather's body cast a cold shadow over the fate of another of Carpenter's friends, Kelly Menjivar.

8

Answers

On May 24, 1981, led by Daly City police sergeant Bob Sola, a twelve-member search-and-rescue team of Explorer Scouts picked their way through the poison oak-covered hillsides along twisting Crocker Avenue where the missing Kelly Menjivar used to run. They were looking for any sign of her, but there was debris everywhere, and piles of garbage containing false teeth and soup bones only confused the issue.

Over two hundred persons had been interviewed in the search for the missing high school student—police had spoken with her relatives, co-workers at the Continental Savings and Loan in Carpenter's neighborhood, her teachers at Mercy High, and her fellow students. Many had recalled Kelly telling them about a wonderful surprise she had for her mother, Juanita, the day before she disappeared on Sunday, December 28, 1980.

On May 23, officers had walked the neighborhood, checking especially with people who were habitual early risers or whose jobs required them to be up early. They asked if anyone had seen Kelly the morning she had vanished. No one had.

348

On Thursday morning, May 28, Municipal Judge William Kelsay amended the complaint against Carpenter to include both Hansen's and Scaggs's murders and extended the gag order imposed by Judge McAddams a week previously into the area of the Marin homicides. "The order extends to *all* homicide investigations regarding Mr. Carpenter in the state of California," stated Kelsay. "Offenders will be held in contempt of court if they violate the order." Carpenter, dressed in a jail-issue orange suit, surveyed the legal jousting silently.

On June 2, a vehicle lineup was held in the parking lot of the Government Center in Santa Cruz. The red Fiat was mixed in with two- and four-door sedans, station wagons, trucks, and other red autos. Both the little-girl witness, Melissa, the twelve-year-old who saw the Fiat after it left Cowell State Park, and Lee Fritz, the Fresno florist, scanned the nearly one hundred vehicles looking for the "foreign boxy-type red car." Fritz's dark, sad eyebrows and down-turned mouth brightened finally. The extralarge mirror on the red Fiat helped him pick out Carpenter's car—"That's similar to the car I saw leaving the scene," Fritz told deputy Fitzgerald. "That's the car."

Because of fears that they might be possible accessories to murder, Karen and Shane Williams had been lying low. She was using the alias of Tracy Meyers when they were finally arrested on Monday, June 1, 1981, in L.A. on bank robbery charges.

Karen broke free and escaped from the patrol car. She recalled, "I didn't have on my glasses, and my vision is like 2200. But I ran though." She was tackled, she later said, "by six cops who jerked me off the ground by the handcuffs so hard I broke my collarbone." Shane was taken to prison on Terminal Island and held in federal custody.

Once again, Karen convinced the police to let her go and, in great pain, set out for Hollywood to see Shane's mother in Studio City. Shane's mom called Karen's father and he arrived within fifteen minutes and went with her to the authorities to discuss any charges outstanding against her under her real name.

"Karen and I grew up in a middle-class environment," Shane Williams later told me, "and I wouldn't call her a bank robber, but she was with me while I was doing it. I had originally invented one cover story where in the process of admitting to my crimes I didn't mention anything about ever having the gun and never having gone anyplace with Carpenter. About a week later they came back and said, 'We have a report that says you were with him here and there.' I invented another story because for a long time I had no intention of coming forward with the gun."

"What finally happened to the missing .38 Rossi?" I asked Brook.

"Yeah, what's so stupid is that gun. Ah! that gun is so dumb. Should have tossed that bastard in the bay."

In Santa Cruz on June 9, 1981, Carpenter pleaded Not Guilty and Judge Kelsay set August 10 as the preliminary hearing date. Prosecutor Art Danner was ordered to turn over to the defense team material that included autopsy reports, witnesses names, physical evidence, recorded conversations of the police surveillance, information of any felony convictions of any of the witnesses, and particulars of any deals the prosecution may have made with witnesses in exchange for their testimony. Once again the judge handed down a gag order and extended it until a verdict was reached in the case, possibly years in the future.

On Sunday evening June 16, two rock climbers were walking through Castle Rock State Park east of Big Basin. They were just off Skyline Boulevard near private property one-half mile from Highway 9. They had come to scale Castle Rock to get a glimpse of San Francisco Bay. Abruptly one of them bent over and picked up what appeared to be a human jawbone from the brush. Inexplicably they took it home with them and kept it until shocked friends convinced them to call Santa Cruz police and show them their discovery. Later they took the police to the exact spot where it was found. The other parts of the skeleton had been scattered by wild animals, but dental records showed that the jaw found on the hillside was that of Kelly Menjivar.

Ana Intriago, Kelly's cousin, was shattered by the discovery. Sobbing, she told reporters, "Mrs. Menjivar has gone into shock. She went blank when police told her the news. She still doesn't believe it's true. She didn't know what had happened. She didn't know what to think until today. This should relieve her of some of that agony."

Kelly's father, Ramon, said, "We didn't expect this to happen to a nice girl like my daughter. We knew something bad had happened but we didn't want to believe it. I never believed that she ran away. Anna Kelly was a good student, an A-1 kid. She trusted everybody. She believed in people. They said he [Carpenter] was a nice man, but look what happened. The system makes heroes out of criminals and forgets the victim. It will be hard for us to forget. After seventeen years, we have a lot of memories."

And just where did Shane Williams put the .38?

"I hid it," said Shane, "out of fear that I would be apprehended with this gun, which I was then convinced had been used in the Trailside slayings. I knew a .38-caliber had been used in the killings and all news accounts pointed to [Carpenter], so I just assumed I had the murder weapon." Before he hid it he made certain that the gun had no bullets in it. "A kid might find it," he fretted.

Shane Williams had strong loyalties to Graham Desvernine, an ex-FBI agent who had assisted Gaddini, Besse, and Keaton in the Trailside investigation after November 1980. Desvernine was a San Francisco detective and a man with whom the youth felt comfortable. When Williams finally decided to divulge the location of the missing gun in exchange for leniency for himself and his wife, it was only natural that he call Desvernine. Shane called Karen from his holding cell and asked her to get in touch with his friend and to ask for Desvernine by his nickname, Dez.

"Now 'Dez' is an old hardball FBI agent," Richard Wood told me, "and a real character. He was doing undercover for years. He's a fascinating guy, a good investigator, and a friend of Williams. I've often wondered if

Williams wasn't a snitch of his, but I don't know that for sure.''

"After the arrest," former Trailside task force leader Lieutenant Don Besse told me later, "everything had calmed down. Around the end of June the secretary in my office got a call from Shane Williams's wife and she wanted to speak with 'Dez' Desvernine. Desvernine was gone and my secretary thought Karen said she wanted to speak with 'Besse,' so I get this message saying 'call Karen Williams.' I call her. I don't think she ever made the distinction between 'Besse' and 'Dez.' She was just following directions.

"Basically Karen told me Shane was in federal prison and he had some information for me and he wouldn't talk to anybody but me. Karen didn't realize I wasn't 'Dez' and so she said, 'It's worth your while to go to L.A.' So I called down there and talked to Bob Robertson, the federal assistant attorney general who was in charge of prosecution. I said I gathered from information I had received in a conversation with Karen Williams that Shane might be willing to talk about the gun. Shane had stressed the importance of what he had, evidence we couldn't get any other way.''

Besse was excited. Here was a man who might voluntarily lead them to the missing gun. The detective flew to Los Angeles on June 30, 1981, to meet with the federal prosecutors, Shane, and his attorney.

"I had talked with the FBI," Besse told me, "and Robertson contacted the federal public defender who was representing Shane, and we made arrangements to meet. An FBI agent picked me up at the airport and drove me over to the courthouse. I went to see Robertson. We talked for a few minutes. 'Do you know what Shane wants?' he asked me. 'No, I don't know for certain what he wants,' I told him. 'The only thing I can think of that he might think is this important is that he might have some information about the murder weapon.' We go to see the public defender. The public defender asks me the same question, 'Do you know what he wants?' I tell him, 'I don't know. I got this call.' I wasn't about to tell the public defender what I was thinking.

"So we go down to the holding cell where Shane is,

myself, the public defender, the attorney general, and the
FBI agent. They bring Shane in. He's got a kind of modified Mohawk-punk haircut. He's quite a talker. Shane
doesn't say anything in twenty-five words or less. The
first hour we're there I probably didn't say anything except, 'Hello, my name is Don Besse.' The first hour went
between the two attorneys and him, a big negotiations
thing about his rights. The public defender doesn't want
Shane to talk to me and he thought he'd get a deal. Shane
had a lot of charges pending against him. I sat back, just
listening, but what I could glean from their conversation
really convinced me Williams knew the whereabouts of
the gun.

"Without that gun we could have made the case but it
would have been a lot harder. Oh, yeah, much more difficult. We had to have Mollie Purnell as the purchaser of
the gun, her giving it to Carpenter, and then Shane, of
course, the person Carpenter gave it to. Without the gun
all we would have had would have been some spent bullets.

"While the attorneys were there they wanted to ne-
gotiate this deal—Shane provides the gun and in return
all charges against Karen would be dropped and he be
permitted to plead guilty to a couple of bank robberies.
'I want,' he said, 'all my other charges dismissed and I
want to be promised a lenient sentence.' The federal
prosecutor says, 'Anything you want, we'll give you.'
The FBI told me, 'You can give him anything you want
if you think it's worth all the bank robberies.' I was really
impressed by that. Here I am, just this lieutenant from
this little department and they're telling me to take this
guy off from bank robbery.

"I don't know why, but I figured he was going to give
me what he had one way or the other. I figured he wanted
to give the information to me. So my bottom line was,
'Shane, the only thing I'll do for you is write a letter to
the sentencing judge telling how you cooperated in a
homicide investigation.' As for Karen, I promised not a
thing. Basically I told him, 'I don't have any control over
federal prosecution. I'm just a nickel-and-dime deputy
sheriff. I will write a letter for you and I'll send it from
the sheriff's office. I will guarantee you no charges will

be pressed against you in Marin County for any crime we find you may have committed. I can promise you immunity from prosecution for any crimes related to David Carpenter that were committed in Marin County.'

"One of the reasons I was reasonably certain that Shane Williams wanted to give me that information was he had made some comments that he was pretty sure he was going to be one of Carpenter's victims and that his wife was going to be raped. Carpenter tried to set that up apparently, but he never got to it because we took him out. But the public defender was saying, 'Don't you see what a con job this guy is giving you? You could get more than that.'

"I was pretty adamant I wasn't going to give Williams any more. So Shane told them that he'd accept what I offered, which was not a whole lot . . . in fact, it didn't do him a bit of good, He still got ten years. Karen's cases were dropped for lack of evidence. The public defender says to Shane, 'If you're going to, you're going to.' Shane asked everybody to leave. Except me. The public defender objected to this but finally left.

"So Shane starts telling me about his relationship with Carpenter and tells me how Carpenter gave him the gun and why he gave him the gun, where the gun was, the whole story. It took an hour because Shane tends to ramble, talks around and around and around. Trying to pin him down was really a problem, but eventually I got the story out of him."

"I revealed the gun's whereabouts," Shane said in retrospect, "in an attempt to get my wife out of jail and reduce the prison time I faced. I thought it might allow me to cut a deal in connection with the bank robbery charges. Carpenter gave me the gun to use in some robberies. I ditched it in a lot several days later when I was linked to Carpenter. I wrapped it in newspaper and put it under some rubble, pieces of concrete and stuff.

"I figured the gun, stashed beneath those chunks of asphalt in a deserted lot would have been found by now. I would have driven a much harder bargain if I thought it was still going to be there. But it was a highly populated area and the gun was very near the surface."

"When I finally determined what Shane had to tell me," recalled Besse, "I said, 'Now look, Shane, I want you to take some deep breaths. I'm going to ask you some questions. I want specific answers and I want you to concentrate on the answers. I'm going to turn the tape machine on and I don't want an hour of rambling on tape.' So he said, 'OK,' and I turned the tape recorder on and I think I got six and one-half minutes that had all the pertinent information—what he wanted to tell me, where the gun is, who he got it from—all the *w*'s. The tape was pretty brief. It gave me hell later. Every defense attorney just racked me because I hadn't recorded the entire conversation.

"Shane gave me directions to the gun. It seems he had stayed at a place on Golden Gate Avenue with some punk-rock friends for a few days. He told me that the house he stayed at was a three-story house and there were three doors on the front porch, one for each level, and the middle door had a BEWARE OF CATS sign on it. The house was next to the Golden Gate Elementary School. He thought it was somewhere around Fulton or Divisadero, he wasn't sure.

"Later on, after Shane and I had finished talking, I left the cell. On the way out the public defender told me that was one of the best cases of negotiations he had ever seen. 'Thanks a lot,' I said, and this coming from a public defender. I was excited and I couldn't wait to be on the plane.

"Shane had put the gun in a vacant lot where a gas station had been torn down. This was just before he was arrested; it had been there for weeks. When Carpenter was picked up on May 15, Shane realized that the gun he had was probably the murder weapon. He was under pressure, since he was going to be picked up at any time.

"When I got back to San Francisco it was probably a half hour before dark. Later a big issue was made of why didn't I call SFPD or call the Marin sheriff's office and have the ID team just get everything and come over. Well, bullshit! When a cop's got that good a lead he goes out and does what he has to do. He finds the gun!

"I was just throwing darts in the dark—this was a real

treasure hunt. I had to backtrack because I didn't know for sure where it was. So I went down and found Golden Gate School. The very next house was a three-story green house. The middle door had a BEWARE OF CATS sign on it. The lot was two blocks, not one block off Golden Gate, but it fit the description perfectly: Shane had described the corner accurately, the wall, the pile of dirt, the phone booth. It was on the corner of Fulton and Divisadero. The lot was just broken-up chunks of dirt and concrete. I had found it.

"Shane said he had discovered some newspaper in a telephone booth and wrapped the gun up. I saw the telephone booth near the vacant lot and I found the broken-up asphalt within a couple of feet of where he had said it would be. I lifted it up and there, wrapped in paper, was the gun.

"I got back to the office by 9:30 P.M. and had Ray Maynard take the recovered gun out to Mike Waller at the State Crime Lab in Santa Rosa first thing in the morning. On July 2, Waller testfired the .38 and ballistics showed that the weapon was used to kill five persons in Marin and two in Santa Cruz."

On Friday, July 31, Marin County District Attorney Jerry Herman charged Carpenter with five of the Trailside slayings and included the additional charges of rape and attempted rape. The most crucial aspect of the allegation was a detailed list of special circumstances, in this case multiple murders, murders committed during the commission of rape, or lying in wait for victims, which could mean the death penalty for the former purser.

Herman specified the rape of May and Alderson, the attempted rape of O'Connell. The DA did not feel he had sufficient evidence to file against the suspect for the stabbing death of Barbara Schwartz or the shooting of Edda Kane on the Sleeping Lady. Meanwhile, Carpenter asked for his sister, who was living with their parents, to collect all his mother's receipts, anything that would help his defense.

Because of the massive publicity and the angry feelings the crimes had awakened in both the cities and the little mountain towns of the Bay Area, a change of venue was granted—to Los Angeles.

It would be three years before Carpenter's first trial, one of the most unusual in U.S. judicial history, would be held.

9

Los Angeles: 1983–1984

"I got married and almost immediately afterward went to L.A.," Stoney Brook told me, "and went right into the trial. I was down there doing groundwork, helping arrange the witnesses, all the exhibits, getting the people on and off the airplanes. The trial was pretty much all I did for two years, getting the ducks-in-a-row kind of things.

"An early issue was the jury selection on October 17, 1983. They were chosen one at a time from a pool. We spent an hour or so with each one. . . . I wasn't allowed to interview prospective jurors but sat in on the selection. . . . That's the nice thing about being a cop. You can just sit there and listen."

California is the only state requiring each prospective juror to be interviewed outside the presence of other prospective jurors. Thus it takes longer in California than in any other state to make a jury selection. The prosecutor, Santa Cruz DA Art Danner, was making sure no juror with a bias against capital punishment, who often tend to favor the defense, would be included in the jury.

As a rule in California when the prosecution is seeking

DAVID CARPENTER ON TRIAL IN LOS ANGELES AS THE ACCUSED "TRAILSIDE KILLER"

the ultimate penalty a bifurcated trial system is conducted in which the same jury that decides the innocence or guilt of the accused determines the penalty in a second and shorter trial called the penalty phase. Carpenter's trial would be different, as we were to learn.

Carpenter's attorney, Larry Biggam, sought both a guilt-phase jury and penalty-phase jury in this trial. Judge Dion Morrow granted this, but with a twist. In order to save time and expense Morrow ruled that *two* juries would be impaneled to hear the case simultaneously.

Biggam, for the defense, was concerned that the mere presence of a separate penalty jury would have an effect on the guilt jury, sending them a message that the case was intended to proceed directly to a guilt phase. He knew it would be, if necessary, an issue he could raise on appeal.

Carpenter's Los Angeles trial would be without parallel in the history of the United States criminal proceedings—in a system never previously employed and in all probability one that would never be used again, he would be judged by *thirty-three jurors at once* (regular jurors and alternates).

After eighty-three days of voir dire questioning, jury selection was finally completed on April 5, 1984. The two juries along with their alternates were sworn in on the morning of May 14, 1984. This had been the longest jury selection in state history. Carpenter's trial to this point had cost $489,000.

May 24, 1984, a Friday, was the anniversary of the discovery of Heather Scaggs's body in Big Basin and also the beginning of testimony in Carpenter's trial. The defendant was wearing a brilliant white shirt accented by a soft powder-blue sweater vest, and from time to time he would straighten up in his seat, hook his thumb under his chin, crook his index finger over his lips as if hushing himself, and look at the spectators in the tightly packed courtroom. His fingers were restless. Carpenter had gotten in the habit of not wearing dark-rimmed glasses, replacing them with clear rims, possibly since those kind of glasses were a key piece of evidence against him, and he was also under judicial order to keep his beard, which he had worn during pretrial hearings and as late as the end of 1983, shaved off. He retained modified mutton chop sideburns.

Buffered from the press and other spectators by an empty row of seats, the penalty jurors and their alternates filled the front row on rubber-cushioned wooden seats. The guilt jury and their alternates, wearing red-dotted badges to distinguish them from the other jurors, occupied the jury box.

Morrow explained to the jury that passing the physical evidence among thirty-three jurors would disrupt the trial and consume too much time and ruled that after both sides had finished their case the exhibits would be theirs to study before their deliberations.

DA Art Danner made his opening statement, a lawyer's preview to the jury of the high points of the case he intends to present. Danner knew that he had to be careful even in a brief (one-hour) opening statement so that he would not have to contradict himself during the course of the trial. He requested that the jurors take detailed notes during the long proceedings. Danner was acutely aware, addressing such a profusion of jurors, that it was much like working theater-in-the-round and said, "Frankly, I'm not sure which way to stand." He quickly adapted to the environment.

"On March 28, 1981," Danner said, "two UC-Davis students, Ellen Hansen and Steven Haertle, spent the night camping in Henry Cowell State Park near Santa Cruz. They went into Monterey the next morning and on returning to the park decided to hike along the Ridge Trail. They headed for the Cathedral Redwoods.

"Along the trail they passed an individual they would see again. The man seemed out of breath, not a regular hiker. As they returned along the trail about an hour later, five hundred yards from the observation tower, they were confronted by the man.

" 'If you don't want to get hurt, do what I say,' " said the man. " 'All I want to do is rape your girlfriend.' The man, who was carrying a gun, ordered the two campers into the bushes, but Hansen called out, 'Don't do it, Steve, he's going to kill us anyway.' Haertle looked down the path, heard shots, and felt that he had been hit. Haertle looked at Hansen and saw that she was fatally wounded, bleeding from the back and head. She had been shot in the shoulder and twice in the head.

"Despite Haertle's wounds, the student was able to reach the observation tower where he gasped out what had happened. Two hikers took him to a van in the parking lot, and drove him to a hospital. Two other hikers, who remained behind, saw a man move along the trail and disappear. These two witnesses subsequently cooperated with a police artist in making sketches of the man they saw. You will have a chance to see their results. You'll see they resemble a person in this room." Danner pointed at Carpenter. "The defendant in this case.

"The wooded trails of Santa Cruz's parks will play a crucial role in the case against David Carpenter," Danner said quietly.

"Haertle's vocal nerve was bruised, and you will probably see that he still loses his voice if he talks for a long time. Haertle will take the stand during the trial and describe the callous killing, and four witnesses who were at the observation deck will identify Carpenter as the man spotted fleeing the scene of the killing.''

Danner told the jurors that a red car seen speeding from the park shortly after the attack on the couple had been identified by a witness as Carpenter's. Danner then moved to events of May 2, 1981, when Heather Scaggs left her San Jose apartment and was reported missing by her boyfriend. She had worked at a trade school with Carpenter and had agreed to meet him that morning to go to Santa Cruz to see about the purchase of a new car and a possible job opportunity.

"Scaggs was to meet Carpenter in San Jose, but she did not keep the appointment,'' Danner told the jurors. ''Her remains were found May 24 off China Grade Road in Big Basin State Park.

"She had been stripped of her clothing. Her purse was gone, although an earring was left behind. She had been shot through [beneath] the eye, and the bullet had entered her head, where it was recovered by a pathologist. That bullet and the ones recovered from Steve Haertle and Ellen Hansen had all been fired from the same gun.''

Defense attorney Steve Wright's opening remarks took only a few minutes. He was co-counsel with Larry Biggam and Jerry Christiansen. ''I'm not going to discuss the facts because the facts will be presented from the witness stand and under oath and subject to cross-examination,'' Wright said. ''I want you to be on your guard to avoid being swayed by photographic evidence that could affect your emotions. I predict that the prosecution will introduce a video re-enactment of the crime, and I ask that you jurors be careful to see that it is factual. I urge you not to decide the case on speculation and theory, but on the evidence.''

On Friday, May 25, Steve Haertle, twenty-three, now a Pacific Gas and Electric economist, was summoned to the stand. The slight slur in Haertle's voice was a side effect of a bruised vocal nerve damaged by a bullet to his neck. His story, his courage, and polite manner had a powerful effect on the thirty-three jurors.

Marin County sheriff's detective Rich Keaton was also moved by Steve's testimony. ''The first time I heard him testify it brought tears to my eyes. He sits in the courtroom and so methodically points Carpenter out. His voice is higher pitched than is normal; I guess syrupy would be the word. You can't help but feel sorry for him, but I've never seen a young man who was able to give such detail as he looked at his attacker in court. He said he tried to remember as much as possible in case he lived so he could identify him later.''

Steve told essentially the same story the prosecutor, Danner, had told in his opening statement. As the young, dark-haired man in the tan suit spoke, Carpenter shifted in his seat nervously, taking off and putting on his glasses which he had been using to read notes from his lawyers, and then methodically sorting through the stack of yellow papers in front of him on the highly polished table, occasionally putting his forefinger to his mouth.

Haertle told of the events of that Sunday, after the couple had driven to Monterey to "poke around the wharf."

"Did you meet anyone as you came up the Ridge Trail?" asked Danner.

"Yes, we did," said Haertle. "He spoke first. He said, 'Ah, we've met again,' and then he pulled out a gun from his jacket. He pointed it at Ellen and me."

At this point all thirty-three of the jurors leaned forward to listen. Haertle's voice was controlled, but the emotion was there all the same.

Steve told how he and Ellen kept trying to move from in front of the attacker's gun. "Then, after Ellen wouldn't let him rape her, defied him, he ordered us to go toward the bushes at the side of the trail. He gestured with his eyes and gun and body."

Steve described how he had edged away from the gun, looking backward, lost his balance, and fallen. Three feet away from Ellen he heard explosions, felt himself being shot, and momentarily blacked out. When he woke on the path "Ellen was facedown on the ground, and her head was in a pool of blood. . . . I picked up Ellen's head to see if she was alive. She wasn't." One lock of Haertle's straight and neatly combed hair had fallen over his left eye.

"Steve," Danner asked, "is the man who you saw on March 29, 1981, the man who shot you and Ellen, here in this courtroom?"

"Yes."

"Can you point him out for us?"

"He's that gentleman sitting right there in the brown sweater and glasses."

"Let the record show that the witness is pointing to David Carpenter."

Now that Haertle had pointed out his client as the man in the yellow-gold jacket on Ridge Trail defense attorney Larry Biggam got to his feet to cast doubt on the sureness of that identification.

Biggam explained to the court that Steve Haertle had recited the story of the events of March 29, 1981, to the authorities seven times. Biggam led Steve through each of these meetings, when, where, how long, and whether or not they had been taped. As Haertle recited his testimony Biggam followed along with his copies of the transcripts of those interviews, ready to pounce on the slightest deviation from previous testimony.

He asked if Haertle had been hypnotized (he had not), and then discussed the layout of Henry Cowell State Park, establishing that fifty minutes had gone by between the meetings between Haertle and Hansen and the man in gold. It was crucial for Biggam to prove his client did not lay in wait.

"Did the suspect walk toward you?"

"Yes," said Haertle.

"This suspect wasn't standing or waiting was he?"

"No, he wasn't."

"He didn't come out of a bush, did he?"

"That's correct."

Haertle repeated his testimony about the suspect giving them orders to go downtrail, and then was asked, "You never saw the suspect actually touch Miss Hansen, did you?"

"No."

Among Biggam's successes during his thoughtful, low-key cross-examination was gaining the star witness's admission that he was an exceedingly poor judge of distance. On the stand Haertle had frequently confused yards and feet. Steve also admitted to Biggam that he had not seen any lettering on the back of the yellow-gold jacket and had identified the tennis shoes as red-striped Adidas, not Nike's. Danner painstakingly repaired any damage done to Haertle's testimony on redirect.

On Wednesday, May 30, witness for the prosecution Leland Fritz of Fresno told how he and his son were on a camping trip in the state park in March of 1981 when they met Carpenter sitting on top of the observation deck watching the hikers on the trails.

"Is the man you saw on the observation platform and driving the red car here in this courtroom?" asked Danner.

Fritz identified Carpenter as the man.

"I looked straight at the man's face for just a second," admitted Fritz during cross-examination by defense co-counsel Steve Wright. "The car was in view for five to seven seconds as it drove past me."

On June 13, 1984, four weeks into the trial, Mollie Purnell testified under immunity that she had lied about the gun "because David told me to say it had been stolen if anything happened." Across the room Carpenter chewed thoughtfully on his thumbnail.

Morrow warned the two juries just before a recess, "Ladies and gentlemen, we will now take a recess with the admonition not to discuss this case among yourselves or with anyone else, nor to form or express any opinion on the case until it is submitted to you. Don't even discuss the weather . . . I am going to ask you, in fact order you, not to talk with any member of the other panel about anything under any circumstances . . . the red badge or whatever it is is to distinguish you from the other group. Congregate separately, the guilt jury in the jury room, penalty in the hall."

On June 20, Marin County sheriff's investigator Ray Maynard took the stand and testified that he had taken blood and saliva samples from Carpenter on the day of his arrest, had been present at the scene of three of the murders in the Trailside case, and in fact had been the investigator on the scene in October 1980 when Anne Alderson's body was discovered. "Her body was found clothed," he said, "near an outdoor theatre in the park at Mount Tamalpais, about twelve miles from the Golden

Gate Bridge. It was almost to the top of the mountain, it's very wooded with hiking trails throughout the area. She was wearing brown leather boots, a jumper, a blue dress, and a purple print blouse. One of the first things I saw at the crime scene was a metal fragment. It turned out to be a bullet near the victim's right foot. Her car was earlier found in a parking lot less than a mile from her body. I found a pair of hiking boots, socks, and a red leather purse in the car trunk and the purse contained her identification." Maynard entered the three Alderson, Moreland, and Stowers bullets and testified only to details of Marin County crimes as would Detective Sergeant Keaton.

Sergeant Rich Keaton set out to give the Los Angeles jury a picture of what the parks in Northern California were like. "We didn't want the jurors to think of this as a park like Disneyland—this is a really remote area," he told me. "At the trial they brought me in with a slide carousel. Morrow was a really down-to-earth man and he says, 'Mr. Danner is going to be showing some pictures of parks. How many pictures do we have?' 'Eighty, Your Honor,' says Danner. Morrow says, eyebrows raised, 'Mr. Danner! At the risk of sounding rude, how many ways can I see a tree?' 'Well, I really think you should see them, Your Honor.' 'OK,' says the judge with a sigh. So I start up the carousel, rushing, and I hear Morrow, 'Sergeant, sergeant, sergeant. You're too quick on the trigger finger. Now slow down and back up.' The defense attorneys are saying the slides are prejudicial, highly inflammatory because some of our slides are of the victims.

"I got through both sets while the judge is making up his mind to admit them. Finally Morrow looks at Danner, 'Mr. Danner, I apologize. As far as I'm concerned, Mr. Christiansen, on your motion to exclude these slides—not only will these come in, but the color photos will come in and the eight-by-tens will come in. It seems to me this was cold calculated murder. He wasn't like a man running amok in the woods shooting people, but was planned—no, they'll come in.' So that kinda made me feel good. This made the impact of a real park and it helped us out."

* * *

Candace Dawn Townsend Brodecky, the woman to whom Carpenter had been engaged, testified. "I met him in January of 1981 and agreed to drive to Sebastopol with him," she told the court. Candy's car had broken down on Van Ness Avenue in San Francisco near the office of Richard Wood. Carpenter had stopped and asked the former barmaid if he could help her, ending up by giving Candy a ride to Marin County. "He stopped the car in an isolated spot near Sausalito. It was," recalled Candy, "actually very near to Mount Tamalpais. It was dark. No one else was around. It was frightening. I felt very uneasy about the whole thing. He asked me to marry him and have sex with him and offered me money."

Candy paused.

"We had sex in the backseat." Afterward they had dinner and he invited her to his parents' home, where she lived with him during the four months before his arrest. She said that Carpenter had borrowed from her a yellow-gold jacket very similar to the one worn by Ellen Hansen's killer.

Richard Wood went down to testify in Los Angeles. He was there for five days, was interviewed by the prosecution psychiatrist, Sanford Samenow, because Carpenter wouldn't agree to "talk with a prosecution shrink," and ended up testifying only twenty minutes.

"One of the attorneys asked me if I had any doubts about this guy's guilt. I looked him right in the eye and said, 'Absolutely not! There's no doubt in my mind.' I was expecting a real damaging cross-examination and he asked me about three questions."

"With so much evidence," I asked Stoney Brook, "why did the trial drag on so long?"

"Well, there's a lot of legal maneuvering more than anything else. A death-penalty kind of case always gets that kind of jockeying. The three attorneys who represented David, Wright, Biggam, and Christiansen, if I was in trouble that's the people I'd go to. They're that good, really excellent attorneys, a lot of integrity, which is one of the reasons I've stayed friends with them all these years. . . . They were doing everything they could to give

him a fair trial, working with a loaded deck. That's all
there was to it.''

Final arguments in the murder trial began on Monday,
July 2, 1984. Judge Morrow explained to the jurors that
the defendant is cloaked in a mantle of presumed innocence. Because of this the prosecution receives two opportunities to prove its case to the defense's one. ''The
jury will first hear a summation from the prosecution,
then a summation of the defense case, and then Mr. Danner will have the final word.'' There was a call for a short
recess, and then the summations were begun.

In his summation public defender Biggam sent a shock
wave through both assembled juries and their alternates.
''Evidence clearly shows David Carpenter killed Ellen
Hansen and Heather Scaggs,'' he said. There was a gasp
from the court.

''That will not be an issue in your deliberations.

''He is a man who was out of control. He's a mess.
He is not capable of weighing the consequences of a decision to kill and is incapable of the planning and pre-
meditation necessary for a finding of first-degree murder.

''Rather, the issue will be whether to return a first-
degree verdict, and whether the slayings were commited
with special circumstances that could lead to the death
penalty.''

In the prosecution's final arguments, Danner said, ''I
think Carpenter should be convicted of first-degree murder because the killings were cold and calculated and
Carpenter shot his victims through the head 'execution
style.' Rape followed by murder is a pattern for Carpenter. He kills, he murders, to avoid detection after he
rapes.

''In admitting the killings of Ellen Hansen and Heather
Scaggs, he [Biggam] opened some very big doors. What
I intend to do is walk through those doors and look
around. . . . It is not surprising Biggam conceded the
murders when you think about what he had to work with.
The victims were attacked in a manner so they would not
live to tell the story.''

Throughout the course of the trial Carpenter had taken
notes placidly, but now, for the first time, appeared ner-

vous. "What does it mean," said Danner across the courtroom, "when he brings the gun to the park. Was he looking for small game?

"What are we talking about if we're not talking about deliberation? He [Biggam] didn't talk about the way he shot people. When you shoot someone in the face at point-blank range, when you pull the trigger and a bullet smashes into your face, no, he didn't tell you about that."

Marilyn Hansen, Ellen's mother, saw Art Danner in the hall after he delivered his final summation. "I had never suspected him capable of such passion and anger. Art was generally cool and calm, at least outwardly, so when he did get emotional or agitated it was notable," she told me. "He was still breathing fast, his chest rising and falling. He was leaning back against the wall. I told him how moved I was by his eloquence. 'It . . . it . . . it's just . . . moral indignation!' he gasped."

Outside the courtroom at day's end Biggam told reporters, "This case has always been a trial for David Carpenter's life. If Carpenter does not receive the death penalty I will consider the defense successful."

One day after Carpenter's own attorney admitted his client's guilt, the guilt jury, eight women and four men, received their final instructions from the judge. Carefully Morrow led them through the rules, item by item, line by line, paragraph by paragraph. The penalty jury, which had heard all six weeks of testimony, had been recessed for the day.

"Assume," said the judge, "Carpenter is of sound mind. You should not consider the five killings for which he awaits trial in Marin County unless you are convinced the defendant committed those crimes." The only face in the room more stern and stonelike than the judge's was the defendant's.

Two paper cards with both possible verdicts already typed out on them were presented to each juror. The guilt jury retired and got in two hours of deliberations before they recessed for the Fourth of July holiday. That evening, under the eye of a deputy sheriff, they were taken to a hotel to spend the night.

On July 5, at 8:30 A.M. the jury returned to the Hall

of Justice and then remained at the hotel once again that night. Early July 6, 1984, after three days of deliberations amounting to just under eight hours, the guilt jury arrived at an agreement. Quickly the bailiff passed the word. Morrow heard rapid steps in the hall outside his chambers, a flurry of excitement. "Your Honor, a verdict has been reached."

Spectators, lawyers, reporters, all rushed to their accustomed places, a silent and intent wave of figures. From a side door to the right, the court reporter and court clerk entered. The jingle of the bailiff's keys could be heard.

"Please, everyone, rise. The court of the Honorable Judge Dion Morrow is now in session." There was a rumble, a murmur, a shuffle of a hundred people rising simultaneously. Carpenter had been brought from his security holding cell and now sat at the defense table, where the mood was both expectant and grim. Biggam leaned over and wrote something out for Carpenter on his yellow legal pad and then seemed to brighten a bit. At the prosecution table the faces were generally unreadable. There was a ripple of unrest in the courtroom.

Morrow spoke: "Order will be maintained during these proceedings." The judge inclined his head in the direction of the paneled door. "The defendant and counsel are present. Bring in the jury, Mr. Bailiff." The room became quiet as the jurors were ushered single file into the court to announce their decision.

"May it be stipulated," said Morrow, "gentlemen, that the regular jurors together with the alternate jurors are each present?"

"So stipulated," came the reply.

Morrow then turned to the jury. "Does the jury have a communication for the court?"

"We have, sir," said the foreman, Frank Aulenta, rising.

"Has the jury reached a verdict in this matter as to all three counts?"

"We have, Your Honor."

"Will you hand the verdicts to the bailiff, please," said the judge, "who will present them to the bench." Morrow scanned the verdicts and said, "The clerk will read the verdicts.'' The clerk began to read: ''Superior Court of California, in and for the County of Los Angeles. The People of the State of California, Plaintiff versus David Joseph Carpenter, Defendant. Verdict, first count: As to count one of the indictment herein, which said count accuses the defendant, David Joseph Carpenter, of the murder of Heather Roxanne Scaggs, a violation of the section pertaining to murder under special circumstances, violation of Section 187 of the Penal Code of the State of California, we, the jury, find as follows . . .''

Though no emotion showed on Carpenter's face his shoulders tensed.

''We the jury in the above entitled action, find the defendant, David Joseph Carpenter, Guilty of the crime of murder as charged in count one of the indictment, and find it to be murder in the first degree with three special circumstances. This sixth day of July, 1984. Frank D. Aulenta, Foreman.''

''And I'm going to ask you, ladies and gentlemen, if the verdict as just read by the court pertaining to the first count is the verdict of this jury. If this be your verdict as to the first count,'' said Morrow, ''you will please respond by answering yes. I will ask you: Is this your verdict as to the first count?''

''Yes,'' came the reply.

''Is there any member of the jury who did not vote for the verdict as to the first count as just read by the court?''

The reply was negative.

The judge then turned to the attorneys. ''Does counsel desire to have the jury polled?''

''Yes, Your Honor,'' replied Biggam.

The judge turned to the jury. ''Ladies and gentlemen of the jury, your name will be individually called, and as your name is called, if you voted for the verdict as read by the court as to the first count finding for the defendant Guilty of murder of the first degree under the special circumstances provision you will please respond yes.'' Each juror responded yes.

Morrow continued. ''The court therefore finds that the verdict as to the first count as read by the court is the verdict of this jury.'' The judge now proceeded methodically to the second verdict of the guilt or innocence phase. "As to count two of the indictment herein, which said account accuses the defendant, David Joseph Carpenter, of the murder of Ellen Marie Hansen . . . we the jury find as follows—we find the defendant, David Joseph Carpenter, Guilty of murder. . . ."

The jury was again polled and each individual response was in the affirmative.

"Very well," said Morrow, "the court finds the verdict as to the second count as read by the court to be the verdict of this jury and orders the clerk to record it. . . .

"Then, ladies and gentlemen of the jury that completes your services to the court in this matter. . . ." Morrow commended their patience and involvement in the difficult and emotional case. He thanked each on behalf of the State of California and the County of Los Angeles and told them that they left the courtroom after having made a great contribution to the cause of justice. "You have conscientiously performed your duties. This jury is discharged and the alternate jurors are discharged."

Immediately after recessing the jury, Morrow set 9:00 A.M., August 15, 1984, for the commencement of the penalty phase of the trial. The judge glanced over at Carpenter, who was gathering up his own documents as the bailiff stood over him. Altogether the ex-purser had been found guilty of murdering Ellen Hansen, attempting to rape her, murdering Heather Scaggs and raping her and attempting to murder Steve Haertle.

This meant the jury had found for three special circumstances—multiple murders, murder during rape, and murder while lying in wait. In the second phase of the trial, since guilt had been proven, the second jury would be required to find for sufficient punishment, either life imprisonment without the possibility of parole or death in the gas chamber at San Quentin.

"We should stop the cycle of violence," said Larry Biggam outside the courtroom. "Right now David Carpenter is going to die in prison. In no way can I excuse his crimes, but we will certainly try to explain them. We will try to explain who he is, where he came from, and why he is here.''

The mothers of the two slain women were in court for the verdict and were hugged by jurors afterward. Marilyn Hansen said she was "proud" of her daughter because she resisted her attacker.

"Her resistance was the beginning of the end for him. Her resistance made it possible for Steve Haertle to live. I think the death penalty is the appropriate penalty in this case. We feel a lot of relief.

"Part of the reason," Marilyn told me later, "we parents went to the trial was to make our kids real, to have an impact." She added bitterly, "Carpenter used his stutter to gain sympathy. He doesn't stutter when he has a gun in his hand. He doesn't stutter when he robs you. He's a big man then. I was told by an expert, one of those in court, that Carpenter is able to control his stammering."

Mary Scaggs was asked if she thought justice had been done.

"No, not completely. Not yet. We knew he raped Heather, but that was not a question in the courtroom."

Over tea and coffee at the Owl and the Monkey Cafe, Richard Wood told me, "I've been involved in some fairly big investigations, drugs, murder, money laundering, but this guy, in my experience, is totally unique, thank God. Thank God there is only one of him. He was truly amazing.

"He still amazes me with the way he carried this thing off and the way he manipulated everybody. He was a master manipulator. He's also just a cold-blooded killer."

Wood was earnest, dedicated, haunted. His dark, penetrating eyes never left mine. There was no doubt he was a shrewed judge of character, yet he felt he had been taken in by Carpenter. I knew for some time he had poured over Carpenter's original file searching for a clue he may have missed in the case with all its mazelike turns. He had found none.

"I had cleared through my supervisors exactly what I was doing in the case and they were aware all along the line what was going on.

"Carpenter had this really straight life going, but he also was good friends with ex-cons. He never mixed the two.

"He wasn't stuttering on the trail was he? I think this guy worked himself up to do each one of these things. I think that's why there was a period in between them. He was just determined to do it and just followed through and did it and then the impulse was satisfied. He is, more than anything, impulsive.

"I don't think anybody's ever explored this guy's sexual problems because I think possibly the whole thing with power and rape really lie at the bottom of this. Rape is of course a sexual crime . . . I don't think anybody can do that unless they've totally dehumanized their victim.

"I also don't think it's an accident that Carpenter started killing people closer to him. I told you that Womack was the guy who broke the case, but in my estimation the guy who *really* broke the case was Carpenter himself. He was the one who split it wide open because he made the first of many mistakes. The biggest of which was killing somebody close to him like Heather Scaggs. I think Carpenter really had the hots for her. As for Candy, why he didn't kill her, I don't know. Nobody can figure that one out. One of the things I wonder about Candy is what his true feelings about her were.

"I think he may have really liked her. This is mere conjecture because with this guy you'll never know. And if there's one person in the world who's not going to tell you it's him. I've often wondered what it would be like to sit down and have a conversation with David Carpenter about all this and get some honest answers."

10

Penalty Phase

On August 13, 1984, as Carpenter's penalty trial began, the depressing news of Captain Robert Gaddini's death at the age of forty-six on July 31 cast a pall over the already grim proceedings. He had been diagnosed at Kaiser Hospital as having lung cancer in late October of 1983, but had decided to remain on the job as head of the sheriff's department's civil division and county jail, following the trial in Los Angeles closely through his last days.

Additional evidence on the five Marin County murders Carpenter had not been tried for would be heard by the penalty jury. Because special circumstances had been proven, Carpenter could be sentenced to death in the gas chamber. The acid-green chamber at San Quentin had not been used for nineteen years. On February 18, 1972, the state court had struck down capital punishment as "cruel or unusual treatment." It was reinstated five years later.

Closing arguments in the penalty trial began on Thursday, September 13, 1984.

As far as prosecutor Art Danner was concerned, Car-

penter was a pathological liar capable of being a loving
grandfather on one hand and torturing his victims on the
other. Danner commented on this later:

"He utilizes all facets of his personality that can be to
the innocent victim very charming and he uses them to
gain the advantage he had in seeking out his victims.
When he learned something about the other person's personality and character he felt was vulnerable, he took
immediate advantage of that and that is in almost every
case. So he's capable of the most devious of ploys and
yet at the same time can be very convincing in the story
he tells.

"If ever there was a case that was appropriate for the
death penalty this is it. You can't review and look at the
facts and know anything about the victims in the case
and see this case unfold and not somehow be touched by
the unbelievable travesty committed by this man on these
victims and their surviving families. This man should be
executed and I believe that. I tried the case based on that
premise and I'd do it again."

The penalty jury reached a verdict of death. On Friday,
November 16, 1984, Mary Scaggs made the following
statement to the court: "I believe the death penalty is a
deterrent. If carried out, David Carpenter will never
murder again." Judge Morrow then sentenced Carpenter
to death in the gas chamber. Carpenter, dressed in a dark-
blue jail jumpsuit, listened solemnly, said nothing, and
was immediately taken to San Quentin near Mount Tamalpais and placed in maximum security.

"I've seen David Carpenter in the East Block," a
source within San Quentin wrote me, "where Death Row
inmates do their visiting. He looks just about the same
as you and I, but predictably enough doesn't look at all
like he does on TV. In fact, some of his features were
strikingly similar to my own pop's. I could tell almost
instantly it was him, though. Can't say why. Even my
visitor could tell.

"Then I heard a few words spoken by him, and that
iced it—an agonizing stutter. Poor bastard. If he's had
that all of his life, and the kids in his neighborhoods
were as vicious as most kids are, he went through his
own private hell. He was in a calm environment and

conversing easily with a lady, and his stutter even under such circumstances was hellish. To a strictly limited extent, one could understand how such a defect could, given the antipathy humans tend to have toward those who appear 'different,' eventually lead to some form of outrageous, and I suppose, outraged, behavior. Sending him in prison blues, looking 'just plain folks,' it was rather hard to picture him terrorizing and slaughtering innocents.

"David Carpenter," my source at San Quentin told me, "is working in his cell about twelve to fourteen hours a day in preparation for his Marin County trial. But I hear other inmates have threatened to do away with him if he doesn't stop pounding on his electric typewriter. He says he just wants to stay alive long enough to prove his innocence.

"I doubt if he is happy in prison, few are, including myself.

"All social traits, all, that you possess and use as a member of society are considered antisocial traits by cop and con alike in this alien environment. To call someone in here a nice guy is a good way to get your nose moved to another part of your face. I can't really tell you about the pen until you've been in it, and once you've been in it I don't have to tell you.

"As for Carpenter, in his first trial he didn't talk with anyone. Now he's changing his strategy, I hear."

Earlier Larry Biggam had said, "I haven't given him up to the death penalty, but he will spend the rest of his life in prison." Under standard procedure, Carpenter's death penalty verdict was automatically sent to the State Supreme Court for review, though Supreme Court decisions take, as a rule, several years to reach a conclusion. Biggam also filed for an indefinite delay of execution. Whereas both state appellate courts nationwide and federal courts reverse an average of 45 percent of the death sentences handed down, the California high court has reversed more than 90 percent in recent years.

After Carpenter made the transfer from Los Angeles to San Quentin to await trial on the Marin County attacks, County Deputy District Attorney John Posey, who had attended Carpenter's penalty phase and sentencing,

went about drawing up the papers necessary to prosecute
the purser on two counts of rape, one count of attempted
rape, and five additional murder charges, the five the DA
felt they could most conclusively prove. The .44-caliber
gun used to kill Edda Kane, the first known victim, had
never been found, and there were doubts about the available evidence in the stabbing of the second victim on the
Sleeping Lady, Barbara Schwartz. A second trial seemed
superfluous to many of the board of supervisors since
Carpenter already had two death convictions hanging
over his head as well as federal and state parole violations.

Four days after his arrival on Death Row at San Quentin, Carpenter met with Deputy Public Defender Frank
Cox and his boss, Larry Heon. The defendant methodically listed what his defenses were, confidently claiming
he could prove he was not the Trailside Killer. Cox was
designated as Carpenter's new lawyer, and on January 31,
1985, filed a plea of double jeopardy, being prosecuted
more than once for the same offenses, on behalf of his
client.

"Judge Morrow," argued Cox, "cited overwhelming
proof of five Marin County premeditated murders when
he sentenced Mr. Carpenter to death for two murders
committed in Santa Cruz in 1980. . . . This constitutes
double jeopardy and Mr. Carpenter is therefore immune
from prosecution for the five Marin County killings."

"Do you enter a plea of Not Guilty?" Judge William H.
Stephens asked.

"Y-y-y-yessir."

"Do you enter a plea of already being once in jeopardy?"

Carpenter replied in the affirmative.

"Do you wish to plead that you have already been tried
and convicted on every charge against you in this complaint?"

Carpenter nodded yes.

Because of Carpenter's speech impediment the county
provided a $366 electric typewriter so that he could com-
municate with his attorney. Immediately afterward Cox
put in a request for a computer for his client, contending
that it would be nearly impossible without it to keep track

of the twenty thousand pages of court transcript and the volumes of information gathered by investigators during the intense manhunt for the Trailside Killer.

Meanwhile, against the advice of his lawyers, Carpenter had agreed to a television interview where he would reveal much of his true personality.

11

Carpenter
Speaks

On August 19, 1985, Monday night, Channel 2's
Ten O'Clock News presented an exclusive interview with
David Carpenter, the first time the convicted killer of
Heather Roxanne Scaggs and Ellen Marie Hansen had
spoken out.

The twenty-two minutes of the interview, to be broadcast in three parts, had been culled from a single two-
hour sitting at San Quentin's Death Row. Elaine Corral,
the interviewer, was dressed in a bright red dress, a long
string of white pearls, and a white jacket. Carpenter was
wearing a prisoner's orange jumpsuit open at the neck,
his white T-shirt showing. At the time this interview was
taped, July 19, 1985, the purser sported a beard similar
to the one he had cultivated prior to his questioning by
Robinson and Womack in Richard Wood's federal probation office. Throughout the interview Carpenter would
stammer badly.

"David Carpenter has been silent since his arrest in
1981," said Corral. "He decided to break his silence
several weeks ago. Everyone from the prosecutor to the
380

mothers of the victims to his own lawyers were shocked by his decision to talk. They didn't think he'd say anything at all until his second trial was over. The shock was soon replaced with curiosity. What would this man say after all these years about the women he was convicted of killing in cold blood? But it was not what he said but how he said it that stands out. We would like to emphasize before we begin that we are not trying to reopen the question of his guilt. A jury has already determined in at least two of the murders that he is guilty. The purpose of this interview is to provide an insight into how this convicted killer thinks.''

PART ONE—DAVID CARPENTER.

DAVID CARPENTER: I've said from the very start that I am *not* the Trailside Killer [at this point Carpenter's voice shook with surpressed anger]. I've said before that they knew before my arrest that I had not killed Heather Scaggs. They knew for sure. They knew positively once they got the bullet from Heather Scaggs's head that I was not the Trailside Killer. By this time they said I had killed everybody that had been killed in the last five or ten years in Northern California and now they were forced to cover up.

ELAINE CORRAL [in voice over]: David Carpenter has suffered from a bad stutter his whole life but there are those who say his stutter completely disappears when he is in control and there's a gun in his hand. Carpenter . . . has been sentenced to die in the gas chamber at San Quentin. His execution date has not been set. . . . during the course of his trial he never admitted any guilt, never took the stand and never talked to anyone but his attorneys.

DC: I have not killed anybody. I have not killed anyone here in, uh, Marin County. I have not killed anyone in Santa Cruz County. I haven't killed anyone in San Francisco. I haven't killed anybody . . . I haven't killed anybody.

EC [in voice over]: Carpenter, however, still faces five more murder charges in Marin County. He's scheduled to go on trial beginning September 13 for the murders of eighteen-year-old Cynthia Moreland and her nineteen-year-old boyfriend Richard Stowers in Point Reyes. Anne Alderson was found on a hiking trail on Mount Tam. She was raped and shot in the head. The following month back at Point Reyes the nude bodies of two more women were found: twenty-two-year-old Diane O'Connell and twenty-five-year-old Shauna May. May was also raped. All of the victims were shot in the head with a .38-caliber gun. Carpenter said he never got a fair trial for the Santa Cruz murders but that the upcoming trial in Marin will be a different story.

DC: When I go to trial I'm gonna prove beyond a reasonable doubt. Something I don't have to do but something I'm going to do to prove that I am not the Trailside K-K-K-K-K-K-K-K-K-Killer. [When Carpenter reached a word that his crippling stutter prevented him from speaking his lips would turn pinker and wetter, his throat would work and veins in his temples would stand out.]

EC [in voice over]: But investigators have linked still other unsolved murders to this man. . . . Our interview took place early on a Monday morning in a holding cell at San Quentin. An armed guard brought him down from Death Row. . . . [to Carpenter] Your attorney said, this is a quote, "David Carpenter is a man who is out of control. He is a mess. He is a personally damaged human being and not capable of weighing the consequences of his decision to kill." Are you a mess? Are you out of control? Are you a damaged human being?

DC: No, no, no. But I used to be.

EC: What's that mean?

DC: All right. I spent the years '72, '73, '74, part of '75 in the therapy program down at Vacaville. And I really got it t-t-t-together for the first time in my l-l-l-life. I got to know who I am and I felt good about myself.

EC: You told a psychiatrist that the way you deal with stress is to rape the nearest female. Is that a lie?

DC: That's a long time ago. I said that when I was probably thirty and I'm fifty-four years old now [he is actually fifty-five]. So you're talking about something that was in a report that is twenty-five years [long stretch of stuttering] you know something I did twenty-five years ago.

EC: And does that describe you now?

DC: No! The thing is this—the same thing you are talking

about is what got me in this situation now. 'Cause when the police picked up my records they picked up my jacket, they looked at my jacket. If there was anybody who should be the Trailside suspect I should be it. There's no question that I was the number-one suspect. My record sucks: There's no question about it. [Carpenter's hands are long and white, and as he spoke he would move his hands up and down and then in sweeping counterclockwise motions like a twin-engine plane.] Nobody will not disagree that my record sucks. It's a terrible record. I am not p-p-p-proud of it. It's there when they picked it up. They said, "Oh, my God, here's the Trailside Killer."

EC: Are you capable of killing someone?

DC: No. That's one thing I could never do. I've done a lot of things in my l-l-l-l-life but killing is not oooooonnn-neooooooonnnnne of them.

EC: Are you capable of rape?

DC: I used to be. Yeah. Right now, no.

EC: You used to alleviate stress by looking for a woman to rape?

DC: In the past. Not now. [Corral's eyebrows shot upward at the answer.] Oh, yeah, yeah, yeah. There's no question. I've never denied what I've done. On everything I've ever done I've always pled g-g-g-g-g-guilty to. [Carpenter slapped his fist into his palm to emphasize each word.]

EC: The prosecutor has described you as a cool and calculating individual. Does that describe you?

DC: No. No. Because as I talk to you you can see the e-e-e-e-emotions that are seething in me. The thing is this—I don't give a damn what he says, all I say is give me a fair trial and let me prove that I'm not the Trailside Killer. That's all I've ever asked for. I want to see these dirty rotten sons of bitches in p-p-p-p-prison. I'd like to see Art Danner and Jerry Herman in prison for the rest of their l-l-l-l-l-lives for what they have done to me.

The face that flashed across the screen was one of fury. Carpenter was watching at San Quentin. "I saw myself," he said later, "and did not like it."

* * *

In the second part of the interview Corral asked, "When Steven Haertle pointed you out in court as the one who did it, did Steven Haertle lie?"

DC: No! No! No! No! [like a series of small yips] Stephen Haertle thinks that I'm the Trailside K-K-K-K-Killer. The thing is this. The most imperfect evidence there is is eyewitness testimony.

EC: But he saw you. Face-to-face.

DC: He saw a person in the lineup, he felt this was the man who k-k-killed. . . . Mary Scaggs, who's Heather Scaggs's mother, believes that I'm the Trailside Killer. She got on the stand and she lied.

EC: Why would she do that?

DC: Because she wants to get her daughter's killer and I don't blame her. Because if it was my daughter I would probably have done the same damn thing. I'd have gotten up on the stand and said yes, that's he, the individual. You see, I can understand where Mary Scaggs is c-c-c-coming from. . . . All of the family members that come to the next trial should listen. We're going to impeach witness after witness after witness.

EC: What about the witness of the trial in Santa Cruz who said he saw you run from the scene and get into a red car and police later linked that red car to you?

DC: There's a lot of testimony here that I can't go into. Because the guy with the red car is Leland Fritz. We refer to him as "Lying Leland."

EC: Do you sit up there and ever have any fears that you're going to end up in the gas chamber?

DC: No. Because I'm not g-g-g-g-g-guilty. I'm not guilty and I can prove I'm not guilty. That's what I intend to do. That's the reason I'm having this press interview is to stay alive so I can prove it. . . . The bottom line is seven people were killed and one person was w-w-wounded. If I can prove that I did not kill one person then I can't have killed any.

EC: All seven Trailside victims were shot in the head with the same .38-caliber revolver; one man had to have done it all.

DC: I became the number-one s-s-suspect because there were a lot of c-c-c-c-co-incidences. I never said that there weren't. What is important to remember is this—who pulled the trigger? If I pulled the trigger then I had to pull the trigger and kill everybody. I can't have killed Ellen Hansen . . . and not have killed Heather Scaggs. They can't say you killed this person and didn't kill this person. [Do they think] I picked up the phone and called one of my friends and said, "Look, I'm the Trailside Killer but I can't go out today. Here's the gun. You go out and you kill someone." It's ridiculous. It's stupid. There's one Trailside Killer. That's all—one.

EC: Carpenter will not talk much about his mother, but it came out at the trial that he was an abused child.

DC: I used to go to school with black and blue marks. Day after day after day. If you were talking about a year's t-t-t-t-time I wouldn't be talking about how many times I got beaten, I'd be talking about how many times I didn't get beaten. If you're talking about 365 days, I'd be beaten about 350 to 355 days a year. I'd get beaten every day.

EC: Summarize how your life has been.

DC: Uh. It's been interesting. I'll say that.

On Wednesday, September 4, 1985, under tight security, the preliminary hearing for Carpenter's second trial opened, a trial estimated to run over a year in time and cost, conservatively, more than one million dollars. Judge Stephens of the Municipal Court presided over the five new charges against Carpenter.

As he had done in the Los Angeles trial, Carpenter did not take the stand during his preliminary hearing. The first testimony came from Mollie Purnell, who had flown in from Key Biscayne, Florida, and was testifying under immunity. A sobbing Evelyn Alderson, seeing Carpenter face-to-face at last, identified a portrait of her daughter in a barely audible voice, "Yes, that's Anne."

The documented material, new and from the first trial, had grown to such proportions that it had to be wheeled into the courtroom in a grocery cart. During the preliminary proceedings the mountain of court documents would grow by another twelve volumes of transcripts; altogether seventy-seven items of evidence and twenty-nine witnesses would be presented.

During the hearing the lawyers for the defense had tried two major arguments: one was that the rape and at-

tempted rape charges should be dropped since there was,
as attorney Stephen Berlin put it, no direct evidence that
the defendant had assaulted any of the victims sexually.
Judge Stephens disagreed strongly. He told Berlin *all* of
the Trailside murders had shown some evidence of sexual
connotation.

A second argument advanced by Public Defender Stephen Berlin was that by trying Carpenter on the Marin
homicide charges using practically the same evidence
used to convict him of the Santa Cruz attacks put the
defendant in a state of double jeopardy. The defense team
had complained of this during the penalty phase of the
ex-purser's Los Angeles trial for the murders of Ellen
Hansen and Heather Scaggs and maintained that evidence relating to the five Marin Killings in question was
used by the prosecution to gain the first convictions and
death sentences. Ultimately this strategy would be rejected in a higher court.

Prosecutor John Posey expressed to the judge there was
"dual intent—rape and murder—in the crime spree." Of
course the recovered .38-caliber gun was the real
clincher. Test slugs fired from this weapon matched in
every way those recovered from the bodies of the Marin
victims and the two women murdered in Santa Cruz
County. The proven owner of the pistol was David Carpenter. The preliminary hearing came to an end on October 10, 1985, as it was ruled Carpenter would be
arraigned on October 24 on charges of rape, attempted
rape, and the murders of four women and one man in
Marin County. Carpenter was present for the judge's ruling and showed no emotion at the result of six weeks of
hearings. Posey had his own theory about the number of
bullets fired on Santa Cruz's Ridge Trail. The fifth
"wild" bullet fired at Haertle had never been recovered.
Posey thought that there had never been more than four
bullets since Carpenter was in the habit of keeping one
chamber of the five-shot Rossi .38 empty.

With the mood of the state's voters favoring capital punishment, both of Carpenter's attorneys made another motion to block the Marin County murder counts against
their client. Carpenter's trial dates were set for mid-July

and then December 1, and while the various defense motions were being considered the second trial was set back even farther.

For some time insiders at the Marin Hall of Justice had been hearing rumors that Carpenter's attorneys were maneuvering to have him plead Guilty in exchange for life imprisonment without any possibility of parole in order to avoid another death penalty. No one could understand why the DA's office would not accept such a deal and save taxpayers over a million dollars.

Then on February 25, 1986, Carpenter abruptly fired his attorney Frank Cox.

"Cox refused to interview key defense witnesses," complained the condemned man. "He was working with someone in the Marin County district attorney's office to cut a deal for me to plead Guilty without the possibility of parole," Carpenter wrote the *Point Reyes Light*.

"He tried his darnest to force/coerce me into taking that deal, based on the fact that I had no defense to put up. . . . I honestly believe he tried to sell me out. I have said all along I am not the Trailside Killer. Things have gotten so bad as of late that I have been forced to write members of my family and ask them to help do investigative work in my case because it's not being done by my defense team."

Shortly afterward, on March 19, Carpenter reversed his decision to fire Cox when Cox's boss, Larry Heon, agreed to personally monitor the case.

"Mr. Carpenter is isolated on Death Row and under a tremendous amount of stress. So are we," said Cox. "Three weeks ago stress caused health problems, forcing me to miss some work. The dispute arose from the stress of having to bring the Marin case to trial with just over a year's preparation. In contrast, Carpenter's defense team in Santa Cruz had two and a half years to prepare their case."

Cox was giving the fight to change the location of the trial his all, commissioning a survey that showed 98 percent of Marin County residents not only remembered the Trailside killings, but of that number an astonishing 97 percent believed Carpenter was "probably guilty." Cox blamed "unprecedented local news coverage," since over a six-year period the media and especially the defendant himself had kept the name of David Carpenter in the eyes of the public.

In Superior Court Judge Richard Breiner's ten-page opinion on the change of venue he noted that the inconvenience was minimal compared to the right of the defendant to have a fair trial, the cost insignificant compared to what a third trial would run years later if the case were reversed by an appellate court on a finding that venue should have been changed in the first place.

On September 13 the State Judicial Council ruled that Carpenter's second trial could be held in either Orange, Santa Barbara, Santa Clara, Sacramento, or San Diego counties. Within five days San Diego was chosen, and February 18, 1987, was set for the start of the trial.

Carpenter now anticipated taking the witness stand in his own defense, saying that he was a victim of a corrupted criminal system more interested in clearing up a case than in solving the Trailside slayings. "I was an easy target because of my long criminal record," he said.

The age of the defendant and two death convictions were not enough to satisfy the prosecution, as long as the possibility existed that Carpenter's previous conviction could be overturned by the appellate court under Chief Justice Rose Bird. Since the State Supreme Court had reinstated the death penalty in 1977, thirty-three of the thirty-six death sentences appealed before the court were reversed, a reversal rate of 92 percent. The court and Chief Justice Bird specifically were accused of being soft on capital punishment by the state's political right wing.

Justice Bird maintained that the current death penalty laws were poorly constructed and rife with constitutional problems, and though she was not the only justice to overturn death sentences she was the most visible, most vocal, and only judge to throw out every death sentence she reviewed.

But all this had changed in 1986. By August, Rose Bird had become California's biggest political issue, and in November Justice Bird and fellow justices Cruz Reynoso and Joseph Grodin were decisively thrown out, the first appellate judges to be so defeated in fifty-two years.

It was obvious that the new Supreme Court, with appointees by pro-death penalty governor Deukmejian, would now begin to uphold more death-penalty verdicts. It was a decisive turn to the right within the mood of the state, and there was now the possibility Carpenter could be executed if the gas chamber were put into operation again. The prosecution remained firm: *no* deals.

This now meant Carpenter's appeals would fall on the ears of a more conservative court, one that would be more inclined to uphold his death convictions for the Santa Cruz murders. Without Rose Bird, the shadow of the green gas chamber cast itself decisively for the first time over the cell of David Carpenter.

"Jerry Herman is a tough prosecutor, a tough DA," Supervisor Giacomini said to me. "I think he thinks Carpenter's killed a whole lot more people than they're even bothering with. I remember Herman trembling with rage in the meeting with us and saying, 'Not only did he kill the people we're charging him with but many other people and if you think I'm going to sit on my hands and let this madman walk, you're crazy!' He was real righteous about it. He said, 'I'm not going to bore you with the other details. He has to be exterminated permanently from society because he's killed many more people than will ever be known. Ever. Probably dozens.'

"But the board has some differences with him on Trailside. We supervisors think it's inappropriate to retry Carpenter. The reasons we do is, How many times can you execute somebody? It's a waste of taxpayers' money. In the early days it was costing us; it was our loot in the beginning. It was later this legislation came along.* Especially with the new Supreme Court, not the old Bird court. We made this contention right away once he was convicted. We said to Herman, 'My God, why are you

---

*State laws were passed in 1983 to provide uniform justice. Government code section 15201 would cover prosecution costs, some of the defense costs, and would reimburse all court costs in excess of $640,000. Penal code section 987.9 covers defense costs. Marin had to absorb $300,000 in the beginning. The $25,000 reward was not reimbursable.

going to spend millions and millions?' Herman said, quite correctly, 'Rose Bird will overturn it.' So we took a hike. We don't think that now. Every likelihood is that the present Supreme Court will sustain the death conviction of Santa Cruz.

" 'So what are we doing? What would you do? Cook him again? We don't understand why it's necessary to do that,' we told him, 'at least until you await the results of the Santa Cruz appeal.' So we're at odds with Herman on that. We think he should take a pass, and the defense was willing to waive time. They have a right to a speedy trial. Waive time means we agree they can be tried after the disposition of the Santa Cruz cases, so we don't think there's any loss in waiting to see what happens.

"Herman makes the case, which is a reasonable one, too, that it gets stale. Witnesses get stale or could die. He is, of course, the elected district attorney and the supervisors are in no position to order him around any more than we are the sheriff about policy decisions. He has every prerogative to do what he is doing. The two trials will easily cost the state three million by the time it runs through the court, maybe five million."

At the end of May San Diego Superior Court Judge Harold Hoffman denied a request by the prosecution to use as evidence the statements made by Larry Biggam during his closing arguments in Carpenter's first trial conceding his client had killed two women in Santa Cruz County. The judge ruled the statements were "too prejudicial to Carpenter." Hoffman also rejected a motion from the defense to suppress evidence, the murder gun, from the earlier trial.

"I had a question," I asked Richard Wood, "about Carpenter's public defenders. They seem to be pulling out all the stops for him. What are they getting from this effort? Are they doing it for media attention, financial gain?"

"No! These guys aren't getting paid a hell of a lot. I think Carpenter has attorneys who really believe in the adversarial system. I think they are saying if this guy goes to the gas chamber, which I understand is the Marin DA's aim, then they want to be able to say to themselves, I have done absolutely everything in my power to make the state prove their case. They've got to knock themselves out because they have to live with themselves. I really have a lot of respect for the way they've done it. The system isn't about defense attorneys lying down.

"I have very ambivalent feelings about the death penalty and this has really changed the way I look at the death penalty. For a long time I was very anti-death penalty, but when this thing with Carpenter happened I said to myself, Perhaps the greatest joy I could get out of this case is watching them drop the pellets on this guy. Now I've come back to the conclusion that I don't think that's going to serve any purpose. He should be locked away forever.''

12

Stoney Brook: Santa Cruz

On May 21, 1987, I visited the Carpenter brown-shingled family home on Sussex Street for the first time since the year of the purser's arrest, 1981.

Elevated, twisting Sussex Street, as it snaked its way past the Carpenter home and descended into the curve of Bemis Street, reminded me of something. The road, with its sidewalks on each side, duplicated the elevation, rises, dips, and turns of Cowell State Park's Ridge Trail and its hardpacked sides leading away from the observation deck.

I stood on the sidewalk and looked up. The plants, which formerly had been tended by Mrs. Carpenter, were dead, and a window on the second floor stood open, revealing a room empty of both furniture and occupants. However, ivy on the fences near the street still thrived. The only thing new about the house was a white, rounded gate at the base of the steep stairs, which must have been added in 1981 to keep reporters away.

As I left I looked back at the elevated house. It was not difficult to imagine Carpenter's father framed in the cold window on the second floor in the rapidly fading light.

* * *

"I have a hunch," Brook told me the following day in his new office in Santa Cruz, "that Carpenter killed those people because he realized if he didn't kill them he was going to get caught.

"I also think the obvious psychological pattern is he goes from strangers to friends, acquaintances, which is obviously going to bring the focus closer and closer and closer to him. It's a form of suicidal behavior." Brook shook his head.

"But I think there's a tremendous story underneath that no one's even touched—the fact this guy was so *invisible* and able to work his way in and was so clever about it.

"A very, very manipulative man, and he's still that way. He's always working at it . . . that's the way life is for him.

"I'm inclined to hold the theory that he sees himself as very bright . . . his nickname was Devious Dave, and guess who gave it to him—he did!" Brook laughed, imitating Carpenter, " 'I was called Devious Dave in prison.'

"That interview he did on TV. Ah, jeez, you're talking about an ego you can't run over with a truck. . . . He fits in with the classical psychological profile of the so-called disorganized mind in the sense you have a passive or nonpresent father, dominant mother figure. . . . Interestingly enough, the sister and brother seem to do all right in life. David, of course, has his stutter.

"They keep saying he was an abused child, but I have a lot of difficulty with that. If you were raised in a Mormon family or if you were raised in a Quaker family— there are a lot of religious groups that are extremely punitive, Italian families are like that, Irish families. But the fact the kid gets slapped up the side of the head or whatever it is, it doesn't always follow you're going to become a serial killer.

"I think a lot of people who commit those kind of crimes just want to commit crimes, that's what it comes down to. There's the type of personality that has that bent for violence. The theory is they eventually grow out of it, but I don't think so.

''Carpenter's a real limp wrist in a lot of ways. He's a real weak person, but he uses his strength of mind to balance that by seeing himself as a much better person than the other people he's dealing with. In fact, he's the kind of guy who would draw bullies to him to abuse him, but what he does in turn is he goes out and finds smaller kids and acts out his own power fantasies on them.

''The reason Carpenter is so dangerous is . . . the fact he thinks it's perfectly OK to abuse other people because that makes him feel good.

''I think what happens in Carpenter's instance, he goes out and gets married, has a couple of kids, got a job— he's a responsible adult. . . . Then the guy goes out to sea, he's in the merchant marine and there's a girl there he makes a pass at.

''Then he had the kids and the pressure of the family. 'What about us?' they said, 'We're home. We need some family support.' Carpenter comes home, takes a job clerking. He'd been a purser on board the ship, a controlling position, had some clout, but now he's got a clerical job with the line. . . . I think he goes through this pressure at home. He'd been going back and forth with the shipping line. Now he's back in the states and he's trying to deal with the kids. It was just more than he could handle.

''I remember hearing the story of one of his ex-wives. The wife was telling me one day he came home and said something like, 'I was driving down the coast highway and I stopped to help some woman who had car trouble and if the police call all I was trying to do was help her with the broken car.' The ex-wife tells me, 'I never put any of that together.'

''I'm thinking to myself, you know, the bastard never quit. He never quit. There are, I bet, hundreds of women out there, who have been victims of David Carpenter that have never been reported. That was in the days, of course, before the Presidio attack. . . . I think what happens is old David, David got into the place where he was working and had to deal with his family and his kids and having to be an adult and he's not an adult. He's a child, childlike in a lot of ways, and that's where the pressure built up and that's what drove him out to start attacking people again.

"I think what happens is that these guys just become dormant like a volcano and there'll be something like they have this kind of resting period, but then there are pressures . . . and it drives them back out there to start doing it again.

"The psychologists tell me Carpenter's got all these pent-up frustrations and angers that are brought about by what happened when he was a child. But all of us have had those kind of frustrations and angers. You go for counseling in order to deal with it.

"This bastard is a classic sociopath. He sits down with these doctors and realizes how to manipulate them. That's where the bright part comes in."

I asked Brook about Roberta A. Patterson, the woman whose tip in the early part of April 1981 broke the case.

"She passed away in 1984 at the age of seventy-two," Brook said. "To this day I don't know what happened to that reward money."

"Did her family get the reward?"

"I would certainly hope so. I sent a letter to the board of supes in Marin County to the good lieutenant up there." The reward was eventually split among four people, including Steve Haertle.

The year before she died Roberta moved from Ben Lomond, which was only two miles from where the last victim, Heather Scaggs, was discovered, and moved to Boulder Creek, where Carpenter had committed a string of violent acts in 1970. In some indefinable way Roberta and David Carpenter did seem linked.

"And what about Shane Williams?" I asked Brook.

"Shane is probably on parole. Seems to me his sentence would be up by now. They really rolled him over light."*

"Is that because he gave evidence about the gun?"

"No. I think to save the hassle of having to go through

*Shane Mitchell Williams was released from Lompoc Federal Prison, December 17, 1987.

a big trial they just let him plead out. Karen they're just letting take a hike.''

"The women Carpenter attacked in the seventies," I said, "mentioned afterward he was kind and concerned."

"I'm sure just before he shot those kids he was kind and concerned," said Brook. "I can almost hear him say it in a very controlled tone of voice—'I'm really sorry I have to do this but I have no choice. I've got this quirk.'

"He's really a pathetic man in a lot of ways."

"As to my new life," Shane Williams told me, "I have to keep my fingers crossed. They don't let you out with much. I think I have a job lined up, but that could fall through. Right now I'm staying with a friend. I have to hope I don't get any parole violations for anything stupid. I'm really looking forward to staying out long enough to see Karen and my son. I think you could say that Karen and I are still in love with each other at a pretty deep level. We're just not living together.

"The only negative ramification about me telling you the whole story and it being published is that Karen has never told her boss about everything and is real concerned about remaining anonymous. She works for a large company. I haven't anything against being named and having the whole story told.

"Karen didn't even ask for any child support on her divorce. She knows when I'm successful I'll kick down for my son 'cause I love him and I call him regularly and talk to him, talk to her. But because we were separated for so long she had to make a life for herself."

"Do you think you and Karen might get back together?"

"Anything's possible in the long run. It's not in the foreseeable future."

13

The Cascade
of Light

Early on the morning of Sunday, May 24, 1987, while a pale, thin moon danced above the TransAmerica Pyramid to the east, the first half of a million people turned out to celebrate the fiftieth anniversary of the third longest span in the world, the Golden Gate Bridge, under which so long ago Roberta Patterson and the purser had passed on their voyage to Japan.

"A necklace of surpassing beauty has been placed around the lovely throat of San Francisco—it is a bridge that sings," said the anchorman on CBS-TV.

Whitecaps whipped up in the chill ocean below, a strong wind came out of the west as eight hundred thousand people walked out on the bridge in the clear and golden light. They could hear the wind whistle through the cables and feel the red-webbed bridge sway beneath their combined weight. The crowd looked down at the ships passing 220 feet below and peered upward at the tapering towers above them.

At 6:10 A.M., the wall of people from Marin met the six-laned wave of people from San Francisco in the center of the bridge, and the walk turned to gridlock. At the point where the slender cables touch before soaring upward again, hundreds of thousands were trapped by their own numbers and their weight flattened out the elegantly arched span, dropping it several feet. But out came the champagne and coffee and vodka and orange juice as 128 yellow biplanes flew over, accompanied by a dirigible. A great wall of clouds began building over the Pacific while beneath the span a parade of sailboats fought both thirty-knot winds and white-capped waves alongside fireboats spraying plumes of water.

Today was also an anniversary of a different short. It was exactly six years ago that the body of Heather Scaggs had been found in the wilderness near Santa Cruz. The sixth anniversary of Carpenter's arrest on Sussex Street for the Trailside attacks had only been nine days earlier.

Nearby, directly north from the bridge, through the Waldo Tunnel, past Marin City and Mill Valley was the prison where David Carpenter was serving out his two death convictions on Death Row and preparing for his San Diego trial.

Maximum-security San Quentin, only five miles from San Rafael and just the other side of a bright-colored grouping of cottages, is a machine-gun guarded and bristling yellow stucco fortress encircled by a twelve-foot-high wall and electrified barbed-wire fence. On Carpenter's return there, he had been taken past the main gate, through the metal detector outside the inner prison yard, and had laced his fingers together, locking them over his bald head while he was scanned from head to foot with a metal detector. Afterward the officers ran their fingers through the remaining fringe and his beard and then shook him down. While his arms were held high over his head he was strip searched. They peered behind his ears, had him lift his testicles to see if anything was concealed behind them or in his rectum.

After the strip search he was showered down, given a close haircut, and outfitted in his coarse denim prison costume of blue sweatshirt and washed-out, baggy bell-bottom blue jeans and canvas hightops. Carpenter had the relaxed air of a man who had spent almost a quarter century behind bars, more at home here than his captors. He was then photographed. Along with his prison number he was given the highest security rating—"Condemned H.V.P."—and, accompanied by armed guards, he had walked toward the maximum-security cell block, his wrists handcuffed to chains at his belly. On the way across the open concrete yard to the elevator of the north cell block it was a tradition for the guards to call out: "Deadman coming!"

As he entered the steel-reinforced concrete block on the ground floor Carpenter shivered, perhaps from the shower he had just taken. Just opposite the creaking elevator was an octagonal, bell-shaped, glass-enclosed, apple-green room—the death chamber, nicknamed The Smokehouse by the inmates. One-half of its diameter jutted into a witness room. Away from the witness area on the far side, out of sight of the spectators, is a holding cell. In this room the condemned man eats his last meal. Nearby is a telephone for the warden that connects the cell with a direct line to the governor's office, in case of a last-minute reprieve.

Behind the glass the chamber contains two unremarkable straight-backed chairs marked "A" and "B." The letters are large and equally unremarkable. Almost two hundred condemned men have been strapped to one of these metal seats and died of cyanide poisoning since the gas chamber was instituted in the late thirties. From 1851 until 1967 the death penalty has been carried out 502 times, 194 of these by lethal gas, the remainder by hanging.

Every one of the 189 men on Death Row knows how the chamber works. The condemned man enters and wide leather straps are wrapped around each of his legs, then one across each forearm, and finally one strap across the prisoner's chest, where a stethoscope is connected.

Two guards man levers. Pulling down on one lever spills a solution of sulfuric acid and distilled water into a metal basin underneath the chair, the other drops a cheesecloth sack filled with six sodium cyanide pellets the size of walnuts. The gas that hisses through the chamber is invisible and instantly deadly.

Carpenter was taken to his cell on Death Row. He was led down two rows of identical, four-and-one-half-by-ten-foot cells. The ever-burning fluorescent light in the cor-

ridor and the naked light bulb overhead in his cell were
as encaged by metal as he was. Even the windows were
covered by chicken wire, though far above and out of his
reach. The wire gave the windows a mysterious, veiled
look. A dim light filtered into the cell, and in one corner
where the wire had been pulled down he could see a
bright blue spot of sky. Impenetrable steel doors slid silently shut behind him.

The bars were painted the same apple-green as the gas
chamber. The nearby shower area, with its pink walls
and tiles, clashed sharply. Carpenter's cell had a narrow
bunk against the wall and a toilet that flushed by pressing
down a button.

The prisoners are allowed a two-hour exercise period
on the rooftop court or in front of their cells. Security is
intense. Even policemen visiting a prisoner are frisked
and asked to leave their weapons at the lockup while they
walk the long brown halls to the interview area. Usually
visitors talk with inmates from behind bulletproof plastic
walls through which twelve speaking holes have been cut
at mouth level.

On this celebration Sunday, while the party was being
held for the bridge, Carpenter lay on his bunk, looking
up toward the patch of sky in the corner of his high cell
window. Beneath this fragment of sky was Mount Tamalpais, where the trails were again peaceful and safe. He
watched as the day grew toward dusk, then darkness. He
could heard the snoring and coughing of the other condemned men.

The party for the Golden Gate Bridge was building
toward a climax. Beneath the bridge bobbed six firework
barges in the violet evening light. Mayor Dianne Fein-
stein threw a switch, and the bridge was slowly illuminated. Aerial bombs could be heard as 7,500 tons of
fireworks, 20,000 shells, began to wash across the sky.
The Golden Gate itself stood out in bold silhouette against
the sky filled with skyrockets, fiery explosions of color,
and powerful searchlights.

To me the lighting of the bridge seemed gradual, slowly
increasing in intensity, stage by stage, or perhaps it was
only an illusion brought on by the clearing smoke of the
rockets. As the new lights swept dramatically upward

toward the north and south towers there was a hush in the crowd of three hundred thousand spectators, an audible sigh of wonder.

Then across the clear span of 4,200 feet, amidst the smoke and searchlights, a golden cascade, like one of the sunset waterfalls hidden deep in the canyons of Tamalpais, began to plunge 220 feet to the water from the underside of the bridge.

In places it was as silver as a painting by Watteau and more golden than the blaze of J. M. W. Turner. As the winds from the east flared out the waterfall into jets and plumes it became a diaphanous curtain that dyed the waves amber. It stood out against the glitter and sparkle and pop of the fireworks like a ghost in the light fog, a gleaming waterfall of light.

Eventually, though, the blaze of showering gold died down, the crowd dispersed, and the bridge became deserted. In the distance, a safe shore amid the cloudy skies, lay the Sleeping Lady.

EPILOGUE

Though at the time Captain Vere was quite ignorant of Billy's liability to vocal impediment, he now immediately divined it . . . yet more violent efforts at utterance—efforts soon ending for the time in confirming the paralysis, and bringing to his face an expression which was as a crucifixion to behold. The next instant, quick as the flame from a discharged cannon at night, his right arm shot out and Claggart dropped to the deck . . . and he lay motionless . . . "Fated boy," breathed Captain Vere in tone so low as to be almost a whisper, "what have you done! . . ."

"Speak! Defend yourself." Which appeal caused but a strange dumb gesturing and gurgling in Billy, amazement at such an accusation so suddenly sprung on inexperienced nonage . . . serving to bring out his lurking defect and in this instance for the time intensifying it into a convulsed tongue-tie; while the intent head and entire form straining forward in an agony of ineffectual eagerness to obey the injunction to speak and defend himself, gave an expression to the face like that of . . . the first struggle against suffocation.

—Herman Melville
Billy Budd

At last there would be an end to the excruciating seven-year wait by the witnesses, families of the slain, and the lone surviving Trailside victim. David Carpenter's second trial began in San Diego on Tuesday morning, January 5, 1988.*

Under, around, and on the clerk's tables and gathered in front of the judge's escarpment were stacks of battered cardboard boxes piled with over five hundred items of evidence. Some of the exhibits were over forty inches high.

The fifth-floor courtroom was windowless.

There were no metal detectors, and as a rule the doors were not locked during testimony. People came and went throughout the day. Kathy Derby, the judge's clerk, Carpenter and his attorneys, Public Defender Frank Cox and co-counsel Steve Berlin, the prosecutor Deputy DA John Posey and his co-counsel Ann Harrington, a special DA,

---

*Jury selection had begun in September of 1987 and had taken three months to complete. This was roughly the same amount of time as that of the earlier trial.

the court reporter, and an army of journalists were all in place by the time Marshal Steve Sharpe summoned the jurors, who were milling about in the hall. As the army of eighteen men and women, twelve jurors and six alternates, trooped into the room I could hear sounds of coughing and foot shuffling. Only after the last of the alternates was seated on the added metal folding chairs before the jury box was there silence.

As Judge Herbert B. Hoffman, formally a prosecutor with the U.S. Attorney's office, took his seat, we all rose. Hoffman was known to run a tight court, but also brought a bemused and deep solemnity to the proceedings.

Carpenter, this time, stood accused of five of the murders in Marin County—Anne Alderson, Diane O'Connell, Shauna May, Cynthia Moreland, and Richard Stowers. The special circumstances, which would call for the death penalty if the defendant were found guilty, were the two charges of the rape of Alderson and May and a charge of the attempted rape of O'Connell.

Deputy DA John Posey promised eighty witnesses for the state, Steve Haertle preeminent among them, while deputy defender Frank Cox and co-counsel, attorney Stephen Berlin, had scheduled roughly half that number. However, the most intriguing possibility was that, for the first time, the accused man might take the stand.

"The strategy in the Santa Cruz case," Posey told me, "is Carpenter does his defense here in San Diego in the second trial. If he prevails in any way—a hung jury or a Not Guilty, then you have some issues, traditional issues that you can argue on appeal. In the penalty part of the trial the jury is not allowed to hear evidence of a violent criminal act that he was acquitted of. Assume Carpenter is acquitted here—that L.A. jury heard five murders so you have an issue as to whether or not, at a minimum, the penalty phase of that trial should be reversed because of that. Certainly if that case had been tried after this case and if he was acquitted there would be no issue— those crimes could not come before that jury."

Prosecution co-counsel Ann Harrington, who had begun the case in late March of 1987, told me, "The evidence against Carpenter was all circumstantial. We [Marin County] had no direct evidence, but like a rope being made of separate strands, all of those things couldn't have happened individually, they had to have happened together."

Judge Hoffman estimated the San Diego trial could take anywhere from three to six months, but because of the complex and perplexing nature of the material, and in order to give the attorneys time to do their homework each night and to enable the jurors an opportunity to retain some semblance of normal life, court would be in session only from 8:30 A.M. until 1:00 P.M., Tuesday through Friday.

Posey would ultimately call only sixty-three witnesses, among the most potent, a sixty-fourth witness, was an inanimate object—the black-barreled .38-caliber Rossi revolver that Mollie Purnell had purchased for Carpenter. While delivering his two-hour opening statement and while questioning Steve Haertle, Posey would hold this second "witness" often. John Posey, who was considered even more humorless than Stoney Brook, was prosecuting his first death-penalty case.

Promising to produce witnesses who could place the revolver in the former purser's hand during the period when a stalking rapist was terrorizing the mountain trails, Posey in his opening statement traced the history of the murder weapon. During this time Carpenter dressed in a white shirt and gray vest, never once looked up from his ceaseless notewriting on his yellow legal pad. Richard Stowers's parents, Joyce and Jerry, Anne Alderson's mother, Evelyn, and Ellen Hansen's mother, Marilyn, were present. As Posey described the deaths of Rick Stowers and Cindy Moreland Mrs. Stowers dabbed frequently at her reddened eyes.

"The five Marin victims were all executed," said Posey. "Each one of them was shot in the back of the head." Up came the cheap, brown-handled gun, every eye and TV camera was on it. Posey had a posture so determined and athletic he appeared much taller than he actually was. Speaking grimly, one hand clinched behind his well-tailored back, his free hand energetically darted forth like a fencer, striking out in the direction of Carpenter.

"Ladies and gentlemen of the jury, you are going to

hear from many, many witnesses in this case. You will be hearing testimony from ballistics and forensics experts as well as a cast of other witnesses, some of whom will not be angels. If murder occurs in hell—which is what this is, these are brutal, savage murders—you're not always going to have angels for witnesses.''

Marin County chief public defender Frank Cox, a rangy, six-foot-one outdoorsman with a mop of graying cotton-candy hair, was familiar with both the trails and legends of the Sleeping Lady. He personally found the Carpenter trial to be the most complex and exhausting case he had ever confronted. When Cox began his opening argument he was as grave and earnest as Posey. Everyone in this case was trying his upmost, operating at their maximum level of competence, and I knew that Carpenter's attorneys would fight all the way to the Supreme Court to see right done by their client, so completely did they believe in the system. ''People ask us, 'Why bother?' '' said Cox. ''Well, I don't believe people should be killed by the state and I hope the jury agrees.

''David didn't do it and we plan to prove it,'' he told the jury. ''In the Santa Cruz case, there was no effort to prove he didn't do it. They called virtually no witnesses for the defense. . . . This time David's enthusiastic about the case. He's looking forward to it.''

Defense co-counsel Steve Berlin rose, adjusted his silver-rimmed spectacles, and conceded with a lowering of his eyes that the random Trailside attacks of a stalking rapist-murderer were the work of one man using the same weapon, but contended that man was not his client.

''Mr. Carpenter is not the Trailside Killer,'' said Berlin. ''We will provide evidence that he was doing something else, somewhere else, while the killer was in the parks committing murder.

''He [Posey] has to prove that he [Carpenter] was at each of the crime scenes and nowhere else. There will be evidence that that was not the case. What Mr. Carpenter was doing during those times may not show him in the best of light. But Mr. Carpenter is not on trial for being a bad person or a less-than-model citizen. He is on trial for murder.'' The prosecution's burden was to prove

Carpenter's guilt "beyond a reasonable doubt and a moral certainty."

Berlin told the jury early descriptions of the killer did not include mention of a stutter, there was variance on the age of the killer, and that all of the evidence against Carpenter was circumstantial.

"In all the important links to Carpenter, you have to take someone's word for it. In the case of [Mollie] Purnell, she bought the gun but that does not mean she gave it to Carpenter."

Throughout, Posey would be delicately balanced on a tight-rope. The slightest misstep might result in a future appeal or reversal. Judge Hoffman had ruled that the jury could not be told the outcome of Carpenter's previous Los Angeles trial for the Santa Cruz murders, his double conviction for murder with a host of special circumstances, that he was on Death Row, of *any* of the defendant's prior convictions, or that he was a prime suspect in four other killings in San Francisco, Marin, and Santa Cruz counties. I later asked John Posey to explain why he couldn't present this information to the San Diego jury.

"Because," said Posey, "the judge said I couldn't. You see, Robert, under Section 352 of the evidence code the judge has the power to exclude evidence if it is prejudicial. He felt the murders had no common mark, that they were not 'similars.' Hoffman cited the fact that $400 was stolen from Heather Scaggs whereas robbery was not an aspect of the Hansen-Haertle attacks. But, I argued, with Heather Scaggs it was the same gun. That was a crucial feature."

On the other hand, Hoffman had ruled that evidence from the Los Angeles tribunal could be presented to the jury by the state.

Since four potential witnesses had already died, among them two gun dealers and one of the 1970 robbery victims, it was decided to have the most crucial witness testify immediately. As the only survivor of the Trailside Killer's murderous attacks, the only living witness, Steve Haertle's testimony was key. In an attenuated, scratchy voice, a result of the lingering effects of a bullet to his throat, the twenty-seven-year-old Pacific Gas and Electric economist and analyst re-created the events of that long-ago March day. Polite, methodical, and more controlled than when giving his emotional testimony in the first trial, Haertle faltered only once, when he identified a photograph of Ellen. Otherwise he patiently, step by step, drew a picture of Carpenter as the attacker.

The defense cross-examined Haertle with the deference due a hero. Cox and Berlin's contention was that Steve's identification was influenced by the composite compiled by Lee Fritz and the other Cowell State Park witnesses. They reminded the jury that Haertle had made only two minor corrections on the composite sketch. Steve did show some confusion about the charcoal sketch which did not have his corrections. Haertle admitted the attacker didn't stutter and did not wear bifocals.

Berlin maintained that Haertle had recognized Carpenter from all the publicity and photographs. "You've seen him at trials and prelims, correct?"

"Yes," said Haertel.

"Thank you very much, Mr. Haertle," said Berlin, turning away.

"I also recognize him from the day he shot me," said Haertle after him.

In early January Carpenter had written a seven-page letter to the *Marin Independent Journal* repeating his litany—"I have an alibi that will clear me of at least one of the murders. If I didn't commit one murder I didn't commit any murders." The letter read:

> *What makes this case of mine so unique is the fact that All of the victims were murdered with the same gun, and, that the prosecution is saying that ONE PERSON committed ALL of the murders.*
>
> *It is the prosecution's job to convince the jury, BE-YOND A REASONABLE DOUBT, that I was the person who was at each of the crime scenes, committing the crimes, on EVERY occasion.*
> *The defense, however, ONLY needs to substantiate ONE alibi, but, could substantiate more, which would, naturally, improve my chances for an acquittal (or) being found not guilty of all of them.*

An alibi does NOT have to be substantiated to be an alibi. So, in an alibi case, the more a person can substantiate an alibi, the more believable the alibi is and the more likely the defendant is to be acquitted and found not guilty. I'll give you this. I KNOW where I was on each occasion when the murders occurred— and I'll leave it there. The prosecution is almost totally in the dark as to what alibis I have or could have.

The upcoming witnesses of particular interest to me are prosecution witnesses No. 14: Jeff Jackl; and No. 15: Reba Lehman. Jackl is/was my friend, and I'm not sure exactly how the prosecution will use him. Reba is a MAJOR prosecution witness who says she saw me with the murder weapon, loaned me her car on March 30, 1981, and other things. You don't want to miss her.

The change of venue was effective. Few in San Diego, as they were caught up in the excitement of the approaching Super Bowl, were aware of the trial, and on some days I was the only spectator in the courtroom. Cox mentioned to me that Carpenter's father had died and that his mother was now "mentally debilitated, senile" and living in a Texas nursing home near her daughter.

From only a few feet away during the days that followed I studied the twice-condemned man. Carpenter's demeanor seemed to vacillate between owlish and simian. His features had by now grown familiar—the hooded eyes, the downward almost sour turn of the mouth, and silklike crown of hair, which fell backward over the collar of the pastel-colored shirts he favored and threaded its way into the thick, almost muttonchop, sideburns— and, yes, the hair was definitely darker now than it was only days before.

I watched Carpenter's hands as, one after another, he sailed yellow notes across the polished surface of the table to his attorneys. He did this with fingers extended and a twist of his wrist. He had worn away the pink eraser of the yellow school pencil, so industriously did he labor. The hands were not the large hands Roberta Patterson's imagination had created over the years, but they were of the most extraordinary paleness. The defendant rarely ceased movement, constantly adjusting his eyeglasses, licking his lips, or drawing his finger across the bottom of his nose.

Carpenter kept a Kleenex tissue on his left knee, and when he had worked too hard in his all-consuming note writing and his eyes would brim over with water he would remove his glasses, tightly pinch the bridge of his nose, and lean forward, bringing his face to the cloth on his knee to rub his glasses and eyes. His attorneys would hunch or actually sink to their knees alongside the bent man and confer practically under the table, reminding me of a band of storks attempting to suck water from an underground stream. Carpenter, after living in seclusion in a special section of the San Diego jail since January of 1987, was once again the center of attention. Each morning he brought his lawyers a cartoon from the paper. I recalled that he used to send Mollie cartoons.

During a recess in the early days of the trial I had remained while everyone else left the courtroom except for the bailiff and the judge's clerk. Carpenter had suddenly taken on a rigid, cold look, and over the normally friendly face came an intentness that was frightening. I followed his gaze. He was looking at a woman who had also sensed his burning gaze, returned it for an instant, and was forced to look abruptly away. When his lawyers returned, Carpenter was again his pleasant self.

I often saw Judge Hoffman, thoughtfully sizing up Carpenter, his eyes roving from the top of the defendant's balding hair to the tip of his toes. Although he was in possession of more facts than the jury was allowed to know, he seemed to be trying to fathom and gauge a virtually unknowable man. As a judge he was alone on that high bench, with no aides (Berlin and Cox were assisted by investigator Jim McFeely and researcher Jay Ruskin; Posey by Don Rose) to help him make immediate and crucial decisions.

Cox was interesting to watch. He always wished prosecution witnesses "a pleasant good morning," and was polite until he began to move in for the kill. Berlin, to me, was a western gunfighter with the drooping mustache of a Texas sheriff, the wheel and stoop of a Groucho

Marx. The pair made a good contrast to the grim determination and unyielding demeanor of the prosecutor, Posey, who sat dwarfed by the mountain of bound transcripts, each relevant paragraph and page carefully marked.

As week three of the trial began, on the morning of Tuesday, January 19, 1988, jurors heard the concluding testimony about the geographical makeup of Ridge Trail where Ellen Hansen was shot, saw photos of the vehicle lineup in which the red Fiat was identified, and some autopsy photos were presented. Carpenter, at the defense table, yawned when clinical pictures of Ellen Hansen were shown.

After Tammy Brinkley had testified about selling two pairs of running shoes to Candy Townsend and David Carpenter, bearded, dark, and frosty Jeff Jackl described his friendship with the defendant and recalled the day Carpenter showed up to help him move and how he had first seen the red Fiat in a little garage in Glen Park.

Reba Lehman, the thirteenth witness in the trial, was an unlucky number for Carpenter. Highly nervous, long brown hair framing a pale anxious face, she took the stand and told about seeing the Rossi revolver. As she was questioned she looked constantly skyward as if looking for the answer to each query, one tiny plump hand brushing her hair away from her face. Posey got the murder gun, walked back to Reba and placed it in front of her. "Looks like the gun he showed me," she said.

Defense investigator Jim McFeely had approached Reba in the fall of 1986 and they met briefly at the Cantina Restaurant. A year later she spoke with John Posey and had now changed two portions of her story. Her roommate *had* seen the gun after all. "I'm not sure when," she said. "It may have been in the living room or someplace else, but I know he saw the gun." During the 1987 jury selection Reba recalled for the first time seeing the gold jacket on the defendant. Her uncle had died and her mother sent her a package of her uncle's clothes. As she opened it a similar yellow-gold windbreaker dropped out and the memories came flooding back. I saw many familiar faces, among them Santa Cruz coroner Dr. Richard Thomas Mason, who was allowed by Judge Hoffman to give his bullet-sequence re-creation, which would point to an execution-style slaying; Stoney Brook, who showed his March 1984 video of Ridge Trail, and of course Robinson and Womack. All were articulate witnesses.

During the fourth week there was sparring over Candy Townsend's forthcoming appearance. Cox and Berlin expressed to Hoffman their intention to probe a conceivable conjunction between Candy's previous attestations against Carpenter and the dismissal of a December 1981 petty theft complaint against her in Billings, Montana, for allegedly stealing a purse from a car-wash patron. Cox was also concerned that Santa Cruz County had paid her food and rent bills for four months in 1981.

On January 21 FBI agent David Hines detailed the week-long surveillance of the defendant, and Joe Henard began a long grilling by the defense concerning the search procedure of 38 Sussex. Henard was already exhausted, having come directly from Boston where he had narrowly missed apprehending a fugitive murder suspect. The next morning, Friday, Henard was still testifying. He flushed with anger at defense implications the .38-caliber bullet had been planted in the bag of key chains.

Throughout the trial Posey seemed to have particularly little patience with Steve Berlin, who reveled in slowly and painstakingly exploring each fact, looking for a chink, making every witness define each term. As Henard finished I heard a hiss of exasperation from Posey. The flow of the trial slowed even more, broken by the long weekend.

On Tuesday, February 2, Judge Hoffman complained to the attorneys about the speed of the trial. Hoffman said, "At this rate we won't be done by summer. We're talking about a case of maybe up to one hundred witnesses and we're doing two a day." Since many of the principal witnesses had yet to testify, the judge told Posey, Cox, and Berlin that he was thinking about having the jury come in on Mondays.

"As you know," Lieutenant Don Besse told me later, "Cox played the tape of my talk with Shane Williams in

San Diego [on February 4 and 5] to the jury. He maintained that I was coaching Shane on what to say, and he based that premise on Shane's halting answers. I thought that was bullshit until I listened to the tape and I thought, He really is doing that. I realized Shane sounded like he did because I was telling him to think about each answer. Don't ramble I told him. I had to explain this to the jury.''

During the sixth week of the trial Shane testified for two days and seemed to love it. In his cross-examination of the ex-bank robber, Cox inferred Williams himself could have gotten use of the murder weapon through an ''unidentified third party'' or through Mollie Purnell. Cox believed that Williams had a motive to lie on the stand in order to help his wife, Karen, and implicate Carpenter in the process.

Co-counsel Steve Berlin was concerned that the testimony of the state's witnesses had taken on a consonance and that their certainty of identification came more from what they were told and had read in the newspapers over the years.

As an essential part of the foundation of the case against Carpenter, Mollie Purnell, the woman who had bought the murder weapon, was called to the stand at the end of the seventh week of trial. Cox and Berlin knew they had to raise doubts about Mollie's veracity.

''Mollie,'' Posey told me, ''was under a tremendous strain. . . . I think day after day the beating that she took on the stand made the jury start to sympathize with her. I forget how many days she was on the stand, four I recall, over and over and over again. . . . The defense was allowed to ask her about a bankruptcy petition she filed in 1979. She had a .22-caliber handgun she said she gave Carpenter—that was not listed in the bankruptcy petition and they wanted to argue that Molly had perjured herself.

''Mollie's father was supposedly well-to-do only they couldn't get the money out of Jamaica. The defense version was she wanted to get down there and get marijuana. They painted Mollie out to be this terrible individual. It's kinda hard to see her like that. I got a picture in my mind having read all of these reports of some really wild people—it was far different when we saw them than the picture created in your mind.''

After eight hours of grueling questioning Mollie Purnell finally lost her temper and snapped at Berlin, ''I don't understand where you're going with this. I purchased the gun for the defendant, and that's it!''

''Didn't you lie to the authorities,'' Berlin asked at one point, ''about Carpenter never having picked up a gun at your house?'' Mollie had spoken with the police on May 16 and June 3, 1981.

''I certainly did. I've told you a million times I signed the statement, but I have also told you, sir, that was a lie! I lied my dear friend. I lied. They told me they were going to tear it up, and here it is, I revised my statement, and I told the truth at the time.''

Stress caused Mollie to become seriously ill over the weekend of February 20 and 21, and the completion of her testimony was delayed. On Tuesday, February 23, Candy Townsend, now married and living in Arizona, was called to the stand and during direct examination she recalled the blue backpack seen by Steve Haertle. However, her memory of the gleaming yellow jacket with its distinctive lettering had dimmed. Candy, looking extremely thin, tanned by the desert sun, and wearing her hair shorter, browner, and curlier, commented that she never wore the jacket, never saw it on Carpenter, and the few times she did see it was in the backseat of his Chevy. Only after having her 1981 testimony from Carpenter's preliminary hearing read did she recall Carpenter having mentioned the death of a woman on the Sleeping Lady as they drove by. ''We talked about that, but I had forgotten about it.''

On Tuesday, March 1, 1988, the beginning of the ninth week of the trial, the rain began in sheets and was a torrent by 8:30 A.M. Like the dark clouds outside, a question hung over the court—would David Carpenter eventually take the stand to testify? Though the light outside was feeble, coloring the corridor pale blue, enough of it filtered through the wide windows to illuminate the cluster of jurors huddled on the benches, reading, knitting, passing trail mix around, and watching the downpour beat against the prisoner-access door five stories below. A rush of wind rattled the windows.

Inside the courtroom I looked at the great, dull bronze seal of California that hung over Hoffman's head. It portrayed a woman in its foreground, San Francisco Bay filled with ships behind her, and a mountain range in the distance. To me this woman, over the days, came to represent those who had died on the trails, and the mountain range became Tamalpais.

Criminalist and forensic chemist Dr. Mike Waller completed his three days of complicated testimony on ballistics and genetic-marker testing. In his intense cross-examination of Dr. Waller, Berlin was at his most knowledgeable and probing. As he paced the courtroom he continued to chip away at Waller's lab results, which showed Carpenter *could* have been Anne Alderson's rapist.

The defense attorney was in an interesting position—he had to discredit the results shown in the genetic-marker tests because of the special circumstances provision calling for the death penalty for murders committed during rape, and at the same time he had to validate the ballistic results done by the same technician, which showed the Trailside crimes were committed by one man using the same gun. Berlin was so effective in establishing for the jury the problems with the ABO-PGM process that a young lawyer next to me commented on it. I was amazed when Cox told me his colleague was not a longtime expert in the microscopic molecular and enzyme-tracing tests but had boned up on it specifically for the trial.

In fact Berlin was so energetic in his questioning of Waller's qualifications that a puzzled Hoffman asked during a morning recess, "You told the jury in your opening statement, Mr. Berlin, that you adhered to the prosecution's position that the same gun was used in each killing, so if you could prove Mr. Carpenter wasn't the shooter in one case it exonerated him in all killings."

"I am further establishing the witness's expert qualifications since, as I told the jurors in my opening statement," said Berlin, "Mr. Waller, in effect, will be our expert."

Joyce and Jerry Stowers, Rick Stowers's parents, often

made the grueling five-hour trip from Tehachapi, east of
Bakersfield, to attend the trial, staying at the Holiday Inn
and supplying their own out-of-pocket expenses, although Joyce told me, "Marin County helped out on occasion."

Mrs. Stowers recalled, "Altogether, I attended five
weeks, Jerry seven to eight weeks. We had never seen
Carpenter in the flesh before and it was very difficult for
me the time he came over to see a display [of the Stowers-
Moreland murder scene] for the jury, leaning up against
the little divider two feet away. It was traumatic. It was
just something that was beyond anything our world had
prepared us for. It brought us closer together, to see ourselves through all this, to lean on each other."

During recess they crossed the room and introduced
themselves to Mr. Moreland, Cindy's father, who was
sitting two seats over from me. Joyce had talked to him
on the phone during their search for Rick and Cindy, but
they had never met before the trial. "It's hard for us,"
Joyce told Mr. Moreland, "reliving this. It opens up the
same old wounds, every wound possible, and starts the
blood flowing again." Ron Moreland, a former high
school teacher, adjusted his hearing aid and nodded.
"Please," implored Mrs. Stowers, touching his arm,
"join us if you want." They returned to their seats next
to Mary Scaggs and Marilyn Hansen, Heather's and Ellen's mothers. Mr. Moreland remained where he was until the morning recess when he joined the Stowers.

As the state's case raced toward completion the pace
of witnesses was brisker. Richard Wood, now a consultant, briefly testified from his log of meetings with his
client, Carpenter, and then Alice Zane, Cindy Moreland's sister, took the stand. Within minutes she had broken into tears. I was very much aware of the Moreland
and Stowers families, now sitting together near the jury
box. It was heartrending to see them reliving the last
moment's of their children's lives. Mrs. Stowers fled the
courtroom, her eyes red and swollen, but forced herself
to return with a brave smile. Ron Moreland sat resolutely, left when it became too difficult, and then he too
returned.

Before Tina Vance's testimony on March 5, Cox expressed to Hoffman his concern that somebody may have made a promise to her in regard to probations and juvenile matters and wondered if there was any benefit for testimony. "When Tina spoke with Brook," asked Cox, "did she expect something?"

Tina Vance took the stand and told Posey, "Carpenter showed me a suitcase of some sort—which I've always called a thief kit—with a gun, some wire, and strips of nylon or cloth in it."

Tina's mention of the wire struck home with the jury. In Posey's mind this was why Vance's testimony was so important. Later, coroner Jindrich told the jury, speaking of Diane O'Connell, "The ligature marks on the victim's neck were consistent with markings that would be left by a cord or wire like you would use to hang pictures."

Posey walked over and handed the .38 to the slight, dark-haired girl. She turned it over and over, placed it down on the witness stand, and pushed it away. "That looks like it." Tina now recalled for the first time on the stand seeing a "big gun" in addition to the smaller-caliber Rossi revolver that she claimed Carpenter had shown her in his station wagon. Tina said she had been sitting on her boyfriend Kenny's lap in Mollie's bedroom when Carpenter showed them a gun in a Crown Royale whiskey bag. The primary reason Carpenter was not being tried for the murders in which anything other than a .38 had been used, most specifically the shooting of Edda Kane, was that no one had been able to place a .44-caliber gun in the defendant's hand.

"Judge," said Posey, "I didn't even know about this until March 2."

Throughout her cross-examination by Cox, Tina was constantly fiddling with the mike, drinking one glass of water after another, and twisting in her seat to look at the jury. She was so flippant in her manner that Hoffman cautioned her sternly during a recess. "Think carefully before you speak. You've testified three times, do it right or you'll be back again."

"Who else saw the gun?" Cox asked her when the jury returned.

"Kenny was the only one who saw the gun. I saw a gun in the house *and* in the car."

"How did it differ?"

"All I can tell you is that it was a bigger gun."

Cox attempted to find the park Tina claimed she and Carpenter had gone to but soon was reduced to exasperation in a pile of maps as the twenty-one-year-old drew a blank. Her answers were given with childish shrugs, sarcasm, and staccato answers. It sounded like Henry Cowell State Park but that was too far away.

On Wednesday Posey called his sixty-third witness, Dr. Richard Waller, who would complete his ballistics testimony on the similar groove patterns on the recovered fatal bullets in comparison with bullets test-fired from the submitted Rossi revolver. Blowups of the striations on the O'Connell bullet and the May bullets were shown to the jurors.

"Were the bullets fired from the same gun?" asked Posey.

"There's no doubt in my mind," said Waller.

With that the prosecution rested its case and the defense feverishly continued to work in order to be able to open its projected seven-week case on Tuesday, March 15. Cox predicted that the defense would be able to raise affirmative evidence that Carpenter was innocent of one of the Trailside murders.

The first defense witness was Oakland private consultant Charles Morton, who was called to contradict police forensic analysis of the four casts made of prints found by Ellen Hansen's body on Ridge Trail. "My impression," he said, "is that they could not match because of the difference in the number of ridges."

"The very first witness the defense put on was a shoe print expert," Posey told me afterward. "The shoes have ridges. It was testified they had the same class characteristics, which they do. There are ridged chevrons at the heel and at the toe and then you have the narrow ones. The thrust of it was Carpenter wore a nine and one-half, so Henard purchased a nine and one-half for the trial. The number of ridges between the heel and toe chevrons is twenty-*nine* on these shoes, but on the footprints found near Ellen's body the count is twenty-*eight*. I think they thought they had us, but there's a catch—it varies from shoe to shoe, not only from size to size, but you can have different numbers of ridges between left and right shoes. On rebuttal we brought in this guy from the FBI and the guy from Oregon who developed the prototype for all the Nike Tennis shoes. Well, it's common practice in the industry to go up or down a size on those bottom soles. Sometimes they'll cut down an existing mold for a smaller shoe size. The only way you can make a match is to have the actual shoe.''

After Cox and Berlin told Hoffman they had witnesses who could provide Carpenter with an alibi it was up to the judge to decide whether their testimony was relevant or even admissible. Ultimately his decision was to allow the first to testify and then rule to limit, accept, or exclude further testimony in this region.

''It's important because we believe there was a person on the mountain,'' Cox told the judge, ''who was a dead ringer for Mr. Carpenter.'' Berlin told Hoffman, ''The man we wish to present testimony about is connected to the killings by wearing a distinctive jacket similar to the one described in the attack.'' Olive Robertson, Rene Josselyn, and Catherine Moller testified they had seen a Carpenter look-alike on the trails.

The Wilkinson family, third-party defense witnesses, had not been, Posey felt, adequately questioned during the preliminary hearing. From the transcripts Posey was not sure what they had seen. They had been the witnesses who had seen a man in a gold jacket in Felton north of Henry Cowell State Park the day before Ellen Hansen's murder. Nobody seemed to have asked them the most important question—''Do you see that person in this courtroom?'' When Posey asked the answer was, ''Of course. He's that man over there—the defendant.''

After a phone call to me by Florence Neuman, Carpenter's family friend of over forty years and his boss at the key-chain warehouse, I was unable to reach her again. I had for some time suspected she would be the alibi witness for the defendant. Sure enough, on Wednesday, March 23, Florence Neuman appeared in court with a piece of paper that she felt proved Carpenter was with her at the approximate time Anne Alderson was killed on

Mount Tamalpais. In January of 1988 she had visited
Carpenter's sister's home in Texas and also seen the purser's mother in a nearby nursing home. "All of a sudden," she remembered, "something triggered in my
brain, that maybe I could find some evidence to bring to
court and the jury to help the case." Mrs. Neuman flew
back to San Francisco and began to sort through the boxes
of records she had brought home after she sold Gems of
the Golden West. In a box of documents from 1980 she
discovered a letter dated October 13, 1980, which Carpenter had, she felt, written. "I'm certain it was at least
4:30 P.M., the last time I saw him that day because I
never leave work any earlier. He was there the whole
time I was. He could have been there until 5:30 or 6:30,
but I can't remember exactly and we didn't have a time
clock.

"He would type the date of the response on the top of
the reply, and this one is dated 'OCTOBER 13, 1980.' "
Carpenter, she further explained, had the habit of addressing letters to customers completely in capital letters. On this date Anne Alderson had been seen alive as
late as 5:30 P.M. by John Henry, and Gems was less than
an hour's drive away from the Mountain Theatre on
Mount Tamalpais. But the letter did strengthen the defense's case.

Marilyn Hansen told me, "Carpenter needed short-
term gratification. He lived hour-by-hour and never
looked too far ahead. I noticed in court how his mood
would change when he received some momentary success, how his whole attitude would brighten."

A condition of Carpenter taking the stand was that he be
allowed to consult his calendar-diary while testifying.
The catch was that Cox and Berlin did not want Posey to
see the diary or ask questions about what it might contain. "Because of the way the law is constructed," Besse
told me later, "the defense doesn't have to give the prosecution anything. The defense can have all the secrets
they want. I think Carpenter is so vain that he probably
wrote a lot of things down in his diary that were real
detrimental to him and his defense. Even though the judge
is supposed to be impartial they didn't want the judge to

see it. You can imagine what was in it knowing what kind of guy Carpenter is.''

Posey thought the defense was trying to put up a shield against any cross-examination. ''The privilege against self-incrimination does not extend that far.'' Cox argued that the diary entries were of an intimate nature and other privileged information and would help Carpenter recall the sequence of events. Ultimately, Hoffman ruled that the diary would remain unseen by everyone except the defendant and added, ''Questions that could arise from any calendar entries related to several slayings similar to 1979 and 1980 Bay Area slayings that remain unsolved should not be allowed—all other areas are fair game for the prosecution.''

During the fourteenth week of the trial, under the examination of Steve Berlin, a well-prepared and relaxed David Carpenter took the witness chair for the first time in his life at precisely 9:30 A.M. on the morning of April 5, 1988. He was wearing a wheat and cream-colored crewneck, long-sleeve sweater, an open-collared pink-peach shirt, and khaki trousers. With his gray sideburns Carpenter tended to blend into the wood-corkboard background. He was still very much an invisible man, I thought.

Hunched over the lectern, Berlin began in an easygoing manner, one which seemed designed to elicit narrative responses from the defendant intended to lead the jury through a two-year scenario of the time Carpenter was on the street after his release. During this recitation Carpenter, in his time, would play many parts and present himself as a devoted, dutiful son, confidence man, loving father, a drug dealer, opera and ballet aficionado, demon salesman, hero in his battle to overcome his crippling speech impediment, and a frustrated dreamer with million-dollar schemes. This would be Carpenter's version of the Trailside story.

During his three hours on the stand, Carpenter would sit with his fists clenched or folded in front of him, constantly adjusting his black horn-rimmed glasses as he read from his personal calendar-diary, phone records, sales receipts, and time cards. Berlin began with May of 1979.

"My name," the defendant began, "is D-D-David J. C-C-C-Carpenter."

"Where did you live in 1979.

"S . . . S . . . S . . . San Francisco."

"Have you ever been convicted of a crime?"

"Yes, sir. I've been convicted of two felonies involving s-s-sex."

"Did you have any associates at Lompoc Federal Prison?"

"Ye-Ye-Ye-Yes."

"I'd like to ask about names people have in prison."

"In prison most people use nicknames. I used," Carpenter paused, "Dave. [Carpenter had actually gone by the nickname he had given himself—Devious Dave.] It's a lot easier."

"Did you have a number of associates in prison?" asked Berlin.

"Shane . . . the 'Greek' . . . We used to get out for a walk," said Carpenter laughing, "for exercise. . . . "

"What was the nature of your relationship with Shane?"

"A friend," responded Carpenter. "Probably my best friend was the 'Greek.' He met Shane first . . . it all seemed to come together."

"While in Lompoc did you become acquainted with a Mollie Purnell?"

"I sure did!" Carpenter laughed. "She headed the Mondo Blair Friendship Club."

"Did you have a correspondence with Mollie Purnell?"

"Sure. I used to call her two or three times a week . . . she was living in Santa Rosa." Carpenter was doing what lawyers call steepling now, placing the tips of his fingers together in front of him in a prayerlike pose. This is considered a sign of someone who feels he is in complete control. My eyes traced the pale blue veins in the back of his white hands.

"What kind of calls were these?"

"In an institution you can only make collect calls. . . . My sister would send her a check for all of my collect telephone calls."

"Did Mollie ever confide to you that she had been paid for those calls?"

"No."

"Was there any contact between Shane Williams and Mollie Purnell?"

"Yes. I think three contacts."

"What is the earliest contact you recall?"

Posey, standing, asked the judge, "I'm going to object until he lays proper foundation."

"Rephrase your question," said Hoffman.

"When did the first contact occur."

"To the best of my memory, February of 1980."

"At whose request was this?"

"At Shane's request . . ."

"Did you make any arrangements about transporting the stuff you had in prison?" asked Berlin.

"I sent all my stock stuff to Mollie [in boxes], books on the stock market."

"Did these boxes contain anything other than stock certificates."

"I don't think so."

"Did you have cause to have anything sent to Mollie Purnell?"

"No, I did not." Carpenter turned toward the jury as he firmly said this.

"Did you ever make any kind of arrangement of having a large gun sent to Mollie Purnell?" One theory was that the .44-caliber weapon used to kill Edda Kane had been hidden in one of the stock books and perhaps been purchased behind bars with stock and drug money.

"No, I did not."

"What were the nature of the restrictions while you were at the halfway house?"

"You had to be there the entire time unless you received permission . . . you had to check in by 11:00 P.M.."

After questioning Carpenter about his family in San Francisco, Berlin asked, "What is your parents' anniversary date?"

"August 6."

"Did you ever obtain a weekend pass to attend an anniversary party?"

"Not that I recall . . . August 6, 1979, was, I think, a Monday. . . . " Carpenter consulted his calendar-diary. "It was my parents' fiftieth wedding anniversary. Because it was my parents' fiftieth anniversary a picture was taken of my three children, Michael, Gabrielle, and Circe, and myself there." Carpenter's pale hands trembled as he held up a three-by-five photo given him by Steve Berlin.

"Did you continue to have a relationship with Mollie?"

"I used to talk to her by telephone because I was usually at my parents' house. She would call from Santa Rosa. There was a pay phone in the halfway house but I don't recall ever using it. I met Mollie three or four times at the place where she worked."

"You've heard Mollie Purnell's testimony about picking up a large gun at her house?"

"That is not true!"

Posey stood abruptly: "Leading the witness, judge."

"Sustained."

"At no time," said Carpenter, "did I go up to her apartment in Santa Rosa. No. I did not."

"Do you by any chance recognize the handwriting on this check . . . exhibit 4 AAAA?"

"It's Mollie's."

"How can you tell?"

"Mollie and I corresponded extensively, some five hundred to a thousand letters."

Berlin, after establishing that the date on the first check was August 2, 1979, asked, "Did you go to Santa Rosa and pick up anything on that date?"

"No."

"Do you know where you were on August 2, 1979?"

"That is one date I have an independent recollection of. I was at the California Trade School in Hayward. I had had trouble with my eye on July 30, was out on July 30, came back on July 31, but couldn't work. . . . I had an eyepatch on when I came back to work on August 1." Carpenter explained he was at school on August 2. "I was there the full six hours. School is 9:00 A.M. through 12:00 noon, half hour for lunch, then work until 3:30. . . . I was required to work six hours every day. If you didn't put in six hours it could be made up at a later date.''

Berlin then showed three more checks drawn on Mollie's account dated August 10, 15, and 17 of 1979. Carpenter stated he was in school the full six hours on those days. Berlin asked Carpenter where he was on the date of a fifth check, August 20, 1979.

"I was taking speech therapy with D. Wayne Smith." Carpenter had had speech evaluation during May through August and had been given a speech evaluation the latter part of August.

Berlin held up Smith's evaluation of Carpenter's history of speech impediments, which was dated August 20, 1979. He then asked about Carpenter's parole from the halfway house.

"On August 6, a Wednesday morning, I was given live-out status. Until September 6 I was officially on parole."

"Why did you opt to live with your parents?"

"I was going to live with my brother, but my father was in his eighties, mother in her seventies. I talked with my sister in Texas and everybody agreed I should live there to look after them. . . . My mother was not [then] legally blind, she could see a little bit."

"Did you have a car at this time?"

"No. My father had given me an old station wagon. My sister was going to give it back to me."

"Did you travel to pick up the Chevrolet?"

"I flew to Big Springs, Texas, on 22 of September 1979. She gave me the car at that time and I drove back to San Francisco in it."

"Did you register that car?"

"Yes, I did. I had to get a smog certificate, which I did, and then had it transferred into my name. [Two weeks later Carpenter applied for personalized plates.] I requested D J CARP."

"I'd like to change the subject, David, and ask you about your speech impediment. How long have you had a problem?"

"I don't ever remember *not* s-s-s-stuttering."

"In 1979 what were your main problems in speech as you saw them?"

"I have partial problems with the letter *m* as in *mother* and *money*. I have particular trouble with *s* especially if I try to say *s.*" There was an explosion of stuttering and spitting as Carpenter tried to say the letter.

"Did Mr. Smith keep a record of appointments?" Carpenter answered yes, and Berlin said, "The Smith schedule is marked six X's and is introduced to refresh Mr. Carpenter's recollection." Berlin requested permission to approach the defendant and handed him the document.

Carpenter noted he had started therapy in October of 1979, and Berlin asked him a key question: "Did you discuss ways to control your stuttering problem?"

"Yes."

"What ways did you use?"

"I have a number . . . ," said Carpenter, adjusting his dark-rimmed glasses.

"What was the one you used most commonly?"

"When I got so I could not talk at all I w-w-w-would whisper because you don't s-s-s-stutter when you whisper." Without being asked the defendant gave a demonstration for the court. Up until this moment he had been stuttering badly, but as Carpenter began to whisper a gleam came into his eye that had not been there before.

"If I *whisper,*" he whispered, "I don't stutter.

"If I *sing,*" he sang, "I don't stutter.

"If I get *mad,*" and here his voice abruptly became loud and angry as he reached over and covered the witness microphone with his left hand, "AND TALK IN A LOUD VOICE LIKE THIS I-WILL-NOT-STUTTER!"

A look of what could only be triumph crossed the defendant's face. When he had changed his pitch no trace of a stutter remained. Those whispered, sung, and shouted phrases had been an unbroken series of distinct words. But even while those last words, "If I get mad . . . ," hung suspended in the windowless room, and as the jury pulled back as one, Haertle's description of the attacker on Ridge Trail must have flashed through their collective mind—"His speech was tense and angry—short orders and commands."

"B-b-but if I talk in my normal voice, I d-d-d-do," Carpenter said, kneading his hands and shaking his head from side to side. "I-I-I-I come to pieces on the telephone."

"Does rhythm have anything to do with controlling stuttering?"

"I read about using a metronome. It has a beat. I began experimenting . . . sometimes using my thumb to keep rhythm." Carpenter began moving his finger back and forth in front of the jury. "When I spoke in a singsong manner, like this, I don't stutter. . . . As soon as I got myself in a pressure situation it didn't work. It all went down the t-t-t-tubes."

When Carpenter spoke about Mollie Purnell in order to discredit her testimony he constantly touched his nose. A lawyer next to me explained that when a witness uses a gesture like that it often indicates they're lying. I had noticed another gesture during stressful questions. Carpenter would use the first knuckle of his index finger to push his glasses back onto the bridge of his nose. Carpenter now explained he had a firm pattern of taking his father shopping on Saturday or Sunday mornings from 9:00 A.M. until 10:30.

"I'm a notorious collector of things, but specifically I saved every receipt I could find so if my probation officer ever asked me where I was on a specific date I could tell him."

"Have you had an opportunity to go over these receipts?"

"I have. Most involve 1979—early 1980. After the first six months I didn't keep as many. Following May 2, 1981, my father had an eye operation and in Christmas, 1979, he was in Big Springs, Texas. Every week I took him shopping with the exception of those weeks."

Carpenter explained what a good relationship he had with Joe Elia and Lane Thomsen, his bosses at the California Trade School in Hayward. "We were very good friends. I attended their annual Christmas party toward the end of 1979. I distinctly recall it because I got a picture taken of me sitting on Santa's lap"—Carpenter looked wistful at this point—"which I *always* wanted to do." He gave out with a belly laugh, but the jury only looked solemnly back at him. He described the photo, which showed him with long sideburns and dark brown hair against a dark background. He said it was hard to see him because he blended into the background.

"In January and February of 1980," asked Berlin, "did you have any contact with Mollie?"

"Yes. I believe Mollie Purnell called me direct at home or at school and left a phone number I could reach her at." He asked permission to consult the phone records. "Yes, January 9, 1980, shows a twenty-two-minute call to one of her friends' home in Modesto. Mollie was excited. She said it was urgent to see me. I met her at a freeway off-ramp."

"What was the conversation?"

"Just a few subjects—she wanted to borrow two hundred dollars to make a trip to Canada to pick up some silver."

"I have here a check drawn on the Continental Savings and Loan dated February 3, 1980, and cashed at the Union Bank," said Berlin.

Carpenter explained he had been interested in stocks and commodities and particularly interested in silver and selling it, at least until the silver market dropped.

Referring to his diary and the phone records and glancing frequently at the jury, Carpenter said, "On March 11, 1980, Mollie Purnell called me collect from a Modesto telephone booth and we spoke for twenty-one minutes. The price of silver was dropping, and she asked my advice. I told her, 'Sell a third. That's money in the bank.' "

Carpenter got a nine-minute collect call from Mollie on April 7. "Mollie had not sold any of her silver," said the defendant, pressing his fist into the lectern. "At that stage of the game nobody wanted her silver—Mollie was broke at the time. She asked me to get her some money, perhaps a partnership in selling marijuana. . . . I would get 30 percent of the profit." Carpenter pushed the bridge of his glasses back with his right index finger. The selling of pot would be a consistent alibi throughout his long testimony. There was never any physical evidence Mollie had *ever* sold drugs.

"Did that arrangement ever come to pass?"

"Yes. I picked up a half pound of marijuana and took it up to her the following Sunday—uh, April 13, 1980."

During the morning recess Posey snipped to Cox, "Something of substance soon, Frank?" When Carpenter resumed the stand he claimed he took his mother to the foot clinic where she got free medical attention. "I took her every second Saturday of the month."

Carpenter told about his three city routes, which included Modesto. "I would stop by and see Mollie. We would talk about her trip to Jamaica and our marijuana transaction."

"Were these topics related in any way?" asked Berlin.

"Yes, they were. Her family came from there. Their land was quite valuable. When she told me she was going to go down there I asked her to look into any good financial possibilities in regard to importing things from Jamaica to the U.S. . . . In May of 1980 Mollie asked me to buy one-half pound of marijuana when I came by on my trip."

"When you delivered the marijuana was she aware of that delivery?"

"Yes, she was there."

Continuing to portray Carpenter as a devoted son and doting grandfather who spent crucial weekends taking his parents shopping, Berlin asked about June 14, 1980, a Saturday. "I took my father shopping," said Carpenter, "and attended a baby shower in the afternoon. First I took Mom to the foot clinic at the California Podiatry Clinic on Ellis Street. I filled out the paperwork because of Mom's eyesight. In 1981 the clinic ran out of funding so she did not continue." This had been, he explained, a way for Mrs. Carpenter to have her blood pressure and other tests done for free as part of the foot examination.

Berlin gave a little smile as he whirled away from his client, placing his right hand over his clenched left hand as he turned. He moved to the second Saturday in July, establishing the same pattern. Carpenter repeated that he was chauffeur to both his mother and his father. Without fail he took his mother to the foot clinic on the second Saturday of each month and then took her shopping in the afternoon. "If she was going to take a bath and get all dressed up she expected to go shopping."

"Where did you go shopping?"

"I took my mother shopping where my mother *wanted* to go shopping. . . . Today we went to the Emporium, then Woolworth's across the street. I remember because we had cake with cream and strawberries," said Carpenter, licking his lips with a smile. "But each Saturday we'd go to a different shopping location. We'd get back at 5:30 to 6:00 in the evening."

Berlin asked about Sunday, July 20, 1980.

"For the first time Jack and Florence sent me to the Alameda Flea Market to sell outmoded key chains. The Alameda Flea Market is located at an old outdated motion picture drive-in . . . but unfortunately I didn't sell many. Jack wanted fifty cents apiece for them, but I sold them for twenty-five cents.

"I was scared to death because of my speech problem. 'Why don't you go over to the flea market so you can practice on people,' Jack explained. I said, 'That's a good idea,' because it forced me to talk to people.

"My experience that first day was scary. I remember that day. Whew!" A hiss of breath rattled the papers in front of the balding man. "It w-w-was *a hell of a day!*" Carpenter's face reddened, his voice quavered then broke as his face contorted in pain and his eyes began to glisten. There was shock on the faces of the jury.

"B-b-but it was the best thing Jack ever had me do. It helped me. That was the thing that got me started. I started to develop self-confidence." the defendant took off his dark-rimmed glasses and began to dry his eyes and then polish the lenses while he spoke. "People were interested in what I had to sell, not what I had to say."

"There was a call from Mollie Purnell to David Carpenter on August 20, 1980, at 9:42, . . . at his home. What did you talk about?"

"We discussed her trip to Jamaica, my first day at the flea market, my speech impediment. We talked about the half pound of marijuana she wanted to get from me. 'From what I understand a lot of stolen goods are sold at the flea market,' I told her. 'It's an idea you might want to invest in'. . . . She asked me if she could come to San Francisco and pick out one-half pound of marijuana. . . . We met the following day and I gave her the marijuana . . . she did mention she liked the idea of going to the flea market.''

Berlin asked about their conversation a week later. ''What was discussed. I gave her one or two names of people to get in touch with and say this person told me to call you.'' Carpenter said Mollie wanted him to accompany her to Jamaica. ''I told her I would have to check with my parole officer. I gave her his name and address. . . . I did not see the letter.''

''Did you tell her what to write?''

''Only write the truth, I told her.''

Anne Alderson's mother, Evelyn, seated in front of the Stowers and to the left of Mrs. Hansen, had watched the proceedings quietly, but as the day ended she was crying as she politely waved off the press. The Stowers family explained to the reporters that they were there for the other victims as much as for their own lost son.

On the next day, Wednesday, Berlin continued.

''What about the second Saturday in August 1980?'' he asked, carefully establishing Carpenter's pattern of driving his parents on the weekends. The pattern, he was hoping, would hold when he reached the weekends of the October and November murders.

''It was a form of paying rent for my living there. . . . I took my mother to the foot clinic, then we went shopping at the Tanforan Shopping Center afterwards.'' Carpenter, in a bland pearl-gray sweater vest and white shirt, seemed more subdued today.

''What about Sunday, August 24, 1980?''

''When Mollie came down to San Francisco, I gave her more key chains. . . . I brought three dozen out-of-date key chains out of the attic—cookies, bears that go 'clap, clap, clap,' great big ducks. Jack also had some Polish candelabras made out of black cast-iron. Just awful! I figured they'd be ideal cover for all the people stopping at Mollie's house. I also gave her some boxes of rocks.''

In September Mollie went to Jamaica. Carpenter had called Wood to discover his permission to accompany Purnell had been denied. ''She owed me money for the marijuana transaction. . . . I could see all of the opportunity there was in Jamaica to make a lot of m-m-m-money.''

"Did Mollie Purnell buy a gun for you?"

"No, sir."

"Did Mollie Purnell ever buy ammunition for you?"

"No, sir."

Berlin then read the records of the long list of phone calls between Carpenter and Mollie from the September 14 flea market to the end of the month. "There were always two topics—one was Jamaica, the other was the marijuana.''

"I had told her I would be there after the flea market. I called her and then hung up. The idea was there were no phone charges on the Gems bill.''

Berlin then asked about calls on September 30 and October 2 and 3.

"During all those calls," asked Berlin, "did you ever say anything to her about going to a store to pick up a gun for you?"

"No, sir."

"Did you travel to Modesto to pick up a gun?"

"No, sir."

"Did you ever obtain from Mollie Purnell a .38-caliber Rossi revolver?''

"No, sir."

Now Berlin began to trace Carpenter's movements on the day Moreland and Stowers had been executed at Point Reyes. He first introduced a fifty-dollar check drawn on Carpenter's account at the Continental Savings and Loan, which the defendant cashed on October 11. Berlin asked what time this was.

"I cashed it at between 9:15 and 9:30 in the morning. I went with my father grocery shopping for one and one-half hours and then returned home. Then I took my mother to the foot clinic at 1835 Eddy—the California College of Podiatric Medicine. I filled out the forms and waited for them to call out her number. I had to fill out the form for her because she was blind.''

"Who filled out those documents?"

"I did."

"What was the first document you filled out?" requested Berlin.

"The screening questionnaire.'' This was introduced

into evidence as exhibit 7-E's. ''My mother received them back and took them home.'' No clinic official or doctor had signed them, but the blood pressure and other readings were in an unknown hand.

''We were at the clinic for half an hour, somewhere in there.'' Carpenter explained how he had filled out the form in Francis Carpenter's name because of her glaucoma. The defendant explained his mother had been number sixty-seven in line, had a blood pressure reading, a diabetes test, and had omitted the remaining tests. They made plans after the foot clinic to go to Sunset Gardens, the Goodman Lumber Company, and Floorcraft. ''Mother had a list of things she wanted to buy. Shopping with Mother took considerable time because she had to feel everything and she would want to pick it up and hold it and would get out a large magnifying glass she carried along with her to see the products up close. I was at Sunset Gardens an hour to the best of my recollection.''

''Did you buy anything?''

''I remember specifically buying an orange pot.''

''Why do you remember that?''

''Jack Neuman was always buying things. He got a deal on some rubber plants . . . my mother wanted to put the plant in a regular pot instead of a box. We got into an argument over the size of the pot. Over the years she kept complaining it was too small,'' he said, rolling his eyes, implying that even at this moment his mother still considered it too small.

Berlin showed the empty clay pot to the court and Hoffman, joking, asked if the plant was going to be admitted into evidence as well. The jury laughed. Berlin showed Carpenter the signature on the Visa statement and asked if it was his.

''This looks like it. On this occasion my mother was mad at my father and she wanted to use his money. 'We'll show him,' she said. 'We'll spend his money.' So we used his Visa charge and filled in the name of Elwood A. Carpenter.''

''Who was Elwood A. Carpenter?''

''He was my father. He died in 1984. . . .'' At this Carpenter became emotional and his eyes filled with tears. After a moment he polished his glasses and then pushed them back into place with his thumb. Berlin asked him what they had bought.

"We bought fertilizer, two heavy sacks. Eight to ten items were rung up on the register."

"When did you leave Sunset Gardens?"

"I thought it was between 12:30 and 1:00." This was close to the time of the shots heard by the two hikers.

"Where did you go next?"

"To the next block. Farmer's Market. My mother wanted to see if they had any fresh fruit. We were there ten to fifteen minutes. Then to Goodman's Lumber. We got a dessert, but I don't remember where . . . we arrived home at 5:45."

"At any time on October 11, 1981, did you ever go to Point Reyes National Seashore Park in Marin County?"

"No, sir."

Berlin moved to the day of Anne Alderson's murder, October 13, 1980, Columbus Day. "Where were you on that day?"

"I got to work at 8:30, 9:00. I was at work the entire day and Monday evening. It was Jack's first day back after a long sickness."

"Did it change the routine of the day?"

"It most certainly did! When Jack came back he was angry at everyone. He spent the day screaming at me."

"Did you stay in the office?"

"On that specific day I stayed at the warehouse. . . . There was an unusual amount of garbage for that evening."

"Did Jack and Florence leave before you?"

"They always left the same time as me."

"What time did they leave that day?"

"Between 5:30 and 6:00 P.M." This was the estimated time of death of Anne on the side of the Sleeping Lady.

"Is there any doubt in your mind on October 13, 1980, you worked at Gems of the Golden West?"

"No, sir," said Carpenter, looking toward the expressionless jurors. "In regard to supper—my mother and father were there. They had already eaten. They would leave some food for me. I would warm the food up." He made a call to Mollie Purnell, his only one of the evening.

"Did you at any time go to Mount Tamalpais State Park?"

"No, sir."

"Was there in the later part of October anything that would have ended your relationship with Mollie Purnell?"

"No, sir. . . . I went to Mollie's on Saturday afternoon, October 25. It was about a two-hour drive to Modesto." Tina Vance's testimony that she had seen a Thief Kit with gun and wire on this weekend has been damaging. Now Carpenter would present his side of the story.

Carpenter said he arrived in Modesto at 1:30, bringing with him a one-half pound bag of marijuana. He found Trudy Preston, Tina Vance, and Kenny Baughman there.

"Did you have with you a firearm?" asked Berlin.

"No, sir."

"Did you display to Kenneth Baughman a firearm of any sort?"

"No, sir."

"Did you display to Tina Vance at any time that weekend a firearm?"

"No, sir."

"What happened after Mollie and Adam arrived?"

"I went down to Kentucky Fried Chicken. I brought it back and we had supper."

"Did Mollie seem surprised to see you?"

"No, she was expecting me."

"After dinner were you aware of any phone calls?"

Posey interrupted and complained Berlin was leading the witness. Berlin rephrased his question. "Did you hear a phone ring?"

"Yes . . . around 8:15 to 8:30." Records were consulted. The time was 8:20.

"On October 25, 8:20 P.M. There was a three-minute phone call. Who answered?"

"Mollie answered the phone. Kenny Baughman's mother had called Mollie Purnell in regard to the fact that the car was borrowed."

"One additional phone call," said Berlin, "on Sunday, October 26, at 8:36. Who was present?"

"Mollie Purnell answered. I was there. I was in the kitchen and talking to Mollie when the phone rang . . .

all the kids were upstairs, sound asleep. She discussed it with us immediately afterwards. 'Kenny Baughman's mother is saying you and Tina stole the car,' Mollie told them. Both Kenny and Tina said Jim Wolfe had loaned them the car. Mollie turned to me.''

"Was there any discussion of Tina returning with you?"

"No, sir." Carpenter said the phone rang at 1:16 P.M. while he was present. "Jim Wolfe said the car was taken without permission. The evening before Mollie and I sat around and bagged the marijuana. We divided it up according to who would get it. Sunday morning the kids were out selling it. . . . After the 2:07 P.M. call I told her I didn't like the way the whole thing was coming down. By now I found out Tina was only fourteen. . . .

" 'We got a car that's stolen here in Modesto.' [Carpenter told Mollie.] 'I'll take the little girl to San Francisco and if Kenny's not in San Francisco by 7:00 I'm putting her on the bus . . . I'm looking out for the kid. . . .''

"At any time did you say anything about a modeling career to Tina."

"No, sir," said Carpenter, ". . . we left at 2:30 to 2:45.''

"Did you take anything back to San Francisco?"

"Yes. I took back all of the key chains I could get my hands on.''

"Did you display a handgun of any kind?"

"No, sir."

"Did you display a handgun to Tina alone?"

"No, sir.''

"Did you display a handgun of any kind to Adam and Kenny together?''

"No, sir." Carpenter also denied they had stopped in any parks or that he had shown a Thief Kit to Tina. "We arrived in San Francisco around five. . . . Mollie called to say Kenny was going to get Tina." Consulting his records, Carpenter explained Mollie had called him from a pay phone at 5:32 P.M. "It was a direct trip from Modesto to San Francisco with no stops." Tina was having tea and salad and vegetables with his parents, Carpenter told the court, when Kenny arrived around 8:00 P.M.

Berlin asked if, after Mollie's move to Sacramento, their relationship had continued. "We would talk about Jamaica," said Carpenter. "There was no further key-chain dealing or marijuana dealing with her."

On the second Saturday in November, Carpenter explained that as usual he had taken his father shopping and his mother to the foot clinic. Afterward they had gone to Sears to see about a sale on vacuum cleaners his mother had read about in the paper. "We got the salesman's card—so if we decided to get the vacuum cleaner we could call later in the afternoon to put the order in with him."

Berlin now asked, "Based on your recollection as refreshed, what did you do on Thanksgiving Day, 1980?"

"My mother and father and I went over to my brother's . . . where we had dinner."

Berlin asked Carpenter where he was the following day, November 28, when O'Connell and May were executed.

"The upstairs toilet in the upstairs main bathroom broke and I installed all new works in it [flexible metal replacement parts from Floorcraft]. It took me between 10:00 A.M. and 2:00 P.M. to do it because I'm not very good with plumbing."

"Were you able to find anything to corroborate this?"

"It was quite a project, but I don't have anyone to corroborate my being at home. I had a witness, my father, but he has since died, and I don't have any way of proving that I was there between 10:00 and 2:00."

On December 31, the last day of 1980, Carpenter worked with Florence Neuman all day, and on January 4, 1981, he made his final trip to the Alameda Flea Market. "I realized I was going to stutter whenever I met a strange person. I got to thinking. I could become successful in business as 'the stuttering salesman.' . . . I tended to relax more.

"On Monday, January 19, I had a change in attitude. I started to sell, . . . going in with the rack, setting the rack on the counter, and *selling!*"

"When you went out servicing accounts did you have a stutter?"

"Yes, sir."

"When you got a new client did you have a stutter?"

"Yes, sir," said Carpenter.

Carpenter began his third day of testimony where he left off the day before. "I just met Candy when I got off work . . . [January 21, 1981]," he said. "I did not take her to Mount Tamalpais."

"Did you, later that night, take her to Sebastopol?"

"No, sir."

"Did you, later that night, take her to a place called Johnnie's?"

"No, sir. After I met her back on Golden Gate Avenue I drove in my Chevy station wagon up Highway 101 north to Petaluma en route to Guerneville. . . . She had made it really obvious she was willing to exchange sexual favors if I was to drive her up to Guerneville. Around Petaluma, 7:15 to 7:30 P.M., somewhere in there . . . I suggested we stop and get something to eat. Before we got something to eat we engaged in sex in the back of my Chevy. We returned to San Francisco."

"Did you propose marriage to her at any time that night?"

"No, sir. Candy had taken a course at a school to be a bartender and she wanted to work as a waitress in San Francisco. She was only going up to Guerneville because that was the only place she had to stay. I invited her to stay at my place for a few days. . . . she was agreeable and went with me to my parents' house on Sussex. Candy lived upstairs in her own room and I continued to live downstairs in my room. . . . she had jobs during this period. She brought a whole carful of clothes with her . . . she had a red jacket, a blue one, including one particular [yellow] jacket . . . the Western Bar jacket." Carpenter described the now-familiar jacket to the jury.

"Did you ever wear it."

"Yes."

"On what occasions?"

"Candy was wearing it and I had had my blue jacket stolen and I had no jacket to wear. I used to wear it at night when I walked my dog. . . . I wore it quite a few times."

"Did you ever wear it outside of San Francisco?"

"No, sir."

"Do you know what became of the yellow jacket?"

"No."

"Did you ever make any explanation as to what happened to her jacket?"

"She lost it one night while drink. . . . I never told it had been stolen."

"Did you ever wear a baseball cap?"

"Yes."

"Did your father?"

"Yes," replied the balding defendant. "Most of the baseball caps were up in my father's closet. One was a specific Oakland A's cap." Berlin handed him a similar one and Carpenter pulled back his head while he looked at it. The cap was mostly green mesh, solid cloth on the sides with a white A's symbol on the brim. "Mine was mostly solid, with mesh in the back . . . but I wore watch caps most of the time . . . probably had about four. It's a knit cap, like a ski cap."

On Valentine's Day Carpenter bought Candy an engagement ring. "I became officially engaged that day. . . . No foot clinic to go to that day. . . . On December 1980 was the last time Mother went to the foot clinic."

Berlin asked Carpenter where he was on March 19, a day the Trailside Killer had evidently been casing the Henry Cowell Redwoods State Park. The defendant produced records that showed he had punched in at 8:27 A.M., had lunch between 12:03 and 12:30 P.M., and 2:15 P.M. was written in in pen. "I was working in the building."

"How long," asked Berlin.

"It's hard to say." His records for March 26 were introduced: "8:59 A.M. until 8:25 P.M."—a long day. On May 8, when he met with Womack and Robinson at Wood's office, he did not punch out.

"March 24 was the last day I shaved," said Carpenter. "That evening I worked late and I stayed in the trailer and I had forgotten my razor. The very next day I purchased my Fiat. Because the Chevy was getting old and consumed quite a bit of gasoline [I bought the new car]. It was a 1974 four-door Fiat 124 in good shape except for three things: a leak in the transmission, the hood latch was broken so if you drove over twenty mph the hood would raise up . . . and all of the smog equipment had been removed.'' Carpenter held up the pink slip with the added notation—''sold 1974—as is, no refund.''

Now Berlin had Carpenter re-create the events of Saturday, March 28.

''I got out of bed at 6:30 A.M. and took the car out to Montgomery Ward in Daly City to get a smog certificate. It opened at 7:30—first come, first served. I got there at 7:15.'' Carpenter told how he left the car, took rapid transit home, arrived there at 10:30 A.M., and then took his father shopping. He ended up at Gemco with Candy about the time the Fiat was ready. ''Candy specifically wanted to buy a pair of running shoes. She was looking at a pair of Adidas. While we were there I noticed some Nike's on sale for $19.95.'' The defendant agreed the shoes Henard had purchased as exhibits were ''identical'' to the pair he had purchased. ''I picked up the car at 2:15 and got home at 3:30 to 4:00 P.M.''

''Were you at Henry Cowell Park that day?''

''No.''

''Do you smoke cigarettes?''

''I don't smoke cigarettes unless they are marijuana.'' A smile.

Now Berlin asked Carpenter where he was on March 29, the day Ellen Hansen and Steve Haertle were shot on Ridge Trail.

''I was home until around 11:00 in the morning. At 11:00 I was picked up and went down to some place in the Redwood City hills . . . it was a residence. I met there with four individuals.'' Carpenter left these people unidentified. ''We discussed some of my ideas for my adult key chains. . . . I returned to the house at 3:00 in the afternoon.'' A one-way trip to Santa Cruz takes between 90 and 120 minutes.

''Were you at the Felton Gas Station and 7-Eleven at 1:30 P.M.?''

''No, sir. I was studying until around suppertime. We ate at 5:30 to 6:00. Mother, Dad, Candy, and me were at dinner. I called Reba later that evening. After supper I received a call from my friend up in Sacramento regarding my adult key-chain idea. . . . I decided that since I was going to go up there I didn't want to drive my Fiat with its transmission beat up and since I was going to discuss my key-chain proposal I wanted to look as prosperous as possible. I wanted to borrow her [Reba's] BMW. 'Is this in relationship to getting my rugs back,' asked Reba. 'Absolutely,' I lied . . . I called Joe [Elia] and told him I'd got hurt playing with kids, hurt my neck throwing kids in the air. This was a lie. On Monday I drove my Fiat to Reba Lehman's house because I didn't have a parking permit. I could leave my Fiat sitting there and not worry about having a cop give it a ticket.

"I returned to San Francisco, went to the bank, dropped off my parole report, and missed work. I lied because they needed me and I had so much happening in my life.

"Once in your life!" Carpenter pounded the witness table with his fist. "You've got a chance to be rich. . . ." Carpenter's stutter vanished, his voice thickened, his face reddened and contorted and he began crying. "And damn it, I wanted to be rich!—That was a million-dollar idea! I was fifty years old and I didn't have much. I had a chance to reach for that opportunity and I took it!" Carpenter regained his composure.

"Mrs. Frank was not interested in the proposal. I went up to Lake Tahoe and gambled and returned to Sacramento after that and I continued to see my friend that evening. . . . I was stopped by my boss at work. I had gotten a neck brace and told him how I had hurt my neck. I returned to work the next day."

Carpenter told how he had returned the BMW to Reba, locked the car, and put the keys on the front tire. He then went to the bank to deposit the $300 he had won, returned home, and called Reba to see if she had gotten the car and keys. "The first thing she wanted to know was what success I had had."

Berlin now asked about April 4, the day the Trailside Killer was thought to have returned to Ridge Trail. "I loaded the van for Jack and Florence and did bookkeeping until 7:00 to 7:30, working for free."

The jury took a recess, and Berlin made a formal complaint that Posey had been making facial contortions of disbelief and rocking in his chair during Carpenter's testimony. There was an angry exchange between Posey and

Berlin after which Hoffman said sternly, "I don't believe Mr. Posey has been guilty of any flagrant misconduct. I do object to his looking to the jury. I don't think that's proper."

"I'm simply exasperated at having to stand up constantly to object to leading questions by Mr. Berlin. . . . Despite my constant objections they continue to ask leading questions. . . . I'm beginning to feel like a jumping jack here, Judge."

"Some trials like this keep you in shape," said Hoffman with a smile, and then turned to Berlin to say, "I'll see about getting some oil for Mr. Posey's chair."

When the jury returned, Carpenter told why he broke up with Candy Townsend. "The final straw occurred on April 8. She called me at 3:30 A.M. drunker than a skunk. Couldn't find her car. She wanted me to come down and find her car. She wanted to drive home so I had to physically put her in her car and drive her home . . . after that time it was agreed she had to leave. I left her a note telling her she had to be out during a specific time frame. April 30 Candy moved out. She asked if she could leave clothing there, so I put all her clothes in the closet.

"May 8, Friday, I went over to my parole officer, Richard Wood, and I was interviewed by Sergeant Womack and Officer Robinson. They asked me what vehicle I had access to on Saturday, May 2. The only vehicle I had access to on that particular day was my Chevy station wagon. My fiat was in the shop." After Wood took his picture, Carpenter went for a meeting with Shane and Karen.

"Karen called me collect Sunday morning at 11:00. Said she had been arrested for bank robbery, was in San Francisco jail, and asked if I would come down and bring her some money.

"That evening Shane called and asked if I had heard from his wife . . . he explained to me he had robbed a bank and had been successful in getting away. I thought that Shane had stopped robbing banks and was selling marijuana. I didn't think of selling pot as a 'biggie.' . . . I went over to see Shane at the Trinity Plaza. . . . I only knew that Shane had robbed that one bank. . . . Karen called and said she had gotten out. I gave her my address and said take a taxi over here.''

The defendant explained he didn't see the Williamses the next day but did speak on the phone. ''I went to the Plaza but they weren't there, so I returned home. Shane called me and invited me to supper.

''On Wednesday, May 13, after work I drove down there.''

''Did you show them any guns?'' asked Berlin.

''No, sir.''

Nine surveillance photos were exhibited and the defendant took a pointer, left the stand, and showed the jury where the trio had parked. After he had gotten what he came for—he claimed it was a marijuana stash—Carpenter turned the alarm back on, locked both doors, and joined his two friends standing outside. ''I gave Shane and Karen most of the marijuana. I was there at the Trinity Plaza for twenty-five minutes, then left and went home.''

Berlin's long journey through the trails of Carpenter's parole now came to an end. Carpenter told the jury that on the morning of his arrest he was wearing the same rounded-bifocal glasses he had gotten from Dr. Wright fourteen months previously.

Carpenter now looked teary-eyed. ''At the time of my arrest, I had marijuana on me. I had an album of Wagner records—you see, I was going over to Jeff Jackl's for supper that night.'' Inside his house he had four to five bags of key chains, some saying HOT PANTS or FOXY LADY.

In covering the two-year period of his parole, Carpenter had given an alibi for each of the Marin County murders. His only witnesses were his deceased father and his elderly, blind mother, who was suffering from Alzheimer's disease. Three unsigned questionnaires from the podiatric clinic and a letter dated the day of Anne Alderson's death were additional evidence. That letter, Posey knew, could be troublesome, and he had already subpoenaed Florence Neuman's Gems of the Golden West records of 1980.

A hung jury was Posey's worst fear. ''If someone on the jury,'' he told me, ''seizes upon one of Carpenter's sweet little stories and hangs it . . . but we had a very intelligent jury. They could really sense what was going on.''

''I did not kill anyone,'' said Carpenter, responding to Posey's aggressive cross-examination the next day, Friday, April 8, but admitted he had hiked on the Marin trails after joining the Sierra Club in 1979. ''Between January 1980 and September 1980 I hiked in Point Reyes National Seashore about five times and took as many as twenty-five hikes on Mount Tamalpais.'' Usually, Carpenter said, I hiked alone. Many times, he admitted, his hikes took him past the Mountain Theatre, where Anne Alderson had last been seen alive.

''Isn't it true, Mr. Carpenter, that you feel threatened by women?'' asked Posey.

''No, I do not.''

''Isn't it true, Mr. Carpenter, that you dislike women?''

''No, it is not.''

''Isn't it true you took Candy Townsend up to Mount Tamalpais to show her where a woman was murdered?''

''No, I did not,'' responded Carpenter.

''Isn't it true, Mr. Carpenter, that you asked her to have sex with you for money?''

''No, I did not.''

On the afternoon Hansen and Haertle were shot, March 29, 1981, Carpenter claimed to have been with four men showing them his ideas for adult key chains portraying heterosexual and homosexual acts. He named them for Posey: Little Junior, who was 6 foot 2, Big Junior, Monk (also known as Vincent)—he knew them only by these nicknames—and an old prison pal named William ''Bill'' Johnson. Carpenter described each man's appearance and their cars but said, ''I have no idea how to get in touch with them. They're drug dealers who wanted to launder their money in a legitimate business. When you're dealing with people like that, Mr. Posey, you don't want to know who they are.'' The defense team had been unable to find any of the four.

''Don't you know the street addresses of any of the men?'' asked Posey, ''in particular Little Junior, who drove you to Redwood City, to the location? [Guido's house.]"

Carpenter shook his head no.

"Is that because there is no Little Junior? In fact, it's a lie about Little Junior, isn't it, Mr. Carpenter?" said Posey, arms clenched behind him.

"No, sir."

"In the seven years since your arrest . . . have you ever tried to find the house where the meeting took place?"

"I never had a need to," replied Carpenter.

"How about the fact that you are facing charges on five murders, Mr. Carpenter!"

"John Posey didn't talk down to the jury," Mrs. Stowers told me. "He let them know he thought they were reasonable people. Listening to Carpenter on the stand— the gangsters, Big Junior, Little Junior—I felt his story was so outrageous that he didn't even consider anyone's intelligence. He also took a dislike to the judge's clerk, Kathy, who was experiencing her first death-penalty trial. He wanted her out toward the end. I called Carpenter the original second-story man—a second story for everything."

On Tuesday, April 12, Carpenter's fifth day on the stand began. As he was shown photos of his room he claimed the police had staged evidence in both his car and closet. He admitted he had a bag of key chains, but, "It was in my room, either on the floor or behind the dresser next to the furnace."

"Did you ever carry a bullet in a bag?" asked Posey on cross-examination.

"No, sir. I can't imagine any person carrying bullets in a bag of key chains."

"Did you ever carry bullets with you at any time?"

"I never had any bullets to carry."

Posey showed Carpenter the photo of his bedroom closet that Mel Peterson had taken during the search of his room. Carpenter told the prosecutor that a liquor bottle and most of the clothing was not his but Candy's.

"Are you saying someone put those items there?"

"Well, Mr. Posey, since Candy's liquor bottle and other personal effects are in there, yes. . . . Since she was the one who had a drinking problem . . . and I remember them being on the other side of the room and now they're shown in my closet where they had no business being. I would say that unless God put them there, the police m-m-must have.''

"Did you buy those new tennis shoes because you believed the police would be searching your house . . . you wanted them to believe those were the ones you had?''

"No, that wasn't the purpose of buying them, I bought them in March.''

Unable to account for the missing yellow-gold jacket, Carpenter ventured Candy "may have lost it when she was drunk. She had a habit of that.'' His faded blue bell-bottom jeans were in the dirty clothes hamper when Henard and Layden searched the house, theorized the defendant.

Posey showed Carpenter a driver's license photo showing him wearing glasses exactly like those found by the body of Barbara Schwartz. "What happened to those glasses?'' Posey asked. This was one of the few questions Carpenter did not even attempt to answer.

Carpenter had told the police that when he was robbed in Sacramento the man had used a .38-caliber gun. Reading the report Posey asked him, "A .38? How did you know it was a .38?''

"Well, I'm familiar with .38's.''

"How did you come to be familiar with .38's?''

"Well,'' said Carpenter, "I see them on television and in the movies.'' He paused and when he saw that this was not going down well with the jury, said, "I also know about .38's because I was up with Elia and Thomsen at their ranch in Mendocino and they were shooting .38's.''

Carpenter's testimony resumed on Wednesday, April 13, as Posey questioned the defendant about the foot clinic where he claimed he took his mother on the day Moreland and Stowers were murdered.

"That was a long time ago,'' said Carpenter studying the forms he had filled out for his mother at the podiatry college. They were unsigned.

Posey and his co-counsel, Ann Harrington, told me later how they were able to discredit Carpenter's "Hong Kong letter" alibi. "The Hong Kong letter came from Florence Neuman," said Posey. "She came in, brought me this little index card. It said, 'Inquiry, September 20—Reply, October 13, 1980.' She says this meant that Carpenter had to be at Gems at the time Anne Alderson was murdered. I asked her where the actual letters were. She said, 'I couldn't find them.' It looked kind of believable when you watched her. She's kind of a scatterhead. Some of the letters were at her home and some were at Gems, which had been repurchased.

"So we did a subpoena *ducus tekum* for all the records. We served it on Gems and discovered that Florence Neuman had personally come in and gotten the records and had some at her house. Ann and I went to Marin and started going through all these boxes of files trying to pick out things, but there was just too much given the time frame. One of the investigators, Ted Lindquist, was there and I told him about the Hong Kong letter to the Guida Metal Factory. Well, he sat in the office all day and just started going through the boxes. We're back in San Diego and in the late afternoon we got a phone call from Ted. 'Guess what I found?' he said. 'I found the letter, but the catch is the letter isn't the way they say it is.' Early the next morning Ted flew down with the box of letters."

"That letter was so typical of Carpenter," said Ann, "insofar as he handled the evidence in the trial. . . . the true statement of facts was exactly the reverse as presented—'inquiry' meant a letter of inquiry from Gems to the Hong Kong factory, and 'reply' meant a reply from Hong Kong."

"I can just see Carpenter," said Posey, "sitting down and suddenly making that suggestion to Florence about using the Hong Kong letter—the thrust of it was that the letter was mailed from Hong Kong [by Yu Kwun Cheung, factory manager] on the same day that Carpenter was supposedly sending out a letter to reply to it."

On Thursday, April 14, the defendant's seventh day on the stand, Posey sprang the trap. "I knew Carpenter was going to be on the stand a long time, and when Ted walked in the courtroom Carpenter knew something was up. Ted had one of the boxes, and Carpenter got this strange expression on his face. He had started piecing together what was happening and I was trying to get him to make an absolute commitment [to the letter] and he did.

"I came back to the letter again to see what he would say. He started doing this, pushing his glasses back over and over and saying, 'Well, let me see, let me see . . .'

"He knows we know something," Posey told me, "and it was annoying him. I just handed him the letter. Most people if you caught them they would react. Carpenter just brushed it aside, absolutely angry."

"I guess, it wasn't that day," said Carpenter, "but I thought it was."

Posey questioned Carpenter about the Marin victims.

"Did you," asked Posey, showing the defendant a picture of Anne Alderson, "shoot her in the back of the head after raping her?"

"I've never seen Anne Alderson. I did not shoot her and I did not rape her."

Posey then showed Carpenter pictures of Stowers and Moreland and asked, "Did you lay these two people down on the ground on October 11, 1980, and shoot each one of them in the back of the head?"

"No, sir."

Posey displayed pictures of O'Connell and May and asked, "Did you lay them on the ground on November 28, 1980, and shoot each one in the back of the head?"

"No, sir."

"Did you say, during an interview of KTVU Television on August 19, 1985, that if you killed one, you killed them all?"

"I believe I did s-s-say that. Yes, sir. I believe the whole statement was that for me to be guilty, I would have had to pull the trigger on every single one. I couldn't have just done it on one or two or three and not pulled it on the rest and that was because the same gun was used each time."

"At the end of the interview you said, 'There's only one Trailside Killer, just one.' Are you that one Trailside

Killer who took this gun and shot all those people in the back of the head?''

"No, sir.''

Posey walked over and picked up the yellow-tagged Rossi with a red band on the barrel and carefully placed it in front of Carpenter. "Do you recognize this gun?'' Posey asked.

"I've seen it only in the courtroom. I didn't have any gun.''

Posey told me, "When I finished cross-examining Carpenter and stepped back I knew the case was won . . . the verdict would be guilty.'' But, unknown to Posey, fate had other plans. The day was already lost.

As the sixteenth week of the trial began Posey cross-examined Florence Neuman, suggesting she would say anything to help her longtime friend. The prosecutor produced invoices addressed and dated in all capital letters that had been done after Carpenter left Gems. Mrs. Neuman was angry that Posey hadn't asked particular questions that she had wanted to answer, particularly about the implication that the index record of letters, which she felt had been misrepresented, since the original had been in her possession.

"I want him to ask me about it because it's crucial to this case,'' she said to the judge and then began an outburst. She had taken the reporters' box of Kleenex and began tossing sheets of tissue about. The judge halted her.

"Thank you,'' said Hoffman. "You can be excused.''

"But I'm not done yet. I'm not done yet.''

"Oh, yes, you are,'' said Hoffman.

"Carpenter had a document for October 11,'' Posey told me later. "There were three more cards from the foot clinic that Carpenter had filled out for his mother, and they just didn't sit right with me. One of the cards looked so new we didn't know if it had just been typed or if there was a way to determine that.

"I needed a documents job, so I got hold of Sandra Homewood [documents examiner from the San Diego DA's office]. I wanted to look at the three pencil-written forms from the clinic to see what was going on . . . you could just feel something was not on the up-and-up.

"Sandy got out her microscope and started looking at the three cards and says, 'This one's been erased. You can actually see it with the naked eye.' It wasn't the whole number. There were two erasure marks on the document. One she described as a 'careless erasure'—the other she described as an 'intentional, deliberate type of erasure mark.' On the first you could see the outline underneath the erased number, on the other it looked like the actual date written was '10-10-80.' The zero had been erased and a one had been written in. There was a dash, and when you looked at it under the microscope you could see where it had been extended.

"Sandra Homewood was my last witness, and we put her with a television screen and you could really see once she started explaining it, what Carpenter did." Homewood testified, "The erasures show a conscious effort to remove every bit from the paper. The patching and retouching were done so that someone wouldn't notice it at a glance."

The dean of the foot clinic, a last-minute defense witness, testified after Posey's rebuttal case had ended that the clinic was not open on October 10, but was on October 11, 1980. "Carpenter needed the foot clinic for Moreland and Stowers," Posey theorized, "and what happened I guess is he goofed and put October 10 on those forms because he was looking at a calendar for the wrong year. . . . I have to say everything that was in those records he had an answer for. Where Carpenter truly got tripped up was where he didn't have something to plan for—the finding of the Hong Kong letter and the discovery of the alteration of the clinic document. Carpenter never dreamed we were going to find that original letter.

"Carpenter uses people," Posey told me, "his lawyers and the system and he just kept putting down all these papers. What happens is you just get flooded. You see, from the prosecution perspective we don't have any opportunity to see them before it happens. The judge wants to move it along, and you're under the gun all the time, and that's exactly what Carpenter was trying to pull—sneak that stuff through."

"I assume," said Ann, "Carpenter's lawyers were shocked to see that there were all those erasures and letters and stuff . . . and that ridiculous story about Big Junior, Little Junior, Guido, Chuey Rodriguez, and Monk. Don't forget Monk, he was the 'linchpin,' the 'big cheese,' Carpenter said. It was part of his way of showing disrespect to Mrs. Hansen, who was in the courtroom. When you think about it, the rest of this stuff that he tried to concoct made sense, but it's like, 'I've done this, and now I'm going to add insult to injury'—he told a story no sane person would believe."

"Only his attorneys would know," said Posey, "but I have a feeling the first time they heard those names was on the stand when I started asking Carpenter questions. I think their names are probably the names of people he's known over the years. That could be the reason his attorneys were unable to find any of them, including 'Chuey' who hung out on Twentieth and Mission."

Ann mentioned the various ways Posey had of getting under Carpenter's skin during the trial. "One day when it seemed like Carpenter's hair was changing color again, John would make this obvious attempt of looking at it. He made sure the jury knew he was wondering about his hair. Also, the mention that Carpenter was done in by a woman, Ellen Hansen, who stood up to him, enraged Carpenter. John mentioned Ellen's name as often as possible, often catching Mrs. Hansen's eye. I noticed whenever Ellen's name was mentioned Carpenter would stop writing on his yellow pad."

Posey had seen changes in the personality of the defendant over the trial. "At times it seemed," he said, "as if a shadow were crossing over Carpenter's face. It was like a different person peering out from beneath those glasses each day."

Tuesday morning, May 3, 1988, after ninety-one witnesses and four months of trial, John Posey began his closing argument. He would speak for five hours.

"David Carpenter," began the prosecutor, "was driven by a need for power through violence when he killed five people in Northern California, using the same gun in all the slayings. This is really the story of a gun. That's the evidence that shows this defendant is guilty.

"One witness testified that Carpenter told her, 'There's nothing like the power of a gun to get what you want, but the ultimate goal would be to commit a murder and rape and get away with it.' That's his ultimate goal here in this courtroom, to get away with it.

"He has needs that have to be satisfied. This is a man who manipulates and controls people and gets them into situations and then uses that situation to his particular advantage.

"Carpenter was a methodical, manipulative killer living his ultimate goal.

"His testimony here was an affront to everybody's intelligence.

"He planned these murders. These weren't just people he picked out at random. He noticed them, then stalked them and scouted those areas so he knew where he was going to take them.

"The attack on Richard Stowers and Cynthia Moreland did not involve a sexual attack because it was Carpenter's first test run with the gun. He took them to a secluded spot off the trail, laid them down on the ground, and executed them by shooting each in the back of the head, just like all the Marin victims were killed. There's no eyewitness to this, but the link is made through the bullets.

"His intended victim on November 28, 1980, at Point Reyes was Diane O'Connell. She's the victim he chose. But what happened was his plan went awry a little bit when Shauna May stumbled on the scene. That's why two women who didn't know each other were killed together.

"Carpenter intended to rape O'Connell before killing her, but focused his attack on May because he was so angry about her interruption He left Shauna May alive while he strangled Diane O'Connell. Can you imagine the terror that woman felt knowing what the defendant was doing? You can see," Posey said, holding up a photograph of the murder scene, "where her hands dug into the dirt, which I submit happened as these acts occurred.

And why was she the rape victim? Because she foiled his plan.

"It's from that case of the shooting of Hansen and Haertle that the vital links are made, and once that is made the links appear between him and the Marin murders. The reason he was caught was because Ellen Hansen wasn't going to let that happen. It cost that young woman her life, but because of it, this senseless killing of innocent people ended."

As Posey struggled with a wayward wheel on his towering cart of red bound transcripts a woman asked him which part of the trial he like best. "The end," he said with a sigh as the elevator doors closed behind him.

Mrs. Stowers told me, "That trial took so much out of John Posey. . . . I had heard that he'd never do another death-penalty trial." Lieutenant Besse agreed. "This case became John Posey. He worked on it for over three years—he's the only one who really knows the whole case. He put it all together, organized it, retrieved it, an outstanding job. Posey is a loner. If he'd had another attorney with him like Cox they probably never would have gotten along—Posey gets real irritated when people try to guide him. Now, with Berlin and Cox there was a lot of infighting.

"Judge Hoffman tried to guide Posey, and Posey really got upset about it. Posey kept saying he thought Hoffman was hostile, but after being there a couple of times I had the feeling that Hoffman realized that the animosity between the defense and the prosecution was detrimental to Posey, so what he tried to do was help out. Hoffman tried to be a referee and keep Posey from doing things that might harm his case. Posey had a 'get the hell out of my way, Judge' attitude. In retrospect some of the rulings the judge made were right down the line and were positive and not negative to the prosecution."

Steven Berlin's closing argument for the defense took up both May 5 and May 4.

"The Trailside Killer and Mr. Carpenter must look a lot alike," Berlin said. "You have to look at the pattern of witnesses building on each others' descriptions so that many of them now agree on an identification initially made by only a few. The original, early statements are the ones that are the most important in the identification part of this case.

"We have testimony from several people who say David Carpenter is not the one they saw in Henry Cowell Park and three are corroborated by instances where the defendant was at work or trade school at the time the Trailside Killer was seen.

"Although we know she, Mollie Purnell, bought the gun, you can't believe beyond a reasonable doubt that she gave that gun to David Carpenter. Her willingness to change her testimony when she's pinned down indicates she's not telling the truth. Any of the hundreds of shadowy figures who at least knew of her through her club could have gotten the gun from her.

"I submit," said Berlin, referring to the chain of events involved in the recovery of the .38-caliber murder weapon, "the gun was not located because of any person linked to David Carpenter and this is still an unsolved set of crimes."

Judge Hoffman gave the jurors ninety minutes of instructions Monday morning and they retired to the jury room to consider their verdict. On Tuesday, May 10, 1988, after only seven hours of deliberations, the jury notified the bailiff they had reached a decision. The courtroom filled. Hoffman took his chair.

When Hoffman was handed the verdict, Carpenter was sitting at the defense table in a gray sweater, striped long-sleeve shirt, and tan slacks, with a stoic expression on his face. Carpenter watched Hoffman intently as he read the verdict to himself, but looked down at the polished table when it was read out loud by Kathy Derby, Hoffman's court clerk.

David Carpenter had been found Guilty of five more murders with a finding of special circumstances of two rapes and an attempted rape. The verdict came just five days shy of the seven-year anniversary of Carpenter's arrest on May 15, 1981. Only four days earlier Carpenter had turned fifty-eight.

Posey thought the verdict had been swiftly arrived at but believed the evidence supported such a quick decision. As Carpenter was led from the court in handcuffs he said to the press, "You can be damn sure this is not the end." Indeed, Carpenter's lawyers immediately began preparing for the penalty phase of the trial, which would begin on May 17 and run a month.

"I guess a lot of what bothered me toward the finish," Joyce Stowers told me, "was listening to John talk about how Rick and Cindy just happened to be sort of like target practice, go out and put some bottles on the back fence—people meant so little to Carpenter; he just had no regard—you know, but you could drive yourself over the edge if you try and think what happened. You try to avoid that.

"I can't imagine Carpenter and his friends having a steak cookout and discussing how to hold a gun, how to rob—it just boggles my mind, having a nice barbecue and discussing . . ." Joyce choked back a sob. "The end," she continued, "has been a long time coming. After it was over Jerry and I were able to drive to the cemetery in our home town for a private family moment."

"Marilyn Hansen wrote a beautiful letter to the judge," Hoffman's young clerk, Kathy Derby, said, "and sent him a copy of a book of poems by Ellen Hansen. They are beautiful, beautiful poems."

On Tuesday, May 31, the defense portion of Carpenter's penalty phase trial opened with a parade of childhood friends who testified to the defendant's terrible childhood. On June 9, a psychologist testified that Carpenter committed the murders during a psychotic state triggered by resistance on the victim's part to his sexual advances. "I don't think he planned to murder," said the psychologist, "I think he planned to rape." The following day Carpenter's children Gabrielle and Michael testified on his behalf. "We're all he has," said Michael.

On June 14, John Posey cross-examined defense witness professor Craig Haney of UC-Santa Cruz who agreed that Carpenter committed execution-style slayings because of untreated psychosexual problems. "I think that's part of his life and affects who he is and what he does," said the psychology professor.

The penalty jury, after eight and one-half hours of deliberations reached their verdict. On Monday, June 27, 1988, Kathy Derby read aloud their recommendation that

Carpenter be executed in the gas chamber. Frank Cox, in referring to the condemned man's childhood of physical and mental abuse by parents and peers, said, "What we're dealing with here is volcanic explosion of rage that was pent up inside of him for years." Now it was up to Hoffman to follow the jury's recommendation or to sentence Carpenter to life in prison with no possibility of parole. The judge designated July 19, 1988, as the day he would administer his sentence.

"After the verdict," Joyce Stowers told me, "Jerry wanted to speak to the jury and thank them, but they came back into the jury room. He stood there a while, but they had all left. I know they didn't want to speak with the defense attorney. Jerry had driven all night to be down there. He was anxious to get started back but still had wanted to talk to them. Toward the end one of the jurors did ask Jerry why he was on crutches. Throughout the trial they had been very aware of us. I think they quickly sorted out who was who there—Mrs. Hansen, Mrs. Scaggs, who was very ill and died at the end of the penalty phase. We felt it was very important the kids were represented by someone, all of us as a group. We have a greater understanding of how the system works, and it does work—not as smoothly and quickly as I would like. I don't know within my lifetime or in Carpenter's if he will actually be executed, but we do know he won't be out on the streets."

By July Carpenter had grown back his beard and stood before Hoffman. The judge handed down a second death sentence in an uncharacteristically long one-hour-and-ten-minute speech. "Mr. Carpenter is, without question, a serial killer and a habitual criminal likely to commit violent acts against others," he said. "The court agrees with the prosecution's view that these crimes were committed with calculated viciousness, and each one after careful deliberation. Two previous periods of incarceration from 1960 to 1969 and 1970 to 1979, had no effect on his criminal activity."

Carpenter had sixteen boxes of appellate material he wanted to keep with him and take to Santa Cruz. "It's up to the appellate council to take care of that stuff," said Hoffman, dark eyes flashing beneath white hair and black brows. "As far as I'm concerned, you're going to San Quentin."

As the judge spoke, Carpenter was very, very angry. It was amazing how his personality changed from the time the guilty verdict came back, through his penalty phase, and then on to his sentencing. Four of the jurors had shown up to see the sentencing, and they noticed his anger too.

"The lack of remorse on Carpenter's part," said Kathy, the court clerk, after sentencing, "the total lack of remorse. And hatred. The way Carpenter was looking at the judge you realized then this was a man who could go out and kill those people.

"The whole courtroom cleared out after the verdicts for death came in. And there was just Mr. Stowers. This lonely man sitting in the heart of this big courtroom.

"I looked over at him and he slowly got to his feet and came up to me and he gave me a big hug and then he started crying. It was so hard for me, being a clerk of the court, to go up to these people and tell them how sorry I am and I finally did. And I held him for the longest time," said Kathy, who was so like the children who had been lost, "because at last it was over."

But it was *not* over. The very thing that Judge Hoffman had feared, admonished, and threatened against daily had already come to pass—contamination of the jury.

On March 26, 1988, during the guilt phase of Carpenter's trial, juror Barbara Durham and her husband, Ron, were dining in a rural eastern San Diego County restaurant with local businessman Michael Lustig and his girlfriend, Donna Jean Duran. At this time Mrs. Durham allegedly told Lustig and Duran, "I'm not supposed to know this, but the defendant has been convicted of doing the same thing in another county and has been sentenced to death." It was not until July 21 that Lustig told his attorney, Michael Evans, of the conversation. Since this improper knowledge was in direct violation of the judge's pretrial ruling, Evans contacted Carpenter's lawyers, who filed a motion for mistrial in September.

On February 21, 1989, Hoffman held a special hearing to discuss the dilemma. The judge knew that if he ruled that juror foreperson Durham knew of Carpenter's pre-

vious conviction his next step would be to determine what
effect, if any, that knowledge would have had on the verdict. By April 12 Hoffman had decided that the defendant's conviction had been tainted by jury misconduct
and gave Posey until May 1 to say why a new trial should
not be accorded to Carpenter. "I think we need to proceed very carefully," Hoffman told the court, "because
I am absolutely convinced the evidence, beyond a shadow
of a doubt, shows Mr. Carpenter is guilty."

On Wednesday morning, June 14, Hoffman ruled,
"The court reluctantly has no alternative other than to
grant the defendant a new trial. This is an absolute travesty that such a result could have happened in this case.
Regrettably, I have to make this finding. Everything was
done by the court to keep improper knowledge from the
jury—and that is exactly the information that Mrs. Durham had. Having that knowledge Durham would have to
say, 'What difference does it make? He's going to die
anyhow.' "

The endless turns of the case had worn down the victims' families. The end had seemed so conclusive that
its escape had left them breathless. But the pain was so
real and the experience so devastating that they had united
in their determination to make their presence felt through
whatever trials lay ahead, however far away.

"As the case stands now," Posey told me in his office,
"it is a tragedy." After unsuccessfully arguing that Durham's improper knowledge did not alter the jury's verdict
he began at the beginning again. He filed his appeal of
Hoffman's decision to the state Supreme Court and, far
off, the wheels of justice began to turn, almost imper-
ceptively at first, but steadily and relentlessly.

Selected References

Arrigoni, Patricia. *Making the Most of Marin, A California Guide.* Novato, Cal.: Presidio Press, 1981.

Barich, Bill. "Board-and-Care." *The New Yorker,* October 8, 1987. A profile of Larry Looper and Kathy Sofos.

Berger, Joseph. *The New York Times,* October 28, 1984. Interview with Dr. Alan James Fox and Dr. Jack Levin, authors of *Mass Murder.*

Carroll, Jon. *Northern California.* Singapore: Apa Productions, 1984.

Chapin, William. *The Suburbs of San Francisco.* San Francisco, Cal.: Chronicle Books, 1969.

Coastal Parks Association. "Kule Loklo and the Coast Miwok Indians." San Rafael, Cal., 1976.

Dalbey, Alice F. *Visitor's Guide to Point Reyes.* Riverside, Conn.: Chatham Press, Inc., 1974.

Doss, Margot Patterson. *A Walker's Yearbook.* Novato, Cal.: Presidio Press, 1983.

Fairley, Lincoln. *Mount Tamalpais, A History.* San Francisco, Cal.: Scottwall Associates, 1987.

Futcher, Jane. *Marin, the Place, the People.* New York: Holt Rinehart & Winston, 1981.

461

Gilliam, Harold. "Mount Tam." Sunday *San Francisco Examiner and Chronicle,* September 20, 1987.

Gilliam, Harold, and Philip Hyde. *Island in Time.* New York: Scribner's, 1974.

Harris, Bill, and Neil Sutherland. *San Francisco from the Air.* New York: Crescent Books, 1986.

Hart, John. *San Francisco's Wilderness Next Door.* San Rafael, Cal.: Presidio Press, 1979.

Hoover, Rensch & Rensch. *Historic Spots in California.* Stanford, Cal.: Stanford University Press, 1970.

Kock, Margaret. *The Walk Around Book.* Fresno, Cal.: Valley Pub., 1978.

Levine, Richard M. *Bad Blood: A Murder in Marin County.* New York: Random House, 1982.

Leyton, Elliott. *Compulsive Killers.* New York: Washington Mews Books, 1986.

Magary, Alan, and Kerstin Fraser Magary. *South of San Francisco.* New York: Harper & Row, 1983.

Margolin, Malcolm. *The Ohlone Way.* Berkeley, Cal.: Heyday Books, 1978.

Martin, Don, and Key Martin. *Mt. Tam.* San Anselmo, Cal.: Martin Press, 1986. Maps by Bob Johnson.

Mason, Jack. *Early Marin.* Petaluma, Cal.: House of Printing, 1971.

———. *The Making of Marin (1850-1975).* Inverness, Cal.: North Shore Books, 1975.

———. *Point Reyes, The Solemn Land.* Point Reyes Station, Cal.: DeWolfe Printing, 1970.

Olmstead, Nancy. *To Walk with a Quiet Mind.* San Francisco, Cal.: Sierra Club Books, 1975.

San Francisco Institute for Stuttering. "Stuttering," a pamphlet. San Francisco, 1987.

Sifakis, Carl. *A Catalogue of Crime.* New York: New American Library, 1979.

Snyder, LeMoyne. *Homicide Investigation.* Springfield, Ill.: Charles C. Thomas Co., 1977.

Taber, Tom. *The Santa Cruz Mountains Trail Book.* San Mateo, Cal.: Oak Valley Press, 1982.

Trail Map of the Mt. Tamalpais Region. Oakland, Cal.: Erickson Maps, 1980.

Whitnah, Dorothy L. *Point Reyes.* Berkeley, Cal.: Wilderness Press, 1981.

Wollenberg, Charles. *Golden Gate Metropolis*. Berkeley, Cal.: University of California Press, 1985.

Wurm, T. G., and A. C. Graves. *The Crookedest Railroad in the World*. Berkeley, Cal.: Howell-North Publishers, 1960.

Sources

The material in this book was drawn over a four-year period from taped interviews with many of the principals in the case, primarily the investigators and families of the victims, court exhibits, court transcripts, police reports, personal notes, telephone records, letters, newspaper and television reports. David Carpenter's narration of his own story is taken from his seven days of testimony in San Diego between April 5 and April 14, 1988, his published letters and interviews, and psychiatric and prison records. For reasons of narrative flow the witches' curse against the Trailside Killer was placed closer to his arrest than actually was the case. Other sources were:

Marin County sheriff's department's and Santa Cruz police department's incident reports and files. Included in these reports are ballistics and crime lab results, autopsy reports, genetic fingerprint comparisons, and suspect files.

My visits to all of the hiking trails and scenes of the crimes, as well as David Carpenter's San Diego trial.

Composite sketches and police diagrams of the murder sites. I was allowed use of FBI photos of the suspect's arrest on May 15, 1981: Numbered W5A through W20A.

The following files on David Joseph Carpenter were consulted in the preparation of this book: FBI file S100 65 A. Federal Bureau of Prisons files A-29796-M and 0 2876-136. Federal Bureau of Prisons Medical files A-2876-M and 28796-136. Social Security file 553-34-9918 and CI&I file #540287. Pacific Bell phone record 1979–81, for Purnell and Carpenter.

In addition to my handwritten notes taken at the San Diego trial of David Carpenter during January 5 through July 19, 1988, the following court transcript volumes and pages were consulted:

For Shane Williams, volumes 75–76, pages 12071, 12078, 12080–12088, 12092, 12101.

For Candy Townsend, volume 81, pages 12656–12657, 12668, 12675, 12697–12698, 12744–12745.

For Karen Williams, volumes 74–75, pages 11933–19935, 11945–11946, 11953–11954, 11961–11968.

For Molly Purnell, volumes 78–79, pages 12354–12358, 12566–12567, 12570, 12587–12588.

Steve Haertle and David Carpenter in volume 107, pages 15944, 15948, 16059, 16077, 16100, 16218, 16062–16063, 16071, 16070–16071, 16063, 16213, 15864–15865, 15791, 15779–15980, 16053, 15902, 16220, 16113. In volume 109, pages 16220–16223, 15864–15865, and 16225. Volume 56, pages 9433–9470.

Newspaper and television accounts of the Trailside case, including reporters' notes and unpublished stories. Reporters who wrote stories on the investigation were: Teresa Allen from the *Marin Independent Journal.*

"Murder and Madness," by Teresa Allen, Monday, April 22, 1985, in the *Marin Independent Journal.* pA6.

"Murder and Madness," (part II) by Teresa Allen, Tuesday, April 23, 1985 in the *Marin Independent Journal.* pA5.

Teresa Allen and Mark Evje's reports on the San Diego trial in the *Marin Independent Journal.*

From the *San Francisco Chronicle:* Charles Raudebaugh, Erik Ingram, Carle Nolte, Don Wegars, Bill Wallace, Jerry Carroll, Charles Petit, Harry Jupiter, Susan Sward, Paul Liberatore, Steve Maganini, Robert Popp, Jack Viets, and Bill Workman.

From the *San Francisco Examiner:* Jennifer Foote, Jim Wood, James A. Finefrock, Lynn Ludlow, Laurie Itow, John Todd, Carol Pogash, Peter H. King and Caroline Young, Mike Lassiter, Lewis Leader, Mireya Navarra, and Stephen Cook.

Guy Wright's *San Francisco Examiner* columns on October 26, 1980, and October 8, 1981.

Dave Mitchell's interviews with David Carpenter in the *Point Reyes Light,* August 29, 1985.

A Travesty of Justice by Marion Irving. A nonfiction book in progress. Various family documents and floor plans of the McDermand home were provided by her. Court transcripts of Mark McDermand's trial: William Simmon examination, pp. 883, 887, 888. Mark McDermand examination, pp. 1033, 1034, 1035.

Mark McDermand Appeal, #A011139 1Crim. 23406. November 19, 1984.

Article on Reno Taini in *North County Peninsula*/North News Section. December 1980.

Kenneth Cory, state controller. "Advance Payments and Reimbursement for the Cost of Homicide Trials," a report, October 1986. PC 15201. PC 987.9. Ch. 32.

KTVU-TV, television interviews, August 19, 1985, with Elaine Corral speaking with David Carpenter at San Quentin in a taped interview from July 19, 1985. Portions of these interviews were introduced into evidence and shown to jurors at David Carpenter's San Diego trial in 1988.

Files on the *Fleetwood* Registry #60159. Owned by U.S. Department of Commerce; launched Moore Dry Dock in Oakland, California, December 4, 1944.

Letter from Santa Cruz Sheriff-Coroner Al Noren, dated May 27, 1981, #812218, to Roberta Patterson. Noren wrote: "I would like to commend you for your outstanding community spirit in providing us with your information about David Carpenter who was subsequently determined to be the self-styled Trailside Killer."

Index